Alternative Modernities in French Travel Writing

Anthem Studies in Travel

Anthem Studies in Travel publishes new and pioneering work in the burgeoning field of travel studies. Titles in this series engage with questions of travel, travel writing, literature and history, and encompass some of the most exciting current scholarship in a variety of disciplines. Proposals for monographs and collections of essays may focus on research representing a broad range of geographical zones and historical contexts. All critical approaches are welcome, although a key feature of books published in the series will be their potential interest to a wide readership, as well as their originality and potential to break new ground in research.

Alternative Modernities in French Travel Writing

Engaging Urban Space in London and New York, 1851–1986

Gillian Jein

ANTHEM PRESS

Anthem Press
An imprint of Wimbledon Publishing Company
www.anthempress.com

This edition first published in UK and USA 2019
by ANTHEM PRESS
75–76 Blackfriars Road, London SE1 8HA, UK
or PO Box 9779, London SW19 7ZG, UK
and
244 Madison Ave #116, New York, NY 10016, USA

First published in the UK and USA by Anthem Press 2016

British Library Cataloguing-in-Publication Data
A catalogue record for this book is available from the British Library.

ISBN-13: 978-1-78527-181-6 (Pbk)
ISBN-10: 1-78527-181-4 (Pbk)

This title is also available as an e-book.

CONTENTS

ACKNOWLEDGEMENTS

This book would not have been possible without the generous support of Trinity College, Dublin, and the Ussher fellowship, which allowed me to undertake the doctoral thesis from which the monograph eventually derived. I would like to express my warmest gratitude to David Scott, for his inspiring supervision during that period, his love of cities and of travel, and for his support throughout the project's nascent stages. Johnnie Gratton and Jean-Xavier Ridon made constructive suggestions with regard to publication. Bill Marshall extended his enduring support, open-hearted advice and conversation, and still encourages me to think on a 'broader horizon'. The publishers at Anthem Press, and Brian Stone especially, are owed special mention for their patience, understanding and personalized support in helping me see this project through to its end. Others have been involved in helping me retain (some) sanity throughout the years of this book's development: Yvonne-Marie Rogez, Alison Kapor, Greg Kerr, Daisy Connon and my brother Karl all provided friendship and heart. I want to express gratitude to Heather Mallory for her intellectual passion, warmth and for allowing me to use her wonderful Manhattan apartment; Carmel Mangan for her kindness and hospitality on Long Island; Barbara and Huw Thomas for their generosity in London; my parents for their enduring wisdom, love and encouragement; and Linda Knowles for her comradeship and our meanders through Paris, London and Dublin.

Finally, Ronan Devlin deserves more thanks than can ever be expressed here. This book is dedicated to our daughter, Robin, who, I hope, will one day walk these cities with us.

INTRODUCTION: APPROACHING
THE CITY

Each city is made of meetings, of contacts and of exchanges. Each city is made of chance and organization, of orders and disorders, of chaos and reorganization in an imperceptible flux of internal mutations. Each city is a complex organism.[1]

Chamoiseau 2002, 16

Every story is a travel story – a spatial practice. For this reason, spatial practices concern everyday tactics, are part of them [...]. These narrated adventures, simultaneously producing geographies of actions and drifting into commonplaces of an order, do not merely constitute a 'supplement' to pedestrian enunciations and rhetorics. They are not satisfied with displacing the latter and transposing them into the field of language. In reality, they organize walks. They make the journey, before or during the time the feet perform it.[2]

Certeau [1980] 1984, 115–16

Long before the age of the megalopolis, movement has defined cities. As complex constellations of people, objects and signs, cities are spaces where social, political and historical relations undergo constant negotiation and where the realities and representations of urban life are in persistent and dynamic states of becoming. This is to say that each person's experience of the city organizes an intricately shifting site for the production and exchange of meaning. Simply walking through the streets – choosing a particular path to follow, avoiding certain others – involves many acts of interpretation and mediation, ways of practising urban space that the average urban dweller undertakes everyday, often without a second thought (Certeau [1980] 1990). As the most complex human appropriation of the natural landscape, cities are remarkable for their mobile entanglement of bodies and objects and for the peripatetic production of meanings around such entanglements (Madsen and Plunz 2002). What happens, however, when we begin to reflect on these movements of and through a city? How do we position ourselves – historically, spatially, subjectively – so that we might begin to understand the changing environment that surrounds us, and our place amidst the different cultural and historical uses made of that environment? And how, furthermore, do we begin to articulate and communicate to others such reflections; how, in the end, do we find a position from which to re-present the urban experience? The moment we begin to ask these questions we are led down a more fundamental, if seemingly naïve, path of enquiry to ask: What is a city? If the opening line of Chamoiseau's quotation emphasizes interaction and exchange, the urban writer follows this by emphasizing the unpredictability of such trajectories of identification, inscribing these within a broader organic system of relations. This organic system, moreover, is not a state of being as such, but one of becoming, an intensive non-fixed 'flux of internal mutations'. In other words, cities constitute one of the most complex spatio-temporal sites of identity formation, a formation Certeau refers to as our 'spatiality' (Certeau [1980] 1990; Tally Jr. 2012, 2014). The interrelation of space, time and subjectivity in the city is 'organic' in the sense that space, time and the human are in consistent and systemic movement, but these moving relationships are by no means 'natural' in the sense that they might follow some preordained ahistorical or acultural schema; culture and its attendant mechanisms of organization and collectivity are at the heart of the city's implication in the histories and meanings of human society.

In terms of studying this relationship between the city and society, much has been written across the disciplinary fields on the relationship between the space–time of the urban environment and its inhabitants.[3] From philosophers to urban planners it is the experience of *dwelling* that dominates discourses exploring meanings for the city. This book, by way of contrast, focuses on urban travel and even more specifically the experience of the French urban traveller in the modern cities of London and New York to explore the notion of exchange intimated by Chamoiseau in quite literal concert with Certeau's idea of narration as a moving, spatial practice. If every story is a travel story, then, this book delineates such 'narrated adventures' in a tangibly concrete way to focus on the French traveller's experience of the modern urban environment as it emerged in the West from 1851 onward. Why the French traveller? In the first instance, as we shall see, the traveller brings into awareness a very material set of alternative interpretive positions from which to view the modern city as it emerges from this period onward. On the most basic level, for the traveller, the city is geographically positioned within a broader series of locations, a destination situated between the points of departure and return. Correspondingly, the spatio-temporal borders of the inhabitant necessarily differ from those of the traveller; the outsider who enters, engages and departs the city within more temporally and spatially restricted frameworks. In addition, the French urban traveller's narrative bank is more often than not informed by distant preconceptions of what the modern city is or ought to constitute, of the city's role in creating the conditions for what we typically associate with Western modernity. As we will explore, the French traveller brings to bear on London and New York perspectives of political, historical and ideological difference, which combine to weave threads of externality into the fabric of these cities' modernity. In examining the relationships at stake in the traveller's negotiations of the city, then, this books seeks to trace the emergence of networks of representation informing understandings of urban modernity as a mobile constellation of intersections, or 'crossings', between different national, cultural and historical identities.

Crossings

This book's more particular focus is on the relationships between representations of space (the built environment as conceived by architects, planners and governmental agencies) and the interpretive frameworks alive in travel writing's production of modern urban 'spatial practices' (Lefebvre [1974] 2000; Certeau [1980] 1990).[4] I am concerned here with the prismatic interrelation of travel writing and the urban environment as open, mutually engaged modes of making meanings for modernity. Analysing travel and travel writing as spatial practice is intended to bring the interpretive tactics of the travel writer into dialogue with a set of methodologies not always commonly associated with literary engagement. Rather than literary theorists per se, it is the work of sociologists, philosophers and cultural geographers, and their ascertainment of the importance of representation to the organization of meaning (and, by extension, of power) that I lean on here. These critical doorways into travel writing are unpacked in more detail in the chapters that follow, for now it suffices to say that this approach places concepts of urban space–time and the travelling subject's interpretive engagement with the urban situation at the heart of the enquiry.

These general comments aside, the reader might ask why London and New York? Why these cities? First, the framework of French perspectives on London and on New York establishes a contextual mesh to discuss better the themes of interest to this book, namely exchange, movement, meaning-making and their bearing on urban modernity. More than this, however, the exchange enabled by this bringing into dialogue of French perspectives on two capitals of modern Western culture unbinds traditional or monolithic readings of urban modernity as a homogenous, undifferentiated entity. The contextual interchange assembled here means that urban modernity may not be reduced to any single monolithic narrative for 'progress' or 'civilization' – terms central to our modern 'social imaginary' (Taylor 2004) – and the inherent alterity of the traveller creates alternative positions from which to view modernity in the West. In this way, we will speak of 'modernities' in the plural to challenge better universalist notions of 'civilization' and of 'modernity'. Of course, the three cities of Paris, London and New York have become so inimical to conceptions of Western modernity as to be a marketing cliché. However, it is argued here that the complexity of the traveller's position in these urban encounters problematizes the homogeneity of a term such as 'modernity' by bringing into view the intensities of the different interpretive positions enabled by this crossing of contexts. For example, in the first instance, London presents a more tangibly industrial manifestation of modernity than either that of Paris or New York. Politically, too, the architectural manifestations of England's constitutional monarchical government present a touchstone for contrasting French articulations of their own long battle with the legacy of the French Revolution and the fraught coming of age of Republicanism. London's social, environmental and political scene from the 1850s to the end of World War II places the French traveller into contact with an urban alterity that brings into view a wider horizon of comparative and contrastive positions on modernity, with the traveller interpreting and constituting 'modernity' as an expression of urban alternatives to the French experience. As Nancy Green puts it, 'as much as travel and cross-cultural study may tell us about other places and other cultures, they yield inherently comparative tales, structured by a perspective that often tells as much about home as about the foreign country' (Green 2002, 424). Correspondingly, New York brings into awareness yet other tensions inherent in French conceptualizations of the modern self on an increasingly transnational and technologically mediated global scene in the twentieth century. Here it is the emergence of consumerism, the falling away of traditional modes of eating, walking, working, and the materialization of a global powerhouse that continues to dominate our imagination of modernity that cause the French to question the precise shape of their own and American culture.

Moreover, as Western civilization recognizes its relativist position in the midst of other cultures throughout the world, representations of modern Western cities take on new significance as sources for understanding more precisely how the codes and value systems of modernity come to circulate. The view of the traveller renders us aware that modernity's meanings are not reducible to any singular urban model, and while for Walter Benjamin (1969) Paris constituted the capital of the nineteenth century, from the French perspective it becomes clear that London and New York represent alternative models for the cultural, visual and architectural expression of modern Western civilization (see Arens 2007). The particular interest of the travel account as a source to examine the emergence of the imaginative geographies of the modern urban environment hinges, therefore, on the necessarily binary position from which the French traveller apprehends these other urban centres. French travel accounts not only build on the established literary and (later) cinematic edifices of London and New York, but, in addition, the perspective of the travel writer as outsider very often serves as a dual, Janus-like position from which to form, challenge and renegotiate ways of understanding and representing modernity (Culler 1981; Healey 2003). Central to this book, then, is a concern to examine the evolution of a French cultural politics and poetics of space and place in relation to London and New York, and to consider how French imaginative geographies of these cities are revealing of urban counterpoints via which to cope with and create new ways of imagining and practising culture in the modern era.

Questions of Interpretation

From an ethnological perspective, as a locus for the organization of human relations, cities are privileged in the complexity of their semiotic and sensory networks governing possibilities for signification.[5] Cities are spaces where paradigms and possibilities for conceiving and living reality are circulated via the interactive spatio-temporal networks of the urban social world and the built environment. As spatially, temporally and socially complex organizations, cities are, therefore, intimately connected to the idea of human civilization. Already in antiquity, the notion of civilization is inseparable from its built manifestation as the city. As Richard Sennett ([1994] 2002) has shown, to speak of a city in ancient times was to speak of civilization, and the development of what has traditionally been termed a 'civilization' requires some kind of urban organization alongside that of a writing system for the management of the city's transmission of meaning. Urbanists and historians have demonstrated extensively how cities constitute a means of spatializing the codes of a particular culture's model of civilization. Buildings and public spaces, for example, facilitate the embodiment of moral order, codes for 'right-living' and the hierarchical power structures pertaining to a civilization's meaningful negotiation of the world. In antiquity, however, the shape of such organization speaks of a very different social and symbolic order to the secularized, transnational and market capitalist orders giving Western modernity its particular shape. The cultural and moral order behind much city planning in antiquity was based on a relationship of the sacred to the profane – for instance, the sacred or cosmological order of the universe informs the use and meaning of geometric layouts in ancient cities. However, as we shall see in subsequent chapters, in modern city planning, urban space–time is organized along other, largely more 'profane', axes. Paramount among the modern organizational axes is 'movement', whereby architectures of transport, circulation, exchange and the engagement of the public with these architectures become guiding principles. In other words, in the way that ancient city structures allow us to grasp the meanings of social life and its organization in antiquity, architecture and urban planning in the modern period are correspondent modes of rendering legible specific versions of Western modernity.

While we will explore further along in this chapter the idea of 'versions of modernity' or what I have termed 'alternative modernities', it is worth remaining with the notion of legibility in the urban environment for a moment so as to move towards a more precise understanding of how travel writing is involved in the production of 'imaginative geographies' for modern urban life (Said [1978] 1979). As stated earlier, given the complexity of representational and interpretive interactions in the urban lifeworld, establishing a firm definition of what a city *is* at all becomes an elusive project. Hubert Damisch sums up the problem when he states: 'the city is not a thing, nor can it be reduced to a substance'[6] (1996, 34). Not a finite or bounded 'thing' – not a material 'object' – the intricacy and mobility of a city's relations establishing networks of meaning between people, places and times, mean that it is difficult to define spatial, temporal or imaginative boundaries for the modern metropolis. For these reasons, legibility becomes an important issue for the modern urban traveller; how to negotiate, to understand and, in turn, to render the urban experience meaningful to a potential reader become central problems in the travel account.

To bring the point into focus, we might consider the emergence in the industrial period of a distinction between the terms 'city' and 'urban' as two related but differentiated ways of experiencing metropolitan space that each give rise to their own hermeneutics. With the rise of the industrial city there develops new modes of social organization, and likewise new methods for understanding such organization (Schivelbusch [1979] 1986). Urbanism as a field of enquiry comes into being with the crisis of traditional ways of life, brought about first in Britain and then America by the industrialization of society and its correspondent transformation from a primarily rural to an increasingly urban mode of organization. The indeterminate character of modern boundaries and the difficulty with defining the limits of modern urban spaces is rendered clearer when we contrast the modern city with spaces of representation in cities during the medieval and Renaissance periods (Kostof 2001, 2004; Rossi 1982; Sennett [1994] 2002). In the medieval era, as the main function of the city consisted in its capacity as defence fortress, the architectural limits of the city constituted an imposing and heavily symbolic presence; the city walls were exceptionally visible lines of demarcation in the physical and imaginative senses, and the city's physicality was active in reminding its inhabitants, visitors and attackers of where it began and ended (Kostof 2004, 28–34). During this period, the ideal city is a contained city: a clear (preferably circular) unit, its spatial arrangement directed at erecting a symbolic order in which the circle and the symmetrical represented universal harmony and the classical ideals of antiquity (see Tafuri 1976; Kostof 2001). In contrast, it is the lack of definition, embodied by urban sprawl, the creation and amalgamation of the suburbs, and the relative depletion of the European city centre during the industrial and post-industrial period that challenges the conception of the city as a neat totality. Even at an elementary level, definitions as to what constitutes a 'city' differ depending on where one finds oneself, so that in France while any agglomeration surpassing 2,000 inhabitants merits the name 'city', in Denmark a city exists once the number of localized people is over 250, in Japan this number must be over 30,000 and in Egypt over 11,000 (Fijalkow 2007, cited in Stébé and Marchal 2010, 12–13). As urban networks of uses and users become ever more complex, a holistic, all-encompassing experience of any modern city becomes intangible, and correspondingly the issue of urban legibility or meaning comes increasingly to the fore in the experience of urban space. Despite this fugitive intransience – or rather because of it – it is during this period that urbanism emerges as a disciplinary framework through which to attempt to comprehend the shape of the city.[7] For the traveller, who is very often motivated by a desire to see (or even, 'to do') the 'whole' city, questions of how to read the city, how to make sense of its layers, and correspondingly, how to render it legible to a reader become intensely problematic in the modern period.

Urban Spaces in Travel Studies

Tracing representations of London and New York by French travel writers from 1851 to 1980, this book contributes to a growing body of work that analyses travel and travel writing beyond the Anglophone context, and engages a body of writing in questions surrounding specifically French material, cultural and aesthetic modalities for interpreting and representing modern urban life.[8] While the city has formed a key theme for scholars of literary fiction,[9] the urban environment has been relatively neglected by travel studies.[10] Although a number of studies have been published at the time of writing, debates in travel studies (for the Anglophone and Francophone contexts at least) have tended to focus on sites of colonialist expansion and postcolonial aftermaths in the vital effort by Western scholars to come to terms with the ethical consequences of racial subjugation and empire. If not postcolonialist in its subject matter, this book owes a substantial theoretical debt to postcolonial methodologies for their understanding of the crucial role played by representational strategies in the formation of cultural identities. Most notably for our context, postcolonial theory has been pioneering in the articulation of ways in which the cultural politics and poetics of imperialism 'places' bodies within an ordered, ideological spatio-temporal schema (see Clarke 1999; Forsdick and Murphy 2003, 2009; Fowler 2007; Kuehn and Smethurst 2008; Ni Loingsigh 2009; Youngs and Forsdick 2012). The potential for interpretive attitudes and representation to order the human lifeworld through the imposition of a delimited meaning set is a fundamental premise of the analysis here. While this book does not deal specifically with postcolonial spaces and identities, its 'ways into', or approaches to, the texts studied are indebted to critical discourses emergent from the postcolonial theoretical scene. More specifically, I borrow and reorient contextually the idea of 'imaginative geography' as first developed in Edward Said's highly influential *Orientalism* ([1978] 1979). For the ways in which it appropriates and builds on phenomenological approaches to space,[11] Said's work is important to this exploration of French travel writing's interpretive positions for apprehending urban culture in London and New York. Said's theory of 'imaginative geography' is underwritten by the assumption that space is more than a set of Euclidean coordinates or a stable, neutral container housing the mobilities of culture and temporality. In the latter objectivist understanding, space is effectively (and artificially) disengaged from time, and by implication from culture, serving merely as a backdrop against which the socio-historical agents of culture mobilize meaning. Said, along with more contemporary cultural geographers (Massey 2005; Cresswell 2004, 2006; Anderson 2009; Soja 1996, 2000), troubles the opposition between the material, the temporal and the symbolic by positing that space exists in terms of what we might call, following Jacques Rancière (2004), a 'politico-aesthetic' relationship. His work explores, therefore, the mutual entanglement of aesthetics (understood broadly as the sensory vehicles producing visibilities and invisibilities, normalities and abnormalities) and productions of spatialized sensibilities in the institutional, political and, ultimately, cultural arenas. In such a schema, the material spaces of architecture are invested with what Said, after Gaston Bachelard (1957), calls a 'poetics', with the result that the concrete dimensions of space are endowed with values, emergent in tandem with a particular historical, ideological imagination or, in other words, space is culturally *located* (Bhabha [1994] 2010). It is through this imaginative mesh that a range of cultural meanings are enacted and confirmed in space. Through this imaginative process, space becomes meaningful in a way that is inseparable both from the cultural politics of particular social groups – whether these be on a local, national or global scale – and from the aesthetic procedures through which identities and roles are made visible (or invisible) to others (see Rancière 2004). Architectures, as spatial organizers of such aesthetic distributions, emerge and re-emerge in dialogue with culture, and this dialogue is largely enacted through representation as the human practice through which material spaces are related to the symbolic.

Said goes further to suggest that meanings of space are not simply individually constructed from a singular intimate connection with certain architectures – the space of the home being the point of origin for Bachelard's thesis – but that spaces are rendered meaningful within wider social frameworks; material spaces emerge from the discursive paradigms that create cultural meaning. Space, as Lefebvre has demonstrated ([1974] 1991), iterates (and re-iterates) social meaning – boundaries, borders, frontiers, entrances and exits – with the result that institutional and domestic spaces are all engaged in framing operations of inclusion and exclusion (see also Foucault 1975, [1982] 2001; French and Hamilton 1979 and Rancière 2004). Through such aesthetico-spatial manifestations, the built environment is a major force in the consolidation of power networks in a society. From this theoretical standpoint, Said proceeds to the analysis of the 'Orient' as a place that emerges materially through the representational processes of European cultural construction – the colonial imagination being the specific target of Said's critique. From within this framework, the space of the 'Orient' comes into being via the colonial imagination of 'otherness' translated spatially into the architectures of everyday life which serve to maintain distance and difference through their spatial separations of 'Us' / 'Nous' and 'Them' / 'les Autres' (Todorov 1989).

For the purposes of this analysis, the final departure of Said's thesis is reoriented and its theoretical focus turned westward to ask the question of how meaning for the modern cities of London and New York circulates in and through the spatial practices of French travel writing. In borrowing the term, 'imaginative geography', I refer then to those categories through which French travel writing maps a material and symbolic territory that circulates meanings for modern urban life – through walking and writing the city's streets, re-presenting its architectures and people – and making sense of these in relation to attendant value systems, ideologies and institutions. In doing so the analysis suggests that travel writers are at once practitioners and producers of the city. In the way that they negotiate the urban landscape according to either conscious or unconscious socio-historical motivations, urban travellers participate in the synchronic and diachronic unfolding of the modern city's meanings at a particular juncture in space and time. As Certeau puts it, 'Turning a corner in the city is to the urban system what turning a phrase is to language'[12] (Certeau [1980] 1990, 151). Concomitantly, travel writers are producers of the modern city because, not only do they participate in pre-existing representations of London and New York, the traveller also reproduces these urban spaces through the act of writing, intervening in existing discursive meanings either to confirm or reinterpret these in accordance with their motivations. The term 'imaginative geography', then, can be expanded and understood as the mobile, porous collection of spaces of representation (narratives, images and memories) that individuals and collective groups share and modulate across time. This imaginative geography is a sense-making apparatus, and by extension, each new representation contributes to the evolution of the symbolic sphere. Furthermore, the circulation of these representations of space opens out possibilities for conceiving new material spaces and new practices that articulate spatial identity (or 'spatiality') by ordering and reordering ideas such as 'home', 'abroad', 'movement', 'belonging', 'progress', 'decline', 'nation' and 'civilization'. It is within this complex nexus of negotiations, then, that an 'imaginative geography' of the modern city emerges.

The Politics of Poetics

Travel, as a departure from 'everyday life', is an action that initiates dimensions of experience to defamiliarize the world, but the modes via which this defamiliarization takes place, or the extent to which the unfamiliar is permitted to endure, are neither ontologically nor discursively stable. The role played by travel writing in imperial contexts, for example, in bringing that which is foreign into the familiarity of language, is central to the discursive production of hierarchical systems (Campbell 1988; Keuhn and Smethurst 2008). Thus the reproduction of tropes, stereotype and the assumption of authorial transparency lay out not only the historical schema according to which another culture may be read but cognitively – and, in the case of colonial expansion, empirically – map the spaces of everyday life in terms of sameness (Spurr 1993; Appadurai 1996; Bhabha 1990). It is this encoded discourse that leads us to revaluate what is at stake in the poetics of travel writing within this formerly minor genre. Paul Smethurst (Keuhn and Smethurst 2008, 2–3), in his introduction to *Travel Writing, Form, and Empire*, suggests that examining 'imperial form', in its particular literary manifestation as tropes, metaphors and other representational practices, reveals how these devices were essential to the endurance of what Michel Foucault (1966) terms the 'order of things' – those foundational structures of knowledge on which imperialist discourse was erected. It is through this formal mesh that the discursive production of space in terms of Western binaries becomes visible, binaries such as self/other, the West/the rest, nature/civilization and authentic/fake. These binaries work to stabilize the strange, to reduce the potential radicality of mobility inherent to the act of travel. Through binary action, alterity is demobilized and codified in terms that render it legible in accordance with imperialist necessities. It is this act of codification that, to move the discussion of form beyond the colonialist context, is referred to in this book as a *legislative mode* of travel writing. Adapting Zygmunt Bauman's (1987) term 'legislative' to describe the tradition of the intellectual as social actor whose authority gains meaning from a modern, collective belief in the Enlightenment era's grand narratives of progress and universality (Lyotard [1979] 1984; Jameson 1991), the designation can also be used to describe the discursive apparatus that such a world-view produces in travel writing.

One of the overarching arguments of this book is that travel writing in urban space throughout this period demonstrates a shift in the traveller's hermeneutic methods of comprehending spatial identity and urban reality. Adapting Bauman's use of the terms to reflect our context, this shift may be referred to as a movement from 'legislative' to 'interpretive' modes of travel. These modalities will be discussed further in the next chapter, for now Roland Barthes's analysis of the imagination of the sign provides a useful starting point for unpacking the resonance of these terms. What I refer to as the 'legislative mode' of travel can be understood as the traveller's attempt to resolve and stabilize the meaning of (and for) the other, or what Barthes refers to as 'symbolic consciousness' (Barthes [1962] 2002, 461). The 'interpretive mode' of travel, on the other hand, exhibits through its form an awareness of the artificial, or constructed, relationship between the sign and its object, and this reflexivity opens the possibility for destabilizing the above legislative procedures. This interpretive mode of travel can be equated respectively with Barthes's criteria for identifying the 'paradigmatic consciousness' (Barthes [1962] 2002, 462–63),[13] understood as an associative, or 'vertical', apprehension of the sign – the possibility of one sign being substituted for another – while the syntagmatic consciousness recognizes the sign on a combinatory, or 'horizontal', level. These different modes of travel, both the legislative (syntagmatic) and the interpretive (paradigmatic), exhibit this concern with sense-making and legibility, but the manner of aesthetic approach has very different consequences – particularly as regards the ethics of signifying otherness – for the imaginative geography of the city that emerges. A syntagmatic consciousness of the other would presume a steady universality of epistemological parameters, while a paradigmatic approach to alterity would insist on the possibility of alternative ways of knowing existing within the shared human lifeworld.

This last point brings us to the epistemologies at stake in travel writing. The extent to which the West consistently reproduced knowledge discourses that reinforced its imperialist domination of other cultures is well documented by colonialist and postcolonialist critique (Campbell 1988, 1997, 1999; Ni Loingsigh 2009, Forsdick and Murphy 2003, 2009; Bhabha [1994] 2010). As already stated, having evolved largely in relation to sites of colonialist expansion and postcolonialist aftermaths, the theoretical frameworks for travel studies have been in the main elaborated with the colonial and postcolonial contexts in mind (Rojek and Urry 1997a). But, as we shall see, these operations are also performed internally, and for our purposes, in French productions of London and New York. In attempting to demarcate the development of spatial and social practices attributable to Western variants of 'modernity', anthropologists point to the need to consider the relevance of cultural practices that are 'closer-to-home' (see Pétonnet 1982; Althabe 1984, 1990; Hannerz 1983). For instance, within the field of ethnology (which has much in common with certain strands of travel writing) scholarship has increasingly redirected study towards the 'home' culture. This is important because until recently the core (if problematic) ethnological question – the nature/culture divide – was explored almost exclusively through examining so-called primitive cultures. Breaking from this traditional model, the anthropologist Marc Augé (1992, 22) argues that 'there is no reason to think that the problem of the real, empirical object, or the problem of representation, might differ whether considered in relation to a great African kingdom or a Parisian suburb'.[14] As Augé points out, ethnological attempts at understanding a culture's networks of significance are as applicable to a modern Western city as to any other manifestation of culture. This observation on the object of study allows for consideration of the travel journal in concert with other texts contributing to the circulation of power and discursive hegemonies in and by the West, and Augé's point is important to this book's approach in two ways. First, he argues for the necessity of approaching European identity from within, inferring its cultural, historical locatedness as a set of shifting symbolic practices. Second, Augé's work, building on the theories of Lefebvre ([1974] 2000) and Certeau ([1980] 1990) on urban space, invites a rethinking of the interconnections between built space and its practice, understanding this interconnection in terms of processes that produce spatial identities. The meanings of urban modernity in the West are, therefore, so many struggles over inclusion and exclusion, 'internal' clashes for power over meaning, and reveal the contradictions and difficulties in establishing a position from which to speak of and to others.

To summarize then, the underlying premise of the readings presented throughout this book is that the aesthetics of the travel account – its stylistic devices and changing forms of representation – are fundamental to an understanding of how particular socio-political discourses operate in and on society (Hall 1997 and Rancière 2004). In this light, 'aesthetics' is employed as a term in possession of meanings beyond an insular study of poetics in a purely literary sense. Instead, 'poetics' as it is used here acknowledges the cultural impact of representation, is cognizant of the ways in which modes of writing are engaged in rendering the city legible and, equally, recognizes the importance of the aesthetic in establishing tropes through which urban space becomes meaningful in relation to political and cultural networks of power (Gandelsonas and Morton 1980; Hamon 1989; Lamizet 2002). It is in this sense that the term 'representational strategies' is used to refer to the nexus of aesthetics and culture operational in the travel text. In this wider sense, and as shall be explored further in subsequent chapters, the operations of the travel text practise space, situating (seemingly) objective geographies in particular moments in time through their imaginative mapping of London and New York; a mapping which is always both spatial and temporal and which participates in the creation of a cultural politics of space and place. An entry point into the texts under discussion, therefore, is how the varied narrative forms of travel writing throughout this period engage in the production and reproduction of meanings for modern urban cultures, and the question guiding the analysis is how, and with what results, space is rendered legible (Lynch 1960; Soja 1984).

Alternative Modernities

So as to qualify the use of the term 'modernity' here, we need to signal first of all a distrust of the general moniker 'modern metropolis' to encompass both London and New York, as it risks blurring the vast differences between both cities' respective processes of modernization and their various cultural trajectories. I have used the term as much as possible in specific reference to a particular city. We begin with the year 1851 as this date marks a watershed in the nineteenth-century era of empire, urbanism and tourism, and constitutes an important temporal signpost from whence our questions around travel and the representation of urban space assume a principally modern form, and where travel and urbanism become critical social and symbolic foci in and through which meanings for Western 'modernity' are constructed.[15] In 1851, the United Kingdom's census reported for the first time in recorded history that a country's urban population had outstripped that of its rural demographic.[16] And from May to September of the same year, Victorian London, the most densely populated city in the contemporary world, hosted the 'Great Exhibition of the Works of Industry of all Nations', an event that embodied several of the cultural and political themes weaving the particular textures of Western modernity – progress, transparency, imperialist ambition and transnational mobility (Berger [1972] 2008; Mirzoeff 2006, 2011).[17]

The conventional use of the (deceptively simple) term 'modernity' embraces some of the most complex technological, intellectual and political revolutions in the history of Western culture (see Savage, Warde and Ward, 2003; Sennett [1990] 1993, 1996). The signification at the core of the word is taken here to correspond with the interactions at stake in what Marshall Berman ([1982] 1988, 16) (in reference to Edgar Allen Poe, perhaps) calls 'the maelstrom of modern life'.[18] To outline briefly first of all, these interactions include: advances in the physical sciences (from microbiology to astronomy) that have changed (first Western) conceptions of humanity's place in the universe; the advent of technology with the industrialization of production, bearing consequences for environmental infrastructures and Western understandings of temporality as the pace of life quickens and creates new foundations for corporate power; demographic upheaval, with its roots in sources as varied as civil war, famine, colonialism and the economic requirements of the capitalist Western world, and its creation of transnational identities, leading to the reappraisal of understandings of cultural heritage and the singular identitarian cohesion of the 'nation'; urbanization – looked at from the perspective of the Western world in this case, but for which non-Western societies have their particular discourses of displacement, poverty and cataclysmic upheaval, as well as their own architectural manifestations (not least of which include townships overlooked by skyscrapers); mass communication and the consequent speeding up of events as we gain more access to the (mainly) surface images of non-proximate societies, and the age of the 'global village' (McLuhan 1962); increasingly powerful nation states and bureaucracy in the latter half of the nineteenth century, and the revision of these in light of decolonization and globalization, along with the emergent interdependency of states for economic, political and demographic stability in the later twentieth century; and finally, the incessant redefinition of our world in material and aesthetic terms by individuals and communities attempting to make sense of the institutions and exterior forces that more and more articulately we have come to recognize as governing factors in the paths our lives take. All of these processes can be called 'modernization' and contribute to the condition we refer to here generally as 'modernity'. Berman puts this general understanding rather more poetically when he expresses that:

> To be modern is to find ourselves in an environment that promises us adventure, power, joy, growth, transformation of ourselves and the world – and, at the same time, that threatens to destroy everything we have, everything we know, everything we are. ([1982] 1988, 15)

Moving towards a closer definition of what is meant by the 'alternative modernities' of this book's title and the particular inflections imparted to the term the aim here is a modest one. While the term 'modernity' has been notoriously difficult to pin down, both in terms of debates with regard to its origins as well as discussions as to its moment of closure, I am interested in the ways in which modernity has been negotiated and the different inflections imparted to the experience of modernity in urban travel writing. The reason for this is that looking at modernity from the 'bottom up' as it were reorients it towards a located phenomenological experience, implying its openness to change. This situates modernity in a minor sense, and moves its interpretation away from a more traditional narrative of modernity as an acultural series of inevitable, universally applicable processes resulting as a universal consequence of the secular outlook that emerged with the European Enlightenment, the attendant rise of rationality and its instrumentation in social organization, and the development in the West of a scientific consciousness. In taking this position I follow Charles Taylor's work when he argues that this latter understanding of modernity is neglectful of cultural perspectives, and supposes that the shape of modernity will be the same for all societies. In this acultural narrative, societies are plotted along a linear scale of relative progression towards a unique manifestation of the modern. Taylor makes a convincing case that modernity has been understood largely in an acultural sense which he defines as 'an operation that is not defined in terms of the specific cultures it carries us from and to, but is rather seen as of a type that any traditional culture could undergo' (2001, 172–73). In another sense, modernity is accounted for within this culture-neutral framework as the material outgrowth of 'increased mobility, concentration of populations, industrialization, or the like' (173). The main issue that Taylor has with such a perspective is that it is universalist and heavily Western centred in its prognosis, and within it 'modernity is conceived as a set of transformations which any and every culture can go through – and which all will probably be forced to undergo' (174). Typical proponents of such a theoretical position who have been significant in shaping the discussion around modernity include Emile Durkheim's idea of the transition from mechanical to more 'organic forms of social cohesion' (174), Alexis de Tocqueville's idea of the progressive creep of democracy and Max Weber's belief in rationalization as a steady process.

Taylor does not dismiss the phenomena identified in the acultural theory of modernity, rather he *locates* or relocates these phenomena spatially and temporally as belonging specifically to a Western experience of modernity, as constituting the intellectual and material sensibilities that have given Western modernity its own site-specific tenors and organized its temporalities in accordance with historically and culturally constituted trajectories undergoing specific transition. To critique this acultural narrative of 'modernity' as a monolithic and homogenizing transition that all societies undergo in the same way, Taylor draws our attention to the cultural specificities which acultural theory tends to screen out. The cultural theory put forward by Taylor begins by decentring the experience of modernity as universal. In a relativist move, Taylor proposes that 'we see our [Western] culture as one among others' (2001, 175). In this model, Western modernity is energized by its own peculiar moral, spiritual and social tenets, or in Taylor's terminology, 'its own positive visions of the good – that is by one constellation of such visions among available others' (175). Taylor's argument rests on the idea that a specific constellation of cultural norms and desires produce the particular effects or renditions of modernity as it becomes actual in one place at any one time. Thus as we shall see, the idea of the 'good' in Victorian London emerges socially in French debates about questions of poverty, the people and human dignity in the urban environment, and politically in understandings of the right or not of kings to govern. This idea of the good differs greatly from the way in which social and political questions are formed in twentieth-century New York. In addition, it is important to note that in both cases such ideas are already filtered for us through the perspective of the French traveller who radically detaches these value systems from their 'naturalness' by drawing them into comparison with their own particular French narratives of urban modernity. This is to say that there are cultural systems of understanding (of interpretation and rendering) that differentiate the experiences of modernity. Thus, rather than speak of modernity in the singular, we should, Taylor tells us, talk about '"alternative modernities" that relate both the pull to sameness and the forces making for difference' (182). This pull is evident in travel writing where, on the macrolevel of social institutions, the modern city may be understood as a collection of traits that a certain society amalgamates as its character, as its norm – the traits the traveller might identify as 'typically' English or American. On the microlevel, by contrast, the shape of modernity is subjectively filtered, interpreted, represented so that its prismatic relativism emerges. Thus, the approach taken here is not to say, of course, that travellers do not attempt to account for a culture in macroterms or that they relinquish the dream of an objective stance from which to comprehend the whole and interpret the fragment for the whole. Rather, the concept of 'alternative modernities' allows for the discussion of the traveller's shifting modalities of interpretation by looking at the representational strategies deployed in their accounts. The key to allowing for the emergence of alternative modernities in the Western context is, I would argue, to examine the differentials of identity and its construction through the poetics of the travel text, so that what comes into view is the differentiations of modernity as understood in a selective variety of times, spaces and subjective positions, 'modernity as lived from the inside' (Taylor 2001, 182). In tension with the idea of 'modernity' as a macrostructural, organizing concept (Appadurai 1996, 2002; Augé 1992; Jameson 1991), therefore, is the individual traveller's micro-level practice of this broader ideological horizon (see Cronin 2012).

Expectations, Chapter Outlines

Rather than adopt a singular theoretical perspective pertaining to a discrete discipline – whether aesthetic, sociological, ethnological or political – this book moves between such disciplinary frameworks to articulate an understanding of the modern city as a porous entity that is at once planned and practiced. This is so that London and New York might become visible in terms of a mobile set of mutually affective interferences between diverse objective conditions (architecture, art and technology; their geographical situation; and social and economic function) and the range of travel practices active on individual and collective levels. Introducing the tension of micro, subjective practice is imperative if we are to locate critically how these travel practices thread their weave through the geographies of dominant, governmental spatialities of modernity, and demonstrate how the specific spatialities of the French traveller in London and New York problematize the notion of any singular macrocosmic vision. In addition, the travel accounts under discussion here bring to light the profound enmeshment of aesthetics (namely writing, architecture and the objects of urban life) with networks of wider discursive frameworks of dominant sense-making apparatus (institutions, ideologies and the material expressions of governmentality). The works chosen here constitute a locus for the often disjointed and contradictory relational determinations that imbricate everyday action and 'representational spaces'[19] (Lefebvre [1974] 1991, 39) in both the development and deconstruction of dominant modalities for understanding difference and sameness in the modern context. It is in this sense that we can consider the traveller as participant in the production of 'alternative modernities', for the manner in which the experience and writing of London and New York during this period engages the French traveller in at least a two-way model of communication, in which their practices of the city penetrate those of England and the United States. The urban environments of these countries are seen to reflect and refract through the traveller's modes of seeing from a position of difference, so that London and New York perform and are performed as alternative geographies for the negotiation of meanings for modernity.

If we think in terms of alternative modernities, Dilip Parameshwar Gaonkar tells us, we agree that modernity 'arrived not suddenly but slowly, bit by bit, over the longue durée – awakened by contact; transported through commerce; administered by empires, bearing colonial inscriptions; propelled by nationalism; and now increasingly steered by global media, migration, and capital' (Parameshwar Gaonkar 2001, 1). This is to emphasize the significance of travel, exchange and mobility in simultaneously defining and undermining boundaries for knowledge, and its role in inaugurating the modern period. In order to situate better the link between interpretations and representations of the other in the reformulation of Western modernity, we might revisit briefly some important historical moments where travel has been instrumental.[20] From the Renaissance period onward, travel has altered ways of perceiving space and time in fundamental ways (Campbell 1997, 1999; Reichler and Ruffieux 1998; Augustinos 1994; French 1992) – transport technologies allow for the traversal of ever-greater distances in ever-reduced time frames (Urry 1995, 2007), movement distorts or reframes spatial awareness (Virilio [1980] 1989), with the result that the local and global are no longer easily differentiated categories (Appadurai 1996; Sassen 1998). Epistemologically speaking, travel has played a determinate role in shaping the paradigms by which the West has interpreted, represented and colonized the world, and by extension, travel has been instrumental in the successive crises that have reformulated frameworks for knowledge (Scott 2004), so that travel writing forms a valuable touchstone in locating the emergence of alternative modernities and for analysing the ways in which cultural upheavals pertaining to the development of different Western cities have been understood. Of these upheavals, the profound transformation of the West's living environment from an agriculturally dominated to an extensively urbanized space is the change that has produced the most profound effects on social and cultural experiences at the levels of the conceptual, the pragmatic and the representational (Lefebvre [1968] 2003). In light of the elephantine expansion of the Western metropolis since the industrial revolution, and in particular the emergence of London and New York as what Jane Jacobs ([1961] 1962) called 'great' and Saskia Sassen (1991) 'global' cities, it is not surprising that such urban conglomerates, with their 'urban' behaviours, architectural novelty and sensorial intensity should become important performative destinations for travellers in our period.[21]

As stated above, this book draws on Lefebvre's ([1974] 2000) terminology for articulating spatial agency, and 'travel' is understood here as a 'spatial practice', an act-enabled modality for negotiating and making sense of the world in relation to an elsewhere. As will be explored in the following chapters, frameworks shift in response to changes in cultures of travel – in relation to society's expectations and ideas of travel (the 'ontology of travel' [Urbain 2000, 142]), as well as in response to practical, technological developments – such as advances in systems of transport – that alter the travel experience (see Cresswell 2006). Urban travel writing as spatial practice, then, produces a shifting geography of modernity, weaving places together, and calling us to recognize the city in its 'innumerable collection of singularities'[22] (Certeau [1980] 1990, 147).

It is important to point out at this stage that the corpus under discussion here is not intended to be representational of any notion of London or New York as 'entities' in and of themselves. Exhaustion of the body of travel texts to these cities, even within the framework of French and Francophone examples, would be an enormous task and would in any case elide the particular concerns of this book. The writers examined here have been chosen for the ways that their writing brings into focus the cultural and political tensions at stake in understanding and practising these cities. Furthermore, due to the infamous textual richness and hybrid textures of travel writing, I have focused on texts where the material structures of London and New York – their streets, architectures and urban artefacts – have constituted the loci for the traveller's negotiation of the city. For the urban travellers discussed here, certain buildings and circumscribed places are often crucial in attracting, orienting and providing meaning for the metropolis. Not only do these architectures perform as simple motifs for a city, they often – whether through their concrete manifestation of technological progress, urban decay, gentrification or social segregation – provide the most immediate, visual and spatial point of contact with the culture visited. As will be discussed further in relation to the differences between the experience of the inhabitant and the traveller, the symbolic potential (as opposed to the everyday functionality) of architecture is consistently activated by the travel experience. Furthermore, all of the texts under discussion here call into question the possibility for understanding urban modernities in any singular sense, and have been selected for their revelation of the tension between the discursivity of monumental urban forms and the microlevel of urban practices. These texts bring into relief how urban travel writing consists in the intertwined nexus of the former 'spaces of representation' with the latter 'representational spaces' (Lefebvre [1974] 1991, 38–39).[23] With these concerns in mind, real rather than imaginary journeys are privileged here because it is in the tension inherent in such representations of the 'real' that the travel journal's overt relationship with the creation of imaginative geographies for experience comes into view.

In order to unpack further the general remarks made throughout this introduction, and to situate the readings of the travel texts within a conceptual framework, chapter 1 is theoretical in scope, engaging with urban theory on the one hand and travel studies on the other. The intention here is to read across disciplines so as to facilitate an integrated analysis of how travel writing participates in the articulation of urban spatialities. This first chapter, 'Producing the City', sets out the frameworks that have informed critical understandings of urban space and the city, resulting from the question of what a city is, and on what conditions its organization and codification depend. Despite the simplicity of the question, the aim here is to determine what it is that makes the urban experience different from experiences of any other of the possible spaces that the traveller might encounter. This opening chapter engages with the work of Lefebvre ([1974] 2000) and Certeau ([1980] 1990), in particular, to lay the terrain for the critical vocabulary of the analysis that follows, unpacking the lineage of terms such as 'space' and 'place', 'representations of space', 'spaces of representation' and 'spatial practice'. The chapter moves on to explore these ideas in the context of travel writing, delineating particular modalities for the traveller's exploration of city space, and demonstrating how the traveller's practice of the city differs from that of the urban inhabitant. The latter part of this chapter differentiates between historical categories of urban travel and urban travellers and the particular (often ethical) difficulties emergent in travel writing's different representational guises. Of these, two main trends in epistemological and aesthetic approach emerge which, as already stated, I have named respectively the modalities of 'legislative' and 'interpretive' approaches to the space of the other.

The four further chapters of the book take up the questions posed at the outset of this introduction through a reading of a geographically oriented corpus of travel texts in connection with key historical transitions within the period. Organizing the chapters geographically better enables us to explore the myriad ways in which one particular city can be spatialized, and reveals more directly the degree to which 'place' is mobilized and unsettled through the act of representation. Chapter 2, 'Urban Oppositions: The French in Nineteenth-Century London', looks at Victorian London through two travel texts – Jules Janin's 1851 account, *Le Mois de mai à Londres et l'exposition de 1851 / The Month of May in London and the 1851 Exhibition* and Jules Vallès's *La Rue à Londres / The London Street* first published in 1876. This chapter takes two very different experiences – that of the tourist and that of the *émigré* respectively – to explore how the varying conditions and motivations of these travellers produce combative versions of French national identity, and lead to the emergence of two divergent topographies of imperial London. The chapter which follows, 'Revealing and Reconstructing London', moves the analysis to two texts from the interwar and post-war period respectively, Jacques Dyssord's *Londres secret / Secret London* (1932) and Alfred Leroy's *Londres et la vie anglaise / London and English Life* (1946). This chapter presents another set of oppositional perspectives for reading the city, but which have their basis in contrasting forms of the tourist encounter. The analysis charts Dyssord's exploration of the darker side of metropolitan life; his fascination with London's East End, and the carceral space of Holloway prison. It places this 'dark tourism' (Lennon and Foley 2000) in dialogue with the 'beaten track' practised by Leroy as he restricts his tour to the parks and monuments of 'Brightest London'[24] to explore narratives of deviant authenticity and post-war nostalgia that circulate within tourist discourse of the period. Chapter 4 moves the book to New York and in this respect corresponds to the twentieth-century dislocation of a geopolitics dominated by European imperialist expansion and the establishment of a new global political order increasingly dominated by a capitalist market economy and American foreign policy. This chapter, 'Wandering Geometry: Order and Identity in New York', examines Paul Morand's *New-York* (1930 and Jean-Paul Sartre's series of essays on New York published in *Situations III* (1949) and written in 1945. The focus is on the traveller's encounter with the geometry of New York's built environment; at once a means of lending visual and material sensory order to the city, the prodigious geometric patterns of New York City are also central to both of these renowned travellers' ideological frameworks for the identification of a specifically 'American' set of values and an exploration of the implications of capitalism for the future of humankind. The final chapter, 'Writing around the Lines: Interpretive Travel Writing', examines Georges Perec's *Récits d'Ellis Island / Ellis Island* ([1980] 1994) and Jean Baudrillard's *Amérique / America* ([1986] 2000) and suggests a shift in focus from the previous travellers' codes for rendering legible the spaces of the city. Here we examine the poetics of the travel text to demonstrate how stylistic devices function to 'poach' / 'braconner' (Certeau [1980] 1990, 239) on other legislative modalities for rendering otherness so as to insinuate difference, instability and multiplicity in the text's spatial arrangements. In so doing, I argue that these later travel texts open onto a reflexive and ethically engaged space of mobility suggestive of the other's singularity and their existence beyond the possibilities for legibility.

A number of shared questions give shape to each of the above chapters and are based on a concern to effect a situated approach to urban travel writing worked in tandem with analysis of the aesthetic frameworks of the text's construction. These questions ask how spatio-temporal shifts and technological changes in the environment have been instrumental in constructing individual and collective responses to the modern urban universe, how these responses have informed negotiations of the city and brought into play representational strategies and tactics via which urban space might be appropriated and understood. This book asks how the city has produced certain modes of travel practice and modalities of travel writing in particular with response to urban architectures that have tended to direct the physical, perceptual and imaginative possibilities for understanding modern Western society. It asks how travel writing reveals differentiated conceptions of French culture in relation to the foreign cities of London and New York. And, finally, it looks at how travel and travel writing produces urban space, so that through bringing into dialogue urban travellers as far apart as Jules Janin and Georges Perec, we might insert travel studies within the wider debate about the ways in which place is entangled with questions of individual, collective and outsider identities. This will enable us to explore the means through which the practice of space in travel writing enmeshes aesthetics in questions pertaining to such identities, the distribution of power in society and the possibilities for intervention in the dominant discursive distributions of urban modernity. This book is an exploration, then, of how the spatial practices of travel writing engender and encode urban space and ensure the city's persistence as the prevailing expressive and organizational tool for collective understandings of Western 'civilization'.

Chapter One

PRODUCING THE CITY

The only thing that is radical is space we don't know how to inhabit.
Lebbeus Woods, cited in Alison et al. 2007, 7

Recognizing the inexhaustible quality of the urban flow of goods, capital and people that inform metropolitan life and in order to approach a means of interpreting urban travel writing, it is helpful to engage with a number of influential theoretical approaches for understanding cities. This chapter explores theories of the city along two main axes: first, as a material condition of the planning perspective, which is to say an urban environment concerned with function and place-making; and, second, as a narrative space, a space of practice where meanings are performed by subjects in places across space and time. Both of these axes correspond with common modes of differentiating between 'place' and 'space' thus facilitating a position from which to understand the interaction between ideological processes at stake in the strategies of urban planning and the 'tactics' of representation (Certeau [1980] 1990, xviii) in the travel account.

Theoretically speaking, the functionalist perspective, or how to manage urban environments, was the key perspective identifying modern cities as special entities that required new social, infrastructural and architectural arrangements. The identification of 'modernity' with the emergence of the city preoccupies the work of influential twentieth-century urbanists such as Georg Simmel ([1903] 2006), Louis Wirth (1938) and Max Weber ([1922] 1958, repr. 1969). In this view, 'what is distinctly modern in our civilization is best signalled by the growth of great cities' (Wirth 1938, 1) and, further, the shift from a largely rural to a predominantly urban society was understood to be 'accompanied by profound changes in virtually every phase of social life' (Wirth 1938, 2). In these sociologists' conception one of the central factors shaping these changes at a macrostructural level was the new economic relations of production. Cities were largely conceived from the point of view of their marked economic drive, as the 'seat of the money economy' (Simmel [1903] 2006, 12), the centre for financial, economic and capital accumulation, and thus as the driving force behind new distributions of labour, which had far-reaching effects on individuals and forms of social interaction. Simmel, for example, saw the ascent of money and capital as productive of modern 'psychic currents' and a 'number of characteristic mental tendencies', leading him to determine that the 'modern mind has become more and more a calculating one' (Simmel [1903] 2006, 13). Weber's complex structuralist typology of the social and infrastructural elements of the city emphasized the anonymity of urban life, thus building on the work of Simmel and the earlier writings of Ferdinand Tönnies ([1887] 2001). Tönnies had distinguished between *Gemeinschaft* (community) – understood as a grouping based on mutual bonds and togetherness – and *Gesellschaft* (society) – groups that are instrumentally maintained by individual members' aims and impersonal monetary connections. In all cases, the distinctions and meanings of life in the modern urban environment are articulated in opposition to a (supposedly) organic set of intercommunal relations characterized by pre-modern, rural societies, and suggested that communitarian arrangements were eroded and possibly destroyed by the rise of urban market societies. These sociologists thus saw modern cities as spatially concentrated power structures and identity catalysts, formative in the psychological, political and economic constitution of those dwelling in them. From this perspective too, the city is conceived as operational on multiple levels to produce ideology, understood to mean the range of ideas that urban institutions incarnate and their procedures for materializing such ideas in the space–time of human social relations. Sociologically speaking, then, urban infrastructures are seen to order urban spaces, and combine to produce a spatio-temporal organization conditioning urban practice at the experiential level. With their emphasis on the macrostructures organizing urban life, these theories tend to present the modern city as pivotal in the decline of a more affective life expressed in terms of 'organic', personalized and perpetuating relationships. In his famous essay, 'The Metropolis and Mental Life', Simmel writes that 'the essentially intellectualistic character of the mental life of the metropolis becomes intelligible as over against that of the small town which rests more on feelings and emotional relationships' (Simmel [1903] 2006, 12). He saw the industrial city as productive of a 'fight with nature' that had been going on between the individual and social forces since primitive times, but which had attained to new extremes in the age of the metropolis, thus giving birth to the 'metropolitan personality' (11). As opposed to these communitarian, affective ties, the modern city replaces such forms of social interaction with individualism, commerce, industry and relationships based on monetary value or abstract public opinion. Finally, although Wirth is careful to identify the growth of the city in this period as a specifically Western phenomenon, very often the sociologists of the German school tended to universalize urban phenomena and talk in terms of 'the city', considered as a singular rationalized site with shared consequences for the organization of social relations across cultures. Taylor, for example, draws on Weber as an influential proponent of what he terms the 'acultural' narrative of modernity, commenting that for Weber 'rationalization was a steady process, occurring within all cultures over time' (Taylor 2001, 174).

Attempting to harness a broader encapsulation of the city, Yves Grafmeyer (1994) proposes the following definition: 'The city is at once a territory and a population, a material framework and a unity of collective life, a configuration of physical objects and a nexus of relations between social subjects' (8).[1] Grafmeyer's definition is useful for the way it combines two orders of reality where, on the one hand, the city is static, a fixed entity circumscribed by material frameworks, and on the other, it is a dynamic space composed of individuals and interrelated groups of social actors. This tension is expressed in Henri Lefebvre's distinction between 'habitat' and 'living',[2] which makes room to acknowledge cities as constituting at once a kind of morphology of designed environments, but one which is never neutral and cannot be understood in a purely ratio-scientific sense. Space for Lefebvre consists in moving collections of ways of living and engaged existence in and through space. Lefebvre's influential book *The Production of Space* is, therefore, a central text in foregrounding the insufficiencies of considering space as a container that might be either neutrally classified or the outcomes of its presence predicted. Lefebvre argues that:

> 'human beings' do not stand before, or amid, social space; they do not relate to the space of society as they might to a picture, a show, or a mirror. They know that they *have* a space and that they *are* in this space. They do not merely enjoy a vision, a contemplation, a spectacle – for they act and situate themselves as active participants. They are accordingly situated in a series of enveloping levels each of which implies the others, and the sequence of which accounts for social practice.[3] (Lefebvre [1974] 1991, 294)

This understanding of space as inseparable from its human perception and practice – and, by implication, space as living systemically in layers of practice that produce social space – heavily informs this book's understanding of the ways in which spaces produce meaning in tandem with human interaction. The city for Lefebvre is a language, a semio-logical system, and most importantly, what he calls 'an *œuvre* of certain historical and social agents, the action and the result' ([1968] 2003, 102–3). The œuvre is linked to the formal qualities of the urban environment and its capacity to generate multiple levels of experience that transcend functionalist separations – creative activity, for example, information, symbolism, the imaginary and, significantly, play – these are all 'particular expressions and *moments* which can more or less overcome the fragmentary division of tasks' (147). These moments are akin to the spaces of improvisation which Jane Jacobs describes in *The Death and Life of Great American Cities* ([1961] 1962), where the streets con-stitute balletic performances, and are filled with potential for play, contact and encounter. The urban œuvre, according to Lefebvre then, constitutes the myriad ways in which the city is employed, 'the eminent use of the city' ([1968] 2003, 66), and this emphasis on practice positions itself in opposition to the broader strategies of urban planners and urbanization as planned modality, which tends to realize the city in terms of exchange value, productive of fixed concomitant modes of consumption and the organization of social life as a direct result of this economy. In Lefebvre's words:

> The thesis of an inert spatial medium where people and things, actions and situations merely take up their abode, as it were, corresponds to the Cartesian model (conceiving things in their extension as the 'object' of thought) which over time became the stuff of 'common sense' and 'culture'. A picture of mental space developed by the philosophers and epistemologists thus became a transparent zone, a logical medium. Thenceforward, reflective thought felt that social space was accessible to it. In fact, however, that space is the seat of a practice consisting in more than the application of concepts, a practice that also involves misapprehension, blindness, and the test of lived experience.[4] (Lefebvre [1974] 1991, 297)

1.1 Practising Place

Unpacking further these ideas around practice and agents' use of the urban environment, we begin by underscoring a theoretical difference between the terms 'space', 'place' and 'site' as they are used throughout the chapters that follow. After Certeau ([1980] 1990), a 'place' or 'site' is understood here as somewhere that is, first of all, geometrically circumscribed, namely that does not permit two things to occupy the same position at once, and that distributes things in distinct locations, so that a 'place is thus an instantaneous configuration of positions', and 'implies an indication of stability' (Certeau 1984, 117).[5] 'Place' in the urban context is remarkable for its architectural and delimited qualities, where infrastructures and points of entry or enclosure determine the geographies of possible pathways through the environment. Furthermore, 'place' implies the singularity of identity. 'The law of the "proper" rules in the place', Certeau explains, 'the elements taken into consideration are *beside* one another, each situated in its own "proper" and distinct location, a location it defines' (1984, 117).[6] Place implies an ordered configuration of positions, and in many ways here Certeau's definition can be approximated to a Euclidean conception of finite dimensional space. Recent work in human geography has sought to move away from the ratio-scientific definition which Certeau bestows on 'place'.[7] Indeed, when I talk of 'place' later on I will not usually refer to Euclidean containers, but rather to an anthropological understanding of 'place' as a site of collective meaning and shared history, which I will elaborate further in the next sections. However, Certeau's first distinction is an important set-up for the way in which 'space' will be used throughout my discussion. To distinguish better the existence of 'place' as static or absolute, Certeau reappropriates the term 'space' so as to introduce movement, *practices* and the inscription of meaning (as narrative) through human engagement with place. In this engagement, 'place' becomes 'space' or is 'spatialized' so that 'vectors of direction, velocities, and time variables' (117) are constitutive in producing its mobile, modular quality.[8] 'Space' is animated, defined by happenings and as such constitutes 'the effect produced by the operations that orient it, situate it, temporalize it, and make it function in a polyvalent unity of conflicting programs or contractual proximities' (117).[9] Space, conceived in this way, implies further the rejection of absolutes with regard to time, the subject or agent, and space, and invites the consideration of space–time from a cultural point of view, as culture – and cultural difference in particular – is significant in determining the myriad uses of place so that it becomes space. Certeau effectively reorients space to the dimensions of human experience, of what it means to be situated – subjectively, culturally, temporally – and implies the potentialities of place, drawing it nearer to a series of processes that place undergoes through being lived and experienced. As Certeau states, 'In short, *space is a practiced place*' (1984, 117, emphasis in original).[10] In this scenario, space is opened out to its full phenomenological potential, inserted into the strong qualitative differentiations of human agency, and by extension into the modes of expression that human beings employ to make sense of themselves in the world. Certeau's stance on space is intricately entwined therefore with anthropological and philosophical perspectives of the human being as articulate agent, notably engaged in the search for meaning (see Taylor [1989] 2004, 2001). Certeau posits that human practices are all manners of living that articulate ways into meaning, and that ordinary life materially and corporeally engages in the production of important distinctions that enable the self to situate itself in relationship to the world. Space conceived as practiced place thus positions the human subject as an agent whose identity is inherently spatialized as well as temporalized, and it is in this sense that we speak of 'spatialities' to refer to the inseparability of space from human identity and the sense we make of our lives. If we are talking of sense-making, we are, Certeau reminds us, talking essentially about narrative, and the transformation of place through practice into space, is akin for Certeau to the reciprocal semiological processes involved in writing (place) and reading (space). As he puts it, 'Thus the street geometrically defined by urban planning is transformed into a space by walkers. In the same way, an act of reading is the space produced by the practice of a particular place: a written text, i.e. a place constituted by a system of signs' (117).[11] In drawing the analogy between the city as text and the walker as reader of that text, we arrive at the first level through which travellers, as readers of the city, can be understood. The modes of reading, or 'strategies' and 'tactics' engaged in the emergence of legibility, will be discussed further below. For now, it is sufficient to point out a further layer in this schema wherein, with the production of the travel text, the spatiality enacted by reading the city and articulating its meaning in written form engenders a moving narrative matrix of interlocutionary forces. It is in this sense that the travel text provides a rich source for understanding the emergence of peculiarly modern Western urban lifeworlds, for the way in which, as an interpretation of foreign places in relation to home cultures, it reinforces the awareness of the travelling subject as interpreter, and of the city as multiplying the modalities of sense available to that subject. Drawing out the implications of the city as an accumulation of spatial practices means viewing it as a performative interaction of spaces, temporalities and subjects, or a 'theatre of narratives' (Schulz-Forberg 2005a, 267). In other words, a city constitutes a culturally situated agglomeration of stories, myths, memories and interpretations that pool to form a discursive and intimate physiognomy. Seen in this way, cities not only store narrative but, through the production of new representations and frameworks for meaning, are active in the modification of such narratives.

Both of these perspectives – the discursive aculturalism of functionalists and the narrative intimacies of Marxist poststructuralists – have constituted influential ways of thinking through the physical and imaginative geographies of the modern city. But well before our period, both function and narrative are identified by sixth-century scholar Saint Isidore of Spain in his book *Etymologies* to be fundamental to an understanding of the word 'city', wherein he distinguishes two strands of meaning. The first strand, the *urbs*, signifies the built environment or stones of the city representing the material, objective dimension of the town, while the second strand, *civitas*, reveals the city's role in the elaboration of social networks of meaning and denotes the emotions, rituals, value and belief systems which are formulated among these stones (see Sennett [1990] 1993, 11).

1.2 Meaning-Making in the Urban Environment

One of the essential differences of the city from other geographies and the reason for its attractiveness to the traveller from the mid-nineteenth century onward is founded in the inseparability of the city from the weave of diverse human practice and the presence of urban signs that seem indicators of modernity. In order for a city to exist, a collective has had to lay the stones for its construction, while the reasons for its growth and design are always the result of complex social appropriations of space and time. Spiro Kostof emphasizes the deep, sometimes invisible, geographical and social factors which determine the precise shape of the city's individual features:

> The fact is that no city, however arbitrary its form may appear to us, can be said to be 'unplanned'. Beneath the strangest twist of lane or alley, behind the most fitfully bounded public place, lies an order beholden to prior occupation, to the features of the land, to long-established conventions of the social contract, to a string of compromises between individual rights and the common will. (Kostof 1991, 52)

Urban arrangements emerge as an outgrowth of a discursive system of power structures and embodied values, and thus, by extension, constitute an architecturally organized manifestation of societies' power structures and frameworks for signification. In other words, cities are heavily engaged in the transmission of cultural codes through architecture, which are then either activated, perpetuated, ignored, reappropriated, misinterpreted or, ultimately, destroyed by practitioners of the city. If we look for a moment at the large-scale social shift constituting a general feature organizing modern Western cities, we can see that the growth of capitalism and its new requirements for labour in the West needed the realization of new forms that gradually came to replace the organizational principles of the medieval hamlet, borough or village. The urban theorist Jean-Pierre Frey (2000, 106) comments on the arrangement of these earlier cities saying that 'the image of their overall organization was easily accessible to everyone, their regularity being of the order of an emblematic topology, schematic but orchestrating, without significant dissent, the coordination of tasks.'[12] The dominant model for Western social relations being capitalism, social consensus understood at this level of simplicity is largely redundant in a system operating according to the global, highly mediated logic of market forces.

The emergence of the middleclass in Europe from the late Renaissance on meant that primitive capital gains were progressively invested in the legal appropriation of land and in industrial enterprise (see Savage et al. 2003). As such, a large number of symbolic strategies of communication were annexed to the proliferation of this power structure, resulting in the emergence of a modern urban architecture and infrastructural organization for cities. The level of activity, the increasing diversity and density of the city's institutional and economic life becomes explicitly entwined in the architectural configuration of the urban landscape. Frey (2000, 16) identifies the emergence of a Western architecture with the progression of capitalism:

> Architecture was born in the West, with the Renaissance, at the moment when the medieval city saw its consensual order dislocated by the development of a capitalist economy which would modify the social structure and the place of social groups in space, particularly with respect to the different relations that each of them established with the localization of their activities.[13]

In this schema, the singularity of the architectural masterpiece (the medieval cathedral, for example) passes from the hands of the masons and guild carpenters to a group of planners and architects whose authority is based in abstraction: the urban plan. The emergence of architecture, as Frey understands it, is inseparable from the progressive emergence of the individual, the new social being for whom meaning seems to lie in the rationalization of relations, and for whom, it has been argued, a new geometric, method-ical and totalizing architecture was needed in order that they could understand, signify and thereby inhabit meaningfully this brave new world (109). In this sense, architecture becomes the transcription tool of an ideological demand that sets in motion a clearly defined urban system of societal relations. More generally, architecture is a discursive mechanism, wherein changes to urban space on the synchronic level accumulate over time to give the city its history, its diachronic order, contributing to the visual emergence of the spatio-temporal urban palimpsest (see Raymond 1984). At this point, we might emphasize once again that cities such as Paris, London and New York were among the first to combine such conditions of urban life, but that these cities each lived their own national histories which duly affected the way in which such architectures were con-structed and perceived.

Within the historical and cultural vernaculars of individual sites, cities can be thought of as the holistic expression of a particular society's social imaginary. By the term 'expres-sion' I wish to imply here the reciprocity of the socio-spatial relations that come into play when we begin analysing representations of the city such as those of urban travel writing. Commenting on these relations, the geographer Michel Lussault reflects on the necessity of understanding the city as an organic, multidimensional space:

> From the outset, the city must be thought of as a *systematic*, *multidimensional* organization where all of society's aspects are articulated and inseparable, which is to say that its temporal, social (the group of individuals), individual (the individual as the smallest complex unit of society and its logic), economic, political and spatial elements are all connected. Space plays a specific and important role in this schema, making *visible* the *components* of this organization and the *principles* and *modalities* of their combination. It converts the order and logic of the urban into tangible signs, forms, structures, in short it organizes material – at once infinite in the details of its fabrication and, when considered generally, fairly simple and limited – *through* the stories and figures that stage the order and logic of urban space.[14] (2000, 31, emphasis in the original)

From this perspective, space is understood in its visuality as a configuration of signs in circulation. These signs are narratively organized in conversation with the life of the city. Urban space here then, as Foucault recognized, 'is fundamental [in the constitution of] all communal life' (Foucault [1982] 2001, II: 1101).[15] Furthermore, the urban lifeworld of modernity problematizes the idea of an archetypal mode of social order. By arche-typal I mean the notion of an immediate historically prefigured community that would (through prescribed ways of inhabiting and interpreting the meaning of the world) allow the subject to exist within a stable set of frameworks and, by extension, allow that com-munity to propagate a self-contained, immutable set of criteria for meaningful living. Through its bringing together of cultures, religions and nationalities in social and work space (whether through internal or external migratory patterns); its layering of tempo-ralities in architectural and infrastructural space (the passing of time articulated explicitly by the museum or monument, and implicitly by successive architectural styles standing side by side, wear and tear); and its wider insertion into a transnational and interlinked network of similar urban conglomerates, the modern city is instrumental (although it is by no means the only causal factor) in propagating the collapse of transcendental, universalist notions of the 'correct' way to live, or the 'right' thing to believe.

In modernity, then, space can no longer be thought of as fixed or immobile (see Massey 2005; Cresswell 2004), rather its assemblage is dependent on certain spatial practices or 'spatializations', which, by extension, imply the mutuality of theory and material realities. Foucault goes on to explain how it is impossible to delimit a 'rational', objective space from space as it is lived:

> We do not live in a kind of void, inside which we might situate individuals and things. We do not live inside a shimmering kaleidoscope of the void, we live inside a system of relations which define the irreducible placement of one next to the other [...].[16] (Foucault [1982] 2001, II: 1574)

In other words, theory (the abstract space of architects and planners, for example) does not flow, detached, above the pragmatic, empirical space of the city, nor, concomitantly, can the inner life of the urban inhabitant be completely extracted from the exterior space of architects and planners. Inextricable from one another, this interconnection has profound implications for the construction of meanings for identities (individual and collective) and for the organization of the urban world and human existence within it.

Lefebvre is the pioneer in elaborating the above position through his establishment in *The Production of Space / La Production de l'espace* ([1974] 1991) of a theory of *spatial practices*. In this influential work, Lefebvre carves out a place within theory that considers the use and representation of space as key to the ongoing production of individual and collective identities. 'Spatial practice', simply put, constitutes fields where space, ideology and representation intersect along both synchronic and diachronic axes to generate meaning, or in other words, 'spatial practice' refers to the production and reproduction of spatial relations between objects and subjects. With particular attention paid to the urban context, Lefebvre of course rejects the idea that space is an 'empty container' or 'abstract category', and instead conceives it as a mode of *perception* in the multisensory phenomenological sense, one that is, furthermore, inseparable from the subject's ontological sense of being in the world. This position constitutes an important rejection of the ratio-scientific, Neo-Cartesian idea that space is entirely shaped by the singularity of authoritative planning or – in the Neo-Kantian frame – that space operates as an inert backdrop to the life of its practitioners. Throughout the chapters that follow I conceive of the act of travel as one such spatial practice, and argue that the modes of perception engaged by the traveller are productive of particular ways of being in the city for our period. In addition, for this book's exploration of the relation between the pragmatic practice of travel in urban spaces and the representational practice of urban travel writing, Lefebvre's theory of space and spatial practice is especially useful in its identification of two modes of spatial production involved in the construction of meaning in the urban environment. These modes constitute, first, 'Representations of space' – or space as it is *conceived* – which are implicated in the relations of labour, its organization (or, in Marxist terms, 'production'), and to 'the "order" which those relations impose; hence to knowledge, to signs, to codes, and to "frontal" relations'[17] (Lefebvre [1974] 1991, 33). For our context, this includes the space of the urbanist, the planner and the architect as well as social engineers and bureaucratic institutions – the spaces that the urban travel-ler encounters at the level of perception. This is 'place' as Certeau understands it, albeit in a less directly Marxist tone of voice. The second mode consists in 'Representational spaces', which refers to space as it is lived through 'its associated images and symbols and hence the space of "inhabitants" and "users", but also of some artists [...]. This is the dominated [...] space which the imagination seeks to change and appropriate' (Lefebvre ([1974] 1991, 39).[18] Once again, for our context this can be understood in terms of the dialectical relation between the spatial practice of the travel writer (their interpretation of the city through walking, through writing) and the representations of space – the signs, codes and architectures – that they encounter in the modern city. Lefebvre's spatial theory reassesses, then, the notion that the city can be considered solely in terms of a definable and discrete unity, or as a site where detached technocratic ideologies shape reality at will, to think instead about urban reality as a process of interaction between variously motivated spatial practices. These three categories – spatial practice, repre-sentations of space and representational spaces – have been provocative in the fields of geography and sociology and are clearly instrumental in the spatial theories of Certeau as well as in Foucault's archaeology of power and discourse. Insofar as Lefebvre's model tends broadly to distinguish professional or institutional practices such as planning and the built environment from the spatial practices of everyday life and from the symbolic meanings erected in spatial forms, it promotes an understanding of the city as a space where pragmatic and symbolic boundaries shift in relational negotiation between institu-tions and practitioners. Lefebvre's spatial typology then, enriches our analysis of travel and travel writing as fields where urban space, ideology and representation are impli-cated in the generation of meaning and identity.

1.3 Representations of Space I: The 'Figured City'

The urban traveller's practice of the city is generally ordered in response to a series of privileged nodes or sites. These are the places featured in the guidebook (for example, monuments and official buildings) that have a privileged status in tourist discourse. Cities, in this schema, consist in compartmentalized networks of officialized places, designed and planned with an aim to coordinate a certain (ideological) scheme for living (Lefebvre's 'space of domination'), to produce what M. Christine Boyer terms the 'figured' city (1995, 82). The figured city constitutes a network of urban sites that are highly conceptu-alized, as conceived by urban planners, architects and politicians. For Boyer, this idea of the 'figure' encapsulates a notion of the city composed as 'a series of carefully developed nodes generated from a set of design rules or patterns' (81). These sites seek to regulate meaning in the urban landscape and, very often, impose a hierarchical structure whereby certain of the city's places are privileged over others through material strategies ensuring cultural and/or political hegemony. They represent an architectural selection and an organized conceptual design that contribute to what the urbanist Kevin Lynch (1960) calls the 'imageability' of the city. As the term suggests, 'imageability' is attentive to the potential for an urban site to be configured perceptually and thus remembered. The urban planner aims at making the environment holistically visible to its users by organizing places in a clear, often diagrammatic, manner. Lynch argues that these designed sites are essential to the subject's feelings of stability, saying that 'a good environmental image gives its possessor an important sense of emotional security. He can establish a harmonious relationship between himself and the outside world' (1960, 4). In this view, 'imageability' is inseparable from how the subject understands his/her place in the outside world; the architectures and spatial arrangements of the city are conceived as legible entities, not merely implicated in the physical structuring of the city, but contributing to the production and assurance of meaning for the individual. The affective significance of spatial design is further emphasized by Lynch, who states that 'a distinctive and legible environment not only offers security but also heightens the potential depth and intensity of human experience' (5). The constitution of the object through its arrangement in terms of an overall structure is thus what makes up the taxonomy of the architectural sites of the city, allowing urban space to be read, to connote, and to establish meaningful correspondences between subjects and their environment. While Lynch is speaking here from the point of view of the urban planner, the conception of physical space in terms of its legibility is important to an understanding of how shared imaginative geographies or meaningful communities are in their turn produced. In the light of Foucault's (1966) emphasis on the role of language and classification systems in providing or indicating the underlying infrastructures determining meaning for a particular civilization, the city can be understood as a place that offers itself to interpretation and, by extension, its semiotic and situated framework materially codify ideologies and engage urban users with these artefacts. For our purposes, the relevance of considering the city as a collection of legible nodes lies in its pertinence to the traveller, who very often refers to the city as a textual assemblage, moving between degrees of legibility and illegibility, with the travel account evidencing varying moods of pleasure or anxiety in correspondence with the urban semiological experience.

1.4   Representations of Space II: Constructing Cultural Codes in Architecture

Since the late nineteenth century, identification of the constructed quality of the ideological frameworks providing meaning for humankind in society has been the consistent problematic in the evolution of discourses and methodologies within the human sciences. The role which material constructions have in shaping and communicating ideologies has preoccupied critical theorists as well as architects (see Norberg-Schulz 2000; Paquot 2000; Raymond 1984; Rossi 1982; Tafuri 1976). Within this debate, Foucault's work on space and power has had a resounding influence. Foucault's (1975; [1967] 2001; [1982] 2001b) philosophy of space is of relevance to an analysis of urban travel writing for how it emphasizes the architectural object's implication in materializing a dominant power structure's economy of the sign. The construction of legible sites and their role in the consolidation of ideologies is at the heart of Foucault's concerns with architecture. His work on the ideological constitution of a public site builds on Lefebvre's ([1974] 2000) conception of space as production, while developing further how architecture and the institutional arrangements of space are implicated in the emergence of a 'site', understood to mean the material choice and perpetuation of one discursive 'truth' over another. From this perspective, planning and architecture function to allow for the production of a conceptual 'order of things' (Foucault 1966);[19] a topology shaping the meaning of the city according to the hierarchical structure of its privileged fragments. Essential to Foucault's thought is the idea that these configured sites are exclusionary; they are privileged to the detriment of other spaces within the city. The figured city symbolically excludes unplanned spaces whose meaning or function is not easily discernible. By extension, the organization of the urban landscape via the institutional control of architecture is seen as crucial to the *governmentality* of the city. To govern, in this sense, is to structure, through place, fields of meaning within the city; to control the semiotic and hermeneutic possibilities organizing the field of physical and conceptual action of others in society. The figured city as it is ordered by governing bodies is, therefore, the outgrowth of an authoritative social logic that produces and perpetuates modes of human categorization, categorizations that manifest themselves spatially in both material and immaterial ways (Kostof 1991, 43). For instance, conditions like zoning and house prices relative to location consolidate material differences in social class, while self-image, accent and notions of belonging to one class rather than another are some of the less visible results of spatial positioning (Goffman 1963, 1971; Jacobs [1961] 1962; Sennett 1996). These divisions are seen as crucial in the creation of schematic characterizations, whereby the individual becomes 'the symbolic inhabitant'[20] (Foucault 1975, 232), or a sign with a designated position within the overall spatial production of the city.

But the ways in which the city directs the cultural practices of its inhabitants need not always be as conceptually determined as it is in the case, for example, of an authoritarian government strategy. Augé (1986) points out that even the most quotidian of architectural structures – the public transport system – enmeshes the urban individual in ritual codes of conduct and mnemonic symbolism that structure lives and, to a greater or lesser degree, control the movements of any individual. The physical sites of the city are all engaged in the erection of systems of value and hierarchies of meaning within the urban universe and, to a greater or lesser extent, function as mechanisms of power instrumental in the production of spatial strategies of control so that dominant discursive operations ensuring coherence and cultural hegemony are maintained. Architecture functions in this schema to delimit the boundaries of the possible interpretations of the self and others, as well as to direct the collective spatial practice of a culture towards accepting the prevalence of a certain discourse or reality over another. Certeau elaborates this attempt at authoritative direction by drawing an analogy between architectural practice and language:

> The geometric space of urbanists and architects seems to have value as the 'correct sense' constructed by grammarians and linguists with a view to establishing a normal and normative level against which to refer to 'figurative' deviations.[21] (Certeau [1980] 1990, I: 152)

In this way, urban planning performs in a similar way to a standard grammar, providing the structural elements as well as the regulations for the construction of sites of conventionalized meaning.

Rationalized surfaces present the world as a coherent entity, cutting off possibilities in the arbitrary and the plurality of human experience in an attempt to streamline reality in accordance with a conceptual schema, and, as with a standard grammar, this normative function is crucial in guaranteeing the transmission of shared cultural meaning within society. From the urban planner's perspective, to practice urban space, then, is equivalent to practising a discursive, conceptual strategy.

While Foucault's analysis of disciplinary architecture aims at understanding the development of power structures in the eighteenth and nineteenth centuries, the work of Gilles Deleuze extends Foucault's approach to the twentieth, and is increasingly relevant too for spatial understandings in the twenty-first century. In his essay *Post-scriptum sur les sociétés de contrôle*, Deleuze terms Foucault's objects of study as 'disciplinary societies'[22] wherein the prison provides the analogical model for the State's architectural manifestation of its power over competing ideologies and which 'precede the organization of the great places of enclosure'[23] (1990a, 240). For Deleuze, discourses of power no longer exert their influence through such obviously carceral structures. Rather, with the twentieth century, Westerners enter the age of '*societies of control*' (1990a, original emphasis).[24] Deleuze sums up the difference between these strategies of organization (enclosure versus control) in terms of their relative concreteness:

> Enclosures are *moulds*, distinct mouldings, but controls are a *modulation*, like a self-deforming moulding that changes constantly, from one instant to the next, like a sieve whose meshes shift from one point to another.[25] (242, emphasis in the original)

Architectures of control are essentially intangible and, through their intangibility, more pervasive; they consist in the conception and construction of the city as an undulating site of networks; as facilitator of the circulation of certain affective deterrents to 'bad' behaviour – the CCTV camera, the fear of attack, the invisible processes of data tracking, for example. This shift, from tangible confinement to the omnipresent evanescence of control, finds its ultimate expression in the replacement of the gold standard, guarantor of monetary value, with the stock market, where money is only ephemerally manifest as credit and its value subject to stock holders' whims. This is also named in terms of a shift from an industrial to a post-industrial mode of urban organization.

Another example of this shift that preoccupies the work of both Deleuze and Paul Virilio ([1980] 1989) is the ability of contemporary architectural technologies to regulate the temporal reality of environments. In the modern city, time can be conceived in terms of temporal rhythm regulated in conjunction with the development of systems of transport, hours of business and the development of machines allowing the citizen to go further faster. The physical acceleration of urban life is, therefore, radical in its alteration of spatio-temporal perception, as the ratio of time taken to distance covered is profoundly distorted and, likewise, this acceleration radicalizes psychological and physical expectations with regard to accessibility and distantiation. Perceptually, space, as it is experienced through technologies of travel, differs radically from an 'organic' or stable experience of the city. In the former case, the environment is highly controlled and the body very restricted in its movements, with the medium of transport usually moving at considerable speed (at least at a rate beyond what is possible for the human body).[26] Virilio's ([1980] 1989) work has been demonstrative of the radical effects that new, post-industrial forms of spatial practice have on time. In the urban context, one obvious example of this is the effect that technologies of transport have had upon the temporal structure of city life. With the evolution of high-speed trains, trams, the expansion of rail and road networks among others, the ratio of distance covered to time taken has been profoundly readjusted. In different ways, these readjustments alter the expectations of both the inhabitant and the visitor with regard to the conventions of the pace of everyday life within the city. The inhabitant anticipates the 'normal' length of time a journey should take with respect to the functioning of the infrastructures of the urban transport system. Improvements or deteriorations in the working of the system continually alter his/her temporal and spatial reality. For the traveller, the process is as fundamental to urban practice but for somewhat different reasons. The traveller, coming from one spatial condition (home) to another (the foreign city) is in a comparative position; the foreign transport and the structure of time are altered in relation to another 'ground'. Furthermore, it is also important to underline the equation of corporeal disengagement from space with abstraction in Virilio's work; the disappearance of humans from their environment and their abstention to a purely intellectual space. In Virilio's view, the physical abstraction attendant upon urban societ-ies has profound consequences for a person's knowledge (physical as well as spiritual) of the exterior world and their sense of self within that world. 'The development of high speeds', according to Virilio, 'culminates in the disappearance of the consciousness of direct perception of phenomena that informs us about our own existence' (Virilio [1980] 1989, 117).[27] Such a perspective evidences a nostalgia for an 'organic' physical connec-tion with space where the body physically endures travelling from one point to another. In the context of this assessment of architecture's role in the reinforcement of capitalist logic, the replacement of real boundaries with virtual networks of restraint can be ren-dered semiotically as the gradual loosening of the sign from its referential object. The sign is no longer grounded in relation to an actual object, what could be termed 'reality'; instead, the signifier becomes meaningful only through its relation with other signifiers. This is an important concept for Jean Baudrillard in America for example, but it is also emergent in the earlier travel writing of Paul Morand. Speed (spatially and temporally) reduces reality to signs; to speak in postmodern terms, reality enters simulation, lend-ing itself to the experience and interpretation of the city as a network of free-floating signifiers.

1.5   Representational Spaces: From the 'Figured City' to the Lives of Spaces

In spite of the governmental strategies for distributing processes of place-making, these exist in persistent renegotiation with the spatial practices of what Lefebvre and Certeau have termed 'everyday' or 'lived' spatial practices. While conceptually the city may be rendered as a diagrammatic whole by cityplanners and architects, this relatively stable and controllable abstraction is always in persistent dialogue with the practices of the city as lived experience, or the 'chance-grown' or 'geomorphic' spaces of quotidian life (Kostof 1991, 43). Concerned to open a space of analysis to challenge Foucault's theory of disciplinary power, Certeau asks, 'But with regard to these apparatus producing disciplinary space, what *practices of space* correspond to them, from the other side, where one plays (with) discipline?' (Certeau [1980] 1990, I: 143, emphasis in the original).[28] Certeau identifies three critical operations at work in rendering the city a strategy-driven discursive space in order to lay the foundation for his own critique of such a space. These three points identify the criteria for the creation of the figured city. The first of these is 'the production of a *proper* space'[29] (Certeau [1980] 1990, I: 143, original emphasis): or the rationalizing of space through the elimination of any physical, mental or political 'pollutants' that would compromise its coherency. Second, 'the substitution of a non-time, or a synchronic system, for the evasive and stubborn resistances of tradition' (143).[30] The opacity of the past and any future uncertainty is flattened out so that the city might seem impervious to history, a schematic whole always making sense and eternally transparent to the present. Third, the last stage in the creation of the ideal conceptual 'city' is 'the creation of a *universal* and anonymous *subject* which is the city itself' (143, original emphasis).[31] Here, actions formally attributed to various individuals or groups become attributable to a global, invisible entity: 'the City'. This is the City as allegory, a single agent to which all action within the real city can be attributed (see also Attali 2001).

However, these strategies for managing the city as a neat, conceptual package are in perpetual tension with other spatial practices that do not 'fit' this overall plan.

The fallacy of the plan as a unifying, synchronizing tool has also been disputed by architects. Aldo Rossi argues that human intervention (which he refers to as 'artefacts') must be considered in conjunction with urban design if the formation of the city is to be understood:

> The principles of architecture are unique and immutable; but the responses to different questions as they occur in actual situations, human situations, constantly vary. On the one hand, therefore, is the rationality of architecture; on the other, the life of the works themselves. When an architecture at a particular moment begins to constitute new urban artefacts which are *not* responsive to the actual situation of the city, it necessarily does so on the level of aesthetics; and its results inevitably tend to correspond historically to reformist or revolutionary movements. (Rossi 1982, 116)

The architect's statement is significant here for its recognition of the primacy of time as a disruptive force in the figured city. 'The spatialization of the expert's discourse'[32] (Certeau [1980] 1990, I: 134) is essentially a mythologizing strategy on the part of the dominant, a ruse to make one ideology seem 'natural', true, and in order for this myth to be consolidated it is necessary to simplify history in terms of this discursive ruse. Certeau writes of these 'modern mutations of time into controllable space', saying that 'scientific writing, the constitution of a proper place, [as] bringing time, the fugitive, back to the norms of an observable and legible system' (Certeau [1980] 1990, I: 134).[33] Sites such as official monuments and museums are obvious examples of this as their procedures materially package narratives for easy consumption, spatializing myriad individual stories into coherent wholes. However, the reinscription of time into the spatialized framework of the city asserts the importance of a diachronic axis in the production of urban space, temporalizing whatever conceptual or structural shape the city takes and placing this structure in dialogue with moments of historic importance, thereby further inscribing potential change into the city's future. In this manner, the causality behind the structure is unveiled and the selection of its components exposed as an exclusionary system of relations. Reinscribing time to urban space shows that there were (and still are) always other potential schemas for the city's arrangement in the present; time thus dispels the myth of inevitability. In order to discover the conditions and complexities of spatial production, it is therefore necessary 'to rediscover *time* (and in the first place the time of production) in and through space' (Lefebvre [1974] 1991, 91, emphasis in the original). Time is presented here in terms of *human agency*: individuals and institutions involved in the 'tactical' (Certeau [1980] 1990) negotiation of urban places, inserting mobility and possibility into discursive distribution. The time implicated here is neither linear nor progressive, nor does it dispel engagement with the technocratic, arranged time of urban life as organized by grander structures. Rather Certeau posits a conception of the city that acknowledges spatial practices which are not necessarily traceable, quantifiable or rational but kinetic and chaotically energetic.

These actions, or 'tactics'/'tactiques' as Certeau terms them, modify the conceptual city by the introduction of 'urban practices'/'pratiques urbaines' (Certeau [1980] 1990, I: 142). Examples of these activities include walking the streets of the city, shopping, eating, drinking, cooking and, importantly for our context, travelling and, more complexly, writing. The latter activity will form the basis of the next section of this chapter where we will explore the tensions emergent in the representational act, which effectively moves between strategy and tactic, a move that can be identified aesthetically in terms of 'legislative' and 'interpretive' modes of writing. For now, while the macrostructural and microstructural forces of governmentality seek to present the city as a coherent whole, a tactic 'inserts absences in the spatial continuum' and, according to Certeau, 'retains only those pieces it chooses: its relics'[34] (Certeau [1980] 1990, I: 153). In this respect, the quotidian actions of people contribute to the fragmentation of the 'conceptual' schema of the figured city. Where technocratic design fabricates the myth of the city via the simplification of that space, day-to-day practices augment the city's density, amplifying the detail of the urban space through countless practices that ensure the continuity of everyday life. At the same time, this conscious or unconscious undermining of the regulated discursive sites of the city creates 'holes'/'des trous' (Certeau [1980] 1990, I: 154) in the coherency of the urban fabric as conceived by its architects and planners. Along with telling the 'official' story of a civilization through its institutions and monuments, therefore, the city becomes the place of untold stories, of forgetting, of memories. Walking through the streets of the city, eating, talking, buying, travelling – all spatial practices that are not representable in their instantaneity – transform the urban scene, layering and perforating the coherent and analytical meanings of discursive space.

From the point of view of urban travel and travel writing, this everyday dimension is valuable for its reinstatement of these minor practices as modes of engendering the spatial dynamics of meanings in the city. The emphasis on the unquantifiable allows for a consideration of the travel writer not simply as a figure that reproduces the established discourses of the city but as an active, individual agent implicated in the ongoing production of imaginative geographies of the modern urban lifeworld. Certeau creates a critical space, therefore, where it becomes possible to conceive of travel in terms of a negotiation between circumscribed, discursive routes and other less quantifiable practices, where the 'site' is perhaps abandoned or its status undermined by the traveller's presence. The 'everyday', as a methodological tool thus emphasizes the spontaneous and the unknown, and becomes especially useful in the analysis of travel writing where we can then begin to distinguish travel as a mode of spatial practice, and its representational spaces as tending towards either the strategic or tactical appropriation of the discursive spaces of representation. Indeed, one of the major attractions of the city for the travel writer is precisely that it is a space where the problematic interaction between the discursive orders and everyday elements relationally come into view, and the infinite and constructed mobility of the signifying process are in constant evidence. Understood as a spatial production, the city thus enters into dialogue with the human agents practising its space.

1.6   Travel as Spatial Practice

Meaning in the city is formed and organized, therefore, through the consistent interaction of spatial practices, their movement through representations of space and the materialization of interpretation in representational spaces. This leads us to consider some points of differentiation between the modes of interaction of the traveller and those of the urban dweller, which prove important for distinguishing urban travel as a discrete spatial practice. As I have already mentioned, questions of what it means to *inhabit* a space have been of primary concern to architects, planners and urban theorists since the beginning of the twentieth century, and it has been mainly from this perspective that questions of urban spatial practice have been approached critically.[35] Travel can, however, be differentiated from dwelling, and outlining the general perspectives and practices of the urban inhabitant serves here to foreground some elementary points of distinction with the traveller's contrasting responses to the city's spaces of representation. This will allow us to distinguish the ontological and epistemological criteria that contribute to the traveller's imaginative geography of the modern urban world.

1.6.1   *The Inhabitant*

The most immediate difference between those who travel to the city and those who dwell there is the contrasting relationship both have to 'home'. Home functions symbolically in the first instance as a space where the self finds definition through its surroundings. As Henry David Thoreau writes in *Walden; or, Life in the Woods* ([1854] 1995),

> I sometimes dream of a larger and more populous house, standing in a golden age, of enduring materials [...] which shall still consist of only one room, a vast, rude, substantial, primitive hall without ceiling or plastering [...] a cavernous house [...] where some may live in the fire-place, some in the recess of a window, and some on settles, some at one end of the hall, some at another, and some aloft on the rafters with the spiders, if they choose; a house which you have got into when you have opened the outside door, and the ceremony is over. (Thoreau [1854] 1995, 157)

Here the house functions as a space for seclusion from the outside world, an insular refuge from society and its ritualized definitions of the individual in relation to normative or collective standards. This is the house functioning as 'home', where 'home' is a space for the existence of the self in a state beyond the prescriptive codes of the social order. Meanwhile, in Bachelard's phenomenological analysis, the home is described as a site where a person achieves self-integration:

> The house is our corner of the world. It is – it's often been said – our first universe. It is really a cosmos [...] Thus the house is not only lived day by day, along the thread of a story, in the tale of our history. In dreaming, the various resting places of our lives interpenetrate and guard treasures of days past [...]. Memories of the external world will never have the same tonality as those of the house. [...] The house, in the life of a man, evinces contingencies, it multiplies suggestions of continuity. Without it, man would be a dispersed being.[36] (Bachelard [1957] 2001, 24–26)

Bachelard conceives of the home as a *centre*, and as fundamental for establishing a sense of connection between the intimate world of the self and the external world. Home provides a point of control, or stable measure from which all other experience is derived. Dwelling in the city, the home, as a site of permanence, provides the inhabitant with a relatively stable environment, a background from which the self can be projected and understood in a relation to the environment.[37] Following the work of Martin Heidegger ([1971] 2005), a further symbolic dimension can be added to the Western conception of dwelling. For Heidegger, dwelling is concerned with finding an authentic (*eigentlich*) state of *Dasein*, or being: an existence that can determine its own state of being-in-the-world, or put more simply to be free enough not to conform to what others (*das Man*) in society think or do. From this perspective, architecture ought to be concerned with the act of dwelling as a spiritual state, a poetics of living rather than simple functionality. Heidegger argues that alienation within contemporary society is produced by the separation of thought and spirit, a condition epitomized by the rationalist privileging of technology and calculative thinking. From Heidegger's perspective, to dwell in the city engenders imaginative geographies that are often linked to nostalgia owing to the shifts in domestic life that the capitalist city demands, but also to the idea of a central, stable position from which the world can be interpreted and meaningfully lived in. Heidegger thus offers a topological interpretation of the transcendental.

From this position, we can dissociate qualitatively the inhabitant's spatial consciousness from that of the traveller, this dissociation having importance for outlining a generalized psychology of the different impact that urban surroundings have on the traveller and the inhabitant respectively. To dwell in a particular environment is, generally, to practise that environment in terms of a set of conceptual (and physical) limits that serve to stabilize the territory within which the dweller does or does not *belong*, where the issue of belonging constitutes the source of security or tension in the inhabitant's identity in relation to wider society. This is not to say that dwelling should be entirely distinguished from moving in the general sense. Pierre Sansot raises the question asking, 'Are we sure that moving is the opposite of dwelling?' (1998, 173) before proceeding to answer, explaining:

> It is now possible to move beyond this opposition – at least in certain circumstances. Dwelling is above all developing habits to such an extent that the outside becomes a shell for the individual and the inner space that I am. That is why, in a certain way, people can claim to inhabit a certain bus route from when they start travelling on it every day. (173)

For the inhabitant, the city is inscribed with habit, with familiarity and, through repetition, with a rhythm that ensures the city is experienced as a series of places that in many ways guarantee the relative cohesion of social and personal identity in relation and in difference to others' movements, habits and regular haunts.[38] Coming to issues of the legibility of space, it is the experiential qualities of dwelling that set inhabitants and travellers apart. As Lynch (1960) points out, through regular contact with the urban object, a repertoire of knowledge is constructed by the inhabitant that creates an image and an order of the city: 'There may be little in the real object', Lynch says, 'that is ordered or remarkable, and yet its mental picture has gained identity and organization through long familiarity' (Lynch 1960, 6). The practices of everyday life produce meaning within the environment through routine and repetition; the rituals organizing life on a day-to-day basis forming the identity of the practitioner, while simultaneously producing representational spaces, or an interpretive vision (among a multitude of possible others) of the city. Dwelling, to a large extent, naturalizes the values of the society within which one lives and lends coherency to the environment. Furthermore, to naturalize the codes of meaning production is to practise semiosis somewhat unconsciously. This is not to imply that the urban dweller is unaware of the organization and constructed nature of his/her environment, but there is a greater degree of semiotic awareness inherent in the travel experience, for the travel encounter is an encounter with the signs of difference. The city dweller practises urban space through habitual modes because he/she practises meaning from within. In dwelling, meaning can be seen to contain a degree of stability that is absent (often deliberately so) for the traveller approaching frameworks of habit and regularity from without.

In addition to having an integrated space in which to dwell, the motivations behind the inhabitant's spatial practices of the city are very often at odds with those of the traveller. These motivations engender different meanings through the alternative manipulation of time and consciousness so that the inhabitant and the traveller experience the same spaces using generally different interpretive codes. From a quantitative perspective, then, the space–time of the inhabitant's urban world is organized in accordance with the necessities of everyday life. The inhabitant's universe takes form and is functionally focused within urban spaces concerned, for example, with getting to and from work, the work environment itself, the rituals of going to school, the trip to the supermarket and places for leisure, sometimes to the point where the space is no longer remarked upon and engagement with it takes place in an automatic fashion. These everyday practices tend towards localization whereby the ritual and routine of everyday life organizes the city into personalized categories, which can be seen as supplements to the discursive demarcations of the *quartier*, district or neighbourhood (Lynch 1960). These personal localities will be more or less restrictive and reductive of the city; a commuter, for example, will have a much wider locality than someone who lives and works in the same neighbourhood. The extent of this territory will also influence the inhabitant's depth of knowledge with regard to his/her locality; a commuter will experience a large proportion of it through the medium of public transport, whereby the space beyond the automobile's or train's interior is experienced on a more superficial level than someone who lives and works in that same space (Urry 2007). For the commuter, the spaces of the train or automobile are parts of their localized spatial experience and, correspondingly, the particular qualities and conditions of those transport spaces are instrumental in the commuter's construction of meaning within the environment.

1.6.2   *Travel and the Traveller*

If understanding what it means to inhabit a space has been much debated, recent scholarship has also highlighted the difficulty of the term 'travel' and proved hesitant in deciding when exactly one becomes a 'traveller'. The question of what travel is and, just as importantly, what it is not, reveals a concern for definition (Buzard 2005, 43–61). Some engagement with this question yields useful directional results in the analysis of travel as an urban spatial practice. One of the main motivations for placing disciplinary boundaries on the term *travel* originates with the explosion in academia of areas of research such as 'Cultural Studies' and 'New Historicism', 'characterised', as James M. Buzard sees it, 'by a studied avoidance of explicit disciplinary claims' (Buzard 2005, 46–47). The debate is ongoing, but addressed here are questions of relevance to establishing a preliminary set of paradigms for interpreting the traveller's response to the urban environment.[39]

Asking what it means to travel, Buzard formulates two questions, asking, 'what is this "travel" we study?', and 'how do we know when someone is "traveling"?' (Buzard 2005, 43). Is it enough to equate 'travel' with movement? If one understands travel in this way, then the daily commute of the urban dweller must be taken into consideration. However, while this use of the term 'travel' may be of some use to sociologists, ethnologists and urbanists interested in the constitution of routine and ritual within the urban dweller's everyday life, it is not as helpful to an analysis of travel writing. As outlined above, the general ontology of commuting is importantly linked to familiarity and repetition; if commuting is of relevance to our discussion, it is so from the perspective of the outsider who is interpreting and textually translating his/her observations for reading by a public unacquainted or less acquainted with the ritual. However, this point of comparison does lead us to the first distinction contributing to a differential framework within which the texts under discussion can be justified and approached: the idea of defamiliarization.

Primary to the act of dwelling is a large degree of familiarity with one's surroundings. The notion of the 'everyday', as understood by Certeau and Lefebvre, tends to exclude the experience of travellers, who, in the search for elsewhere, are inclined to place themselves outside the range of the quotidian. This exclusion is not unproblematic. As stated above, the traveller often includes accounts of daily life within his/her writing – the daily practices of the inhabitant are of acute interest to the outsider granting an ethnological dimension to travel writing. In addition, in our contemporary and extensively mediatized world, what might have once constituted the great Unknown is now itself virtually unknown, with the result that the strange is never without some degree of familiarity. However, the notion of 'defamiliarization' proves useful as a critical basis from which to approach urban travel. We note, first of all, that the term has been associated with travel as the act of placing physical distance between oneself and one's homeland. Georges Van Den Abbeele (1992) has studied the various uses of spatial metaphor in describing thought-worlds and states that 'to call an existing order (whether epistemological, aesthetic, or political) into question by placing oneself "outside" that order, by taking "a critical distance" from it, is implicitly to invoke the metaphor of unconventional thought as travel' (xiii). Correspondingly, physical movement has long been ascribed to the development of a critical consciousness in relation to one's society. However, the metaphorical use of the term 'travel' proves too broad a concept to capture in any finite analysis. With an appreciation for the poetic value of Robyn Davidson's (2000, 4) assertion that 'the metaphor of the journey is embedded in the very way in which we conceive of life – a movement from birth to death, from this world to the next, from ignorance to wisdom', Tim Youngs (2004, 179) argues that 'to extend travel metaphorically to any and every life event, and to the nation itself, is to dematerialize travel and to make of it a huge and empty metaphor'.

For our purposes, the term 'defamiliarization' has been restricted and considered in relation to a lived encounter with the city. Such a limitation serves to direct the study towards material encounters with the city in order to explore the ideological and aesthetic implications of urban form within specific spatio-temporal contexts. This perspective is grounded, therefore in a study of the tension between the real and the representational. Experiencing the city on a day-to-day basis, the inhabitant gains a certain intimacy with his/her environment. Familiarity, whether conscious or unconscious, gained through repetition, constitutes what Augé (1986) has termed the rituals of the contemporary city or spatial practices that construct meaning through the mechanisms of repeated confirmation over an extensive period of time. The absence of this type of reflexive knowledge is one of the most significant associations for a concept of what is means to travel. More than mobility across space, a qualification for thinking travel lies in its quality as a modality for negotiating the world in terms of a departure from everyday practices. Travel can be thought of as a radical act in the extent to which it proposes dimensions for experience that defamiliarize the world.

The reasons for the lack of familiarity that the abstention of the everyday entails may seem obvious, but these elements are of crucial importance in the construction of the traveller's urban universe. The first of these reasons is temporal: normally, the traveller has only a limited period of time within which to experience the city and, therefore, does not have time to build a relationship with it whereby familiarity would in some senses naturalize the urban space. A reduction of the temporal complexity of urban experience is achieved spatially through place selection: a confined number of key sites to be visited in order to have experienced the 'essentials' of the city. This spatio-temporal reduction forms the ideological basis at the heart of the urban travel industry whose function it is to 'sum up' the whole of the city. Through this simplification, the city is experienced reductively, categorized according to a guidebook hierarchy of 'sites' or monuments. The second consequence of temporal restriction is that there is less time to become accustomed to the surroundings. Thus limited time, or the 'window' that frames the travel experience, tends to magnify the significance of the encounter. This heightened awareness of the environment means that the experience of space is almost always accompanied by an appreciation of its signs' positions within the symbolic order as often the encounter with difference in urban space brings the question of legibility to the fore. In this way, as Jonathan Culler (1990, 2) notes, travellers practice the city in terms of its objects' value as signifiers, not in the more everyday terms of their use-value. These signs of difference demand hermeneutic engagement if the traveller is to 'make sense' of his/her environment, and certainly if the traveller is to represent this experience. The foreign urban space is under constant scrutiny, being interpreted, its meaning being worked out according to either the legislative or interpretive frameworks governing the traveller's models for making sense of the world.

The consciousness of the city as an encounter with signs is heightened for the traveller, as an 'in-betweener' (Borm 2000) is alive to the differences between their own daily existence at home and this new spatio-temporal experience of the foreign city. As such, therefore, 'defamiliarization' – a concept associated with Victor Shklovsky's ([1917] 2006, 781) distinction between artistic language and everyday language – can be transported by analogy to the spatial practice of travel: travel is to artistic language as inhabiting is to everyday language. To put this in another way, travellers do not generally seek out objects for their usefulness, but rather for their artfulness, for the heightened perceptual experience which they bring to the contrastive encounter with the foreign. And the traveller who attempts – not without difficulty in today's globalized world – to remove the familiar from his/her range of experience indicates how travel might constitute a radical gesture in the constitution of identities from a perspective of difference. Conceived thus, contact with the foreign becomes a performative element in the construction or confirmation of alterity within the city. The spatial and temporal reductions of the travel experience are thus instrumental in fashioning alternative positions from which to read and write space.

1.7 Reading the City

Before turning to questions of representation we can specify several dominant ways of using the city, locating urban travel within a historical framework of cultural norms. These modes have contributed to the consolidation of cultural models for travel, and create what we might term an 'ontology of travel' according to which the act of travel is made comprehensible, and whose paradigms direct the experience and interpretation of the urban universe (Urbain 2000, 144). This ontology constitutes a consciousness on the part of the traveller as to the significance of his/her experience in the city, and its subsequent representation in the travel journal. It is largely based upon a network of signs that are loaded with meaning and offer degrees of interpretive access to the foreign urban space. The criteria for the establishment of categorical hierarchies determining the value of the travel experience constitute the anthropological structure of travel's imaginary as it exists within the home culture and as it informs the traveller's motivation. As stated above, the hermeneutic position of the traveller is, therefore, conditional upon the cultural conventions surrounding the travel experience.

Whereabouts in the city the traveller finds him/herself is an indication of the personal motivation behind a particular hermeneutic response to the urban environment, providing an understanding of the landscape of material and discursive conditions within which the urban traveller operates. It can be noted, therefore, that the most traditional distinction, that of tourist/traveller, while providing a convenient binary opposition for traditional criticism and travel writers themselves, should not be seen as unproblematic. Branching the tourist/traveller into spatial tropes we observe their interconnectedness, with the tourist being associated with mass, collective forms of predetermined movement along a 'beaten track', while the traveller resonates with the values implied by the emergence in the eighteenth century of the modern individual, with Romantic peregrination 'off the beaten track'. The significance of both terms emerges, therefore, from the same codex, one informing and inseparable from the other; the traveller trope conditioning the meanings for tourism, and tourism forming the antithetical line that the traveller must avoid. Commenting on this division in their essay, 'Varieties of Nostalgia in Contemporary Travel Writing', Patrick Holland and Graham Huggan assert that 'the distinction [between tourist and traveller] is, at best, specious, although ironically it still proves useful for a tourist industry that takes full advantage of such nostalgic travel myths' (2004, 139).

This illustrates that, as regards a categorization of traveller-types, one must recognize that such a schema can never be considered definitive; there will always be some degree of crossover between motivations and practices. Nevertheless, if one examines the hermeneutic modalities informing the traveller's concepts of what the act of travel means, the categories below stand out as specific spatial practices for different travellers' negotiations of cities. The groupings below clarify some of the main motivations behind travel and the interpretation of urban space, and have been developed along four major lines, 'the pilgrim', the educationalist', 'the tourist', and 'the nomad', although, as we shall see, these variants overlap and mutate within the writings of many of the travellers studied throughout the course of this book.

1.7.1   *The Pilgrim*

There are two semantic strands defining the word 'pilgrimage' that are helpful to a critique of urban travel. The first states that a pilgrimage constitutes 'a journey to a shrine or sacred place as an act of devotion, in order to acquire spiritual merit or as a penance'

(*Penguin English Dictionary* 2004). The second defines it as 'a long journey or search under-taken for sentimental reasons, out of duty, as a process of self-discovery etc.' (*Penguin English Dictionary* 2004). The importance of the figure of the pilgrim for the history of Western travel has been noted by William H. Sherman (2002, 24) who comments that 'the pilgrimage was the dominant medieval framework for long-distance, non-utilitarian travel'. The first great city of pilgrimage is, of course, Jerusalem, whose popularity as a destination for the Latin West grew after the fall of Rome in the fourth century AD. For the pilgrim the reality of the city fades into the background, experience of the pres-ent mattering less than contact with the representations of space that resonate with (in the case of Christianity) the Jesus Christ narrative.[40] Jan Elsner and Joan-Pau Rubiés (1999, 17) point out that:

> In effect, the Holy Land became an imaginative geography in which pilgrims could roam through the world of scripture in three dimensions, as it were, with every site testifying to the truth of the text and recalling a Biblical tag or quotation.

It is in this sense that Jerusalem became an imaginative topography, where even the most desultory object could operate as a marker of previous presence.[41] The pilgrim's experience of the city becomes equivalent to a textual performance, which in the case of the early Christians was a biblical one. For the pilgrim, the journey guaranteed the literalness of the events of this text, and pilgrimage constituted the constant reaffirma-tion of the sign's attachment to the object. Space becomes meaningful here through the pilgrim's projection of the sacred text onto the physical landscape, with the effect that they create a series of symbolic nodes that resonate with the biblical narrative. Such projection created a literalness, or an equivalence of territory and text, that was to mark Christian religion throughout the medieval and early modern periods. Its demise can be traced to the onslaught of doubt, which alternative truth models insinuated between the bond of object and sign. More importantly for our context, this literalness produces representational spaces that are conflictual and thus potentially socially transformative. Within the ideological regime of religious signs, space is imbricated in relations of power that as Foucault would have it, constitute the world in terms of 'a hierarchical collection of places' (Foucault [1982] 2001, 1572).[42] Thus contestation over the imaginative geog-raphy of Jerusalem determined social relations within Western civilization for centuries, as well as Europe's relationship with the Middle East; medieval crusades were motivated by Christianity's conceptual geography and spaces of representation, a geography which continues to inform contemporary geopolitical conflicts.[43] In the general sense then, pil-grimage is less about 'putting the world on paper' than it is about an imagination, percep-tion and, ultimately, practice of the world as sign (Sherman 2002, 17).

In addition to being instrumental in shaping early nineteenth-century itineraries –evi-dent for example in Chateaubriand's *Itinéraire de Paris à Jérusalem* ([1811] 1968)[44] – medi-eval pilgrimage also engendered a world vision that informed later interpretations of the urban landscape. Foucault explains this mindset as a way of seeing the world which:

> Always took for granted the signs that came before it: so that knowledge could dwell entirely in the gap of a sign discovered or affirmed or secretly transmitted. It [divination] has as its

task to uncover a preliminary language left by God in the world, and it is in this sense that by some essential implication it divined, and it divined from the *divine*.[45] (Foucault 1966, 73, emphasis in the original)

This notion of a prelapsarian language, lost since the Fall, engenders the West's obsession with the 'centre' as a locus of knowledge, a site where the sign corresponds transparently with the objective world. Western philosophy has arguably yearned for the sign that confers meaning to all others – the mythical 'transcendental signifier' – that in turn corresponds to an unalienable anchor: the transcendental signified. Until the Renaissance, the Bible and Jerusalem functioned in such a manner; that Jerusalem proved (at different historical points) to be unattainable served to reinforce this yearning as well as the idea of the city as possessor of ultimate 'Truth'. The epistemological doubt which successive philosophers and alternative theological perspectives cast on this truth model has become the story of Western identity since the Reformation, and its effect has been the creation of an omnipresent feeling of nostalgia distinguishable in Western travel writing since this period (see Scott 2004, 1–15). From the point of view of the pilgrim, the centre of civilization is always elsewhere.[46] In more contemporary terms, this nostalgia can be identified in the critical reaction to the collapse of the 'grand narratives' of the Enlightenment in an age of capitalist consumerism, and is an important feature in interpretive travel writing. In contemporary terms, this nostalgic urge for a stable relationship between signs and their objects so as to make the world transparent and coherent, suggests a reactionary urge in the face of the heterogeneity of global culture (Holland and Huggan 2004, 139).

1.7.2   The Educationalist

From the late seventeenth century on, the secularization of knowledge and the influence of empiricism changed the emphasis and motivation behind travel. The widespread importance of John Locke's *An Essay Concerning Human Understanding* ([1690] 2008) revised theological concepts of human knowledge and marked a crucial point in the development of critical epistemology through the promotion of the idea of the human mind as a 'blank slate', and the conception that all knowledge is produced from the 'impressions' of the five senses. 'If knowledge is rooted in experience and nowhere else', Buzard points out, 'travel instantly gains in importance and desirability' (2002, 37). Empiricist concerns displaced book learning as the dominant mode for gaining information and understanding about the world, and thus, *seeing* and experience were invested with authority as forms of learning. This constituted a development in travel practice, which was now (among other things) motivated by a desire to acquire an empirical, practical education. Humanism, while it encouraged travel and favoured reason and empirical evidence as paths to truth, still largely took the authority of its truths from textual sources. Indeed, its motto *ad fontos* or 'to the sources' promoted the consultation of old manuscripts of the Ancients as a 'new', pre-Christian set of paradigms through which secular meaning could be imparted to the world. In order to read these ancient texts it became necessary to travel, and many scholars across Europe made their way to the libraries of monasteries housing the works of philosophers and scientists of ancient Greece and Rome. This made travel 'something like an obligation for the person conscientious about developing the mind and accumulating knowledge' (Fussell 1987, 129). Travel with a view to 'knowledge gathering' was of course important for the development of other disciplines within the human sciences, most notably geography, the natural sciences and ethnography. Travel became valuable as a social commodity as it was perceived as necessary to the education of young aristocrats and a burgeoning middle class (very often the only people who could afford to travel prior to the mid-nineteenth century). In this narrative, travel secured its social importance in constituting part of what it meant to be 'civilized'; a social imaginary that produced both discourses of imperialistic superiority and counter narratives of profound doubt and insecurity in relation to other cultures.

Most important for the development of approaches to travel for our period is the establishment of the grand tour.[47] In the late seventeenth century and up until about the 1850s, this round trip of Europe was undertaken by 'a substantial upper class with enough money and leisure to travel' (Withey [1997] 1998, 7). In Buzard's estimation, 'The Grand Tour was, from start to finish, an ideological exercise' (2002, 38). While the itinerary shifted over the centuries (most notably from the period 1790–1815 during the Napoleonic Wars on the Continent) cities figured greatly in the grand tour. From Paris one might travel to Geneva, moving across the Alps as quickly as possible to Turin or Milan, proceeding down to Florence and then on to Rome and Venice. The tourist could venture as far as Naples. The return journey usually consisted of visits to Strasbourg, the German university towns, Berlin and Amsterdam. In its most reduced form the tour consisted of visits to Rome, Florence and Venice, these urban centres being seen as essential to the education of the upper- and middle-class gentleman and gentlewoman.[48] It is not surprising that the city, as the space epitomizing civilization, was an essential stop in the pedagogical itineraries of the elite classes. Originally, the ancient Greek word for 'urban' *'aesteos'* signified 'end' or 'spiritual', its weight as an element of social classification becoming clear when one considers that the word for 'rural' translates as 'uncouth' or 'crude' (Sennett [1994] 2002, 36). Several approaches to the city have their origins in the intentions behind the grand tour. The first is intimately connected to the classical tradition and comparative and contrastive opinions on ancient civilization in relation to contemporary French society. From this perspective the tour was intended as an agent in the development of a historical consciousness via which the French could articulate ideas about their own metropolitan universe. It was hoped, as Buzard observes, that 'personal experience of the places made famous by the Latin text which the traveller had read in school would seal the bond between ancient and modern empires' (2002, 40). The figure of the ruin and the varieties of its representation across the nineteenth century is one image that illustrates the degree to which travel to the sites of the ancient city was not always positive in its outcome, and it can be seen that the pronounced instability of France's contemporary political and cultural situation was crucial in the motivations behind depictions of the ruin. Furthermore, in relation to travel from 1851 onward, the ruin was a contemporary figure on the urban horizons of both Paris and London, which were undergoing modernization as a result of intense industrialization. As we shall see, the discourse of the ruin is often transferred to the modern city, where the paradigms for interpretation are constructed within a teleological framework auguring the 'inevitable' rise and fall of metropolitan civilizations.

Another educational facet of travel was its association with the cultivation of one's artistic taste and social etiquette. Travel was undertaken with a view to enhance one's cultural capital and status within society. This period establishes the figure of the European collector as someone with an education in the principles of 'correct taste' and with the financial means to accumulate sculptures and paintings from the Continent. These collections, open to the select viewing of an ever-increasing number of connoisseurs, can be seen as forerunners of the modern museum, whose ideological implications shall be discussed more fully in subsequent chapters in relation to Janin and Perec. It is useful to note here, however, how the metropolitan identities of both Paris and London during the Grand Tour period became linked to the idea of the metropolis as a point of cultural convergence, or world-centre, so that the idea of civilization expanded to incorporate cultural multiplicity and contrast. This convergence is central to the notion of what a Western metropolis should constitute. Its implication for the foreign city is clear – for the French and English grand tourist, other cities were places where one could gather 'a good deal of cultural booty' (Brewer 1997, 207): an attitude one might term 'artistically-imperialist'.[49] Travel as a form of cultural accumulation was by extension constitutive of the imperial capital, as we shall see when discussing the Great Exhibition of 1851.

A further feature of the grand tour important to interpreting urban space is the development of the idea of the 'picturesque' and the 'sublime' as conceptual modes for experiencing geographical space. In the latter half of the eighteenth century and throughout the nineteenth, the cultural idea of landscape developed so that, in some ways, landscape became a function of the ideals of the Gothic and Romantic movements of this period. The gentle, sloping landscapes favoured by the grand tourist were replaced by a penchant for wilder, untamed regions. Valleys were thus forsaken for the mountainous areas of the Pyrenees and the Alps, and the soft climates of the Mediterranean for the harsh weathers of Scotland and the more Northern countries.[50] Once again, the representational space emergent from these more rugged journeys is influential in relation to the urban environment. The picturesque, understood in terms of a philosophical discourse, was primarily concerned with experience as an aesthetic apprehension of the environment configured around contrasting ideas of the beautiful and the sublime. Edmund Burke's *Philosophical Enquiry into the Origin of Our Ideas of the Sublime and the Beautiful* ([1757] 1998) denied that rationality was involved in an appreciation of the beautiful or the sublime, and stated that their experience was one of subrational sensation. Briefly, beauty was characterized by soft, gentle contours (the rolling hills and green valleys favoured by the pastoral tradition) and inspired desire and acquiescence in its onlookers, while the sublime inspired 'agreeable horror' and agitated the senses towards self-preservation (epitomized by the Gothic horror genre). Both of these extremes were seen as emotional forms of transcendence, where contact with such landscapes might provide access to an inner truth. The picturesque mediated between these two extremes and contained elements of both the placid and the wild. The appropriation of this anti-rationalist philosophical ethos produces representations of urban space along two major discursive lines that can be noted here for their influence on nineteenth- and twentieth-century travel writing. The first gravitates around a negative pole: the traveller sees the modern city as a rationalist, utilitarian entity and, therefore, completely outside of the bounds of aesthetic experience. This positions the city within a framework of opposition to the natural or organic, a contrast significant in Leroy's London of 1946 and Sartre's negotiation of New York the year before. The modern city is represented as a space of frenzy, of mercantile exchange and the mechanical. In a discourse propounding Nature as a means of transcendence and authentic experience (after Jean-Jacques Rousseau (1712–1778) – as an antidote to the corruptions of urban society),[51] the city is practised in antonymic terms, whereby urban(e) civilization is equated with decadence, perversity and the inauthentic (see Rousseau [1750] 2011). In this scenario, 'progress' is tantamount to distancing humans from their natural face and thus equivalent to a loss of humanity, with the result that the city becomes the space of profound crisis in humanity's relationship to the world.

The other main perceptual strand whose development may be traced to eighteenth-century theories of the sublime is that of the modern city as a space of terrifying monumentality and thus of heightened emotional stimulation. This aesthetic of transcendence, a tenet of monumental architecture, is one the main thrusts behind the Modernist and Futurist conceptions of the city which were elaborated extensively, not only by architects such as Mies Van Der Rohe and radical futurist artists like Marinetti, Umberto Boccioni and Antonio Sant'Elia, but also by travel writers. The sensory exhilaration which spaces of the modern metropolis provide produces accounts of it as a figure of profound possibility, a hope for transparency in humanity's relation to the world: a distinctly liberal attitude that figures prominently in the texts of writers such as Paul Morand in 1920s New York. Tropes such as the placid and the primitive function extensively in representations of the urban universe, whose fascination often lies in the contradictory proximity of these two extremes. Elements of such a discourse can be traced to the travel writing of Gautier in London (1852) and, of course (as fellow city-lover Walter Benjamin recognized), to the poetic and prose works of Charles Baudelaire ([1857] 1972, [1869] 1987).

1.7.3 *The Tourist*

With the emergence of an increasingly influential middle class in the nineteenth century, travel became more accessible and desirable than ever before. However, it was not until the growth of capitalism and industrialization, and particularly after the introduction of paid holidays in the 1930s, that tourism changed from being an activity exclusive to elites into 'an activity scandalously accessible to a deindividualized, metaphorically liquid mass' (Buzard 2002, 47). Nevertheless, from the mid-nineteenth century onward we have the emergence of Baedeker (the first guide on Belgium being published in 1843) and the establishment of skiing holidays (the Club Alpin Français was created in 1874) and holiday camps in Switzerland (1875).

Throughout the latter half of the nineteenth century too, the material possibilities for travel alter considerably and produce new modes of spatial perception. Increased speed and decreased cost were the cumulative result of steam power, both on the rails (the first major rail networks were built in France between the years 1850–1860) and on the water. The relative ease with which tourists could now move across and within the foreign landscape was furthered by the appearance of marketplace institutions and facilities easing the financial and physical hardship traditionally associated with travel, such as Baedeker and the Touring Club de France (1890). With the development of mass tourism in the early twentieth century, access to the picturesque, the beautiful and the sublime extended beyond the custody of the privileged few, and with this extension emerged the paradoxes that have marked the act of travel ever since. The emergence of mass tourism has, of course, seen the emergence of mass critique, with the proliferation of the industry and its attendant transformation of the landscape all contributing to the conception that tourism destroys the very thing it sets out to observe; so that the impetus for tourism threatens to destroy the possibility of tourism (Rojek and Urry 1997a, 1). This 'desperate evil' (Rojek and Urry 1997a, 1) of tourism is summed up by James Buzard:

> Disruption of the pristine regions of prelapsarian travel would result not simply from the new railway lines, with all their attendant noise and smoke, but from the unwitting collective action of the ticket-holders themselves who, in their very numbers, would kill the things they loved. (Buzard 2002, 48)

Tourism also becomes a discursive force in its own right – equipped with its own architectural spaces of representation – that seek to package the perceptual possibilities of travellers, largely through the erasure of the signs of difference. In that it constitutes an industry conditioning spatial practice, tourism functions in the manner of a discursive mesh, analogous, in Foucauldian terms, to a kind of governmentality of the space it seeks to market. Therefore, while defamiliarization is a primary feature for distinguishing the practices of the traveller from those of the inhabitant of the city, when dealing with the tourist the unfamiliar is carefully packaged and controlled. This has been one of the essential mechanisms of tourism since its conception. As Buzard points out, 'the new service industries undertook to insulate their clients from all but "expected" forms of difference' (Buzard 2005, 58). Tourism's appeal lies in the extent to which it makes another culture and territory accessible and secure, which it does largely by marketing its clients a highly controlled set of expectations through regulated distribution of a collection of textual and visual signs, and satisfying expectations by directing the flow of human traffic along the 'supervised' trajectory of the 'beaten track'. Through this controlled repertoire of images and texts, tourism provides places of symbolic contact with the city well before the 'trip' is ever realized, and thereby familiarizes foreign space for its own ends. In this way, the tourist industry's strategies are comparable to those of the medieval pilgrim, for whom places were immediately transparent by their insertion within a ritualized set of semiological criteria that produced meaning for the landscape. In a similar fashion, the tourist is engaged in a ritualistic confirmation of the city that is enabled by the technologies of representation accompanying the journey, most notably the guidebook, the camera, and increasingly today, the camcorder, the mobile phone and the internet.

While technologies accompanying the tourist on his/her travels have evolved considerably over the last two hundred years, the principal force behind a tourist's spatial categorization of the city can still be identified in the schematic design of the guidebook form. Tourism, like any ritual, is engaged in the reduction of complexity, revising the world to meet its requirements for meaning. This reduction has an important temporal dimension when it comes to tourism. This temporal limitation is one of the major reasons for the growth in popularity of the guidebook. In the way that it performs as an amalgamation of the city, the guidebook generally functions in accordance with principles of hierarchy, wherein the locations 'worth seeing' are enumerated. As appropriated by the guidebook, urban space becomes legible in terms of a series of value-laden 'sites', places of historical interest or cultural importance, which often exist outside the range of the everyday urban life.

Furthermore, as well as providing a spatial summation of the city, the guidebook not only organizes the physical itinerary of the tourist but also explicates the stops along that itinerary, and is thus involved in structuring the narrative and temporal relationship which the tourist has with the city. Crucially for the tourist, the guidebook presents a concentrated form of the urban environment, dividing space both textually and visually into manageable units that proffer themselves as the 'essentials' or 'must sees' which purport to capture the city in its entirety: a minimum of information inserting such 'sights' into a discourse that makes these spaces transparent to the outsider. In this sense, the guidebook provides a key to the steps one needs to take in order to have 'seen' Paris, London or New York. The popularity of certain sites and certain cities over others constantly shifts with respect to fashion, politics and economics, while the guidebook's function – to amalgamate the city, to sum it up (ideally in under two hundred pages) – remains consistent and deliberately predictable in form. From this perspective, the attraction of the guidebook lies in its convenience; one can say that one has 'done' a city when physical confirmation of the designated sites has been achieved – usually through incessant photographing or '*clichés*' of particular sites as proof of having been there. In this way, the guidebook provides a definite set of criteria that serve to validate the tourist's trip: a textual and oftentimes visual mirror authenticating the tourist's experience of the city through mediated reflection. Essentially, tourism as a spatial practice can be seen as a (increasingly pervasive) remnant of what Foucault terms the analogical model for producing knowledge of the world – a model based in resemblance, where one sign refers to others similar to itself, and thus for the construction of reality in terms of similitude (Foucault 1966, 45). In one scenario, tourism operates from a principle of hierarchy, with places gathering importance through their capacity to reproduce the expectations set up by the guidebook and the bank of previously established images that the tourist has at their disposal. It is for this reason, perhaps, that the metropolis, as an efficacious 'summary' of a culture's entire civilization, figures highly on the list of tourist destinations.

The guidebook functions for the home culture, too, in that its narrative participates in the construction of the monument, ensuring its constant reaffirmation through the appreciation of the 'tourist's gaze', and signalling to the inhabitant the importance of the 'site' on a national or international scale (Urry 1990). From the tourist's perspective, by creating an official blurb to accompany the urban site, the guidebook becomes a crucial point of access to pre-established meanings for the city. In rendering the site legible, the tourist is reassured as to its identity and thus to his/her own in relation to it. By dispelling the unknown, the discursive strategies of the guidebook assuage the fear which dislocation through travel might bring. The uneasiness of fragmentation or disorientation is denied by the guidebook, whose textual strategies – colour coding, maps, integrated histories – all combine to create a place that is accessible, coherent and transparent. Thus, 'an object seen for the first time may be identified and related to not because it is individually familiar but because it conforms to a stereotype already constructed by the observer' (Lynch 1960, 6).

The guidebook, the bank of urban and national stereotypes, and the collective imagery pertaining to the metropolis, all have consequences for the depiction of the 'reality' of the city. The speed and transparency that characterize tourism are also exclusionary in the extent to which these aspects seek to eradicate the intimacy, the unexpected and the unconsciousness of experience that feature in the everyday life of the metropolis.[52] The tourist industry, then, is (as Roland Barthes (1957) recognized) part of societies' myth-making processes, which consumerism employs to render the world a less antagonistic place in which to dwell, processes that lead Augé to refer to holiday-making as an 'illusory kaleidoscope' (Augé 1997, 14).[53] These general points provide a preliminary framework within which the travel journals of Janin (1851), Leroy (1946) and Morand (1930) can be approached, while issues surrounding the tourist industry's influence on later twentieth-century urban travel writing will be examined in relation to the writers Perec and Baudrillard.

1.7.4 The Nomad

If travel as practised by the tourist is engaged in the confirmation of certain established discourses proliferated by interested parties, the notion of an 'authentic' traveller, someone who wanders off the beaten track, can to some extent be considered a response to these discourses. The romanticized ideal of the intrepid explorer can be seen as a further discursive trope emerging from a profound doubt that the tourist is in fact travelling at all. Within this discourse, any pretence to 'travel' comes to depend on the isolation (preferably within expansive, alien geographies) that assures distance from the tourist. As Urbain (2000, 146) comments:

> These travellers – whether they be inexhaustible pilgrims, persistent runaways, or wandering poets – are all convinced that the only true experience of travel is to be found in the association of the travelling self with the experience of other worlds that are spatially remote, immense, empty and isolated.

In this schema the tourist emerges as a parody of what it means to travel, and by extension, there develops a utopian self-image of the traveller who defines him/herself in contradistinction to such a parody. The 'nomad mind'[54] is glorified as the seeker of unadulterated space, of space uncontaminated by Western civilization.

Nomadism is perhaps best understood in the light of Deleuze and Guattari's (1980) concept of 'nomadic becoming', which in the context of travel is the equivalent to a state of mind, not a figure but a figuration (Jokinen and Veijola 1997). The feminist theorist Rosi Braidotti (1994) has appropriated this conceptual usage of the *nomad* for her own gendered critique of theory, but her point is relevant for determining the anti-tourist in terms of an attitude rather than as a pragmatic exploration of space. Braidotti argues that:

> Though the image of 'nomadic subjects' is inspired by the experience of peoples or cultures that are literally nomadic, the nomadism in question here refers to the kind of critical consciousness that resists settling into socially coded modes of thought and behavior. [...] It's the subversion of set conventions that defines the nomadic state, not the literal act of traveling. (5)

Although the idea that theoretical nomadism can claim referential support in the actual activities of nomads has been refuted, nevertheless, the identification of nomadism as a travel type allows us to identify certain tactical practices of the city that present an alternative to the discursive modes of thought and practices of the tourist.[55] It must be noted, however, that the discourse of the nomad emerges from within the context of the debate surrounding tourism and is thus more of an anti-discourse if one will. As Buzard explains:

> Through varieties of what the sociologist Erving Goffman has called 'rôle distance', modern travellers and travel writers identified themselves as anti-touristic beings whose unhappy lot it was to move amidst and in the wake of tourists, *for one of whom they might even be mistaken*; on the increasingly beaten path of Continental travelling, self-differentiation, not imitation became a guiding purpose. (2002, 49, emphasis in the original)

Within the urban context, such attempts at self-differentiation become increasingly important as the anonymity of the crowd and the speed of an increasingly accelerated urban life threaten to submerge the individual. And, somewhat paradoxically, in their search for individuality, the nomad calls to mind another anti-touristic being – the *flâneur*. The decelerated city, as produced through the rhetoric of the strolling *flâneur*, can be seen in terms of a reaction to the pace of the urban tourist, someone whose style of response to the urban landscape signals a desire to escape the frantic pace of the modern metropolis. The *flâneur*'s crafted practice of the city provides evidence of a discourse that snubs the tourist's scheduled style of response to the urban world. The *flâneur* is the traveller expert in the diminutive journey, he deliberately seeks to read the city in its detail, and to transgress the conventional urban routes as they are organized by the guidebook.[56] In this way he positively and actively validates the city, revealing through pauses and in-depth decipherment of signs a more personal, singular and impressionistically fleeting vision of the city. The *flâneur* is a considered stroller: walking with a deliberately measured pace, noting everything, allowing the urban landscape to stimulate the inner eye. The *flâneur* is thus (consciously) immune to the frenetic rhythm of the city streets, and in order to protect a measured pace will spend hours wandering in the covered arcades of Paris, hidden away from the circulation of the crowd and the traffic, or along the massive boulevards which provide ample space to pause and focus one's attention on something or someone in particular. Walter Benjamin remarks on the Parisian fashion of taking turtles for a walk: 'The *flâneurs* liked to have the turtles set the pace for them. If they had had their way, progress would have been obliged to accommodate itself to this pace' (Benjamin 1983, 54). The *flâneur*, therefore, determines and creates the material conditions for his spatio-temporal experience of the city, studiously placing himself out of step with modern existence, reacting against the rapid pace and the condensed humanity of the city, and by extension implying his cultural and intellectual superiority over the tourist. However, by virtue of the *flâneur*'s conscious attempt to differentiate himself from the fluidity of the crowd and to assert his individuality, he becomes a figuration, a recognizable social 'type', and thus part of the representational space of the urban universe. Moreover, the identity of the *flâneur* as a distinctly male figure in the urban environment raises issues for the ways in which women were restricted from experiencing the city in this way. While the male walker is thus associated with a kind of intellectual, studied experience of urban life, during this period, the only women who walked the boulevards unaccompanied were generally 'street walkers', to walk on the street as a women was thus to become part of the paraphernalia for sale.[57]

Returning to the nomad, in positing vast, uncivilized spaces as the only spaces worth travelling, a certain anxiety emerges when the potential disappearance of such spaces becomes conceivable, an anxiety attendant in much urban travel writing. Urbain detects a certain degree of tyranny in this type of traveller, and describes him/her as someone 'whose anger is not momentary but reflects a constant sense of mourning' (Urbain 2000, 148). For the nomad, the city functions as a critical stimulus – within the discourse of nomadism, the city emerges as the prime culprit in depriving humans of nature, the deserts and the unknown, and is, therefore, implicated in the demystification of the world. Confronting the enemy, however, is also a reason to visit, and one of the motivations for the nomadic traveller's visit to the city lies in the fact that the industrial or postindustrial panoramas of the city serve as spaces within which to develop a critique of urban civilization. In the face of the increasingly technological manipulation of man's relationship to his environment, the nomadic traveller reads the city through a lens of nostalgia for a 'primitive', untainted vastness. The city's order and highly mediated landscape are antithetical to a point of view that valorizes expansiveness and laments the thoroughness of previous explorers that has left nothing (for Western eyes) to discover. In this way, as we shall see in relation to the later twentieth-century explorers of the metropolis, with its overtly mediated landscape extensively appropriated by the sign, the city often provides a territory where the nomadic traveller might engage critically with modernity.

To conclude this section, we have seen here how the motivations behind the traveller's interpretation of urban space vary across time as well as space, developing in correspondence with general discourses on the nature and purpose of travel, as well as responding to technological developments that alter the perception and experience of the world. From the experience of travel as spatial practice that negotiates various spaces of representation in the city, we move now to the travel writer's translation of these perceptions into text and come to urban travel as a representational space.

1.8 Representational Space, Writing the City

1.8.1 Issues of Genre and Modes of Representation

Space begins thus, with only words, signs traced on a blank page.[58] (Perec 1974, 21)

Given the multifaceted hermeneutics of travel, it is not surprising that contemporary critics have had problems agreeing on travel writing's status as a genre. Lorenza Mondada (2005), for instance, situates the material conditions through which we construct our interpretations of the travel journal by pointing out that heterogeneity is only problematic in the light of developments within academia. For Mondada, 'The very notion of academic discipline is posterior to the wave of success of travel accounts throughout Europe, which predate the institutionalisation of knowledge when Universities were organised in the nineteenth century' (2005, 66). The concomitant separation of knowledge areas such as that of science, art and ethics gives rise to disciplinary specialization, which is a recent development when compared with the travel account, 'an ancient genre located well upstream of this later division of knowledge' (2005, 66). In this light, the notion of genre when it comes to the travel account proves extremely problematic. Jan Borm enumerates the variant strands of composition that have come under the denotation 'travel writing':

> Among the wide range of terms in use are: 'travel book', 'travel narrative', 'journey work', 'travel memoir', 'travel story', 'travelogue', 'metatravelogue', 'traveller's tale', 'travel journal', or simply 'travels' (*The Travels of Sir John Mandeville*), and, in a different vein, 'travel writing', 'travel literature', 'the literature of travel' and 'the travel genre'. (2004, 13)

In light of this extensive taxonomy, Borm argues that travel writing cannot be considered a genre in any conventional sense, and instead refers to travel writing as 'a collective term for a variety of texts both predominantly fictional and non-fictional whose main theme is travel' (Borm 2004, 13). Youngs echoes such concerns in *Travellers in Africa* showing how travel writing 'feeds from and back into other forms of literature' (1994, 8). Travel writing can be viewed in a reflexive sense, therefore, as a form of writing which demands attention be paid to its modalities of representation for the very way in which these cross traditional generic categories.

The need for a referential designation, however, is argued by Schulz-Forberg (2005b) who justifies the use of the term 'travel writing' stating that, while travel writing has adapted in relation to changes in literary and scientific discourse, it is nevertheless classifiable as a genre 'since travel writing has been written according to a clear set of rules' (14). According to Schulz-Forberg these rules are based upon the hybrid nature of travel writing, its generic identity being founded on its mediation between the scientific and objective and the personal and subjective. To varying degrees, and in response to historical and cultural developments, travel writing possesses traits relating to contemporary fields of analysis such as autobiography, history, anthropology and ethnography among others, a scenario in which hybridity becomes a defining characteristic. In addition, another of the genre's traits is its relationship to the real, and its concern for authenticity. Schulz-

Forberg identifies the paradox at the heart of this quest for the 'authentic' experience and the voice via which to convey it, pointing out that in travel writing the authentic is reliant on the individuality of the experience, requiring the subjective presence of the author to validate its status as a 'true', 'scientific' account.[59] This leads to the affirmation that 'the subversion of the genre is […] part of its fundamental characteristics' (2005b, 15). Indeed, if one is to follow Gérard Genette's (1986) method for conceptualizing genre, then the hybrid nature of travel writing does not preclude its collective identification as a body of texts that exhibit similar representational concerns. As Genette suggests, 'the mixing or mistrust of genres is a genre among others' (1986, 158).[60] This mixing of genres is one of the important features of travel writing, and one that makes it a particularly rich field for transdisciplinary approaches to questions of representation, such as the dialogue between urban studies, architectural discourse and practices of writing presented here. In particular questions regarding narrative voice and the construction of cultural perspectives within the travel account require that we examine travel writing's relation to fictional, autobiographical and ethnographic modes of voice.

1.8.2 *Fiction*

By using *travel writing* as an umbrella term to refer to a large body of works, the distinction between fiction and non-fiction is not made by Borm above. As this book focuses on *lived* rather than *fictive* journeys, some conceptual boundaries will be laid down here in order to confine the multifarious term 'travel writing' and to clarify the generic debate outlined above by limiting the use of the term to refer to journeys that have taken place and where the concern at the heart of the work is to transmit an account of this journey. However, in light of the fact that a dogmatic and clear-cut distinction between fiction and non-fiction is difficult – if not impossible – some further explanation can be helpful to situate this position more clearly. The distinction between fiction and non-fiction is, to a large extent, a theoretical construction. For instance, Aristotle's notion of *mimesis* refers not only to works of fiction (its most common exploitation by critics), but also to non-fiction. Aristotle's *Poetics* suggests that the transformational effects of *mimesis* are at play in any narrative. According to Aristotle: 'Since the poet, like a painter or any other image-maker, is a mimetic artist, he must represent, in any instance, one of three objects: the kind of things which were or are the case; the kind of things that people say and think; the kind of things that ought to be the case' (cited in Borm 2004, 21). Here, the reference to 'the kind of things which were or are the case' can be taken as encompassing works of non-fiction, implying that the literary is active within any narration. This observation has been at the heart of twentieth-century developments in criticism in the human sciences; in the field of history with the advent of the 'New Historicism'; in anthropology with the work of Lévi-Strauss ([1958] 1996), and more recently in the ethnographical work of James Clifford (1986, 1988). Structuralism, poststructuralism and semiotics have also been instrumental in undermining the hermeneutic stability of works of non-fiction.

Hans Robert Jauss's suggestion of looking for dominant aspects within a work or genre can help to bring into focus what is meant by 'travel writing' and to situate individual works in relation to discursive strategies within autobiography and ethnography. As Jauss argues, 'the introduction of a notion of the dominant which organizes the system of a complex work allows for the transformation of what we call 'a mix of genres' into a methodologically productive category' (Jauss [1970] 1986, 44).[61] An example illustrates how one might identify a 'dominant aspect' within the work. For instance, there is a clear difference in the reader's response to 'New York' as it appears in a novel such as Louis-Ferdinand Céline's *Voyage au bout de la nuit* (1932) and its representation in Paul Morand's travel journal *New York* (1930). This response is intuitive for the most part but it indicates that while a clear-cut distinction between fiction and travel writing is problematic, the reader nevertheless does not confer the same ontological status to Céline's third-person narrator Bardamu, as she does to the traveller-journalist Morand. In this schema, the major point of generic differentiation lies essentially in the absence of a 'referential pact' in *Voyage au bout de la nuit* (Borm 2004, 15). Following Jauss, Borm goes on to define the travel journal as:

> *Any narrative characterized by a non-fiction dominant that relates (almost always) in the first person a journey or journeys that the reader supposes to have taken place in reality while assuming or presupposing that author, narrator and principal character are but one or identical.* (Borm 2004, 17, original emphasis)

The reader of the travel journal thus has a certain horizon of expectations based on the presumption that the text is predominantly concerned with an actual individual's account of a journey which he or she made in spatial and temporal reality. But this horizon of expectations does shift depending on the period in question. Paul Fussell, in *Abroad*, has pointed out that 'in the seventeenth century the travel book was so commonly regarded as a repository of wonderful lies that in 1630 Captain John Smith felt obliged to modify the word *Travels* with the word *True* when he published *The True Travels, Adventures and Observations of Captain John Smith*' (Fussell 1980, 165). In our case, given that the texts under discussion here have been selected on the basis that they have a non-fictional dominant, I use the umbrella term 'travel writing' to refer to the body of texts discussed here and the terms 'travel journal' or 'travel account' to refer to particular works within this collective.[62]

1.8.3 Literary Presence

The concept of the dominant aspect of a work is not to deny of course the presence of a literary element within travel writing. As mentioned above and as recognized by Genette, a clear-cut distinction between fiction and non-fiction in any narrative work borders on the impossible and consists largely in theoretical construct.[63] In other words, any narrative form involves stylistic choice, processes of selection and exclusion, as well as the linguistic and literary devices available to the author. The presence of the subjective voice implies the use of a *style*. While in scientific forms of narrative, this voice is generally elided in the aim to achieve an 'objective' (and thus more authoritative) position from which to speak, paradoxically, in travel writing, the subjective voice is seen to provide testament to the journey's having taken place as described, and thus lends a sense of authoritative verisimilitude to the writing. While operating within the historically contingent set of conventions and generic norms inherent in any system of representation, the inevitability of choice and composition imply this subjective dimension. This is particularly pertinent to a genre such as travel writing where the narrator purports to describe an exterior world. The contingency of the written sign is, therefore, placed in tension with the notion of an objective, impersonal real. Just as Certeau extends this notion of style rhetorically to the individual's practice of the city, style has significance for the travel writer in that the exposition of representational choice also renders problematic the notion of a transparent relation between text and world. The presence of style can be seen, therefore, to undermine any narrative's transparency in relation to the real. In later interpretive travel modes, the deliberate obscuration or questioning of reality through the text's poetic gestures becomes in itself a powerful comment on the constructed nature of political and cultural normativism. In the light of Said's *Orientalism* ([1978] 1979) and the advent of postcolonial criticism, writers such as Caren Kaplan (1996), Steve Clarke (1999) and Syed Manzurul Islam (1996) have pointed out that a narration's deliberately reductive version of reality does violence to the cultures it encounters. This is to highlight the ideological tensions of representation which, in the wake of structuralist and poststructuralist criticism, have rendered problematic any account attempting to represent 'reality' as though it were, on the one hand, objectively transparent, or on the other, subjectively malleable. The presence of the individual element that is style necessarily imperils the coherencies and straightforward relations between text and world, ideology and actuality, signs and their objects. As Michel Beaujour has recognized, 'literary description always opens onto another set, so to speak, "behind" the this-worldly things it purports to depict' (1981, 39). With this in mind, the aesthetic dimensions of travel writing as representational space form a crucial part of the discussion in the chapters that follow. The reason for this is two-fold; first, the tension between the subjective and the objective has had significant consequences for ethnography and history, fields which have important links with travel writing. Second, travel and travel writing raise important issues with regard to the meaning of the self/other encounter. Given that many of the writers under discussion here show particular concern and awareness of these issues, it is useful to introduce some of the paradigms within which this 'autobiographical dimension' of travel writing will be considered throughout the chapters that follow.

1.8.4   Autobiography

This tension between the subjective and objective narrative voice is analogous to the expressive tendency within travel writing to gravitate between the generic poles of autobiography and ethnography respectively. Autobiography is problematic as a genre, having complexities of its own with regard to fiction, memory and identity. Furthermore, the tendency amongst critics, as Loredana Polezzi points out, has been to neglect travel writing's autobiographical worth and see 'travel writing as a minor genre whose importance is mainly to be found in the instrumental role it played in the development of the novel' (2004, 121). While the travel journal may inform our biographical knowledge of the authors discussed here – some of whom have written significant works of fiction – this book does not set out to construct a 'portrait of the artist'. In addition, none of the features examined in the travel journals under discussion shall be approached from a psychoanalytical perspective. The reason for this being that travel journals are studied here for their function in relation to issues concerning conditions for the construction of urban meaning rather than the individual intricacies of the authorial personality per se. In this manner, the representation of the individual is considered in terms of the tension between the self and urban modernity, and the self's search for meaning in the city.[64]

However, while this book veers away from a reading of travel writing as autobiography, it is nonetheless useful to point out some of the features common to both genres for the problems they raise with regard to issues of identity and the self/other relation, and the implications of these for the practice and representation of space. The central overlap between the genres of autobiography and travel writing can be simply understood in terms of a shared mode for constructing subject and object positions: from the point of view of the reader, in both genres, one expects the synchronicity of author, narrator and protagonist, while the object of narration is presumed to have actually taken place (Polezzi 2004, 122). Issues of genre aside, on another level, travel and travel writing are also implicated in self-discovery as well as self-mutation and, in the extreme, the loss of self (Scott 2004, 80). Leaving one's home culture potentially places the subject in a certain limbo. The new, the other, holds no memory for the traveller and, lacking the reflective dimensions of 'home' – 'the not-I that protects the I' / 'le non-moi qui protège le moi' (Bachelard [1957] 2001, 24) – the traveller is vulnerable (often deliberately so) to misrecognition of the other. In this scenario, travel writing becomes a space for exploring the principle of mobility involved in shaping an identity (Scott 2004, 82). In the presence of urban difference, identities are rendered mutable, where intense semiotic complexities and networks of exchange make difficult the preservation of an integrated self, and the traveller unaccustomed to such a barrage of signs is especially vulnerable to these forces. In *Soft City*, the travel writer Jonathan Raban comments upon how shifting identities constitute an integral part of urban life:

> In the city, we are barraged with images of the people we might become. Identity is presented as plastic, a matter of possessions and appearances; and a very large proportion of the urban landscape is taken up by slogans, advertisements, flatly photographed images of folk heroes – the man who turned into a sophisticated dandy overnight by drinking a particular brand of vodka, the girl who transformed herself into a latter-day Mata Hari with a squirt of cheap scent. ([1974] 1998, 59)

This passage illuminates how the city's sensory mishmash of signs and people enables the breakdown of distinctions between dream and real life. Within this 'emporium of styles', class and cultural determinisms are easily unravelled (Raban [1974] 1998, 64). The spatial practices of urban life, engaged to a very large degree with the action of the sign, are continually exposed to the possibility for alternatives; one sign can be substituted for another, one social circle abandoned and another entered into with a change of dress, of café or hairstyle. And it is this flexible circularity of these more minor representations of space and its social orders that allows individuals to live out their fantasies, and to enter social arenas hitherto beyond their range of experience. As Barthes observes in his essay '*Sémiologie et urbanisme*':

> The game is a theme that is very often underlined in enquiries about the [city] centre. In France there have been a series of enquiries investigating the attraction of the suburbs to central Paris, and from the periphery it has been said that Paris, as a centre, has always been meaningfully lived as *the privileged site where the other resides and where we ourselves are other*, like the place where one goes to play.[65] (Barthes [1967] 2002, II: 1285, my emphasis)

This possibility of becoming other is one of the major attractions of the city for the traveller, but it is also, as we shall see, one of the most daunting.

1.8.5 Ethnography

The search for the origins of ethnography as a scientific discipline has led to an enquiry into the modes of narration and description at work in the earliest travel accounts. This search has been approached from differing perspectives that are shaped largely by how critics define the function of an ethnographic account. Recently, within the field of ethnography, a debate has emerged over definitions of the exact object and methodologies of the science. Those working in the field of travel writing have also contributed to this critique. A brief review of these analyses and the questions they raise for travel writing will situate the approach taken to the urban practice of the travellers examined here.

Let us begin with the ethnographer James Clifford's delimitation of 'ethnography':

> As an academic practice it cannot be separated from anthropology. Seen more generally it is simply diverse ways of thinking and writing about culture from a standpoint of participant observation. (1988, 9)

Joan Pau Rubiés (2002) finds this definition useful in that it helps to identify an ontological shift in the travel writing genre. This shift constitutes the movement away from a concern to entertain the home readership with fantastic tales and/or an undiscriminating moral condescension towards other cultures and the genre's movement towards an attempt at objectivity, as well as an increasing tendency to reflect relatively about another culture's social and spatial organization. Because the travel writer participates directly in a society through observation of the other culture, and writes down their diverse reflections, Rubiés, in keeping with Clifford's (1988) definition, ascribes the term 'ethnographic' to Renaissance travel writing. In doing so she identifies possible circumstances and evolutions in narrative techniques and self–other reflection that have contributed to the development of the human sciences in Europe. It has been widely recognized that the intellectual transformation of Europe during the Renaissance was in no small measure the result of a response to discoveries of the New World, which awakened colonialist desire and scientific and cultural curiosity about the Other. Narrative accounts of the foreign landscape and its peoples contributed to moral and scientific debate shaping Europe's identity in response to this previously unknown entity, and became crucial to the Enlightenment project for a world-historical science of humankind. Rubiès argues that the contingency which Renaissance exploratory travel introduced to Europe created the need for a greater rationalization of European identity and its categories for knowing the world. Soon after these discoveries, scientists and priests began making the journey to the New World, and their intellectual methods for gathering information and making sense of the Other greatly influenced the development of taxonomic strategies of classification and categorization that have been crucial to Western methodologies of knowledge since the nineteenth century at least.

Other critics have been concerned to differentiate more specifically between the genres of ethnography and travel writing. This is a position originating from a deep concern not to simplify either genre, and to remain lucid about the problematic status of any narrative purporting objectivity. Borm (2000, 80), for example, points out that if one were to accept Clifford's loose disciplinary boundaries for modern ethnography, this would necessitate extending the definition to include journalists as ethnographic practitioners. For Borm, Clifford's definition would imply that ethnography is a practice that could be ostensibly traced back to antiquity. Out of a similar solicitude, Campbell discerns that 'people have come to use the word "ethnographic" to refer to just about any eyewitness representation of non-Western people at home. But the word also refers to a genre that did not exist in the sixteenth century' (1999, 48). Most critics do agree, however, that the narration-description dichotomy is of great importance to identifying a work as a scientific ethnography or a travel journal.

Debra Picchi's maxim for the ethnographer provides us with a point of contrast useful for identifying the travel journal. In the context of her critique of anthropology graduate student Florinda Donner's *Shabono: A True Adventure in the Remote and Magical Heart of the South American Jungle* (1982), she identifies the distinguishing feature of the ethnographical position as a 'commitment to the documentation of relationships between behavioural variables on a cross-cultural basis' (Picchi 1983, 674). This statement provides a general axis along which lines can be drawn to provide at least some, if not definitive, clarification. Mary Louise Pratt describes this axis as the 'narration-description duality', and identifies it as forming the basis for both travel journals and ethnographies. She distinguishes between these two forms, arguing that:

> Ethnographic writing as a rule subordinates narrative to description, but personal narrative is still conventionally found, either in the separate personal volumes or in vestigial form at the beginning of the book, setting the stage for what follows. (Pratt 1986, 35)

Identifying shared traits found in travel writing and ethnography, and determining their degrees of dominance within the genres, is helpful for the questions these traits raise with regard to the traveller and representation (see Campbell 1988). Augé's description of the activities of the ethnologist provides a useful starting point from which to extract the points of intersection between 'mere travelers' (Malinowski 1961, 11)[66] and the scientific ethnographer. Augé helps illuminate the remarks made by Pratt above in the effort being made here to tentatively demarcate the two genres. In *Non-Places / Non-Lieux* (1992) he states that:

> From the off, the field ethnologist's practice is that of a wanderer of the social, a manipulator of levels, a comparativist on tiptoe: he cobbles together a meaningful world, if needs be by exploring, through hasty study, intermediary worlds, or by consulting, in the guise of a historian, supporting documentation. He attempts, for himself and for others, to know who he can deign to speak about when he speaks about those with whom he has spoken.[67] (22)

Clarifying the methodology of the professional ethnologist, we note the relevancies of the practices described in this passage for the travel writer seeking to represent the foreign city. In a similar manner to the ethnographer, the travel writer too collects data, reads the city and gathers signs in order to piece together a coherent representation. Likewise, the travel writer will very often consult archival sources for assistance in gaining access to the meaning of the sights/sites of the city, with such background providing information on the initial dilemma of what the travel writer should be looking for, and later providing access to historical or social significances of the environment. The ontological position from which these activities are carried out does, however, differ when the point of reference is the travel journal and the traveller, and this is where Pratt's outline of the ethnographer's description-orientated account is helpful. For the dominant aspect of the travel book, while difficult to determine, is definitely not that it should be predominantly discursive and scientific. The ethnographer's method of categorization and description is traditionally inscribed within a set of scientific criteria whereas, superficially at least, the travel writer has more freedom of choice and expression when it comes to developing descriptions of the city he/she visits. Borm once again clarifies the point:

> Thus travel books seem generally less scientific in terms of their outlook and narrative strategy: there is only a limited amount of footnotes (rather than a systematic and frequent use thereof) in travelogues and at least in contemporary travel books no precise page references seem to be a rule. It is true, however, that certain (contemporary) travelogues contain bibliographies, stressing their erudite dimension [...] without turning them into scientific monographs though. (2000, 93)

The question is, therefore, integrally related to readership. The ethnographer is writing for a scientific, professionally trained audience, and while travel accounts can be read in such a manner, the same level of adherence to methodological practice is not expected. The travel writer is also more free to voice his/her subjectivity without too much objection from the reader, whereas the acknowledgement of subjectivity within ethnography has formed the very basis of ethnographers' own critique of the discipline, leading ethnographers such as Clifford (1988), Geertz (1988) and Augé (1992) to reconsider the epistemological basis of their 'science' and the conditions of its possibility. This paradox – the necessity of personal experience (and, therefore, a subjective viewpoint) and the scientific attempt at achieving an objective (and, at least in aspiration, a universal) stance – is, however, a trait clearly relevant to the travel writing under discussion in the following chapters. Moreover, in relation to authors writing in the latter half of the twentieth century, this paradox is often consciously explored. An analysis of such explorations enables an engagement with wider disciplinary debate over the status of modes of writing, the ethical consequences of such writing forms and whether it is possible to move beyond a nihilistic reading of the travel text.[68]

The next point Augé makes concerning the voice of the ethnographer acknowledges this critique, and for our context it highlights two specific issues regarding recent scholarship on travel and travel writing. While travel writing may not have the same scientific problematic as ethnography, when it comes to narrative voice, it is nevertheless fruitful to address the 'innocence' of the travel narrative. This line of enquiry highlights some important questions regarding the representation of reality and its implications for Western identity. The first of these questions has to do with the possibility of ever achieving a sufficiently objective stance so as to be able to represent the encounter with another culture. The objectivity referred to works on two closely interconnected levels: the social and the individual. How can one represent another when one's own methods of representing are embedded within a culturally configured set of discursive strategies? How can one ever reach beyond one's subjectivity? And, importantly, from what authority does one speak? This concern, for an authoritative position from which to speak, is dependent upon the discursive strategies that a culture (in this case European) uses to convince readers of the 'truth element' in its representations. Geertz pinpoints this authority as having its basis in the idea of presence:

> The ability of anthropologists to get us to take what they say seriously has less to do either with a factual look or an air of conceptual elegance than it has with their capacity to convince us that what they say is a result of their having actually penetrated (or, if you prefer, been penetrated by) another form of life, of having, one way or another, truly 'been there.' And that, persuading us that this offstage miracle has occurred, is where the writing comes in. (1988, 4–5)

For instance, even the statement, 'I do not know how to describe', frequently encountered in travel journals, does not prove that the narrator is unable to narrate – it does not invalidate the message whatsoever. Quite the opposite, this conceptual vacuum is meaningful in that it implies two statements: 'I was there to witness', and 'I do not understand what I have witnessed'. Both of these utterances serve to distinguish the construction of knowledge in travel writing from that of geographers or traditional ethnographers. Use of the first person singular and verbs of visual identification operate as guarantees of the traveller's presence *in situ* (the subjective, testimonial dimension of the travel account), but at the same time the use of verbs of perception, such as 'to see' constructs a certain 'authentic' relation between the space and the traveller, lending the narrative an objective, impersonal dimension (see Mondada 2005).

Geertz's point has relevancy for another key aspect of travel writing – the way in which the travel journal is read. Modes of reading are, of course, conditional upon the historical and cultural shifts in what a reader expects from the travel journal, and these shifts have often been conditioned by changes in relation to other modes of writing about travel. The development of the guidebook in the nineteenth century, for example, took some of the responsibility off the traveller to enumerate facts such as where to stay and what places to visit, and likewise readers came less and less to expect the presence of such lists in the travel journal, which then tended towards a more impressionistic, descriptive and personal style of narrative (Buzard 2002, 49). The second issue is one of responsibility. Representation is implicated in the construction of impressions, ideas, but also in the pragmatic politics of one culture towards another, and the writer is, therefore, faced with ethical issues concerning the present and future identity of the culture he/she describes. All of these questions are relevant to the analysis of travel writing, and scholars such as Campbell (1988, 1999), Mills (1991), Kaplan (1996) and Clarke (1999, 2000) amongst others have produced cogent critiques of travel writing, engaging it in a debate on the ethics of representation. As Steve Clarke (2000) points out:

> A travel book necessarily refers to that which cannot be immediately and tangibly verified: an elsewhere. Travel reference is to do with world-coherence: the book projects a world, and it is the ethics of inhabiting that alternative domain that are primarily at stake. (115)

Many of the writers under discussion here are engaged in similar critiques of their scriptural activities. If, as Clifford points out, we know that 'we can no longer know the whole truth, or even claim to approach it' (1986, 25) how is it even possible for writers to write? This question moves us along to the ethical issues at stake in travel writing, and implicates the aesthetic, or literary form, as a mode of 'sensory distribution' (Rancière 2004) that insinuates form in the creation not only of points of view, but of an experience of common life in the city. In what follows I want to specify two opposing operational schemas for apprehending style in modern travel writing and that promote an understanding of the bridge between form and spatialities of experience of the other: the legislative and the interpretive modalities of travel writing. The identification of these modalities permits a nuancing of the forms which defamiliarization assumes and implicates these forms in the ideological production of the space of the other.

1.8.6   Legislative and Interpretive Modes of Travel

Borrowing Zygmunt Bauman's (1987) terms *legislator* and *interpreter*, these stylistic operations are adapted and rearticulated here in relation to a cultural shift engaged in questioning established discursive hegemonies for representing alterity. This shift is reflected in travel writing as the genre moves between legislative modalities – of the tourist, the pilgrim or early ethnographers for instance – that are consistent with a narrative form that contains social space through established codified binaries, and an interpretive textual mode, a writing that reveals the contingent and constructed nature of these binaries through the use of reflexive literary forms. Travel, as a departure from 'everyday life', is an action that initiates dimensions of experience to defamiliarize the world, but the modes via which this defamiliarization takes place, or the extent to which the unfamiliar is permitted to endure, are neither ontologically nor discursively stable. The role played by travel writing in imperial contexts, for example, in bringing that which is foreign into the familiarity of language, is central to the discursive production of hierarchical systems. Thus the reproduction of tropes, stereotype, and the assumption of authorial transparency lay out not only the historical schema according to which another culture may be read but cognitively – and, in the case of colonial expansion, empirically – map the spaces of everyday life in terms of sameness.

It is this encoded discourse that leads us to revaluate what is at stake in the poetics of travel writing within this formerly minor genre. Paul Smethurst (Kuehn and Smethurst 2008, 2–3), in his introduction to *Travel Writing, Form, and Empire*, suggests that examining 'imperial form', in its particular literary manifestation as tropes, metaphors and other representational practices, reveals how these devices were essential to the endurance of what Michel Foucault (1966) terms the 'order of things' – those foundational structures of knowledge on which imperialist discourse was erected. It is through this formal mesh that the discursive production of representations of space in terms of Western binaries becomes visible, binaries such as self/other, the West/the rest, nature/civilization and authentic/fake. These binaries work to stabilize the strange, to reduce the potential radicality of mobility inherent in the act of travel. Through binary action alterity is demobilized and codified in terms that render it legible in accordance with imperialist necessities. It is this act of codification that, to move the form beyond the colonialist context, will be referred to here as a *legislative mode* of travel writing. Adapting Bauman's (1987, 2) term *legislative* to describe the tradition of the intellectual as social actor whose authority gains meaning from modernity's collective belief in the Enlightenment era's grand narratives of progress and universality, the designation can also be used to describe the discursive apparatus that such a world-view produces in travel writing.

To rest for a moment with the cultural context in which Bauman conceives this legislative model operating, we can elaborate to say that this model operates on the assumption of a preconceived model of a collective order according to which the other can be described and, in the case of imperial operations, according to which the social system of another culture can be shaped and administered. Bauman observes that this position leads to the 'establishment of a relatively autonomous, self-managing discourse able to generate such a model complete with the practices its implementation required' (1987, 2). This model of order and its discourse perform through Western ideological formulations, gathered together under Fredric Jameson's (1991) concept of the 'grand narratives': a litany consisting in the autonomous subject, its truth, its freedom, history, teleology, progress, power, economy and sex or, as Baudrillard would say, 'all the *real*'s big numbers' (1987b, 46). These epistemological strategies for making sense of the world have been sundered by the rise of theory, and reframed in travel writing critique as strategies for abstractly translating alternative cultural traditions in terms application to Western Europe – what the anthropologist Steve Tyler names as the Hegelian and scientific fusion of horizons, 'which reduces all traditions to the shape and interests of Western discourse' (1984, 328). In aesthetic terms, this world-view is revealed through the literary modulation of other cultures as quantifiable, and made manifest in travel writing as an approach to space that seeks to render alterity legible. The aim in legislative travel writing is to re-present space in terms of a stable collection of locations, sites and situations, with the effect that the space of social life is produced in terms relative to the same. The assumption of a transparent, coherent relationship between the code of language and the exterior world, or between the sign and its referent, works to immobilize space as it brings the meaning of alterity under control. This is a mode of writing travel in which, Smethurst states, 'instability and potential disorder are necessarily suppressed within the knowledge structures that give *form* to imperialist discourse' (2008, 2). Legislative travel writing consists, then, in a mode of producing space that frames and strategically positions other cultures within the epistemological boundaries of sameness.

It is from here that the notion of legislative travel may be connected to the ethics of engaging with the social space of the other's urban environment. Legislating for another is only possible when the ground from which one speaks is epistemologically stable and connected to a hierarchical or 'Archimedean' position from which to speak (Clifford 1988). The legislator for Bauman epitomizes the authoritative position of the Western intellectual during the modern period, a position grounded in the belief, among others, that the world was knowable, that what was yet unknown would be known and that all cultural trajectories could be plotted along the moral axis of the West's progression towards the democratic ideals of freedom and equality. However, the ethical codes pertaining to such a system situate value on the basis of exclusion, those who are not yet in the fold of this form of social life merely need to be convinced of its 'truth value', or else they are, by definition, morally inferior and should remain outside. In transferring Bauman's terms to the critical terrain of travel writing, the notion of an ethical code takes on a spatial dimension as interaction with others is linked to processes of rendering alterity legible, and the imposition of a cohesive order on alterity becomes indicative of a comprehensive, unilateral vision of the world. This is a form of travel writing in which contingency and instability are suppressed in favour of the paradigms of order and synchronicity. The legislative travel narrative corresponds to an ethical engagement with space in which the social, political and cultural elements of elsewhere are written by means of formal operations that are primarily reductionist in their relationship to the external world. Put another way, this coding paradoxically allows travel to remain stable; mobility for the most part is rendered neutral through the application of epistemological or ontological frameworks that permanently assert the hegemony of ideological discourses of Western Europe's modernity.

In opposition, interpretive travel writing can be considered as an emergent, self-conscious encounter with space, a representational form that recognizes the risk inherent in writing's pertaining to a transparent relationship with the real, to reduce and stabilize space. Interpretive travel writing can be thought of as 'tactical' (Certeau [1980] 1990) poetic forms that make normative representations of space appear in another register. The precise formal qualities of such a writing is discussed in the final chapter in relation to Perec's and Baudrillard's representations of New York, for now it is useful to qualify these forms theoretically as attempts to undermine legislative frameworks in certain distinct ways. First, interpretive travel writing, more than a stabilization of space in coherent legible form, points rather to a locus of enunciation, drawing reflexive attention to its own linguistic limits and very often seeking to transcend such limitations by poetic tactics that work at the edges of language – through the installation of silence or the double-take of parody, for instance. Second, rather than mastery or legibility, the tactical poetics of an interpretive travel account will operate by 'isolated actions, blow by blow'[69] (Certeau 1984, 37) recognizing its insufficiency as a dominant mode of representation. Rather than a claim to authority or authenticity this account is one of deficiency and subjective presence. Finally, the interpretive travel account is an act of 'poaching'/'braconnage' (Certeau [1980] 1990, 239); it works within the discursive organization of legislative space to blur its (alleged) transparency through stylistic reappropriation. In the chapters that follow we discuss the aesthetics and politics of our travel writers' use of legislative or interpretive modalities for negotiating the city, and how these modalities contribute to the emergence of modern spatialities in London and New York.

Chapter Two

URBAN OPPOSITIONS: PRODUCING FRENCH SPACE IN NINETEENTH-CENTURY LONDON

Oh! What iron, oh! What copper and steel, what cogs and wheels, what tireless machines and invisible horses! What an occasion, what miracles, what a future![1]

Janin 1851, 3

In this chapter I draw some of the theory already outlined into dialogue with two urban travel accounts to London dating from the latter half of the nineteenth century: Jules Janin's *Le Mois de mai à Londres et l'exposition de 1851 / London in the Month of May and the Exhibition of 1851* (1851) and Jules Vallès's, *La Rue à Londres / The London Street* (1876). As can already be discerned from their titles, both works are concerned with different architectures and spatial arrangements of the city, and indeed both texts exhibit a consciousness of space as a material configuration of modernity. However, the key question here is to examine the distinctions being made by the authors with respect to their differing appropriations of this nascent modern world. As Lefebvre tells us, the modern world consists in a 'problematic' of space that is dual in its aspect, requiring an account both of capitalism and modern social space if we are to understand more precisely the 'tendencies of modernity' (Lefebvre [1974] 1991, 123).[2] Without pretending to attempt to analyse this problematic, I want to take Lefebvre's duality to analyse the texts at hand. In this way, I explore Janin's (1804–1874) engagement with the Crystal Palace as an encounter with a new representation of space in the Lefebvrian sense explored in chapter 1, an architecture that can be seen to signal the beginning of a certain idea of 'global space'[3] (Lefebvre [1974] 1991, 125) in its erection of a space of ostensible transparency – a building assembled entirely from glass and iron girders, the Crystal Palace constructed a void that was to be filled by the gathering together of national objects in a global topography of spectacle. In a second movement, I examine Janin's modus operandi for interpreting what Paul Scheerbart might call this 'glass palace' ([1914] 1971, 14), and how the author's spatial practice is shaped by a political vision of France in the aftermath of the 1848 June Days. Thus, the house of the exiled former king, Louis Philippe the First (and last) (1830–1848), in Surrey constitutes the second geographic node through which Janin's representative space of London includes a critical imaginative geography of France. Vallès's imaginative geography of London too is built around an architectural figure of modernity, in this case not a singular edifice, rather it is the street that organizes the narrative. In this choice, Vallès's reveals an alternative political lens for interpreting London's social space. As an exiled *Communard*, his gaze on London filters the city's landscape to look precisely at the people of the city, who emerge therein as poor substitutions for the mythological *peuple* of Paris. Both travellers read, therefore, through a bifocal lens that frames its subject, London, with an overlay of French political realities.

The focus, then, is on the alternating and, often, oppositional principles of legislative writing which these travellers employ to render London legible. Both Janin's and Vallès's narrative strategies illuminate how modern French interpretations of London were ensconced in emergent moral identifications with the nation state, imperialism and progress, at the same time that these identifications were articulated in (often paradoxical) relation to traditional conceptions of community, history and profound associations of the past. As we shall see, during this period it is clear that there is, in Taylor's words, 'a specific moral direction to Western modernity' (2001, 176), however, this direction cannot be wholly accounted for by the negation of the sacred, cosmological outlook with the emergence of a secular, scientific world-view. In examining Janin's experience at the Crystal Palace and Vallès's exploration of London's insalubrious streets, I want to explore then the tension inherent in the modern experience as one indicative of Western modernity's 'own original spiritual vision' (Taylor 2001, 176), a vision that is invested in different (very often, conflicting) notions of 'the good'. The 'good' is to be understood here as a *differentiated* set of Western understandings of the human subject about his/her relationship to society and the world. In modernity, Taylor observes the emergence of the self as a dichotomous, inward/outward being, and the growing centrality of everyday experience to the meaning of life. In this scenario, meaning in life is no longer completely derived from the sense of one's place in a transcendent, providential order of things. Rather, this development of the self as 'inward' subject moves towards the valorization of sensibility, emotional well-being and a sense of the division between the private and public self. In the same tone, the valorization of everyday life suggests that the 'good' becomes oriented towards finding meaning in a concept of human dignity and, with the development of capitalism, created an affinity between the idea of civility and social order (Taylor 2004, 47). This is a vision that while it is, to a certain extent, causally linked to the material developments in urban culture – extensive mobility, industrialization and the growth of capitalist markets – cannot be wholly explained in these terms. Taylor demonstrates persuasively, for example, how 'external' changes in the material and institutional circumstances of a culture cannot account wholly for the shape of 'modernity' within that culture. For our case, then, while the external forces attendant upon modern societies may exhibit similarities, it is, to follow Taylor, in the cultural, value-laden differences – brought to light by these travel narrative's political representative spaces – that bring London into view as an alternative manifestation of these external forces, or, as one urban modernity emergent amid a myriad of other possible tendencies. In this chapter we shall see, furthermore, that these cultural, and value differences are the precise ones being sought by the French traveller, for it is through the encounter with difference that it becomes possible to articulate a critique of France. A critique which is spatialized through the London encounter.

2.1 Modern Babylon

To contemporaries London possessed a unique identity certainly but it was an identity marked by duality and extreme contrast. While, on the one hand, the wide Georgian streets and neoclassical building façades of the Regency period meant that London was one of the most planned cities in Europe by the 1850s, another image encroached on the orderly architectures that were predominantly present in the West End. The city's split identity was articulated by narratives labelling London as 'Modern Babylon', 'Coketown', or William Cobbett's (1822) 'The Great Wen', and confirmed materially by the structural difference of London, based in the fundamental disparities of demography, industry and wealth that separated the metropolis from the rest of Britain as well as from the continent (Sheppard 1971).[4] Beyond the gamut of Western experiences of human social organization, London defied any encounter with urban space which the traveller may have had before. Between 1801 and 1851 the population of London almost tripled in size.[5] Internal and external migration to London during the period far exceeded that to Paris, which was due in some measure to the fact that for centuries London had been absorbing neighbouring towns and spilling over its Roman walls.[6] By 1811 the city had over a million inhabitants and the rate of growth seemed exponential – the capital had four million inhabitants by 1891. The demographic upsurge reinforced London's well-established dominance over the political and cultural landscape of Britain. Unaccustomed to the galloping expansion of the metropolis, the size of London seemed incredible to visitors (Lees [1973] 1999, 414), who very often attributed a moral charge to the sobriquets they bestowed on it, and connoted the city as containing both the best and worst that civilization had to offer: a 'wen' summoning images of cystic boils on the head, 'Coketown' calling forth images of dense fog, claustrophobic atmospheres, dust and filth, with 'Babylon' positioning the city as decadent and debauched – a point to which we shall return. These appellations contain an eschatological drama of London as a peaking and perverse civilization whose decline is immanent.

In economic terms, too, London was ahead of its French counterpart. Several important sectors, such as the service and transport industries, as well as the large numbers of people employed in commerce and finance, meant that the economic development of London was more diversified and complex than that of Paris (Winter 1993). This was largely due to the physical and financial environment favourable to capitalist development in London – the deep estuary of the Thames provided the city with an international port, and the relative stability of imperial politics fed the city with luxury goods and raw materials from the colonies (Young and Garside 1982). This also contributed to creation within the city of transnational heterotopias,[7] where in Wapping, sailors from all over the world disembarked. Prostitutes were a permanent sight along the docks, and this space's hodgepodge of nationalities and races fascinated French travellers from inland Paris. Vallès, for instance, is called upon to draw an imaginative geography linking Wapping with Messina, Hamburg and Calcutta – other great international port cities of the period.[8] And he remarks on the heterogeneity of the district's soundscape saying, 'Here a thousand languages are spoken, like in the Tower of Babel' (Vallès [1876] 1951, 232).[9] All of these contributed to the image of London as the hub of trade capitalism in the modern world. If Paris was the source of the ideo-logical vocabulary of modernity, then London was seen as the chief economic expres-sion of this modernity (Hosbawm [1962] 1999). And this market aspect of London is central. As a 'complex ensemble of commercial relations and communication networks' (Lefebvre [1974] 1991, 112),[10] London created a hierarchy of levels in national and international terms, it subordinated local and regional markets to the focused space of its capital, while its international port was the largest in the world in this period and the heart of the expanding British Empire.

It is true that a very specific spatial conception of modernity has been generated by Haussmann's spectacular remodelling of Paris's urban infrastructures (Pinkney 1958; Harvey 2006; Harvey 1996). Lynda Nead posits that 'Paris has dominated recent histories of modernity and urbanization. The rebuilding of the city under Napoleon III (1852–1870) and his Prefect of the Seine, Baron Haussmann, has been taken as the paradigmatic model of nineteenth-century urban history and of modernity more generally' (2005, 6). Indeed, Haussmann acted with ruthless decision, demolishing whole faubourgs in the pursuit of clarity and accessibility, all ideas that would become central to the urban ideals of early twentieth-century modernist architects. The île de la Cité was cleared of its warren of menacing streets and its topography was refor-mulated as a bureaucratic architectural hub. Expansive, horizon-reaching boulevards cut through the old quarters, avenues of sculpted trees aestheticizing the military objective of this urban project to make the fiery tempered faubourgs more accessible to government troops. Large squares functioned as nodal points for radial networks of streets, while urban parks clarified the landscape, and performed as unofficial sites for the exhibition of the power and prosperity of Napoleon III's Second Empire (Moncan 2009).

This is the Paris of modernity. However, when Janin left Paris in May 1851, Louis-Napoleon Bonaparte had yet to stage his coup (which would not happen until 2 December of that year). Paris in 1851 was largely as Louis-Philippe I had left it upon his abdica-tion in 1848. Even then, this bourgeois king of the July Monarchy (1830) had not made any major changes to the city since coming to power. In a period fraught with political instability, and a country still trying to come to terms with the French Revolution and its aftermath, Louis-Philippe's project was not one of modernization but of modesty. As Colin Jones succinctly puts it, 'The July Monarchy was more of a finisher than an ini-tiator in matters monumental. Most of its major achievements were inherited projects, many of which had ground to a halt at some stage since 1789' (Jones [2004] 2006, 311). Indeed, a large part of the municipal budget was devoted to establishing churches or restoring already existing ones – structures which do not chime well with the idea of Paris as the capital of modernity. However, what is significant for the emergence of a modern social imaginary in Paris during the period is the central place assumed by *le peuple*, which became an established mythology from this point on. Jones recounts that one of the outcomes of the popular July Revolution in 1830 was that the people of Paris were now represented by their dynamism, virtue and capacity for revolution. This representation emphasized masculine *vertu* / virtue, in a call back to earlier depictions of the French rev-olutionaries of 1789, and of Jacobin heroism under Robespierre's Committee of Public

Safety (1793–94) in particular.[11] This new moral attachment to the idea of an invigorated *peuple* was evident in the urban toponymy. Paris changed sex, passing from female to male in French gender declension. Thus, the allegorical figure of the city as woman – *La ville de Paris* – was abandoned and subsequent adjectives and monikers attached to the city were used in the masculine. Jones provides us with some examples, 'the Left in particular variously lauded and mythologized the city as a majestic "hero", "gladiator", "soldier", "sentinel" and "toreador"' while the Right tended now to describe Paris as '"a tyrant", "a satrap", a "parvenu", "a beggar", "a murder" or a "charlatan"' (Jones [2004] 2006, 314–15). These associations of Paris with violence and revolution will become key to understanding Janin's reading of London.

To return to London, the French often remarked upon the oppositions that London seemed to contain, and this is reflected in the travellers' tendencies to draw dichotomies between the monumental aspect of London's urban order and the fascination with the chaos and insalubrity of the streets in industrialized neighbourhoods such as the East End. On the one hand, therefore, the city constituted the pinnacle of urban master planning – in the eighteenth and early nineteenth century, Georgian neoclassicism and Regency architecture had ensured the clarity of London's urban design. On the other hand, as the century progressed and the population swelled, London's correspondent sprawl made it difficult for architecture to keep up with the necessities of industrial development (see Olsen 1982). Furthermore, the decentralized character of London's local government hampered modernization and a cohesive plan to unify the city spatially was almost impossible. No effective government beyond that of the City of London was installed until 1839 when the London County Council came into being, and this meant that London was ill-equipped, administratively and in terms of its infrastructure, to handle the day-to-day crises of metropolitan growth and change. From the mid-nineteenth century on, change in London happened quickly, and in the new industrial areas this change did not have the rational quality of an overall grand plan (Olsen 1982; Arnold 2000). As Nead observes, 'Modernity for London in this period was a condition of compromise; between local government and private industry, local vested interests and traditional authorities. Modernity was an accumulation of uneven and unresolved processes of urbanization; it took the form of the improved street within a district of slums' (2005, 5). Prior to the chaos that Haussmannian reconstruction would bring to Paris in the 1850s and 1860s, therefore, already in 1851 London was the site of constant and unpredictable demolitions occurring alongside modernizations. Familiar avenues disappeared without their replacements ever lending connective coherence to the city's sprawling topographies. The result was that the clarity of the Grand Manner design, which Regency architects such as John Nash had given London's West End, stood increasingly apart from the sprawl and overcrowded squalor that characterized the East End. These contradictions provide the framework for Vallès's spatial practice and the scaffolding for the representational spaces of his travel account.[12]

The prodigious sprawl and contrasting topographies of London were, of course, important factors in its attractiveness for the French visitor.[13] One trope commonly used to articulate these aspects of modernity was the crowd. Captured as a figure of the modern urban landscape, the crowd is narratively constructed in terms of its capacity to alienate and/or exhilarate the individual. Furthermore, in travel accounts of London, the crowd becomes one of the key tropes for articulating the social space of the class system, regionally structured class divisions and the co-presence of a large urban underclass. In this version of modernity the official rearrangements of the urban landscape are understood from within a more localized and communal framework of meaning than the one put forward by the nationstate (Adams 1994; Attridge 2003). The travel accounts examined here suggest that confrontation with the chaotic states of existence produced by modern London habitually involved a configuration of oppositions – between streets, forms of government, social spaces – for manufacturing meaning, attempts at resolution that result in paradox and contradiction. For one thing, the social space of modernity is not simply constituted by the moulding and organization of space in line with the emergent discourses of power articulated in the nineteenth century through science, mass culture, nation and empire. Meaning for urban modernity is also to be found in the mental space it produces, in the experiential shift undergone by subjects in space. So that in the travel account we encounter a range of expectations, fears, fascinations and anxieties that produce narratives of modernity in the affective sense. For another thing, the social and historical contexts which surround these two French travellers' visits to London in 1851 and 1876 respectively are formative of their interpretations of urban space, and provide the reader access to an imaginative geography of modernity that cannot be abstracted from culture.

2.2 French Travel Writing and Modernity

The attraction of the city for the traveller involves the potential for engagement with the architectures and social spaces that are seen to provide access to the kernel of the other's national identity. The traveller's everyday experience of the city and his/her relationship to the urban community is often, and quite paradoxically, negotiated in relation to the urban environment's symbolic sites or monuments as a visible means of directing the significance of space and time. The discourse of such monuments articulates the individual's modes for comprehending social structure and this occurs through the mesh of comparison, so that London for the French traveller becomes a site in which they might collect evidence of 'Englishness'. In other words, the traveller reads the foreign landscape as a visual array of signs, signs that are appropriate to understanding the wider horizons of an other culture in holistic, totalizing terms. Jonathan Culler, speaking of tourism expresses this idea well when he says that 'the tourist is interested in everything as a sign of itself, an instance of a typical cultural practice: a Frenchman is an example of a Frenchman, a restaurant in the Quartier Latin is an example of a Latin Quarter restaurant, signifying "Latin Quarter Restaurantness"' (Culler 1981, 2). Tourists apprehend the urban object and the inhabitants' practices as cultural signs, reading into these the codes to unlock the 'ultimate' meaning of a particular culture. Evoking Baudrillard's theory of social objects as things important for how they create meaningful relations between people and cultures, Culler underlines the tourist practice as one based in meaning-making, 'rather than needs or use-value'.[14] Travellers, more generally, and urban travellers in particular, are uniquely involved in conceptualizing the everyday experience of the city in terms of signs, and in relating these signs to broader networks of national cultural narratives or normative structures of signification that operate within a French oppositional conception of their own and of London's culture. The travel account reminds us, then, that a passage across the street is a passage through complex, culturally differentiated definitions of identity, of the 'common good' and what this does, and ought to, constitute. The significance of a monument, for example, lies in its materialization of ideals, which inscribes it in the temporalities of the city's imaginative geographies. Most often, the monument resonates as an architectural symbol of the state's discursive strategies of power (its ideals), and produces a space designed to ensure the preservation of such ideals in the future. As José Luis Sert, Fernand Léger and Sigfried Giedion write in their influential 1943 manifesto, 'Nine Points on Monumentality', 'Monuments are human landmarks which men have created as symbols for their ideals, for their aims, and for their actions' (Giedion et al. [1943] 1993, 29). In this final emphasis on action, the authors remind us that monuments are also often 'living' architectural structures, which is to say that are not simply visual artefacts but multisensory, situated structures with which the public interact spatially, mentally, and for our case, representationally. In this sense, the monument moves beyond form to function as the site where ideals enter the realm of performance; through the subject's spatial practice of the monument, ideals become enacted experience. Representations of metropolitan monumentality are, therefore, indicative of the traveller's way of coping with the confrontation of an alternative set of socio-symbolic criteria as articulated by the foreign city.

In modern societies, normative distributions of social space are articulated through the regulation of access to various sites within the city that effectively distinguish the public from the private (MacCannell 1976, 39). With increased urbanization these normative paths of access are made visible through physical divisions; walls, fences, barricades and signs marking the limits of a community, an institution or a personal space. The social ordering of human interaction is, therefore, only one of the ways that the structure of modern society might be understood (Goffman 1963, 1971). For the traveller, who lacks intimate acquaintance with the society being visited, other visible forms emerge as central to reading the social structures of the foreign city. Architectural shows of industry, empire, museums, parks, as well as, decay, refuse, slums and prisons are all important visual nodes for the traveller. The traveller's experience is thus directly engaged with questions of nationality, accessibility, legibility and subjectivity through which the experience of London is apprehended. The travel account demonstrates how public representations of modernity were very often renegotiated and challenged by the perspective of the outsider. The version of metropolitan modernity that emerges from the travel writing examined here is very different from the grand, ineluctable process described by Berman ([1982] 1988) in his version of modernization's grand narrative. It does, however, preserve the vitality of contradiction that Berman identifies as inherent to the modernization experience on a social, cultural and economic level. This makes the traveller's engagement with the monument significant in terms of tracing French subjective responses to collective national narratives and the spatial manifestations of governmentality. In a period that augured the age of empire (Hobsbawm 1989), an outsider's response to another nation's network of symbolic references is revealing of an alternative encounter with modernity's urban expression, and one which does not so easily fit with the idea of either the tourist or inhabitant as unconscious participants or passive consumers of the structures of urban governmentality and their implications for social life. More specifically, we shall see that Janin's and Vallès's representational spaces are organized in the context of the deep political unrest which formed the background of Parisian modernity during the period. It is the idea and expression of 'revolution', conceived in the cultural, social as well as political senses that structure their perceptions of London's urban spaces.

2.3   Jules Janin's Glass Palace

Janin's account *London in the Month of May and the Exhibition of 1851* raises questions for French modernity in relation to that of its rival Great Britain. It becomes apparent that throughout the nineteenth century until the end of World War I, the ideas of 1789 and France's successive political upheavals throughout the nineteenth century[15] condition French narratives for understanding both their own and alternative forms of institutional power (Hobsbawm [1962] 1999, 73). In examining Janin's narrative on the Crystal Palace we will see that not only does the exhibition space perform as a representation of space which produces a certain imaginative geography of the British Empire, it also enables the traveller's application of another set of criteria, structured around a subjective political response to the abdication of Louis-Philippe in 1848, as well as a critique of the politicization of French popular culture through the burgeoning mythology of revolution and *le peuple*.[16] The production of Janin's urban imagery, then, is the result of a transfer of cultural positions, which is to say that his interpretations of the English capital are negotiated from within a value-laden framework relating to France and the home culture. Here the focus is not simply on travel as the conveyance of external motion, but also an assessment of the imaginative geography of the traveller as an intellectual territory that moves between France and England with the result that Janin's representational space is inherently and consistently in motion. This movement is articulated in the first place in terms of wonderment at the Exhibition's spectacular display but also in terms of the harmony of its workers, thus Janin's spatial perception allows him to construct a critique of French political culture. Second, the other major destination for Janin during his time in London is the home of the exiled Louis-Philippe in Surrey, so that here England becomes a space of nostalgic reminiscence on a governmental space that once existed in France – thus infusing the account with multiple temporalities as well as geographies. In the first instance, I will examine the Great Exhibition and its organizers' methodologies for the spatial arrangement of power to demonstrate the significance of the exhibition in creating modern representations of space that articulate an ideal of national and international power through display. The final part of the analysis treats Janin's development of locational hierarchies that result from the author's idealized itinerary.

2.4 A Worthwhile Revolution

In his manifesto *Glass Architecture* ([1914] 1971), the German architect Paul Scheerbart posited the replacement of closed architectures of stone and brick with those of transparent glass:

> We live for the most part in closed rooms. These form the environment from which our culture grows. Our culture is to a certain extent the product of our architecture. If we want our culture to rise to a higher level, we are obliged, for better or for worse, to change our architecture. [...] So many ideas constantly sound to us like a fairy-tale, when they are not fantastic or utopian at all. Eighty years ago, the steam railway came, and undeniably transformed the face of the earth. *From what has been said so far the earth's surface will once again be transformed, this time by glass architecture.* If it comes, a metamorphosis will occur. (32, my emphasis)

While Scheerbart speaks from a vantage point of over half a century after the first of the great world exhibitions opened it glass doors to the public, his perspective on cultural improvement, and the role of transparent architecture in that amelioration, illuminate the opinion of many exhibitors at, visitors to and organizers of the Great Exhibition at the Crystal Palace. Moreover, Janin's 1851 representation of the Exhibition as 'a worthwhile revolution' concurs with Scheerbart's identification of glass architecture as the means to an open society, freed from 'closed rooms'. If circulation, technology and legibility are associated with the architectures and topographies of modernity, then 1851 undoubtedly merits consideration as the year of London's accession to the status of a modern city. A point of departure in architectural as well as cultural terms, the Great Exhibition, housed in the Crystal Palace that was constructed specifically for the event, was the first of its kind to establish models for public and state interaction based in transparency and in a gathering of transnational objects beneath one glass roof. In her article, 'La Ville et l'industrie', Françoise Maille (2007, 1) remarks on the extent of the Great Exhibition's cultural influence:

> The apogee of 'relations' between London and industry was undoubtedly the Great Exhibition of 1851. Londoners' first encounter with all facets of industry, it was equally the first encounter with products and men from around the world. The event caused a stir, but it also made London the site of a vast number of visitors; a little more than six million, a number that most international exhibitions would envy today.[17]

As an officially ordered site that encouraged and directed the collective consumption of modernity, the exhibition constructed such consumption from multiple vantage points through the various national displays which it gathered together under one roof (Urry 1995, 142). Among the 13,000 exhibits from around the world were the Jacquard loom, an envelope machine, tools, kitchen appliances, steel-making displays and a reaping machine from the United States. Many of the visitors who flocked to London came from European cities, and in becoming a centre for international travellers, the exhibition produced space in a way to emphasize Britain as the heart of global modernity, through its display of the state's imperial power, but also, and more fundamentally, to the conception of Victorian Britain as a social space of civilizing institutional bodies (Flanders 2007). From the French perspective, the Exhibition was an occasion that produced a vast variety of publications. These ranged from Ch. Laboulaye's *Essai sur l'art industriel* (1856) – a comparison of French and British accomplishments in industrial invention – to the *Guide de l'étranger à Londres* (Exposition Internationale 1851), a poem 'L'Exposition universelle à Londres en 1851' and a song, 'Le Palais de cristal' by Jean Laudéra (Laudéra 1853) as well as a journal series of 22 issues, *Le Palais de Cristal* (1851). This last declared that its aims were to inform French workers about their rights, and to bring back information about the industrial techniques and objects on display in London so as to enrich French industrial development.[18] In addition, of course, the exhibition fostered a sense of competition between nations, in effect contributing to the emergent nationalism that was to shape French and British geopolitical relations in the late nineteenth century. To take just one instance, the issue of *Le Palais de Cristal* of 7 May 1851 declares its goal to be:

> to make known to the industrial world the part which our nation has often played in these new inventions, in these artistic or mechanical marvels laid before our eyes in the palace in Hyde Park. […] So that while this statue or that jewel, this piece of furniture, or that swathe of silk, might appear under the English section of the catalogue, its design, its execution, could perhaps be the work of French artists or workers hired at great expense by England. (Wednesday, 7 May 1851: 2)

Likewise, Adolphe Blanqui's *Lettres sur l'Exposition universelle* opens with the line: 'Never forget, dear reader, that the Universal Exhibition was a thought born in France' (1851, 10).[19] The French liked to claim that the Crystal Palace could not have happened without its forerunner, 'The Public Exhibition for Products of French Industry' which was organized every few years in Paris. This French precursor to the Crystal Palace approached neither the scale nor popularity of the latter, however, which constituted a major innovation in the development of forms of travel for cultural betterment, exchange, and industrial as well as cultural knowledge with a transnational flavour. This cultural tourism also articulated a modern comparative consciousness around ideas of the nation, national pride, and, importantly, as we shall see in the case of Janin, what should constitute the proper aims of a modern civilization.

Within the comparative framework, Janin's perspective on the exhibition is formed aesthetically through a reappropriation of the word 'revolution' as commonly understood in the French context since 1789. From the opening pages of the narrative the travel writer employs the imagery of revolution and battle to represent the momentousness of the occasion, and roots the word 'revolution' in a comparison that puts the revolution of industry in London in competition for meaning with the successive revolutions of political life in France. Moreover, this revolutionary imagery is ensconced within a socio-political hierarchy that places industrial and economic change in opposition to, and above, political and ideological governmental upheaval. Effectively, this constitutes a bringing together of two strands of modernity – industrial and political revolution – that produced the particular shape of European nations in the period. In Janin's text these two versions of modernity are made to compete with one another, so that the descriptions of the revolution in industrial life on display in the Crystal Palace function to create a more or less explicit critique of French political instability at the time.

Using London as an outpost from which to marshal a critique on instability at home was not unusual in French accounts of the Exhibition. Blanqui's *Lettres sur l'Exposition universelle* opens with a critique of French bureaucracy – in particular, the customs tariffs and complicated procedures for bringing souvenirs back to France from England. But, more significantly, the author uses this ruse to slip in a sarcastic assessment that this kind of administrative mentality is what prevented 'a great country like ours, where the people change their form of government every fifteen years and become a republic, when they are in bad humour' (1851, 10) from being the first to stage an international exhibition on the scale of the Crystal Palace. Coming to Janin, this journalist and novelist was a prolific writer, well known in Paris since the 1820s when he worked for the centre-right newspaper *Le Figaro*, he established his royalist credentials at the *Quotidienne*, and spent a large part of his career working as a critic for the conservative *Journal des Débats*. A confirmed supporter of the July Monarchy and a politically engaged writer, in 1851 Janin positions himself strongly against the idea of popular revolt and republicanism as a form of government. In an expression of his distaste for the tendency in France since the Revolution to politicize each aspect of everyday life, the traveller consistently rejects political discourse as a means to frame his London experience. Instead this account consists in descriptive passages that convey the exhibition as a hub of movement, noise and work. These passages, however, are highly connotative, manipulating the language of revolution to reposition it in the context of the exhibition as a site of productive activity. For example, he praises the French working-class artisans accompanying him on the voyage to England for their grounded conversation: 'the night passed thus in talking, each man about his craft without a word on politics' (Janin 1851, 6).[20] Throughout the journal political debate is represented as impractical and pathetic and, indeed, detrimental to the development of a nation. Instead, cultural order and industrial progress are placed in direct opposition to politics, and this is done formally through the stylistic inversion of the discourse of revolution and battle:

Here, finally, a riot that merits worldly contemplation and smiles from the heavens. Here are some excellent revolutions, worthy of our admiration and respect. We do battle with the most courteous of weapons. We erect, one beside the other, barricades made of masterpieces, we hear only of these people at work the noise of the hammer striking the anvil, or the whining of steam, harnessed to its flaming chariot. Listen! This noise, like that of cannons, that topples cities, it is the noise of craft that makes itself heard the world over, it is the generous efforts of great nations that refuse to be vanquished in this immense battle. Look! In the distance, along all passageways, on every path, across the oceans and the seas, from north to south, from dawn till dusk, across mountains and chasms, by sun and ice, in government charters and at the foot of thrones, in white sweat and black sweat […] you can see surging these armies of workers, busy with feeding, repairing, defending, protecting, growing, to show this world dedicated to conflict, this world abandoned to chance, this world long given over to feeble theories, incendiary and idle evangelists, vagabond preachers, to the wretches who wish to change these tools into daggers, these toiling fires into hungry flames, these workers into rioters. Cowardly flatterers of the most vile sentiments with ignorant hearts, leave them alone, they will say of these hopes, of these glories of our contemporaries only slander, blasphemy, perjury, threats and conspiracies.[21] (1851, 1–2)

The ideological position of this passage is clear, but importantly, it reveals a socio-historical awareness articulating the cultural dichotomy differentiating England's industrial and material revolution from France's ideological, institutional and linguistic one. In the same way that political or social upheaval produce a 'revolutionary consciousness' or awareness of the significance of a happening as an event, so too when confronted with the exhibition's cornucopian spectacle, 'one feels gripped by that profound anxiety that takes hold of the soul at the onset of some momentous event' (9).[22] Here, the exhibition's display and the fervent industrious atmosphere, encourage the visitor's contextualization of his presence in national terms, and cause him to reflect critically about the state of things in his home country.

In effect, the organization of space at the Crystal Palace facilitated greatly the production of a comparative mental space in the foreign viewer. To rest for a moment with the ways in which its architectural and spatial order enabled this, we can say first of all that the Crystal Palace was the world's first exhibition building to be constructed from glass and wrought cast iron. After failed attempts on the Royal Commission's part to find a competition design suitable for the Exhibition as well as failing in their own design, it was finally Joseph Paxton, the Duke of Devonshire's gardener, who designed the 1,848 foot structure. The building was based on his model of a lily house that used the principle of the lily's leaf structure to create a framework for the edifice. The building used over 900,000 square feet of glass and 3,300 iron columns, which meant that it was easy to assemble and could be erected and dismantled efficiently. Monumental in scale – Queen Victoria referred to the exhibition as 'the great monument'[23] (Poovey 1995) – the Crystal Palace, Isobel Armstrong tells us in her evocative study, 'was experienced as an alternative world, a transformative space. The control of light in the building enhanced the sense of a newly made world' (Armstrong 2008, 152). The classic description of the building by Lothar Bucher emphasizes the architecture's liberation from the physical norms of substance; the building is diaphanous, melting into the visitor's lines of sight:

> Instead of moving from the wall at one end to that at the other, the eye sweeps along an unending perspective which fades into the horizon. We cannot tell if this structure towers a hundred or a thousand feet above us, or whether the roof is a flat structure or built up from a succession of ridges, for there is no play of shadows to enable our optic nerves to gauge the measurements.[24]

Furthermore, through the arrangement of objects the exhibition organized materially a simultaneous display of international capitalism while its programme provided a social locus for the ideology and practice of imperial culture. The Exhibition opened on 1 May and ran until 11 October after which point the building was removed and reconstructed at Sydenham Hill in South London. The objects on display came from all over the world, and the building embodied a vision of modernity conceived as a performance on a global stage, with objects arranged according to their national origin. Its importance as a historical event was its being the first public space of its kind to place antique artefacts beside technological prototypes, as well as its bringing together products and people from all over the world for the vast gathering in Hyde Park. This scale and innovation made it a talking point among contemporaries and the paradigmatic model for all future public spectacles (Auerbach 1999). The exhibition's global dimension was distinctly imperialist in nature. Countries with displays included British India, as well as those that had been more recently settled, such as Australia and New Zealand, considered part of the 'new' empire (Hoffenberg 2001).

Tony Bennett's (1995) work, which focuses on the architectures and arrangements used by the exhibition's authorities, notes that this building provided a new technological environment within which artefacts and machines entered the discourse and experience of common cultural life. Indeed, the Great Exhibition broke many of the architectural and organizational conventions for cultural display, and its material arrangements were testament to the imperial power structures that underpinned its organization. The Victorian government imposed its doubly democratic and imperialistic vision on public space, opening the building to the general public, and thus to some extent breaking down barriers of accessibility between high and low culture.

The Crystal Palace, through both its architecture and public protocol, constituted a marked departure from both the restraint and exclusivity that characterized traditional modes of exhibition, as in the cases of the *Kunstkammern*, the *Wunderkammern*, private collections or *cabinets des curieux*. By opening objects to an arena of full public visibility and inspection, this departure gave rise to what Bennett terms the 'exhibitionary complex', a phenomenon paving the way for modern, participatory notions of display sites as places of democratic relation. The exhibitionary complex originates in 'a break with both [the traditional relations of sound and vision] in effecting the transfer of significant qualities of cultural and scientific property from private into public ownership where they were housed within institutions administered by the state for the benefit of an extended general public' (1995, 73). The architectural arrangement of the Crystal Palace meant that not only could the authorities observe the public but equally that the public became observer of itself as a collective entity, a self-reflexive relationship of singular bodies amid a larger collective scene. In this way, the buildings enabled both the functions of surveillance and of spectacle.[25] Within the park, and from elevated vantage points around the glass walls, colonial and class subjects, global visitors and more local inhabitants actively observed one another, 'creating', as Peter Hoffenberg (2001, 17) puts it, 'a sense of community among visitors and exhibitors, a duality to the process of vision'. Also significant was the decorum of the public which, in the presence of the 1,000 extra policemen and 10,000 soldiers kept on standby, proved orderly in its conduct. The exhibition's programme stratified visitors by providing different days for different classes of visitors, and regulated access through varying prices of admission. Bennett observes that 'the exhibition transformed the many-headed mob into an ordered crowd, a part of the spectacle and a sight of pleasure in itself' (1995, 72). In addition, the cultural codes predominant in this democratic space were largely bourgeois and aspirational in the sense that they sought to impose a middle-class moral order on the crowd. The perceived threat of unseemly behaviour on the part of London's underclass was regulated by introducing special manuals that outlined proper decorum for visitors and appropriate modes of dress, and in which the state appealed to a national sensibility not to spoil the overall appearance of the exhibition, but rather to aspire to its aesthetic unity, to integrate with its grandeur, in short, to become a part of it. Mary Douglas, showing how institutions answer a basic human epistemological desire for order and coherence, points out that institutions' encoding of information and processes of categorization delimit conceptual perimeters that 'systematically direct individual memory and channel our perceptions into forms comparable with the relations they authorize' (1986, 46). Bennett picks up this theme of material space as means to produce mental and emotional resonances, arguing that beginning with the Crystal Palace, the exhibitionary complex developed out of the need to respond to the problem of public order and a need for national coherency. The space of the Exhibition was, therefore, to some extent motivated by socio-political disquiet and productive of a vision of cultural coherence on a mass scale, its architectures were engaged with the 'question of winning hearts and minds as well as the disciplining and training of bodies' (1995, 62).

More broadly, Anthony Giddens contends that one of the defining features of modernity is the manner in which social relations are uprooted from local contexts of action. By 'uprooting' (1991, 209) Giddens implies the extraction of social relations from local engagement and their redistribution across wider spans of space and time. In the manner of its organization – its recombination of the collective public's relationship to the presence of the multicultural in both temporal and spatial terms – the Great Exhibition was key in the reconfiguration not only of the public's relation to the cultural object situated in a democratically open arena but also, by extension, to their understanding of the British nation as being at the heart of an imperial and global set of geopolitical relationships. The exhibition's cultural influence, expressed more concretely in statistical terms, demonstrates the scale at which this reconfiguration of spatio-temporal relations took place. It attracted over 6,200,000 visitors and further inspired visitors to extend their cultural education by taking in London's other main historical sites and museums. For example, visits to the British Museum increased from 720,643 in 1850 to 2,230,242 in 1851. This spectacle provided an interactive space for the cultivation of knowledge, allowing visitors to become subjects as well as objects of power (Johnson 1970). Material and communal worlds that were normally invisible or private were made available to the commoner; peoples, wares and machines usually hidden within private domains or behind factory walls were newly available for visual consumption at the Crystal Palace. Furthermore, with the ordered modalities of the display, the exhibition space encouraged visitors to draw commercial and social connections between these new objects so that they might become comprehensible. Governmental modalities for display were interactive at the exhibition (Hoffenberg 2001, 17–19), opening onto new interpretive possibilities for the visitor, drawing into awareness a particular configuration of signs – glass, crowd, industry and the international – that were to underpin ideas of urban modernity and what it meant to be modern, civilized and progressive.

In terms of Janin's ideological motivations, England operates as a space of cultural counterpoint where the enduring existence of monarchy and imperial power in the present provide the traveller with a vehicle for articulating his anti-republican stance and his abhorrence of political instability. Janin's value-system is evident in the extract quoted above. The vocabulary of revolution – 'riots', 'excellent revolutions', 'barricades' and 'hammers ringing out like canon fire' – is employed here to describe the activity of the worker. This emergent proletariat, presented as sculptors of a new world, is associated with positive action through the accumulative enumeration of verbs such as 'feeding', 'repairing', 'defending', 'protecting', 'growing'. The result is that through the production of space in the travel narrative, the word 'revolution' is cleansed of its violent, chaotic or destructive associations to retain its status as a monumental event while acquiring an alternative set of associations that attach it to work, workers and industrial progress. Producing the obedient worker, preoccupied only with his craft (and presumably not with political unions), the contrastive linguistic taxonomy conveyed in the accumulative use of words such as 'incendiary', 'idle', 'vagabond', 'wretches', 'ignorant' and so forth associates the politicized Parisian *people* with decrepitude and moral waywardness. The 'good' in Taylor's sense is clearly articulated in Janin's production of modernity in terms of technological advancement and social order based in class distinction. The diligent, obedient worker is the hero of modernity for Janin, so we see the rejection of the values of Republicanism, with French republicans portrayed as conspirators and hypocrites.

From this reading, we see that our Western social imaginary of the 'sovereign people' so often traced back to the French Revolution of 1789 was a highly contested concept in France until at least 1870. Taylor explains the anxiety attendant upon modernity by the instability that ravaged France after 1789 as owing to the fact that the move from the dynastic rule of the *Ancien Régime* to that of the nation whose power was seen to rest in the people 'had no agreed meaning in a broadly based social imaginary' (Taylor 2004, 113). The fractured social imaginary that shapes the imaginative geographies and political landscapes of France during the period mean that, for Janin, London becomes the single possible site where progress and civilization can attain to modernity, which in this narrative can only persist under the relative stability of England's constitutional monarchy. This latter form of government, by contrast with the idea of popular sovereignty in this period, had achieved consensus over centuries. Janin's social imaginary of London speaks, therefore, to a governmental space that has already been put into practice, and achieved legitimacy and normative status over a long history. In this fraught transitional period then, Janin cannot conceive of popular democratic rule as a tenable shape for modernity as he conceives it.

In this provisional era, where the broad-scale social imagination of the nationstate was still inchoate, Janin's London becomes a space that is modern in its industrial manifestations, therefore, but one still rooted in a tradition with well-established moral credentials. His account is an attempt to persuade readers that revolution and the transition into modernity need not express themselves through violence or a disturbance of the entire social order. In this imaginary, London emerges as a battlefield for progress, harmony and order:

> I vainly wish to describe this noise, this tumult, these cries, this eagerness, activity and zeal. At the tower of Babel there were so many languages that no one could understand the other. But there is no rivalry between these various nations; on the contrary each tries to help the other as best they can. Every day the space is open to visitors and the curious, mingled with workingmen, bother no one. The policemen lend a hand to strangers [...]. There are people

nailing, un-nailing, unfolding, attaching, straining, painting, rubbing, polishing, printing, labelling, all are hurrying![26] (1851, 15)

From within this framework, Janin's associative and enumerative style conveys a sense of hectic urban rhythm along with a heady enthusiasm for focussed, collective labour. The incessant rhythm of his prose sets up a trajectory of imagery that while, on the one hand, it successfully represents the pace and simultaneity of the modern metropolis, on the other hand, in its Franco-Anglo polarization threatens to dissolve into legislative tropes for depicting industrial social space.

The horizontal form of order manifest in the arrangement of national displays at the Crystal Palace, finds its opposing vertical expression in Janin's articulation of the source of Victorian monarchical authority, its capacity to instil order through awe. Janin connects public respect with a 'natural' link between monarch and transcendental power – that of God – so that public order is structured in symbolic relation to the divine. This link recalls Erich Auerbach's assessment of how sacred symbolic attachment is formed

It can be established only if [...] vertically linked to Divine Providence, which alone is able to devise such a plan of history and supply the key to its understanding...the here and now is no longer a mere link in an earthly chain of events, it is *simultaneously* something which has always been, and will be fulfilled in the future. (1957, 64, my emphasis)

Vision, technology and progressive order as part of a divine order (embodied here in the person of the Empress Queen Victoria) are envisaged by Janin as mutually generative of the stability he desires for technological modernity. It is the absence of such hierarchical and transcendent systems in France – systems that might enable meaning to be established in relation to past imaginaries of providential order – that cause Janin to lament:

The sentiments of a true people, they surprise us today [...] we other French who founded all of the monarchies of this world and who will never separate those two powers: God and king! – The fact remains that today's celebration would have none of its solemnity and grandeur were it not presided over by the queen. That none would trust this pale sun, if we were not sure that the sun obeyed the queen, and that we could never find a more lofty voice to proclaim to the people of the universe: *Let the battle commence!*[27] (21)

In this citation Janin equates 'a true people' with subjects of a monarch (as opposed to citizens of a nation). The actual workings of monarchy are never pitted against democracy in political or ideological terms; the emphasis is rather placed on ornament and symbolism as the source of the queen's commandment over the respect and order of the people. Her embodiment of traditional, non-secular (and, therefore, in some senses 'pre-modern') imaginaries brings to the public event a reassuring taxonomy of signs and symbolic behaviours. This return to a providential order then contributes to the legibility of the Exhibition's architectures and its social importance in terms of a conservatively authoritative and, ultimately sacred, cosmological order.

That Janin's account of modernity is firmly rooted in a sacred social matrix, which refuses the notion of the popular, secular sovereignty (emergent from the Revolution and so often associated with our contemporary imaginary of modern France), is clear in the way that he tempers his accumulative mass of industrial signifiers with biblical analogies. The result is that London's narrative of industrial progress, articulated through the edifice of the Crystal Palace, emerges as an alternative and improved version of a *eutopian* paradise on earth.[28] The grandeur of the occasion is narrated through a series of comparisons to antiquity and past achievements, with the implication that the failures of the past have been remedied through the application of science, industry and cultural amalgamation. While these images reinforce Janin's ideological position in favour of England, they also serve to stabilize London in its cosmic monumentality – working to counteract the verbal movement of the contemporary scene by framing it within familiar modes of metropolitan representation. In Janin's narrative, the social imaginary he argues as befitting modernity is given further authority through association with ancient civilizations and a series of analogical tropes rooted in the mythologies of ancient cities. The analogies function to allow Janin make sense of what he sees before him, structuring the representation of London so that the geographic imagination is temporalized by looking backwards, and where the past of antiquity constitutes the legitimate model of civilization and social connection. In this way, the narrative of becoming modern is based in prior agreement as to what a great civilization can and ought to constitute.

The Exhibition's accumulation of spatio-temporal fields, achieved through the ordering of objects from different historical epochs, also finds narrative equivalence in Janin's account through his layering of immediate description with citations from ancient texts. Latin quotations intersperse the prose and are sourced from ancient writers such as Virgil or Tibullus, although often such phrases had been recited by more contemporary authors and gained significance through writers such as Chateaubriand.[29] This leads to a certain ambiguity with regard to the authorship of direct impressions. For example, while at one moment Janin offers advice on the ways to interpret the density of London's simultaneity saying, 'there is no legitimate way to study and understand a city where we are led by our fantasies. Accept it as it shows itself to you' (116),[30] at the next his prose is patterned with references to past images that speak to a need to restore sense through the established signs of intertext:

> What was Shakespeare talking about when he described old England? *A swan's nest in the midst of a great swamp!* – What did the ancient poet mean when he said that London was filled with Babylonian men and women, whom he would send to eternal damnation? 'An enormous mass of bricks, smoke and ships, a smoky and dirty city, lost amid a forest of masts, the scattered solitude of pointy steeples, a gigantic dome like a madman's calotte!' Of these two images which one is true?[31] (117)

Untangling the array of references here demonstrates the extent to which Janin's imaginative geography of London is grounded in old tropes that circulated consistently in France throughout the period. The reference from Shakespeare is taken from *Cymbeline*,[32] also cited in Chateaubriand's 'Shakespeare' (1836).[33] The poet referred to is Lord Byron, and the citation that follows a weak translation of Canto X, Verse LXXXII of his satiri-cal poem *Don Juan*.[34] The imagery appropriated here – a forest of masts, a mass of brick and smoke and ships – is also employed by Théophile Gautier's travel account who vis-ited London in 1847. A slight diversion into Gautier's work at this stage helps to illustrate the connotative territories becoming established through the repetition of key tropes in French narratives on London.

In *Caprices et Zigzags* (1852), a collection of articles previously published by Gautier and compiled by the editor Victor Lecou, the image of a vast estuary vaulted with the masts and riggings of marine vessels is transferred onto three metropoles – the ancient city of Nineveh, whose ruins were housed in the Louvre, the present city of London, vis-ited by Gautier in 1847, and the future city of Paris as imagined by the writer in the essay 'Paris futur' / 'Future Paris'. Confronted by the silence and absence inherent in the ruin, Gautier reconstructs Nineveh in line with the fate of Babylon, and therein suggests the inevitable decline of all great civilizations. The reconstruction of the fate of Nineveh can be read as a warning to the modern Babylons of Paris and London. London for Gautier has an 'Egyptian air' / 'air égyptien' and is reminiscent of Thebes and Babylon, while the descriptions in the visionary essay 'Paris futur' are strikingly close to those of contem-porary London and, indeed, to his imagination of Nineveh in the past. The Paris of the future will obtain to modernity by aping present-day London, and like London will pos-sess harbours, where ships from the West Indies will dock. And, while in contemporary London 'you will discover a prodigious alley of ships' masts extending to infinity, an inex-tricable jumble of apparel […], of ropes, bringing to shame the most entangled ivy of the virgin forests of America for its being so densely knotted' (107),[35] in future Paris 'one sees a jumble of masts, of ropes more entangled than a virgin forest in America' (315).[36] One city recalls another; all three metropoles are portrayed as Promethean giants, inte-grating the most exotic in nature, the most ambitious and monumental works of man, and the most impressive architecture and machinery; language reconstructs the cities in terms of one another and thus multiplies the relevancy of this image in terms of the eventual decay of metropolitan civilization, as was the fate of Nineveh.

Urban modernity, in this case is mapped in terms of well-established narratives reproduced consistently across the nineteenth century in France. Swan and spleen, beauty and death, progress and ruin are images that re-emerge time and again in relation to London and Paris. Flora Tristan employs them in *Promenades dans Londres ou l'aristocratie et les prolétaires anglais* ([1840] 1978), while Charles Baudelaire draws on this visual repertoire to describe the urban landscape throughout both *Les Fleurs du Mal* ([1857] 1972) and *Le Spleen de Paris* ([1869] 1987). Alexandre Dumas also, in his *Causeries* (1857), uses the Shakespearean image to describe London. When one considers that over the nineteenth century there were over 6,000 individual titles (not including reprints) published in the travelogue genre, the proliferation of intertextual reference is perhaps not all that surprising. Travellers very often consulted previous works on the places to which they travelled, either prior to or following the trip, and this is consistent with engendering and consolidating both the material appearance of the tourist site as well as founding a legislative aesthetic of the city's representa-tions. More specifically here, while Janin leaves these citations unreferenced, they enter the text in a manner that blurs the line between Janin's interpretation of his immediate surroundings and the connotations previously attached to metropolitan life by either ancient philosophers, other travel writers or well-known authors. The use of an established bank of signs, then, is one of the strategies that Janin employs so that the metropolis becomes legible according to a prescribed set of literary nodal points, facilitating the traveller's assimilation and active appropriation of the sprawl and simultaneity of the city.

The use of conventional urban images and the authority of the past are often ways for the travel writer to reassure the reader as to his cultural authority on the place visited, as well as to satisfy her expectations of the narrative. But it would seem that drawing on the signs of the past in order to interpret and convey the significance of the present moment is as political for Janin as it is a question of appearing cultured to his reader. The portrayal of industrial and cultural harmony, as well as economic productivity and scientific progress, is framed as a consequence of England's monarchical system of government. The latter is not only associated with majesty and grandeur, but further viewed as the reason for the orderliness and respect which the crowd observes and the queen commands at the exhibition: 'The English respect and adore each other, on their knees, through the person of their queen. They look at her with the same gaze with which they look at themselves' (20).[37] Furthermore, monarchy is seen here to add symbolic weight, and thus stability, both to the physical needs of the people and to their sense of 'imagined community',[38] the sense of belonging to a national whole. As Janin points out: 'to think badly, or speak badly of the queen [...] they would compare that to a free man slapping his own face!' (20–21).[39] The spectacle of the Exhibition not only visually aestheticizes the objects on display (from ruins to machines),[40] but also synthesizes empire and nation, integrating subjects and travellers alike in a shared, simultaneous experience within its glass walls. In addition, as Bennett (1995, 68) observes, the exhibition served to create a sense of shared communal interest: the public became not only observers of, and were observed by, the Empire on display, but also became observers of themselves as part of the crowd, or as Hoffenberg puts it, 'they displayed and were the displays' (2001, 246). This sense of belonging is doubly important, for both the creation of a great spectacle, as well as for initiating a non-institutional form of surveillance – that of self-regulation – whereby the public's pleasure in becoming part of the spectacle ensures its sense of responsibility for the smooth running of the proceedings, so that it might become 'a society watching over itself' (Bennett 1995, 69).[41]

2.5   An English Pilgrimage to a French Past

In this narrative, the various 'truths', which successive French governments struggled to embed in post-revolutionary French society, are revealed in their fragile nascent state. This travel account exposes the moment when alternatives to French republicanism and imperialism are still at work and relevant to the creation of counter-narratives for determining the good for French civilization. Here, England essentially becomes a vehicle for the exploration of 'what might have been', a lament for the alternative of a monarchical

France. Janin's ideological identification with England transfers to his representation of himself as subject who travels. He does not feel ill at ease or homesick upon his arrival in London, and his feeling of comfort emerges in stark affective contrast to his sense of alienation with regard to France and his adopted city of Paris in particular. Born in 1804 in Saint-Étienne in eastern central France, he began his education there before moving to Paris to continue his education at the lycée Louis-le-grand, one of the most prestigious educational establishments in France.[42] After years of relative poverty, Janin would eventually became well known as a novelist and, more significantly, as a dramatic critic for the *Journal des Débats* (1831–1873). His ambiguity with regard to political principles throughout the alternation of governments in France during this period earned him the moniker 'le petit Janinus' (see *Le Corsaire*, 6 May 1830). His support for the so-called July Monarchy of Louis-Philippe I meant that he was sporadically criticized throughout his career, notably by Baudelaire who addressed him saying: 'You do not love truth […] neither its metre, nor its rhyme, all of that would require taking too much care for you to achieve it' (Baudelaire 1983–1985, 2: 232).[43]

Janin was consistently critical of popular urban society in Paris, viewing native inhabitants of the city disparagingly and distinguishing them from his idea of the 'true Parisian' / 'vrai Parisien'. Here we see the developing association of Paris with a person who is cultured, while native Parisians are represented as slaves to the modern city's requirements.

> There are no true Parisians in this world except those Parisian who were not born in Paris. […] The Parisian from Paris is so willing, fake, noxious, idiotic and silly so as to give pleasure. […] The Parisian from Paris is the dupe of the city where he was born. […] It is he who lights it, who repairs it, who fills its prisons […] who bloodies its strikes.[44] (Janin 1836, I: 25)

This assault brought on native Parisians (which, from the above, implicates the poorer inhabitants of the city) is, in this case, a justification for this outsider's sense of belonging to the city, and to his acceptance into the cultural elite of Paris as a kindred spirit. More generally, it further suggests that identification with modern urban social space is based less on any original connection through birth, than on acquisition, the insertion of strangers into a social space seems to be based on shared cultural interest, status and social relationships established by choice or necessity. This is a peculiarly modern and urban form of interrelation and identity formation, then, grounded as it is on a social imagination of cultural, economic and political forms of belonging. And the city, as the space where such networks can thrive, becomes key during this period in spatially disrupting the immediate connection between birthplace and notions of belonging as rootedness. Urban space permits, indeed requires, the reformulation of networks of belonging along the lines of shared socio-cultural interests, and paves the path to transnational communities.[45] This idea is important for Janin's ease of identification with imperial London; the cultural and political order that he finds there inspires in him an admiration for the British public and their government. It also implies that in the wake of Louis-Philippe's abdication, and the political uncertainty that accompanied Louis-Napoleon's populist ascension to power, Janin acquires a certain distance from his French roots.

The sense of distance from home and of cultural alienation engenders an imaginative geography of England filled with nostalgia. While nostalgia is generally defined as a kind of wistful longing to return to a time in one's past, or one's homeland, Janin's nostalgic representational space is unconnected in any mnemonic way to England. Rather, the presence of monarchical stability in the figure of Queen Victoria, evidence of production, international prestige and industrial display become the objects through which Janin constructs a space of identification with England. The spectacle functions to confirm Janin's ideological dislocation from contemporary France, on the one hand, while, on the other, it enables identification with England's social imaginary. The identification emerges through the representative mapping of his ideological affiliations with the abdicated July Monarchy onto English space. England, as the site of Louis-Philippe's exile, is also for Janin, then, a site of modern pilgrimage. A pilgrimage to the supposed lost stability of monarchical order (although the Orléanist king Louis-Philippe was a decidedly weak monarch) and nostalgic therefore for a governmental world-view based in centuries old tradition.[46]

It is noteworthy that Janin's visit to Claremont in Surrey takes place on a Sunday as this day's significance resonates in tension with the emergence of secular and capitalist temporalities in modern France, where Sunday was no longer observed as a day of rest. Sunday is, as we shall see later in this chapter, a recurrent point of ideological orientation for Vallès too. In Paris, the post-1848 growth of secularism meant that Sunday was no longer granted special status, with the result that the rhythms of the city were undifferentiated from one end of the week to the next. In London, however, where Sunday still retained its status as a day where shops and businesses closed, the relative desertion and quiet of the inner city on this day when compared with the working week, meant that it created an alternative symbolic and spatio-temporal experience of the modern city. The observation of Sunday reveals the trace of a Christian cosmology constituent of another layer in the complex weave of modern urban space. The differential space–time of an English Sunday is represented by the traveller in terms of the contrasting socio-political orders of France and England, and as a means to construct a value-laden critique of modern French social space. Janin was a devote Catholic, a fact that makes the erasure of Sunday's special symbolic difference in France even more meaningful to him. England's Sunday for Janin in the present, therefore, becomes a representative space that resonates with past experiences of Sundays under the July Monarchy, a period when this day was still observed in law. In the passage that follows, Janin's anti-republicanism manifests itself in nostalgia for the past experience of Sundays in France. The traveller paraphrases the Bible, naming Sundays as 'the chosen days' / 'ces jours choisis' (1851, 61) and, perhaps with some contradiction, he seizes the opportunity to fill the day with errands, while at the same time lamenting the absence in Paris of such liberty:

> And yet, here I am (in London!) where a Sunday will be kept by me as the most complete day in all my days. I want to make of it a marble monument, a bronze divinity, to place it on the tomb of all the beautiful Sundays that have flown from me and from here on, this one will console me for all those days I have lost.[47] (61)

There is the sense that time is being regained here on English soil; the narrator's loss of his sacred social space in Paris means that London becomes a geography where this loss can be restored, if only for a time. The piece, however, anticipates the recurrence of this feeling of loss, so that England's Sundays become inscribed into the traveller's projection of himself in the future. This spatio-temporal hiatus in London therefore resonates profoundly with the traveller's sense of self, with his religious sense of identity as a Catholic and with his political worldview as a supporter of the July Monarchy. Sunday also performs as a trope for the traveller to maintain the more politicized representational space of his comparative critique of England and France.

From such a perspective a simple visit to Surrey is transformed into a pilgrimage: an errant knight's quest to honour the tomb of the 'king who is no more'[48] (61), the exiled Louis-Philippe in Weybridge House, at Claremont in Surrey, and to pledge allegiance to the former queen, Marie-Amelia. At Claremont Janin is reunited with his ideal vision of France, and here the thus-far superior image of English monarchical culture is supplanted upon the traveller's encounter with the living remnants of the Orleanist monarchy. Janin effectively talks as though he is visiting his King, paying medieval homage to the figure that embodies his sense of order and says that 'my first duty and my strongest desire *and* all my allegiances, hardly have I arrived in London, but they compel me towards Claremont' (61).[49] In this way, while the representation of the exiled and relatively impoverished French queen stands in contrast to the spectacular grandeur of the British empress, the feudalistic language used here is suggestive of a return to an imaginary geography of medieval codes – honour, chivalry and courage – the effect is that we become aware of how Janin's self-understanding and imagination of modernity is deeply embedded in the social matrix of tradition and conservatism, underpinned by a language of pastoral simplicity and virtue. The landscape, as he approaches the former monarch's residence, is rendered in idyllic pastoral terms, and Janin's gentle ridicule of an Englishman's remark that the sun would certainly shine for Queen Victoria's opening of the Exhibition, is inversely employed here with the greatest sincerity as he approaches the home in exile of the fallen French monarch:

> Everything in that moment was celebration and joy, where the sun (it is rare) lit with its bright ray so many little feet and spring gowns running around on the lawn […]. These French lilies blooming suddenly on the English lawn, the recent loss of the old king's daughter, he who was king at our maturity and our last defence against the vile passions that leave us forsaken and murder us.[50] (64–65)

The consistent use of hagiographic imagery to describe Queen Amelia romanticizes the past. In a notable representation of her arrival 'incognito' (16) at the exhibition, the traveller's description takes the form of a hyperbolic elegy:

> Oh August queen. She remains, and she will be until the end, our queen! Each man saluted her as she went by. All brows were bent before this benevolent majesty and before this courage that is more than human. They say, however, that in the crowd, one or two voices hoarse from gin tried to babble a few couplets of the *Marseillaise*! Indignation silenced them and contempt chastised them.[51] (16–17)

The queen is elevated to saintly status; people bow their heads, the fact of her presence even silences those who reject the politics she represents. Janin's language thus renders the exiled royal family sacred, or 'more than human' through the act of travel as pilgrimage which functions to reconnect icon and object, monarch and bodily presence. There is, furthermore, a considerable temporal ambivalence on the traveller's part towards the present. First, Janin insists on referring to Amelia as 'our queen' and himself as 'her humble subject' / 'son humble sujet' (66), although these titles are no longer valid. Their use here reinforces the nostalgic tone of Janin's representative space. As Svetlana Boym tells us, 'in broader sense, nostalgia is a rebellion against the modern idea of time, the time of history and progress' (Boym 2007, 8), and so Janin's England provides a geography where the time of the French past can be recovered through presence – the presence of the royal family in the here and now – and so the French present can be denied through Janin's spatial practice. His movement through English space therefore sets up a temporal vector towards the French past, a symbolic mapping that activates alternative histories. Second, as with the use of classical citations to express the present, Janin draws analogies between Amelia's personal appearance and Renaissance portraiture, these signs resonating with immortality, her synthesis with art rendering the passage of time and its events meaningless (66).[52] This might be read, perhaps, as a form of defence – a means of refuting the relevancy of contemporary France. London provides a space where the French past – 'that forgotten grandeur: majesty! That divine force, the respect!'[53] (23) – might be revisited. Here, the discursive strategies of the traveller create a legislative space that embellishes the paucity of the former French monarch's material conditions. The emotive pilgrimage, which Janin and his companion embark on 'in silence, seeking the traces of royalty, on the beaches, on the lawns'[54] (66) relocates Janin within an ideological and cultural sign-world that makes him feel at home temporally as well as spatially.

2.6 Avoiding the Everyday

To finish our commentary on this account, we might return to the question posed by Janin earlier as to which sign (swan or spleen) is the more representative of London: 'Of these two images, which one is true?' (117), the traveller immediately responds saying, 'For myself, I readily opt for the swan's nest in the middle of a great lake. I am not going to bother (to what avail?) seeking out a dirty, smoke-filled city' (117).[55] The traveller determines, therefore, to avoid any encounter with the working river 'in the midst of that mast-filled forest' (117),[56] and to explore the (then) faraway and leafy suburb of Richmond upon Thames. He justifies the exclusion of the industrial, metropolitan zones of the city by disclaiming the authority of the traveller to pass judgement on the social problems generated by modernization, saying that we should 'leave to the future saviours of humanity, to the modern evangelists, to the vagabond *Christs*, the task of railing against Babylon: a traveller passing through has no right to stop and preach at every crossroads' (117).[57] However, in circumscribing travel practice in this manner, Janin effectively delimits its socio-political potential, rendering it an activity that is meaningful solely within the categories of the aesthetic and the pleasurable. Importantly, he avoids sabotaging his elegiac account of either the city or its government, and thus consolidates his own spatial hierarchy of the urban environment. This consists in excluding any chaotic or unregulated areas of the city so as to direct the reader towards sites providing more straightforward codes for interpretation – the pastoral, the sacred, the monumental or the monarchical – sites easily reconciled with his image of England as bastion of tradition:

> Let us go rather along the poetic banks and look for joyous traces. […] Yes, and he who knows how to remember will be charmed walking along the happy banks of this fresh Thames […]. Believe me friends, in everything one should go towards the beautiful and the great; beware of irony and paradox, and when you walk beneath these old oak trees, witness and confidant to so many illustrious loves, don't go then and ask the old tree how many people have hung themselves on its branches.[58] (119–120)

In the same way, therefore, that orientation towards spaces signifying a lost past refutes the temporal validity of the fledgling French democratic system, so too here, the social spaces of the slum and overcrowded industrial tenements of the urban landscape – spaces that complicate the ideal of English modernity as viewed by Janin – are disregarded. Janin's image of himself as a traveller passing through, as someone who cannot engage with the reality of social life, makes travel the excuse for remaining located in the spectacular versions of modernity, that are well-ordered here in line with governmentality. Effectively, Janin dismisses the ability of the traveller to understand the social space of everyday life, so that travel remains necessarily an exploration in icons, and, furthermore, a practice of confirmation; Janin's spatial practice tallies with his ideal of the good being rooted in a system of providential order. Janin's circumscription of London's social space depends, then, on the mutual delimitation of the travel project – on that project's reduction to a set of easily legible sites that combine to confirm Janin's predetermined ideological position, the conservatism of which corresponds to the imaginative geography of the conventional tourist. This necessitates Janin's undermining of other travellers who approach London from a different (often, opposing) perspective. He concedes that what one might term 'contrarian' tourists[59] have honourable intentions, but ultimately rejects any outsider's ability to comment on areas of the city that are not legible in positive terms:

> Most of our humourists, […] hardly arrived in London, have nothing better to do than to descend to the vaults of sin and night, to see, with their own eyes, how the dogs bark while justice limps along after them! Naturally, all of the good instincts of French writers, of those men who incarnate honour itself, emerge disgusted and horrified […] and naturally, this indignation is transmitted, in the liveliest manner, on the French front pages, where they pretend to speak of London and England! Is it just, however, before seeing anything else, to bound to these scornful places, so as to draw conclusions against a government, strong enough to hold these railleries in contempt, and who with a disdainful stamp of its foot could flatten this underground parody, if it were to cause the least trouble?[60] (121)

Thus, Janin presents us with the model of a tourist, whose rigidly bounded travel practice enacts a legislative mode of reading the city erected on oppositional contrasts between France and England. It is a French past that organizes the traveller's negotiation strategies for interaction with England's alterity. Janin's travel practice is inseparable from the author's stance with regard to material circumstances in France in May 1851 and is, therefore, directed in accordance with a specific political vision. Here then, physical and narrative modes of urban practice are organized in accordance with an ethos of monarchical politics and culture as the ideal form of government and nationhood. These function as the basis against which to perform a critique of France, and, in concordance with such a model, the reduction of London life to the legibility of its monuments serves to reinforce the governmental dominance of imperial and industrial strategies for the organization of urban life.

2.7 Jules Vallès's Topographies of Exile

Before beginning an analysis of the work *The London Street* ([1876] 1951) by Jules Vallès, it will be helpful to examine the problems that Vallès's situation raises in relation to the categories by which one defines a traveller. Crucially, what distinguishes Vallès (1832–1855) from the other writers examined throughout this analysis is his politically enforced position in London as an exile. A prominent activist and creator of the socialist journal *Le Cri du Peuple / The Roar of the People* ([1848–71] 1953), Vallès's journalism was often controversial in its critique of Second Empire France. He was forced to flee Paris when his involvement with the Commune in 1871 resulted in his being condemned to death. He subsequently sought asylum in London until he received amnesty in 1880 under the Third Republic, upon which he returned directly to Paris, thereafter making journeys back to London for editorial purposes (Gallo 1988). Taking these biographical details into account, it is impossible to consider Vallès within the same qualitative critical framework as one would a tourist. Where tourism implies leisure, Vallès, an impoverished writer, was continually (often desperately) engaged in communication with French publishing houses during his exile in London in an attempt to continue to earn his living as a writer. Furthermore, tourism implies freedom of choice on the part of the practitioner, and the 'elsewhere' of the tourist is intimately connected to the pleasure principle, which is based on anticipation 'especially through day-dreaming and fantasy' (Urry 1995, 132) of pleasure. As we have seen in the case of Janin above, the activity of tourism often involves the intensely motivated delineation of places to the exclusion of any other space that might infringe on either the pleasure principle or threaten the traveller's world-view. There is some ambiguity with regard to Vallès's attitude to England before he was forced into exile. When he first visited London in 1865 prior to his expatriation, his writing of this event reveals a sense of impasse when faced with the simultaneity and sensory overload of the modern metropolis. Vallès writes:

> After three weeks staying in London, I realize that to be able to speak about England, I'd have to spend ten years here. – I looked and I did not see; I listened and did not hear: I only like to speak about what I have heard and seen. I laughed at myself and sailed back across the sea.[61]
> (cited in Bellet [1975] 1990, I: 793)

The vastness of the city was a challenge not only to the visitor however, for, as Stephen Inwood (2005) points out, the biggest components of the urban landscape – Westminster,

Islington, Stepney, Lambeth, St Pancras, West Ham – were the size of Edinburgh, Bristol or Sheffield, and the scale of the metropolis meant that intimate knowledge of it by either visitor or inhabitant was a rare and difficult achievement. Along with this, fewer than two million Londoners were in paid employment, and many of these, including about three hundred thousand domestic servants, slept where they worked. It remained that while trips to London's shopping districts, to a central London theatre or music hall, or Regent's Park Zoo or the Crystal Palace (relocated at Sydenham), might take Londoners away from familiar territory once or twice a year, in general life in London was conducted on a small-scale, local level (Inwood 2005, 2). Moreover, from the 1860s on London was undergoing extensive structural changes in both its forms of metropolitan government and its physical appearance. To take but one example, the construction of the world's first underground railway in 1863 reconfigured the visual appearance of the city and reorganized the spatial relations between the urban population and their city. Excavations through residential and commercial areas altered the shape of the city's landscape irrevocably. The destruction of streets during periods of construction exposed the foundations of the city, and provided urbanites with unprecedented views of their metropolis (Nead 2005). Unlike the demolition and reconstruction of Paris, London's expansion was equivocal and piecemeal, taking place over longer periods of time, and creating a series of juxtapositions – the old alongside the new, the wreckage of the ruin alongside the sublime quality of the scaffold – with the result that the constant disfiguration of the urban landscape made it impossible for contemporaries to feel that they knew their city in any holistic or finite manner.

In this schema, knowledge of London was a precious commodity, and reporters, social reformers, tourist companies and cab drivers devoted much time to cultivating urban legibility.[62] Vallès's statement, 'I realize that to be able to speak about England, I'd have to spend ten years there', is illustrative of the overwhelming task that interpretation of the metropolis presented. Furthermore, beyond the vastness of London itself, Vallès also felt his status as visitor made his experience inauthentic, and did not provide him with any position of authority from which to speak about the city. Authenticity in this framework is associated with both the self's sense of mastery over what he sees, and a faith in his ability to interpret it. But it is also related to the representations of space that are accessible to the traveller who only rests briefly in the city. The sense from Vallès's citation above is that the city of everyday life – where ordinary people live in correspondence with the rhythms of the work environment in its burgeoning capitalist state – remains inaccessible. By contrast, the representations of space that the monument, museum or administrative centres of the city in the West End provide are articulated by Vallès as representational of an order reductive of the above everyday spaces. This reduction then leads the traveller to respond that the tourist's experience is essentially a journey in mythology; a spatial practice that remains orderly cannot be one of understanding or critique. Thus the self cannot be an authentic self in this view, but is conditioned to repeat what others have said, without the ability to form its own view of the modern city. Heidegger's conception of the 'they' and its relationship to the modern self comes into view here. The 'they' in Heideggerian terms is equivalent to mainstream cultural consensus, it is everyone and no one as opposed to a definite named other. The self is in constant negotiation with this 'they', so much so that for Heidegger most of our lives are spent in a state of 'they-self', an inauthentic mode of existence wherein we passively accept the prevailing view of the 'they'. As Heidegger expresses it, 'The Self of everyday Dasein is the they-self, which we distinguish from the *authentic Self* (Heidegger [1927] 1962, 129). Authenticity of the self thus derives from being able to form one's own point of view; to be true to one's self. Furthermore, this equation of authenticity with depth in spatial terms (leaving behind the beaten track) and with longevity and personal experience in a temporal sense, alerts the reader to the emergent sense of the modern individual that we will encounter in Vallès's account.

As he set off on a trip to London in 1865, he writes, 'I do not have the dubious honour of leaving in exile, nothing requires me to perform the role of an exile' (cited in Bellet [1975] 1990, I: 771).[63] The dramatic irony of this statement with regard to Vallès's imminent future is pointed. At the same time it reveals the meaning attached to the term 'exile' in France during this time. London had been the capital of the French who were forced to leave the home country at key moments in their country's history, where their identities posed a threat to the current regime in power. Huguenots left France for London throughout the seventeenth century, while more recent émigrés included those forced to flee France after 1848, the so-called *Quarante-Huitards* or Forty-Eighters. In this passage, Vallès's anarchist tendencies come into view, a devotee of popular democracy and a believer in the sovereignty of the people, his views manifest in his desire to have a 'valid', socially esteemed (from the insurgent's perspective) and authoritative position from which to speak about the city. It also problematizes the notion of choice, for it is clear from the above that Vallès would have preferred the officially sanctioned status of expulsion, which would prove his social anarchist credentials, to that of his current freedom. At this stage in Vallès's work, therefore, the reader finds a romantic attachment to the imagination of exile, which emerges more prominently in *The London Street* ([1876] 1951) when Vallès finds himself forced to flee France for London after his involvement with the radical Republican government of the Paris Commune of 1871. Exile is imagined as the form of existence that confirms the complete correspondence of the self's ideals with the self's actions in reality, or in other words the 'dubious honour' of exile is one that indicates the authenticity of the self.

When this trip did become an exile from late 1871 onward, Vallès's attitude towards London had ample time to develop, but while the author may have boasted about *The London Street* to Hector Malot in 1876, declaring that 'this will be the first impartial book on England. Everyone else has lied up until now from Esquiros to Taine. Well, let's say they were mistaken' (Vallès [1862–84] 1968, IX: 129),[64] like Janin, his representative space is constructed through a series of conceptual oppositions. The English metropolis emerges in dialectical opposition to the author's memory of Paris, and it is the city *in absentia*, the home city of Paris, that generates Vallès's meaning for London. The suggestion, prevalent throughout the account, is that *Paris* is the traveller's desired destination. We are aware here too that the Paris that emerges in Vallès's account is equally an imagined geography. London serves to bring into clarified relief the author's spatialization of his political views through the re-imagination of Paris from a distance, so that in effect, Paris becomes 'home' through the writer's dislocation in

London. Dislocation is productive therefore of closer ties to home. Taylor points to the way that, in modern consciousness, it is the validation of the particular that allows for the emergence of a general sense of one's place and importance in the world. In modernity, 'the general or typical now emerges out of the description of the particular, situated people in their particularity' (Taylor [1989] 2004, 187). Taylor explains this through his philosophical analysis of the gradual, contextually complex, substitution in Western Europe of providential explanations for human existence with a secular Humanist world-view across the eighteenth and nineteenth centuries. We can position Vallès's concern with the detail of everyday existence in London in approximation to this emergent emphasis on the particular manifestations of the urban object and person, and see his spatial practice of the modern city then in terms of a search for meaning in a world without transcendental archetypes to provide reassurance as to one's place in the world.

In contrast to Janin, whose London is oriented around the monumental and the archetype of royal power, Vallès's spatial practice is performed as a desire to remember home and to preserve his political faith in the ideals of 1871. Objects and people in their present realities in London recall their idealized versions situated in an imaginative geography of Paris. As Corinne Saminadayer-Perrin (2000, 8) notes, 'to write London is also (especially) to try and conceptualize France, the France of memory but also the France which gave birth to the shock of the Commune'.[65] Vallès is an outsider, albeit an unwilling one, with a perspective on the city framed in terms of his alternative, French reference points for 'home'. In terms of the difficulty, then, of defining the *émigré* experience of the city within categories for conceiving approaches to travel, Vallès's status proves problematic. That his status as an outsider is obligatory rather than voluntary differentiates him from the other authors visiting London, and it is illuminating to place an extreme case such as Vallès's in dialogue with an account such as Dyssord's (1932), examined in the next chapter. This later writer orientates his urban practice along similar topographical lines – his *Londres secret / Secret London* also explores the underbelly of the imperial metropolis – but the motivation behind Dyssord's topography is fundamentally different from that of Vallès's. The former traveller's contrarian explorations of London are poetic, symbolic and driven by curiosity as opposed to any need to make a political statement and, crucially, Dyssord can leave to return home at any time. Vallès's unsparing exposition of London's slums, underclass and bourgeoisie, on the other hand, is defined by the loss of home, the loss of an ideal with the fall of the Paris Commune, and the hardships of everyday life in London.

Vallès's gaze, therefore, implies another possibility for urban spatial practice, one that operates from within the context of the traveller as exile; as banished foreigner, he is an outsider in all senses of the word. Concerning the psychology of exile, Joseph Wittlin has coined the word 'destiempo' (deprivation of homeland) from the Spanish *destierro*, showing how the exile lives both the present and the past simultaneously, with the past life sometimes being more intensely experienced than the present. In this sense, an exile 'moves backwards' (cited in Tabori 1972, 32). In a similar vein Tzvetan Todorov identifies the unique perspective of the exile towards the foreign culture:

What is an exile? It is someone who interprets their life abroad as an experience of not belonging to their surroundings, and who cherishes it for that same reason. The exile is interested only in his own life, indeed that of his own people, but he realizes that, to promote this interest, it is better to live abroad, where one does not 'belong'; he is a foreigner not in any provisional sense but in a definitive one. [Exile] is most definitely not a discovery of others.[66] (1989, 382)

In Vallès's account, the experience of exile consists in the topographical transposition of an absent Paris onto London's everyday spaces. This effectively generates an alternative mode of negotiating the city, wherein London's urban underground is practised from a basis of negative juxtaposition – the spectre of Paris and a sense of loss haunt Vallès's representational space of the London streets:

Oh! It's not the street of France – that chattering, joyous street, where you encounter people all the time, where you are stopped on any pretext. You follow the women and laugh with the men; there one finds uproarious laughter, sunbeams and thunderbolts, the fizzing of irony, a whiff of pleasure, dusty memories.

The London street is either enormous and empty – silent thus like a line of tombs – or packed with human carcasses, jammed with carriages, full to bursting, as noisy as an army camp and a flood of disaster. But these are muted sounds, the groaning of factories, the tumult of animals – not an explosion of life and passion.[67] (Vallès [1876] 1951, 1)

Thus, these opening lines of the account alert the reader to the fact that Vallès's urban lexicon exists within the legislative parameters of comparison. The dynamism of this competitive field informs the entire representational space of London that emerges. This differential structure is quite common to travel writing and the experience of travel, but Vallès's choice of spaces further articulates his sociopolitical preoccupations, as well as his sense of isolation, to evoke an urban landscape devoid of joy or human connection.

One of the motivating forces behind *The London Street* is, therefore, a political value system rooted in the revolutionary radicalism of the French socialist community, and in the traveller's subsequent distance from this community. Ali Nematollahy interprets Vallès's political stance and literary production in terms of an 'anarchic sensibility and [a] refusal of all forms of authority, particularly the authority of the state' (2007, 575). Nematollahy examines a literary tendency in Vallès's work, which he labels 'vitalism' formulated within a context of nascent anarchist aesthetics (576). 'Vitalism' refers here to the belief in the *peuple* as the source of life, of political energy and of popular revolution as the means for restoring equality and harmony to social life. This 'vitalism' is expressed in *The London Street* in terms of an Anglophobic revulsion at industrialist authoritarianism and at the population who seem to Vallès to accept blindly such authority. Vallès belittles the English people's acceptance of such oppressive authorities saying that 'every quarter of a century people with energetic minds have these strokes that one names revolts' (8).[68] These 'strokes' are paltry efforts at the revolution of society in the sense that Vallès wishes it.

In London, Vallès's 'vitalism', or political energy, is not spent calling for revolt or social change. Rather, the vitality in his prose on London stems from the tension he sets up between two differently imagined communities. In the following citation this is articulated within the author's representation of '*le Peuple*' / 'the People':

> We should mourn them. Life in London must be dull and grey, depressing, at the hour when the People have left the battlefield – the People, only grand in the anonymity of those who run or crawl for bread, […], but as we are in the country of selfishness, of phlegm, of discomfort and boredom, when there is not the hubbub of work, there is nothing but the cry of vice: dull, muggy vice, which screams in the grogshops and vomits in corners.[69] ([1876] 1951, 48)

Conceived here as the mythical 'mass' representing the 'common good' or the 'general will' emergent with the French Revolution's radicalization and mythologization of the people as the source of national sovereignty, in this account, the People are reduced to debauchery in England. In effect, as Vallès goes on to note, the burgeoning sense of individualism in line with the development of capitalist space has not produced in Vallès's London a sense of collective social engagement. Vallès's moral order, or his definition of the 'good' therefore resides in his conceptualization of the common people as the source of political meaning. In this logic, therefore, the Londoner's seeming disengagement from politics leaves room only for obscenity or a lack of dignity.

   Vallès's writing is indicative of a modern sensibility that affirms the quality of everyday existence of the common people as the correct basis for the constitution of the state. The centrality of everyday life, as valuable in itself and the ordinary as a moral base from which to strive towards dignity and the 'good' is, according to Taylor, a central feature of Western modernity (Taylor [1989] 2004). Taylor sees the importance attached to everyday life in the modern period as emergent with the Radical Enlightenment of the eighteenth century. The thinkers of the Radical Enlightenment, from Julien Offray de La Mettie, Denis Diderot to Baruch Spinoza, remove the world from the cosmology of providence, and look instead at the world as a neutral domain. This absence of a providential order means that it is down to the individual to know and, thereby, to master the 'causal relations' of the natural world in order to produce the greatest amount of good. This disengagement from a 'higher' power places responsibility for the good therefore in the hands of the individual and ushers in the secular time of modernity, which shifts the focus of moral living away from the 'next life' and places it firmly within the human lifespan. In modernity then, increasing attention is paid to issues of everyday happiness, emphasis is placed on human dignity and equality of the means to live a life free from degradation and violence. An extension of Nature's harmony, the ordinary life of the family, issues of survival and individual rights to liberty and social equality emerge as pressing points of concern in the urban travel account. In correspondence with this attitude, Vallès gives narrative precedence to the description of the particular and the ritual behaviours of the English in daily life.

   Given Vallès's acknowledgement of the difficulties of knowing a culture without having lived there, his narrative demonstrates a familiarity with the less immediately visible social life of London. In a similar fashion to the novelistic form, Vallès scrutinizes the particularities of the streets of London for signs of more general truths about the 'English character'. But unlike the novel, which from the eighteenth century onward tended to resist the modus operandi of archetypal depiction, Vallès's account gathers his observations of everyday life to produce a series of archetypal or stock characters and thus constitutes a gallery of portraits, or representative sketches, against which he can define his political position. It would seem that the experience of exile therefore tempers the experience of the particular. The attraction to the everyday is never singular for Vallès because the locational realities of the traveller's position reverse the material poles of attachment and detachment; Vallès is in London, separated from his political homeland in France. The disparity between Vallès's geographical position and his emotional one, therefore, intensifies the contrastive structures of the account. The everyday is driven towards a wider metaphorical consciousness that difference sets up. From within the juxtaposition of London with Paris, derives a series of urban images laden with archetypal significance that emerges, through the traveller's spatial imagination, as an antagonistic polarity between home and abroad.

Vallès's radical socialism does not equate to some concordance with the French nationstate, but with the spirit of revolt that marks the instability of the French nation during this period and, most importantly, with the French integration of the political and the personal, or what Hobsbawm ([1962] 1999) calls the politicization of everyday life. That the traveller's conception of belonging to France is socially based is revealed by the fact that Vallès does not accuse the English of lacking national affiliation; on the contrary he states that 'their virtue, is that which we in France would call vice, the pride of being English, the awful, heroic chauvinism [...] They are capable of anything, in the name of the nation' (90).[70] In difference to the view of the nation as state of authority, then, the author's conception of the nation and national affiliation emerges from within a conception of the nation as a type of extended kinship – an 'esprit gaulois' (91, my emphasis) – that consists in a horizontal, imagined attachment (Anderson [1983] 2003) of its members. This view rests on the peuple as the source of the good, and resists a vertical, hierarchical and patriotic sense of loyalty to any particular authority pertaining to control such a community under the adage of the 'nation'. Vallès understands English nationalism in terms of an abstract patriotic affiliation that is at once hierarchical and protectionist, seeking to obliterate, or at least to deny, the existence of one section of its population:

> Degrading himself, he [the poor man] shows that he is a man to the ladies, who certainly see it, but the ladies go to swell the crowds of philanthropic meetings, and on their return, they get down to making long johns for the savages – without daring to say 'long johns', they wouldn't utter the word, it's *shocking*. Earlier, however, without blushing they rubbed shoulders with a man whom poverty had reduced to obscenity.[71] ([1876] 1951, 16, emphasis in the original)

The traveller's approbation of such a system is revealed in his correspondence with Malot, where he proclaims: 'The Englishman horrifies me… what perfidious creatures all these lords, conservatives and liberals' (cited in Merker 1970, 687).[72] However, *The London Street* does not dwell on an exploration of English politics or patriotism, and various critics (Lauzanne 1997; Redfern 1992, 155–72; Saminadayer-Perrin 2000, 7–10) have suggested that this is perhaps because Vallès, as a poor jobbing writer, did not have access to the higher echelons of British society. Instead of politics, the primary frame Vallès uses to represent the city is the legislative contrast between the political culture of France and the industrial culture of London.

Rather than a vertical sense of affiliation to the nation state, Vallès's nationalism can be understood, then, in terms of what sociologists term a 'group-relation', that is, a horizontal sense of community that imagines and thus establishes a network of identity connections between the individual Vallès and the social group which we label 'French'. This sense of belonging to a particular group becomes the primary category for coping with the cultural codes of England and, as we have seen, often results in hyperbolic metaphorical transfers and inflexible stereotyping. In opposition to other behavioural scientists, Gordon Allport (1954) has argued that categorization processes that produce stereotypes are not simply driven by malicious intent or a desire to discredit another group. Allport proposes that prejudice emerges from an association between categorization and differences in value, and that such an association is an unavoidable aspect of general cognitive functioning, saying that 'the human mind must think with the aid of categories... Once formed, categories are the basis for normal prejudgment. We cannot possibly avoid this process. Orderly living depends upon it' (20). The legibility of the foreign city for the traveller depends on their being equipped with the codes for its comprehension, where social or political categorization, by means of simplification, functions to render the shifting urban universe less complex, more readily understandable and, in some ways, more bearable. Furthermore, Allport's study proposes that stereotyping is habitually determined by a process of categorizing others in relation to categories associated with the self. The constant frame of reference for Vallès's exploration of London being his imagined connection to France, we might suggest, therefore, that it is his sense of affiliation to native cultural categories that lead to his rejection of English social codes.

However, Vallès's affiliation with France ultimately prevents him from establishing a basis upon which to integrate into English society. In the case of another type of travel experience this might not be so serious – travellers often deliberately avoid assimilating local codes where the latter threaten to restore a degree of familiarity to the other. In Vallès's representation, however, a lack of intimacy and a sense of alienation are suggested by the prevalent use of the metaphor of the prison employed by the traveller to describe general existence in London. This metaphor has a dual symbolism. From Vallès's point of view, London is a prison that keeps its inhabitants *in*, enslaving them to its industrial rhythms, while at the same time English society is portrayed as an insular prison designed to keep the stranger *out*: London as prison prevents Vallès from entering or engaging with the community in any meaningful way. Nor did Vallès's material circumstances help the situation – he barely spoke any English upon his arrival and, furthermore, like many other *émigrés*, he was poor, a fact which prevented him from participating in society with any degree of comfort.[73] Vallès maintained close ties with France during this period, and *The London Street* was first published in serial form for the French journal *L'Evénement* over the years 1876 to 1877. We might suggest, following Cronin, that writing in French during this time, constituted 'a form of homecoming' (Cronin 2000, 32) for

Vallès, while at the same time ensuring that he maintained a certain distance from social life in England.

Vallès's stereotypes of the Englishman's home and the 'typical' Englishman illustrate the degree to which the traveller feels isolated from English society. For example, in his description of a visit to an Englishman's home, Vallès neglects to name the host in question, with the effect that this anonymity furthers the traveller's ability to elevate this particular visit to the level of a general stereotype of English culture in its entirety – as he says, 'it is the depths of the nation that we wish to study' (94).[74] The chapters proceed to enumerate experiences with a view to abolishing the stereotypical image of the English as a hospitable and comfort loving people: the visitor is forced to enter the house by the servants' entrance, required to wait in the lobby and then in the drawing room, and once inside he proceeds to contrast each item of English furniture with a French equivalent. Here we see the object working across cultures to establish meaning for the one in opposition to the other. What emerges from the description, above all, is a sense of lack, that is, quite literally, a lack of the comforts of home, which in the following citation is elevated to hyperbolic proportions:

> There are no bedside tables! *There are none!*
>
> Oh! I know they'll call me a liar! The job of an observer brings its own perils […]. They'll say that I gratuitously slander a nation, that I'm taking unfair revenge for Waterloo. Let them say what they will. I believe it's my duty to warn my contemporaries, I have warned them. *There are no bedside tables*. I, from exile, side this time with my banishers, and from my exile I applaud this immodest receptacle.[75] (98, emphasis in the original)

This is one of the few instances in the account that Vallès mentions his exile explicitly, and it is significant here that in a somewhat ironic mode, he sides with his French 'banishers'. He also acknowledges the possibility that his account will not be taken seriously or viewed as sour grapes, yet, while the piece may be deliberately and ironically provocative, the sense of homesickness is striking, as the stranger calls to mind:

> The sumptuousness of the great wardrobe, heritage folded on the oak shelves, dozens of sheets and tablecloths that are the fortune of the simplest people and honour itself to the peasants throughout the most modest households of France. They [the English] do not know what it is to worship cloth, to respect the sainted laundry, to pray to the pyramids built by our ancestors' stitching that reveals the entire history of our labouring past.[76] (97)

This nostalgic pathos, both the result of a sense of connection to France and the loss of that connection, leads to the idealization of the home country so that *in absentia* France becomes the quintessence of sensuality and vibrancy, with this idealized extreme generating the opposing pole of London as an impenetrable city and the English as an impenetrable culture: 'Their face remains dry like the head of a swimmer who has bet on not wetting his hair; and their forehead inscrutable like the tarred caps of their sailors' (163).[77] Vallès's representative space then produces London as a city of outcasts, through which his own outcast position might be articulated.

2.8   Outcast London

This travel account's opening pages alert the reader to the network of juxtapositions providing the legislative framework grounding Vallès's perspective on London. The book's title, *La Rue à Londres / The London Street*, suggests an inversion of the traditional conception of the tourist guidebook, and an intention to expose London from the level of its streets rather than its monuments. Indeed, the modern urban street becomes the morphological figure on which Vallès constructs his vision of London's industrial society. The urban transformation of Paris over the period 1853–68, which saw the street transformed by Grand Manner architecture demanded reconsideration of the codes via which the street was to be interpreted. In terms of the shape that future industrial cities were to adopt, Paris provided the typical model for metropolitan development (Giedion 1967, 739). The consecutive demolition and reconstruction of Paris intensified the experience of the street for Parisians, and rendered the city unrecognizable. While both London and Paris were undergoing extensive structural change during this period, their ideological responses to and architectural articulation of industrialization resulted in different interpretive codes for legibility in the modern industrial city. With the Haussmannization of Paris, the street became a new modus operandi for understanding the newly industrialized city as a holistic entity, which is to say that the street seemed to reveal codes for understanding the social and political character of the new urban landscape. London too was shaped by national and imperialist concerns during this period, but a large part of the city in the East End lacked the architectural coherency that the radial system of boulevards provided to Paris. The industrialization of London led to the overpopulation of areas ill designed to cope with the resultant demographic and economic explosion. Thus, Paris's architecture provided space, light and air, the elements that would come to form the constituent language of architectural modernity under the Bauhaus and the International Movement. In the East End, by contrast, London's overcrowded streets, condensed slum areas and environmental toxicity presented the urban traveller with large areas around the Docklands that testified to the social consequences of modernization, and these are the areas that prove most attractive to Vallès's socialist sensibilities.

Vallès was fascinated with the street as a visual and cultural code. At the same time that he was compiling notes for *The London Street*, he also attempted in 1879 to set up a newspaper entitled *La Rue / The Street* (which ultimately failed). The street is adopted by Vallès as a means to penetrate 'the soul of this hard nation', to discover 'the dominant quality of the English' ([1876] 1951, 89).[78] And again, like the living room interior, the imaginative geography of London's streets is constructed through contrast with the Parisian boulevard. Commenting on the emergence of codes for appropriating new forms of architecture, Charles Jencks notes that 'the more unfamiliar a Modern building is, the more they [urban inhabitants] will compare it metaphorically to what they know' (2002, 26). Similarly, in order to cope with the unfamiliar environment, this French traveller attempts to map a familiar architectural experience onto the other unfamiliar location. It is the Parisian boulevard that provides Vallès with a cultural frame of reference for the London street, and this imposition of a familiar code onto the foreign city results in a legislative opposition, which Vallès articulates in concordance with the cities' divergent architectures; Paris, imagined as city of light and harmony, thus becomes the major code for oppositional interpretation of the social life, value-systems and 'guiding virtue' / 'vertu maîtresse' of London ([1876] 1951, 89).

There are two levels of narrative structure apparent in *The London Street*. On the one hand, the author's exploration of the city is delineated by the urban landscape's architectural and infrastructural features – the account's table of contents contains chapters with titles such as 'The Street' / 'La Rue'; 'The Walking Street' / 'La Rue qui marche'; 'Le Soho'; Les Docks', 'Le Workhouse', 'Drury Lane', 'Temple Bar' and 'Petticoat Lane'. These chapter headings illustrate the traveller's lack of concern for guiding his reader through a conventional, Baedeker-style repertoire of monuments, pointing instead to a consciousness that recentred meaning around the everyday experience of the city. Furthermore, as becomes apparent from the chapters' contents, the author is preoccupied with investigating the people who inhabit these dilapidated and disreputable areas of the city, so that the travel account functions as a kind of social reportage *avant la lettre*. Both the architectural and social orientations of the traveller combine to form a representation of what Gareth Stedman Jones (1971) refers to as 'outcast London'. As we shall see, these architectural and human elements of the city inform each other so that the representation of the people is often reflexively structured in terms of the architectures and atmospheres of the industrialized city. It is notable, therefore, that the areas of London listed, while all concerned with a specific urban location or architectural hub avoid the controlled, aesthetically beautified and officially ratified monuments of tourist London. As we have seen in relation to the Great Exhibition, the official monument functions to direct the collective imagination and, from the nineteenth century on, to reinforce a positive image of the nation. Instead, Vallès's favours an orientation based on those areas of the city that the governmental and metropolitan authorities of the time sought to remove from the urban landscape.

At this point in London's history, the tourist value of the city's topography was fundamentally different from what it is today. Janin informs us in 1851 that tours of the urban 'underground' (the Tower, the sewers), were available (1851, 155–57) during the period. However, the complex motivating force behind such sites' attractiveness – namely, conversion of the dread attached to these forbidden or historical nether worlds into dissociated nostalgia and, thus, *safe* points of fascination for tourist consumption – was not yet historically removed enough for these tours to extend into the slums and tenements that industrialization was still in the process of producing. The immediate crises of disease, malnutrition, unemployment and overcrowding constituted very real threats to London's working-class population. As MacCannell, in talking about contemporary tourism to former industrial sites, points out, 'the modernization of work relations, history and nature detaches these from their traditional roots and transforms them into cultural productions and experiences' (1976, 91). However, the social crisis produced by England's industrial revolution was neither temporally nor physically distant enough for the authorities to feel comfortable with acknowledging the urban underclass as part of the social space of modernity. For Vallès to portray this underworld at such a point in time, therefore, means that his imaginative geography of London emerges from outside the normative social imaginary of travel in this period. Rather his representation

presents us with a narrative of modernity that exhibits an emergent social consciousness based on a conception of human dignity in the natural equality of the person, and
rooted in a secular outlook that positions man at the centre of the moral universe. This
narrative emerges through Vallès's critique of London's industrial urban culture and its
capitalist value-system.

Vallès's critique takes on a further political dimension when one considers that at
this point in London's history, rather than to integrate, the authorities sought to dissociate the uncouth, impoverished and desperate elements of the industrial urban from
their vision and material articulation of progress. Safeguarding cultural and political coherence meant the denial of anything that threatened traditional, middle-class
ideas of the beautiful, of appropriate social behaviour, and illustrates the Victorian
moralization of the physical expression of individuals in its society. Such denial was
not always consciously undertaken on the part of the authorities; the economic difficulties inherent in free-market industrialization from the 1850s onward meant that
London became competitively untenable for many manufacturers. Often, the answer
to the problems of high rents, expensive fuel, high wages and scarce skills consisted
in an industry's total or partial removal from the capital.[79] This created an employment situation whereby labour in London became predominantly seasonal and, by
extension, meant that for a large part of the year a significant number of Londoners
were unemployed. The instability of casual labour created a considerable 'underclass'
within the capital, that is, a population of the casual poor who lived in slum conditions
and existed in a state of chronic instability and impoverishment. The government
and the middleclass response to the presence of such misery was to moralize the situation and to equate low living standards with low morals. The poor were variously
referred to as the 'dangerous class' or 'the residuum', and governmental reform agents
viewed them as positing a very real threat to the material and moral progression of
middle-class, capitalist civilization (Stedman Jones 1971). The spirit of urgency and
the belief that slumliving led to physical and moral degeneration inspired the likes
of the economist Alfred Marshall's scheme (1842–1924) to remove the chronic poor
from the capital (and the unregulated workhouse) and place them in labour encamp-
ments outside London. Technically voluntary, in actuality this plan forced the casual
poor to move to these colonies by strict enforcement of the laws against overcrowding.
Marshall expresses the prevailing attitude of the middle-class authorities to the presence of this class:

> The suffering caused on the way would be as nothing compared with the ultimate gain; and
> if the suffering could not be prevented, then it should not be shirked. There is no more urgent
> duty, no more truly beneficial work than to deprive progress of its partial cruelty by helping
> away those who lie in the route of its chariot wheels. (1884, 228)

A similar sentiment was expressed by the clergyman and reformer Samuel Barnett who
believed that it was 'a shocking thing to say of men created in God's image, but it is true
that the extinction of the unemployed would add to the wealth of the country… The
existence of the unemployed is a fact and this fact constitutes a danger to the wealth and

well-being of the community' (1888, 753–54). The idea was that once the rehabilitation of the unemployed had taken place in the countryside, these chronically poor families could be resettled outside London as agricultural labourers. The general governmental strategy was, therefore, to create a distinctive social and physical gap between the industrial middle class and respectable workingclass and the chronic casual residuum. Through the tight control of charities, the suppression of overcrowding and the enforcement of sanitary standards, the poor were to be removed from the landscape of urban progress.

The recuperation of this class by the heritage and, more latterly, the tourist industries would have to wait until the late twentieth century. At this point in London's history, Vallès's exposition of this underclass does not emerge from a safe position of either personal or historical distance, nor does it emanate from a (humanist or protectionist) sociological concern with the well-being or improvement of metropolitan life such as that expressed by the industrialist and social reformer Charles Booth (1889, 1891) or the social scientist Friedrich Engels ([1844] 1993). Often, in his novels, Vallès expressed sympathy with those on the margins of French middle-class society, glorifying those working-class men who refused the hegemony of bourgeois authority and convention. Vallès's interest in the working-class rebel stems from a sense of identification with those who were victims of authority and yet strove to fight back and survive. As he commented to his friend Arthur Arnould saying, 'We were not born to be dupes or victims, we who by temperament, looks and heart are with the proletariat' (Vallès [1870–80] 1980, 174).[80] His is a value-system based on the anarchist rejection of authority. However, although *The London Street* is preoccupied with the urban underclass of the English metropolis, there is no sense of identification here, rather, in consistency with the contrastive paradigm set up in the opening line, the poor of Paris and those of London are brought into a generalized, competitive frame:

> French paupers do not prepare one for the paupers of London. Of course, in France there is the beggar with his fat face like that of a monk chased from a convent, or with his bald head and grey beard, like a fallen saint; but it is a trade, that of the beggar, almost a mission, he even has something of the sorcerer. He has his soup rations, his strips of meat. […] The poor of London are not the same. […] Some of them brought to mind those prisoners that the police lead along the roads from squadron to squadron; who walk flanked by two black horses, attached to the saddle; […] and they travel like this, night and day, until the prison gathers them in. Such are the starving English![81] (Vallès [1876] 1951, 15–16)

Vallès recounts the existence of this underclass in order to amalgamate their desultory existence to his repugnance at the social fallout of urban industrialization in London as a whole, and, most especially, to express his sense of personal and political isolation and alienation. Thus Vallès's representational space is framed by a lens focussed on the underworld of London – the London that remained hidden to the vast majority of the city's middle- and upper-class inhabitants and even more so to its visitors – so as to expose better the underbelly of the modern metropolis with a view to expressing an abhorrence of industrialization as well as a sense of personal isolation.

2.9   The Great Maw

One of the major metaphorical recourses that Vallès employs to describe London is that of the prison. Images of closed doors, closed skies and grilled gates proliferate throughout the account, and this seems to reveal, first of all, that Vallès's understanding of affiliation is rooted in a nationalist tendency that is not coterminous with humankind, but resides in a belief that there exist inherent 'natural' differences between people of different countries. The writer comments on what he perceives to be 'the instinctive hatred' / 'la haine instinctive' ([1876] 1951, 91) of the English for the French: 'It is an instinct, *in the blood*, this blood which doesn't flow like Latin blood that glows crimson in the sunlight […] but which pours forth from the stabbed man wounded in the ring or from beneath the hanged man's cap at the gallows (91).[82] Vallès's nationalism is not entirely coherent, however, for here we can see that he combines a notion of community based on the *jus sanguinis* (law of blood) (or what modern sociologists refer to as 'ethnic nationalism') with a territorially based conception of national identity (*jus soli* or law of soil). This illogical confusion is, nevertheless, typical of nineteenth-century expressions of nationalism making it conceivable that the exile's experience of London results in feeling entrapped in a space with which he has no 'natural' correspondence (see Nairn 1977; Anderson [1983] 2003; Seton-Watson 1977; Wegner 2002). More than this, the prison metaphor is projected beyond personal identity with the result that it comes to epitomize London, and the metaphorical associations of the prison are extended to construct an image of the landscape and people of London. Vallès explicitly connects his status as outsider to a position of objectivity, and from this perspective he concludes that London is a prison, albeit one invisible to its inhabitants: 'The visitor, who travels from the cellar to the loft, sees the prison better than the detainee who dreams in his cage, forehead against the bars' (89).[83]

   In the opening pages of *The London Street* Vallès describes the city as the workday finishes and the workers (in this case businessmen) return home. Here, the traveller, in consistency with his vision of London as a closed, insular community, appropriates the architecture of the English home. The writer constructs an archetypal image of the 'typical' Englishman's abode:

> Guarded by railings with fanged spikes, protected as well as a bakery against the famines of 93, this *home* and this hearth! Between the façade and the footpath gapes a dirty chasm, a deep cavern, a railed hole, as for keeping a wolf. Black iron is everywhere or stones grey as tombs, like bones blanched by the rain. At the top of the steps, the wooden face of a door resembling that of a prison or a convent.[84] ([1876] 1951, 9, emphasis in the original)

The image is one of a people living behind impenetrable walls – impenetrable both to the visitor and to the outside world. Within this image Vallès identifies what he sees as an English desire to shut out the city – to literally keep the wolf from the door. In another passage he employs animalistic imagery once again, representing London as a giant allegorical beast that leaves its servants stranded once it has gone to sleep: 'Where can one go when the City has retracted its claws, closed its maw, shut its eyes […]; when the tumult has ceased in the mercenary and merchant camps? (29).[85] The streets are inhospitable, filled with vice or misery, and while Vallès admits that 'It is late, it's evening', he goes on to say, 'but in the daytime, it's the same, it's always the same' (9).[86] This statement – that life in London is essentially stagnant – reinforces the notion that the city's misery and its inhabitants' impenetrable character are eternal states. Even when the sun comes up, or as Vallès disparagingly remarks, 'what they call the sun', the gates remain barred, 'the sun will not force the locks' (9).[87] The architectures of 'privacy' are, therefore, interpreted by Vallès as symptoms of a 'hostile country, walled race!' (10);[88] symptoms of a national malevolence which Vallès evokes using penal imagery:

> What a sinister impression these rows of buildings give, gnawed on by the fog and rain! When the houses of London do not bear the doleful aspect of a soiled shroud, they are the colour [...] of the court dock – these tones of prison or the scaffold. It's awful. I will not recant, one would think they were damned or imprisoned.[89] (11)

While Vallès states that it is not his desire to dwell on such an image, the account is laden with such references, and these are extended not only to the architectural elements of London but also to the social life of the city. From the book's opening lines, it is apparent from the outset that emptiness, silence and inhumanity are critical to Vallès's interpretive landscape of the city. His prose weaves a deathly silence within the urban space, most notably around the Sunday city: 'In England, you hear nothing amid the dreadful calm of a Sunday. It is silent, and not a sound cuts through it [...] a people crushed by a sect [...]. Everything is closed by law' (70).[90] These metaphors of the tomb, the prison, the convent, enclosure, and their attendant sense of suffocation and authoritative, inhuman mechanism facilitate Vallès's filling this emptiness with images of a voluptuous and vibrant Paris. Such silence in Paris is inconceivable, unless it is the result of war – a situation that does not characterize the city. The chapter 'An English Sunday' / 'Un dimanche anglais' opens with the line 'You recall, those tragic hours in Paris, when certain streets were deserted, silent, dark?' (70).[91] While silence is an anomaly in Paris, in London it constitutes a persistent state of existence. Vallès assumes this existence to be a result of London's industrialization and middle-class conservatism. Here we find then, a direct contrast to the values attendant on Janin's experience of the space–time of Sunday in England. The day thus becoming a significant trope around which ideologically opposed versions of urban modernity can be articulated.

Furthermore, for Vallès, London's is an existence equated with death. In opposition to a view of industrialization that associates technological progress with morality and civilization, *The London Street* associates the industrial city with the inhuman and the mechanical, essentially, with death. The physical expressions of London's industrialization – its polluted air, river, weather, the city's slums and guarded middle-class areas – infiltrate the traveller's imagination of each aspect of urban life, with the result that the mechanization of the city is directly transferred onto the representation of the city's inhabitants. As urban time and the rhythms of urban life become standardized through industrialization, so Vallès represents Londoners as a homogenous, undifferentiated group of automatons:

> They run hither and thither like machine *pistons*, they go by each other like ships in the night; they never say a word except: 'Nice morning... terrible weather' depending on whether it's

fine or bad weather – and they carry on about their business, abrupt, straight and energetic. Onward piston![92] (1–2)

The amalgamation of the Industrial Revolution and the urban individual sets up one of the legislative paradigms for Vallès's reading of the metropolis, and creates a narrative extremism that involves associative overstatement engendered within a discourse of the demonological and (although much less frequently) the angelical. It is clear that Vallès views industrialization as aberrant – a pollution of both the elemental and social world, suffocating the city and its civilization. The brutality of the industrial atmosphere is compounded by the imagery Vallès uses to describe the Thames. This great body of water, indeed the life force of the metropolis and the reason for its existence, is dissociated from all traditional associations of water with life or fluidity. In a reversal of the metaphors of liquid movement often used in urban discourse to characterize the street (an artery, a vein, a medium of circulation), the Thames is discussed here in architectural terms – 'the marching street' / 'la rue qui marche' (23) – a metaphor evocative of concrete and, in the light of Vallès's previous characterization of London's streets, of mechanism, filth and deathliness. The monstrousness of the river as it flows through the city is made apparent through an imagined contrast with the Thames at its source: 'At its source the river is clear […] here, it is cloudy and vile as though the crockery of an entire army had been washed in it […] a river bordered by a battlefield, and whose bed is one of coal kneaded in blood' (23).[93] There is a sense, therefore, that beyond the industrial city a natural order remains intact, but that within the metropolitan environment this order has been superseded and, ultimately, corrupted.[94]

Imagining the river at its source can be seen as a strategy for reminding the reader that the city is an aberration and London a depravity. Vallès contrasts the dense opaque waves of the Thames – 'The yellowish waves' reflections like crude gold' (23)[95] – and their demonic weight – 'who so falls there rests there' (24)[96] – with the transparent, sentient rivers of France:

[The Thames] is dense like beer, and one never sees houses gaily washing their heads in it, nor trees dancing sinuously in any part of the Thames, as one does in the green mirror of the Rhone or the blue mirror of the Loire whether in the depths of the countryside or the city![97] (24)

The imagery is striking in its oppositions. In France, houses are represented using an anthropomorphic lexicon, as are the trees that 'dance' exuberantly. Here, the language imbues the scene with suppleness and life. The Thames, meanwhile, is aligned with death, its water a wasteland of the city's expulsions, and anyone who attempts suicide is sure to drown (as is anyone who tries it but regrets doing so at the last moment and attempts to save themselves). The Thames has anthropomorphic associations of its own however:

Are there not a thousand chimneys that cast their foul vapours towards the sky, in heavy curls, in thick plaits, it is the sombre colour of the river, the sad braid of the Thames – Old father

Thames. I saw a head sculpted from stone, dead eyes, moustaches drooping like drenched grass [...] 'This is old father Thames!' an Englishman announced to me with pride.[98] (24)

From this passage, it becomes apparent that the industrial environment is to be blamed for the corruption of the purity of the sky. Industry launches its filthy, braided tail upwards into the sky. Similarly, rather than refer to sculpture as a discrete art object, 'Old Father Thames' is represented as a head sculpted into stone, indistinguishable from the hard, dead material from which it is made – the eyes of the sculpture are dead, its moustache hangs like a river weed, as though off the face of some drowned victim. This characterization, placed before the Englishman's acclamation of pride, serves to align the malignity of the statue with the absurdity of the inhabitants of the city. The representation gives the impression that the people of London are blind to the iniquitous influence of industrialization, that their pride in technological progress is misplaced, and that it is a faith such as this that ultimately keeps them enslaved and deadens them inside. The final nail in the coffin is the river's stench, which Vallès identifies as 'burned flesh' (25).[99]

The diametric opposition of France and Britain emerges, therefore, from within the portrayal of their respective environments. France is associated with transparency and thus with beauty and gaiety; the Thames, however, is the colour of tar and at lowtide leaves its ships lying in a corridor of mud, its impenetrable, metallic sheen is the immanence of death itself. The sky is filled with smoke and the sun never shines, and just as the crowd is dehumanized through the metaphor of the machine, so the perceived lifelessness of the environment is transposed onto the character of the English: 'This water reflects nothing, like the face of the English' (24).[100] The image of Nature as the source and map towards the good is here a discourse that shapes the competing imaginative strands shaping the traveller's meanings for social life. Nature is corrupted through industrialism, and thus its extension, humanity, is too.

And yet, in the end, and on another stretch of water – that of the Channel – the traveller is capable of admitting some positive emotion with regard to England. Distance from England and the prospect of home seem to facilitate a more nuanced perspective on the part of the French exile, and on his journey home he writes:

It is not without sadness that one leaves this sad city. On smoky, dismal London I cast a look of recognition calling to mind the hospitality that the exiled French received there – whose ideas were not agreeable and whose flag was feared. I tipped my hat at the black City, to thank this people, who have never slandered the Queen, for having taught me, I from a republican country, what freedom was.[101] (250)

There is, perhaps, some irony in this statement. Nevertheless, it remains that England proved more hospitable to Vallès's revolutionary politics than his own government. It would seem that Vallès is self-consciously aware here of the manner in which the contrasts with which London provided him enabled a better articulation of his radical views. Freedom in this sense refers to the liberty of expression which England's liberalism afforded Vallès, so that while he cannot identify with the form of nationhood he finds in England, nevertheless he can respect the agency given him. Ultimately though, this account ends without any sense that the traveller's displacement has undermined his sense of identification with France, which he terms a 'republican country' – a statement that naturalizes this form of government in its respect to France; the geographical entity of France and the political entity of the republic are one. The radicalism of Vallès's world-view is evident here, especially given the instability of previous political regimes at this point in time, but Vallès does not seem to be referring to forms of state organization here, rather he infers that the social imaginary of France is, from this point on, inextricably tied to a vision of the Republic.

Bringing together Janin's and Vallès's travel writing highlights the fluidity of perspectives engaged in structuring narratives to make sense of the upheaval which urban modernization brought to everyday life. The consideration of national, cultural and political difference is the central framework of the traveller's practices of the city discussed here, and it is this legislative grid that produces a series of oppositional categories through which the metropolitan universe is rendered legible. In Janin's account the expounding of official – institutionalized – monumentality, as well as his political nostalgia for and idealization of the English monarchical system, function so that travel performs as a register of cultural criticism: in the case of Janin it is present-day France that provides an antithetical perspective to the industrially revolutionized and stable monarchy-governed society of England. In the case of Janin, English economic progress and public order are viewed positively in concordance with an ideological position grounded in an ideal of monarchy's sacred right and its potential for harmony, in opposition to the unstable condition of contemporary French politics. For Vallès, by contrast, the city is viewed through a lens of nostalgia, due to the imposed absence of home, which results in London's representation as an impenetrable and sinister prison. To an extent, both of these discourses operate from a position wherein identity is constructed through a differential series of modern understandings of the common good, in accordance with these writers' contrastive imaginative geographies that are rooted on French soil. But as we have stated, modernity cannot be considered as a seamless flow. In considering Janin's account alongside that of Vallès we become aware of two dominant competing strands of modernity at play during the latter half of the nineteenth century. Urban travel writing here then creates representative spaces of dynamic linkages, which cross territorial as well as temporal boundaries. London is performed as a strategic double architecture, a topography of different French identitarian positions that require the other in their definition, an alternative modernity from which to enact spatially the political birth pangs of modernity in France.

Chapter Three

REVEALING AND RECONSTRUCTING LONDON

Hidden away behind the busy streets and main thoroughfares of the old city of London there exists a secret city of narrow alleyways, timber framed buildings and hidden courtyards that really make for an enjoyable and original experience.[1]

Jones 2008, 1

As we have seen in the previous chapter, in constant tension with the representations of space of London's orderly West End and tourist attractions are spaces of urban disorder, social 'dysfunction', and poverty that continually threaten to depose the institutional and ideological clarity of the figured city. For the French travellers examined in this chapter, spaces of disorder perform in correspondence and contrast with the monumentality of more official sites. Disorder is a trope that provides a key to analysing these travellers' strategies for making meaning for London during the interwar period – in the case of Jacques Dyssord (1880–1952) – and in the immediate aftermath of World War II – in Alfred Leroy's narrative (1897–?).[2] The underbelly of London's metropolitan life in the first half of the twentieth century is at once repellent and fascinating to the traveller and, furthermore, this underbelly is consistently identified with the act of revealing or uncovering, and with the notion of an 'authentic' space, a space of everyday life amid ordinary working people, that posits an alternative social space to that of the public sphere officially sanctioned by monumental or institutional architectures. In the travel account, we are presented with an articulation of itineraries; pathways through the city organized in response to, but never in exact compliance with, the rational logic of the urban planner's viewpoint. Space, at street level, is malleable, shifting in response to the walker's changing perspective, presenting opportunities to confound the diagrammatic stability of the map through the multiple ways in which travellers, as practitioners of space, orient themselves, temporalize places through narrative, rendering places as spaces and making visible the polyvalence of meaning in the city. Certeau emphasizes the potential for space, as practised by narrative, to move away from its diagrammatic clarity and become 'delinquent':

What the map cuts up, the story cuts across. In Greek, narration is called 'diegesis': it establishes an itinerary (it 'guides') and it passes through it (it 'transgresses'). The space of operations it travels in is made of movements: it is *topological*, concerning the deformations of figures, rather than *topical*, defining places. [...] when it marks a stopping place, the latter is not stable but follows the variations of encounters between programs. (1984, 125)

The travel narrative, as a representational space of narrative movement, has the potential to disrupt the figured city. Equally, however, when the narrative rests with a description of a particular place (or, 'marks a stopping place'), Certeau makes us aware of the variety of resonances or contexts that can enter into play. In this way, space is always situated, as indicated by Certeau's use of the term 'topological' to describe the effect of narrative on place. Travel writing deforms place in concert with poetic conventions, historical situations and subjective responses to that place's architectural order, so that meaning is produced through the traveller's interpretive strategies for understanding the encounter with difference. The second pair of representations of London to be examined in this chapter reveal this tension between the sanctioned representations of London and the subjective spatial practice of the traveller. This tension is played out here in terms of a conflict over notions of truth and authenticity. In their idiosyncratic appropriations of concepts of 'truth' and the 'real' they reveal the extent to which the sensory distribution of urban spaces in the travel account rests on the emotive and imaginative geographies of the subjects that engage with the city. In this chapter, then, I explore what I have termed the 'dark tourism' of Jacques Dyssord's *Londres secret / Secret London* (1932) and Alfred Leroy's wartime portrait of the city in *Londres et la vie anglaise / London and English Life* (1946). Both are texts that demonstrate to a high degree the mechanisms of legislative travel, where 'authenticity', or the construction of a representational space purporting to capture the real, conditions the meanings for London in the years before and immediately after World War II.

3.1   The Secret City: Authentic Spaces and Dark Tourism

Jacques Dyssord was the pen name of the poet and writer Edouard Jacques Marie Joseph Moreau de Bellaing. Born in Oloron Sainte-Marie, a small Bernais town in the Pyrenees, his family was aristocratic and religious. After having studied at a Jesuit School in Toulouse, he went on to obtain his law degree. Rather than follow his father's wish to enter a career in the military, Bellaing went to Paris to pursue a writing career. In 1909 he published a collection of poems, 'Le Dernier Chant de l'Intermezzo' under the pseudonym, Jacques Dyssord. Dyssord was alternately a poet novelist, journalist, essayist and playwright and his work was largely influenced by his native Bearn, his bohemian lifestyle and his travels abroad (Austria, Tunisia, as well as Great Britain). He also wrote literary criticism in numerous journals and newspapers. In addition to 'Dyssord', the author also wrote under the names Lazarille and Jean Cardesse. During the French Occupation, Dyssord was attacked for his work with collaborationist Parisian newspapers. He retired from literary life in 1945 and died in 1952 in Villejuif. His travel account of London, published in 1932, is structured around the trope of the 'secret city', which was an axiomatic reference for tourists in the twentieth century. In this analysis of Dyssord's *Londres secret* (written in 1929), we will see how this fascination with the dark, expressed through intimate human interaction in these urban back spaces, is equated putatively with the 'authentic', while the expressions of transparency – technology, modern architecture and public order – are represented as deceptive agents that obscure human beings' relationship to reality.

The nether city implies an alternative to the metropolis of monuments, the 'beaten track' of the regular tourist. This alternative city presents a 'species of space' (Perec, 1974) concomitant with the architectural theorist Anthony Vidler's (1992) category of 'dark space'. Vidler defines the term 'dark space' as the dialectical opposition to the 'bright' or transparent orders of urbanism and architecture. It refers to a space that 'is assumed to hide, in its darkest recesses and forgotten margins, all the objects of fear and phobia that have returned with such insistency to haunt the imaginations of those who have tried to stake out spaces to protect their health and happiness' (Vidler 1992, 167). For Dyssord travelling to London in 1929, the notion of a 'secret' city implies that behind the governmental spaces of the metropolis, there exists another, opaque urban landscape that is, by extension, more 'authentic' than that of the orderly avenues of London's West End. Erving Goffman (1959) has analysed the tendency in modern society to feel that there is a reality more authentic than the one that offers itself to perception. Goffman's structural division of social establishments into what he terms 'front' and 'back' regions are equated to what will be referred to here as categories of 'light' and 'dark spaces':

> Given a particular performance as the point of reference, we have distinguished three crucial roles on the basis of function: those who perform; those performed to, and outsiders who neither perform in the show nor observe it. [...] The three crucial roles mentioned could be described on the basis of the regions to which the role-player has access: performers appear in the front and back regions; the audience appears only in the front region; and the outsiders are excluded from both regions. (144–45)

In Goffman's theory, the seeming transparency of social interaction becomes problematic within modern society. In modern civilization, what is perceived as authentic depends on the structural organization between front and back. For example, a back region, closed to the audience and outsiders, conceals props and preparatory activities that have the potential to discredit the realism of the performance out front. Accordingly, maintaining a coherent sense of social reality requires some degree of mystification. When we talk about social space conceived in this context, and in particular about modern social space, Lefebvre's analysis of the effect of the burgeoning production of images in modern society is pertinent. For Lefebvre, the image of space (photographs in tourist brochures for example, or illustrations in a travel account) obscures the role of time in the production of that space's production. Or in other words, the image erases historical time. The image 'dismembers' space, 'fetishizes abstraction and imposes it as the norm. It detaches the pure form from its impure content – from lived time, everyday time, and from bodies with their opacity and solidity, their warmth, their life and their death' (Lefebvre [1974] 1991, 97).[3] For our context, there is the sense then that the tourist city in some ways organizes the city into front and back regions, dismantles space, separating it from the complexities, illegibility and contradictions of lived time – most concretely evident in the separation of the space of labour and industrial production from the city centre – sanitizing space so as to present it as a coherent whole. However, this space is also productive of the modern desire for 'transparency' – the sense that there exists something behind the façade – but this sense, for Lefebvre, is an outgrowth of the same modern desire for 'readability–visibility–intelligibility' ([1974] 1991, 96).[4] The desire for authenticity emerges in tandem with the sensibility that there is a point at which the dismemberments of modern space will be made whole again. This desire for holism stems of course from the demarcation of space in Western modernity, wherein 'demarcated space necessarily embraces some things and excludes others [...]. Such a space asserts, negates and denies' (Lefebvre [1974] 1991, 99).[5] But it equally provokes a sense of loss, and a desire for restoration – a desire for the 'authentic' as a space that exists behind the rationalization of the sign as image.

Moreover, when applied to tourism, the concept of 'authenticity' is a fairly controversial word. First used by MacCannell as a means to explore tourist motivations and experiences, the concept was introduced in relation to travel in his book *The Tourist: A New Theory of the Leisure Class* (1976). In his discussion, MacCannell draws a distinction between what he terms 'experienced authenticity' and 'staged authenticity', building on Goffman's identification discussed above of 'front' and 'back' regions in the organization of society. In regard to 'staged tourism', MacCannell states: 'It is always possible that what is taken to be entry into a back region is really entry into a front region that has been totally set up in advance for touristic visitation' (cited in Wang 1999, 353). In this scenario, a tourist's experiences of space never exist outside the organization of the signs of difference, and, therefore, can never attain to authenticity even if they are perceived as such. Ning Wang, however, counters MacCannell's arguments through the observation that authenticity is often a term ascribed by the elite, educated outsiders – analogous to tourists in many senses – looking in (Wang 1999 355). In this schema, authenticity is seen in relation to the subject. As Arianna Drumond sees it, 'To the tourist, a staged event may seem perfectly genuine, though to the organizers and performers, the event is indeed staged.'[6]

In the philosophical sense of the term, many writers on authenticity in the twentieth century considered the urbane manners and the bourgeois cultural norms of Western Europe to be inauthentic. This attitude can be traced to Rousseauian ideas of modern civilization as a corruption of the individual. More recently, Heidegger thought that the 'they' as discussed in chapter 2, caused people to behave inauthentically through social pressure to conform to normative standards prevalent in the bourgeois social imaginary. In later life, Heidegger spatialized this conception of authenticity, associating it with non-technological ways of existing in the world, and in his view technology constituted a distortion of Dasein's relationship to the natural world. Etymologically, the word authenticity has its roots in the ancient Greek *authentikos*, meaning 'original, genuine, principal', which can be traced back further to *authentes* – 'one acting on one's own authority'.[7] These original meanings form the basis for the contemporary interpretations of the concept in the spheres of philosophy and psychology, as well as in tourist studies. Authenticity, in these spheres, is associated with a person's ability to remain true to their own personality, spirit or character, which is put under pressure to confirm to social norms. In this schema, authenticity is thus connected with the relation between a person and society. The most prominent authors setting the grounds for this conception are Kierkegaard, Heidegger and Sartre. In another framework – which has been important for the development of the concept in the context of travel – authenticity, as conceived in the context of art, relates 'to the set of qualities that a work of art or an artistic performance should possess to be considered authentic' (Drumond 2013). Two basic qualities lend distinction: nominal authenticity and expressive authenticity. Nominal authenticity can be defined 'as the correct identification of the origins, authorship, or provenance of an object, ensuring, as the term implies, that an object of aesthetic experience is properly named' (Dutton 2003, 259). Nominal authenticity can be empirically tested, and is based on facts, as Denis Dutton points out in relation to the authentication of a work of art. Unlike nominal authenticity, expressive authenticity is more akin to the existentialist sense of the term and has 'to do with an object's character as a true expression of an individual's or a society's values and beliefs' (Dutton 2003, 259). If we apply this to social space, then expressive authenticity becomes an important issue in tourism, in particular when the traveller encounters difference. Here, the attempt is made to identify the extent of the space's conformity to signs typically equated with a community's values, attitudes and traditions, and is reminiscent of Culler's identification of the tourist as a seeker of the essential signs of the authentic. To be considered an authentic space, then, the site of the visit should seem to express the 'true' identity of the community. Furthermore, the object can be audience-focussed too, so that in contemporary manifestations of tourism, for example, there is the expectation that the object be signalled as authentic in order for the tourist to apprehend its meaning and value.

As we shall see, in the modern urban environment, for the French the trope of the 'authentic' is invested further in thinking around London's expression of class difference. There are analogies to be drawn here between the way that Dyssord explores London as a 'secret' space – a social space of working-class life and an architectural space of incarceration – and Goffman's notions of 'front' and 'back' regions. The dominant order organizing urban life can be compared to the back region; this is the space where capitalist relations are effectively managed, and where bureaucratic procedures are determined. These institutional procedures design reproductions of space that allow the imaginative geography of the capitalist imperial city and the nation state to present an image of coherent society. As we have seen in relation to the metropolitan measures for slum clearance in the nineteenth century, the possibility that the outsider, or other, might penetrate this back space is a core motivation in the organizational strategies of the authorities to exclude the public from this arena. MacCannell (1976) has pointed out that the mere fact that these spaces exist generates the belief that there is something being hidden from the general public. Even if there are actually no secrets, such spaces are areas where the secrets to society's inner workings are believed to be kept. It is akin to watching a play; we watch the spectacle unfold before us, all the while knowing that the performance is being carefully managed backstage. In this scenario, the 'backstage' city becomes the object of the traveller's desire – he wishes to unveil, to render transparent, the underpinning structures of society and the 'truths' that others cannot, or will not, acknowledge.

In addition to this, in travel writing, this conflation of 'back' space with the authentic is intimately related to the tourist/traveller opposition or, more precisely here, to Dyssord's conceptual association of conventional tourism with inauthenticity and his corresponding desire to distinguish himself from tourist practices of urban space so as to experience 'real' London and to validate this experience to his reader. Of course, as MacCannell points out, disparagement of the tourist 'is so prevalent, in fact, that it is part of the problem of mass tourism, not an analytical reflection upon it' (1976, 104). Nevertheless, the distinction is a crucial part of Dyssord's practice, and his path through the city is negatively determined by a concern to steer away from 'the beaten track', wherein he joins the conceptual matrix of the 'true' traveller who sets out 'to attain authenticity by being faithful to scripts they have written for themselves' (Golomb 1995, 3). There is of course a well-established social imaginary of the tourist that requires the travel writer to eschew certain aspects of mainstream and mass travel. As Ellen Furlough has put it, 'As consumers, tourists are said to exemplify qualities thought to adhere to mass culture and mass consumption: tasteless, serialized, socially uniform, and culturally passive' (1998, 248). Culler relates this to the image of the tourist en masse that persists in contemporary society, but which was also heavily present in eighteenth-century French travel narratives (see Thompson 2011). Culler puts a colourful spin on things saying, 'Tourists are continually subject to sneers and have no anti-defamation league. Animal imagery seems their inevitable lot: they are said to move in herds, droves, flocks and swarms; they are as docile as sheep' (1981, 1–2). But the search for an authentic space is, Culler goes on to observe, a large part of the tourist experience and, moreover, for an object or experience to be 'authentic' it needs to be distinguished as such. As Culler puts it, 'The authentic is not something unmarked or undifferentiated; authenticity is a sign relation. Even the sights in which the most snobbish tourists take pleasure are not unmarked' (Culler 1981, 6). In order for the tourist or the traveller to understand an object, person or space as constituting an authentic part of a culture, there needs to be an indicator to that effect.

This notion of the mark is important to our next point in relation to Dyssord's proposal to uncover the secret city. Dyssord's representational movement away from the monumental city and an orientation towards the social spaces of the capital's less salubrious quarters is not so much an expression of 'real' travel but is more akin to the sign relations at work in the phenomenon of 'dark tourism'. This is a concept derived from researchers John Lennon and Malcolm Foley, and which is define as travel to sites of death, disaster or the seemingly macabre (see Lennon and Foley 2000; Rojek 1993). Furthermore, according to Lennon and Foley, for a site to be considered 'dark', it must incite a reaction to modernity and 'therefore must relate to an event or catastrophe that has occurred within recent memory' (Yuill 2003, 18). Dark tourism emerges as a concept to describe visits to sites that bear witness to the fallout of modernity, notably Holocaust memorials, war cemeteries or disaster areas such as Chernobyl. In general usage it implies that the disastrous event is historically 'complete' or distant from the present, that the prison, gulag or concentration camp no longer retains its original function and has been converted into a museum or memorial. Dyssord's motivation and travel practice produce a representation of the city through modalities similar to that of dark tourism. From within Dyssord's representational space, the city is depraved, miserable and fascinating in equal measure. Here, I extend the meaning of 'dark tourism' to imply a journey off the beaten track to a space which, for this period, is associated with the suffering of the working classes and sites impoverished by industrialist modernization, sites that at this time remain beyond the realm of conventional tourist sites. Dyssord's journey through the East End of London is an exercise in dark tourism, testifying at once to a social consciousness as well as to a fascination with the heterotopic spaces of London's working-class culture; the language, pubs, eating habits and criminal activities of cockney Londoners.

From the opening lines of the account, Dyssord establishes his travel practice in opposition to the middle-class conception of 'bright' London. After having lost his first East-End guide, he attempts to recruit a replacement from among the middleclasses. He is sorely disappointed, however; theirs is not the London he is seeking:

> Outside of their club, their cricket and their business, they know nothing or want to know nothing, which is the same thing. To listen to them, London since the war has become a model city. The unemployed? Lazy sods who would bankrupt them. The *slums*? Cleaned. Beautiful municipal housing is being erected in their place. What am I saying, houses? Palaces, where the poor wallow in comfort. Prostitution? Inexistent, except for in the French quarter or Soho, where [...] you can count the Frenchmen on one hand. In short, I could expect nothing less than paradise, and there I found myself, from the moment I stepped foot onto the platform at Victoria station. 'Indeed', Panurge would have retorted, and I with him.[8] (1932, 81–82)

The implication here is that middle-class people are idealistic and ignorant about their city, and that they prefer to remain so. Dyssord, recalling the Rabelaisian character Panurge, portrays this class as a flock of sheep revealing his scepticism towards modernization's attempts to create the best of all metropolitan worlds. At the beginning of the twentieth century, this scepticism at appearances presents the opposing hand of the reformist movement's political desire, as well as the architectural modernist movement's sociocultural one; to render the city a perfect model of functionalist living and to purify it of its squalor and decrepitude. Against what Goffman (1959) documents as the 'show' of social life, the presumed existence of another, dark space functions to maintain the polarity that places the alleged 'intimate and real' in opposition to the display of bright space. In terms of what Dyssord equates with the bright city, this is related to the progress made by government intervention in social life and the restructuring of social relations in response to new technologies of energy and transport. The transformation of the dark spaces where London's poorest populations worked, lived and were 'educated' began taking place from the 1880s (see Inwood 2005, 458–65).[9] For example, the London County Council (LCC), founded in 1889, signalled an interventionist approach on the part of the Victorian government and an inclination to abandon its laissez-faire attitude to social life in order to address the effects of industrialization (see Rowntree 1901, 360–61). However, it was really only after the death of Victoria in 1901, and the coming of the Edwardian age, that the Liberals' 'social service state' (1906) attempted deliberately to bring transparency and order into the everyday lives of all of its citizens. The social revelations of Booth, as well as those of the more radical Seebohm Rowntree (1871–1954) in his study of 1901, *Poverty: A Study of Town Life*, undermined the Victorian commonplace that poverty was an outcome of weak character.

Dyssord's account, in its quest for 'truth' in the East End, gives little away of the technological and infrastructural changes that had taken place in London from the 1880s to the 1920s.[10] But, it is important to note that developments contributing to the modernization of London made it a vastly different city, both in attitude and shape, to the one where Vallès spent his exile. Horace Taylor's 'Brightest London' poster campaign for the London Underground testifies to a positive appropriation of metropolitan life, depicting the glamour, diversity and even playing on the contradictions of the city – evident in the paradox of the poster's title: 'Brightest London is reached by Underground'. Dyssord, however, ignores this city in favour of an excursion into the 'lower depths' of the metropolis. The East End is the secret London of the account's title. The bright space of London is deliberately avoided, with the result that the materiality of the East End and its everyday detail provide the basis for a representation of another London, a secret city. However, rather than this dark space eliminating the monumentality and transparency of the governmental city, Dyssord's account functions within the network of contrasts set up between the figured city and its underground, between the middle-class gentleman and the working man, between appearance and reality, in order that the traveller establish his authenticity spatially and socially in antithetical relation to the common tourist. The following section examines the traveller's narrative strategies for constructing this authenticity in connection with the underground city.

The traveller's desire for the authentic, conceived as underground space, is constructed out of a suspicion at society's modernization with its tendency to homogenize and monumentalize space and the correspondent emergence of mass tourism. Foucault ([1982] 2001) has argued that Western society's cultivation of a mythology of power through transparency stems from an initial fear of the dark, and that this fear engenders a fascination with those unbridled spaces – areas of darkness, hideouts, cellars, dungeons – spaces that resist the panoptic eye. Vidler expands on Foucault's hypothesis, noting that 'the moment that saw the creation of the first "considered politics of spaces" based on scientific concepts of light and infinity also saw, and within the same epistemology, the invention of a spatial phenomenology of darkness' (1992, 169). In other words, while the impulse to transparency is engendered by fear of the unfamiliar, with that transparency a more evolved consciousness of the unknown enters the spatial imaginary. We can, furthermore, bring the idea of 'dark tourism' into dialogue with that of Vidler's 'dark space'. Although for Vidler (1992, 173–74) dark space in architectural structure effectively neutralizes monumentality, in the travel context the dark city exists within an established social imaginary and, consequently, is as much a part of the orderly symbolic universe of urban space as any overtly monumental one. The traveller's focus on the secret city, and his dismissal of 'London's handsome face' / 'le beau visage de Londres' negates, to a certain extent, the validity of official monumentality, but, on the other hand, through the strategies of this travel practice, another kind of regulated picturesque appears, so that we might categorize Dyssord's portrayal of London's East End as establishing a series of 'dark monuments', for this contains within it the trace of the bright monumentalism essential for the emergence of its antithesis. These divergent types of monumentality operate within the opposition of the authentic and the inauthentic, where the authentic is equated with something that must be revealed to inhabit a secret space behind the transparency of the representations of space that sanction middle-class behaviours and create modern society's modes of inclusion and exclusion. MacCannell (1976) has understood the identification of the hidden with the authentic thus:

The problem here is clearly one of the emergent aspects of life in *modern* society. Primitives who live their lives totally exposed to their 'relevant others' do not suffer from anxiety about the authenticity of their lives, unless, perhaps, a frightening aspect of life suddenly becomes *too* real for them. The opposite problem, a weakened sense of reality, appears with the differentiation of society into front and back. Once this division is established, there can be no return to a state of nature. Authenticity itself moves to inhabit mystification. (93, original emphasis)

As intimated above, the authentic requires 'markers' so that the traveller can discern where to visit, where to look. The modern yearning for authenticity, of the tourist industry to appropriate all measure of representational spaces into its repertoire, and not least, the publication of the travel journal, leads to the eventual widening of this beaten track so that it comes to encompass the 'secret city'. In this schema, 'dark tourism' can be categorized, its naming verifying its status within the constellation of place as commodity and generative of a travel experience that can be marketed to a particular traveller type. Each discursive appropriation of the hidden city exposes it through more signs, and the emphatic association of the underground with the authentic results in a play of representations. Eventually, within the sphere of the secret city, this heterogeneous local gains picturesque status, understood in the urban context, as a space associated with cultures perceived to be removed from the values and norms of the dominant social class. In so doing, the local everyday spaces of the city's urban underclass enters the generalized realm of the symbolic, where representations such as Dyssord's contribute to the creation of a coherent mythology through the symbolic appropriation of all that stands apart from the 'official' identity of the metropolis. Exploring these issues through an analysis of Dyssord's representation of the East End of London in 1929, we might turn now to the legislative strategies used to negotiate London's 'dark space'.

On this point, Dyssord's localized representation of the English capital in *Secret London* has been compared with Vallès's images of an outcast London examined above (Schulz-Forberg 2005a, 270–71). However, while there is some similarity between the locations visited by both writers, the travellers' status as well as the historical contexts are profoundly different, as are the motivational paradigms within which the authors' respective representations are constructed. Dyssord's position in London in the late 1920s contrasts with Vallès's *exilé* status in the 1870s – in terms of free agency first of all, as well as in terms of the city they both visit. The urban landscape of 1920s London had altered considerably in the 50 or so years separating the two travellers. Dyssord's visit to London is in concordance with conventional definitions of the traveller – he has freedom of choice, and his stay sets up a short-term encounter (April–May 1929). With regard to the authors' respective representational spaces, Vallès's imagery reveals an anxiety in attendance at the birth of modernity; his bleak city is a condemnation of industrialization and its representatives. Dyssord, however, with his self-motivated quest, is afforded the luxury of fascination with, and empathy for, the slums of the East End. Nevertheless, it is noteworthy that the modern city with its technological and social advances barely appears in Dyssord's account, suggesting a deliberate evasion of these bright spaces, as shall be explored later on.

Dyssord's aim – of discovering 'by means other than hearsay, the lower depths of London' and 'in my turn, to rely on the people of this abyss'[11] (1932, 7) – operates within a framework of the picturesque that attaches specific significance to the East End. This reveals a development in the imaginative geography of the modern metropolis, and indicates a different range of markers for designating authenticity in the urban environment. As P.J. Keating has argued, prior to the 1880s there was no sense that the East End signified a particular social consciousness or was any different from any of the rest of 'outcast London' ([1973] 1999, 586–88). It was events such as the publication of Walter Besant's novel *All Sorts and Conditions of Men* (1882), the strike by Bryant and May match-girls led by Annie Besant in 1888, the Jack the Ripper murders in the same year and the London Dock Strike that led to the consolidation of a public image of the East End as an area possessed of an identity separating it from the rest of London – an identity rooted in poverty, debauchery and violent death, and that created an aura of fear around this area of the city. As the end of the nineteenth century approached, the sensational reputation and imagery associated with the East End became more nuanced.[12] An important literary figure in the recuperation of the East End from middle-class vilification was the journalist and novelist Arthur Morrison. In an article entitled 'Whitechapel', published in the *Palace Journal*, 24 April 1889, Morrison rejected two of the commonest stereotypes pertaining to the East End – that it was a criminal ghetto, and that its population consisted only of vagrants.[13] Morrison's study of the East End rejected the 'graphically written descriptions of Whitechapel, by people who have never seen the place' (1889, 20). Morrison's writing, most especially the prose of his early novel *Tales of Mean Streets* (1894), combines the monotony and minute detail of the attention paid to everyday life while also highlighting how poverty engenders its own degrees of respectability and creates hierarchies within the working-class community.

Morrison's success led to an upsurge in the publication of novels and short stories about the East End, and while many authors attempted to create their own unique visions of the area (see Keating [1973] 1999, 599), much of the writing rehashed Morrison by paying lip service to the nobility of the working class. However, novelists were quick to appropriate the East End in terms of oppositional stereotypes with another emergent space of representation, that of 'Brightest London' – the city of civility, speed and middle-class wealth – eventually receding into caricatures of working-class relationships, arbitrary violence and involving some aristocratic hero or heroine en route to self-redemption and class responsibility through their encounter. There were attempts to displace the East-End's monopoly on working-class representations of London, but, as Keating points out, 'by the very nature of its frequency this kind of response merely serves to emphasize the symbolic importance of the East End in this period, too central to be easily replaced, too firmly established for denials to have much effect' ([1973] 1999, 600). The American social reformist Robert Archey Woods, pointing out the symbolic resonance of the East End, stated that 'one feels a sudden chill, as when passing out of a warm breeze into another with a touch of winter in it. [...] East London will still continue to be thought of in a special way as the nether London' ([1895] 1896, 1–3).

Dyssord (1932) echoes Woods's analogy of the East End as a nether world representing 'the lower depth of the city', a dark space outside the boundaries of the middle-class metropolis. In his portrayal, as we shall see, the stability of Victorian narratives of the commoner as debauched or immoral fails; indeed, the conception of 'authenticity' that emerges in Dyssord's depiction of the East End evokes the dialectical notion of Rousseau's that civilization itself is somehow inauthentic.[14]

3.2   The Guide

Exploring what he perceives as the hidden arenas of the city, Dyssord's murky excursion is defined in opposition to a practice oriented around the bright, or orderly spaces of the renovated urban landscape:

> The West-End, a neighbourhood in the West, with avenues lines with rich residences and fairy-tale parks sit adjacent to the most sordid *slums*. The Eastern district, the East-End, running from the thrift shops of Whitechapel to the desolation of the Poplars where in basements scrawny children breath in a viscous air oversaturated with soot and coal, while pathetic groups of those unemployed meander through the mournful streets.[15] (7)

The dark tourist, then, always already exists within a legislative paradigm of dialectical opposition. As Kjell Olsen points out, 'The metonymic relationship between modernity, the copy and the tourist has become an opposition to the traditional, the original and the other' (2002, 176). In this way, the dark tourist emerges as a counter-subjective stance, looking for the sites where authenticity is supposed to exist. Dyssord's travel practice creates an urban juxtaposition wherein the traveller categorically divides the city in two so that the West End and the East End emerge as discrete cities. In the case of the West End, space is represented as homogenized and aestheticized. This city is equated with fiction – its gardens are like those from a fairy tale, those who live there believe that the city has been purified of its undesirable elements. The East End, in contrast, emerges as a space of misery, of decrepitude, but also of character – the alternative face of the modernized metropolis, the space where the environmental and human consequences of industrialization and exclusivity are revealed. For the dark traveller, those areas of the city that do not perform within the middle-class orders of convention, immediately assume an aura of truth.

This type of truth operates appositionally so as to undermine the transparent world of bright London. For example, when the traveller meets his guide, the first question this man asks Dyssord is 'Do you love the truth? (4).[16] The tramp justifies the question by explaining that 'the kind of fishing I do has made me acquainted with unpleasant places. These are not where guides bring tourists…'[17] to which Dyssord replies: 'I love the truth', while adding that he is 'looking him straight in the eye' (6).[18] Here, Dyssord clearly distinguishes himself from the common ideas of the tourist as one who is involved in a transactional, superficial experience with social space. Now constructivist theories in tourism studies have convincingly argued for the breakdown of the binary opposition constructed by MacCannell in his discussion of tourism and authenticity. Their position is that MacCannell's argument does not take into account the extent to which context and agency are engaged in shaping the touristic experience – whether from the point of view of the tourist or 'touristee'[19] – and that understanding tourists as actors engaged in social processes denies the binary of 'authentic'/'inauthentic' its power. Nevertheless, while this may be valid from an academic and anthropological standpoint, it is also true that during this period many tourists themselves construct their experience of the city along the lines of such a binary. Dyssord, in particular, mobilizes the trope of the 'authentic' and the 'inauthentic' as a means to validate his experience, but more than this, the trope becomes a means of engaging in what Taylor has identified as a peculiarly modern form of social criticism that emphasizes the intimate and the everyday as spaces where the truth of modern life can be revealed (see Taylor [1989] 2004). The monumental city, for Dyssord, becomes the fool's paradise of the tourist, while the truth is associated with all that lies beyond officialdom, with what corresponds to the dark spaces of the metropolis: the tourist city emerges as chicanery, against which the city of crime and villainy can emerge as intimate and substantial – the space of everyday interaction (no matter how suspect) – and, therefore, more real. In this scenario, the dark tourist nominates conventional tourism as unsuitable for authentic experience. By extension, hidden urban space acquires a symbolic status of increased value: the secret gains allure because it refuses the assumption that all communication is transparent.

As stated in chapter 1, the tourist or traveller is commonly seen as someone who exists outside the possibilities of such intimacy with the city. Nominating the East End as '*secret London*', implies that this area of the city has restricted access, that its social codes for interaction are specialized, and that its spaces are off-limits to outsiders. The traveller's capacity to enter this community, through the acquisition of a guide, therefore, puts him on the side of truth, adding value to his account, in the way that the more restricted something is the more precious access to it becomes. For the dark traveller to gain access to the secret city he must first ensure his interpretive integrity – he must prove to the reader that he is not a conventional tourist, and that he is prepared to delve into the city's depths (no matter how uncomfortable a position this puts him in) in pursuit of authenticity. This pursuit is constructed representationally as a quest for intimacy with the local population, and with demystifying institutional organizations, such as the prison, places that figure significantly in the lives of this 'deviant' community. Furthermore, in relation to the travel narrative, in order to guarantee the authenticity of his experience, the traveller employs certain strategies via which the reader can identify his account as that of a 'real' encounter.

One strategy for guaranteeing the authenticity of both the practice and narration of the dark city is the presence of a 'genuine' guide. Dyssord uses two guides to aid him in his exploration of London. The first is a beggar, although this man gets put in jail which forces Dyssord to look for another guide whom he finds in the person of John Jarvey, another local East-ender. When Dyssord begins his account, he is outside the Duke of York bar in Whitechapel, awaiting the arrival of the man who has promised to guide him around London's East End. In obtaining a guide, the traveller admits his status as outsider, and with that his limited knowledge of the foreign city, thus ensuring the mutual recognition of his readers. At the same time, however, obtaining a guide implies that the traveller now has unrestricted access to the inhabitant's urban knowledge. Catherine Bertho-Lavenir (1997, 161) has qualified the central role played by the guide in the interpretation of space: 'It is he who is in charge of transmitting a discourse intended to make sense of a place'.[20] Charged with rendering the space legible, the guide must be validated as an authentic member of the East End community in order to justify the authority of Dyssord's encounter. The guide must be a 'real local', preferably esteemed within the community, so that the traveller is assured of his level of penetration into the intimate workings of everyday life. By taking a guide, Dyssord further shifts the trope of the conventional tourist into a realm where a more diverse experience of the city will be offered. By employing a guide, Dyssord positions himself in contact with the 'natives' and, therefore, spatially and temporally incorporated into the everyday activities of life in the East End.

Dyssord communicates Jarvey's authenticity to the reader by emphasising the itinerant status of his guide and by contrasting this with his own social position as a middle-class gentlemen: 'One wouldn't imagine stopping an honest gentlemen in the way that the strange character with whom I have an appointment did' (2).[21] The travel writer further authenticates his account through the use of dialogue. The guide's dialogue is recorded in what appears to be straightforward testimony, and the use of colloquial phraseology furthers the impression that the traveller is in conversation with a genuine East-ender. Added to this, within the first sentences exchanged between them, the beggar reveals his knowledge of the dark spaces of the city, confiding to the visitor that he knows *Wormwood Scrubs*, a prison on the outskirts of the city.

The authenticity of Jarvey needs to be confirmed to the reader, however; if we are to follow Dyssord on his quest we need to trust that he has chosen his guide carefully. In another episode he approaches a female charity representative whom he knows to be acquainted with the slums of the city. The association of middle-class Londoners with deception and blindness sets up the contrastive power of the representation of John Jarvey, a working-class man from the East End. The writer's representation of the female charity worker's reaction to his request that she accompany him to these areas is revealing:

> When I expressed to her my intention to visit these undesirable slums in her presence she *recoiled*. The good Englishwoman that she was, I saw her *take refuge* behind the decisions of her Committee. I knew then that psychological *penetration* is not the forte of the daughters of Eve living on the other side of the Channel. Because these places that she *hid* from me with an offended modesty, such as the Chadwick slum, she should never have doubted that I would not stop until I had visited them. Likewise she was wrong to be so alarmed. Westminster is no worse than Edgware Road, Paddington and other places that seem to be a *repugnant ulcer on the beautiful face of London*.[22] (89, my emphasis)

The language employed here insists upon the notion that the woman is receding, literally, hiding from the truth, and that her concern is to conceal this truth from the traveller. The choice of words such as 'recoil', 'take refuge', 'penetration', 'hid' and 'modesty' reinforces the image of the city as a double space, where the bright city attempts to conceal the dark from the eyes of outsiders, and from itself; the lexicon of concealment constructs a façade, suggesting that behind the bureaucracy of officialdom there lies another, more 'true', layer of London. In a similar fashion to the juxtaposition of the

West End with Whitechapel and the Docks, the representation functions as an inverse standard of concealment by which to establish the legitimacy of Dyssord's East-End guide.

A further technique emphasizing authenticity is the use of direct speech and colloquial language. The replacement guide, Jarvey, is introduced as 'The Londoner who speaks slang the best' (82).[23] Once again this linguistic quality separates this community from those who speak standardized English. Dyssord establishes Jarvey as a more poetic and accomplished guide than those he has considered from the middleclasses: 'This quality [language] does not displease me, far from it. I have always loved slang and those who speak it. There is more poetry in them than a doctor of the Sorbonne' (82).[24] Here, techniques of dialogue can be understood as discursive processes functioning to establish the legitimacy of his account. Slang, as a hermetic linguistic code, draws defined lexical boundaries around its users, at once distinguishing their communication from the standard expression of the official city, and at the same time inhibiting comprehension between social groups. Its appropriation by the traveller, therefore, enhances the legitimacy of his account, while also differentiating him from the common tourist. Furthermore, in a similar manner to the secret, the hermeneutic preciosity of slang adds an aura of underworld erudition to his knowledge of the city. An American expert on slang, Joseph Matthew Sullivan gives us some contemporary insight into Dyssord's opinion: 'Slang is too big, too vital, too much a part of language (and a living part) for us to ignore it. [...] Victor Hugo thought criminal slang worthy of a chapter in 'Les Miserables' [sic]. Every earnest investigator of the underworld agrees with him' (1921, 15–16). This idea of slang as a vital dialect, reinforcing communal identities beyond the standardized world of the official city, infuses Dyssord's account with obscurity and, by extension, with a sense of danger. That the traveller will hazard misunderstanding and being misunderstood, that he will place himself at risk as an outsider in an underworld community, contributes to an image of the traveller as heroic urban adventurer, on a quest for authenticity and in defiance of those who would conceal it from him, and by extension, from the reader. By introducing slang here, Dyssord brings us to the arena of language as a dialogue, of the traveller operating as a prismatic intermediary between the external lifeworld of London, the interpreter and his reader.

Dialogue, as exchange and medium for meaning, is emphasized in order to represent the encounter with Jarvey, the traveller records his dialogue with him in direct speech. Thus particularity and proximity are the conditions within which the traveller establishes his material presence at the scene (see Mondada 2005), this is a form of intimacy that, as I have said, is normally considered outside the range of the tourist experience. Dialogue infuses the piece with the authenticity of direct testimony and reassures the reader as to the actuality of the events that follow. Furthermore, Dyssord often directly translates Jarvey's slang and places the standard meaning beside it in parentheses:

So, John Jarvey continued, drawing on his pipe, many people who have 'had hemp fever' (were hanged) or have gone, if you prefer 'to tend sheep by the light of the moon' are victims of *John Barleycorn* (whisky) or of *Old Tom* (gin). [...] Don't pay any attention to the people around us, *The Crown* is not a 'place' for you. I know another pub where I go sometimes, the *Horse and Groom* where you'll be in excellent company.[25] (83–84)

The lexicon employed here mediates between the transparent and the obscure, and this can be seen as a deliberate strategy on Dyssord's part to infuse the reader's experience with a sense of the unique and the authentic. On this point Cronin explains that, 'If names can get lost or distorted in translation, they can also been seen as "typical" in their untranslatability, their referential uniqueness' (Cronin 2000, 31). Recording Jarvey's subterranean language authenticates for the reader the otherness of this man and his world, while at the same time Dyssord's translations (not least that the entire conversation is translated from English to French) of Jarvey's slang permit the complete legibility of this underworld to his French readers.

Through this translation, furthermore, we can see how the French language is effectively unsettled in the contact zone with cockney slang. Dyssord, composing in his mother tongue, revisits French from the perspective of difference, and leaves multiple traces of the other peppered throughout his account (see Cronin 2000, 35). Authenticity, in this scenario, is also a question for language and puts us face-to-face with the difficulties and choices that the French traveller has to make when searching for a language that will communicate the otherness of experience to the reader, while making it comprehensible enough that the reader can perceive this authenticity. Dyssord must ensure that his reader can mediate between the familiarity of the French language that gives the reader access to English culture, while at the same time ensuring the play of difference remains to the fore by inserting English proper names and other nouns into the text. These perform as stumbling blocks to complete transparency, setting up another of Goffman's back spaces, where the reader is hesitant about the precise relationship between the sign and object – to what does slang refer? – and thus maintains the sense of authentic experience of the travel account. There is a sense here, too, of an unwillingness to translate certain idiosyncratic aspects of English, and in particular, working-class English, into the reader's mother tongue. This goes some way, perhaps, towards a validation of the difference not only between English and French cultures, but also between classes.

The traveller must infuse the dark codes of slang with light, he must articulate the sign object relation – he must ensure legibility after all – nevertheless, these dark codes act as forms of minor collision between the reader and the city. In order for the travel account to communicate its significance to a reader, therefore, it is necessary that transparency and obscurity, that 'bright London' and 'secret London', enter into tension with each other. To appropriate the dramaturgical terminology used by Goffman (1959), the traveller is forced to *stage* the authenticity of his account in order for it to acquire meaning for his middle-class reader. Within this interrelationship of transparency and obscurity, the traveller's agency functions doubly. On the one hand, Dyssord begins his encounter from a point of ignorance, gradually progressing to knowledge as he establishes a network of intimate relations with the community. On the other hand, it is he who uncovers this dark space for his readers, who reveals it as it is revealed to him. In this way, the traveller's decision not to translate certain of the slang words that Jarvey uses, while also rendering their meaning quite transparent, demonstrates the act of translation as fundamental to the travel writer's role as interpreter for his reader (Cronin 2000, 36).

3.3   Dark Tourism and Language

As we have seen, taking a guide adds an air of authenticity and colour to the travel account, but this act also functions to reveal the naivety of the traveller and to establish another level of identification with his reader. Just after he meets his first guide, Dyssord relates to the reader that he is about to explore the London underworld from a position of ignorance, and that in order to do this he will need the guidance of a local: 'My intention being to get to know the lower depths of London by means other than hearsay, I relied on the people of this abyss' (7).[26] This position is similar to that of the reader. First, Dyssord tells us that he is a 'gentleman' / 'honnête homme', out of place amid the dregs of the East End, and thus establishes a social rapport with his (presumed) middle-class armchair traveller-reader. Second, the traveller's implied ignorance at the beginning of his journey is a further mode of identification with the reader.

After rejecting hearsay, and thus establishing his reliability as a narrator, the author's proposal to rely on local inhabitants for information means that he is dependent on these individuals in order for the dark city to be revealed. Through the strategy of ignorance, then, the reader feels she is discovering the dark city alongside Dyssord. The use of the present tense, as well as dialogue, serves to increase the impression of transparency as well as temporality within the account. These techniques suggest that the city is revealing itself across time to both Dyssord and the reader simultaneously, and this serves to create a degree of empathy between the travel writer and his reader.

This impression of simultaneity, while creating a window of transparency into the obscurity of the East End, also produces dramatic tension within the text. The issue of the guide, the traveller's reliance on him, the subsequent loss of the guide, and the potentially dangerous situations in which the activities of the guide place the traveller, all function to create a degree of tension for the reader. By placing faith in the guide's testimony before his own immediate impressions, Dyssord performs here more as an investigator of the urban underground than as an authority figure. Furthermore, the traveller's assumption of the position of investigator suspends straightforward description. The expression accompanying this investigative role is the narrative mode of the question. Alongside descriptive techniques, a large part of the narrative of *Secret London* consists in dialogue. The dialogue is structured by a series of questions put to the guide by the traveller that the guide then goes on to answer. This suggests the traveller's state of anticipation and curiosity, at the same time that it creates these feelings in the reader. The nature of Dyssord's questions also furthers the impression of proximity and locality. Often these questions are directly related to local inhabitants and the immediate social surroundings of the traveller – people of whom Dyssord has heard by reputation, the 'characters' of the East End, or people who catch his eye because of their strange demeanour, drunkenness, furtiveness or social incompatibility. To take but one example, Dyssord asks Jarvey:

– Who are those two men seated at the little table, John? The old man with the bowler hat and the really young one wearing the cap.

He elbowed me and spat at his feet.

– The young one. A *fribbler*. Look at his lips, they're too red, and his effeminate air. There's no doubting it. The other is a pimp. This neighbourhood's overflowing with them, same as at Paddington, retailers without patents.[27] (84)

Thus, the traveller unveils London to his reader as he has it unveiled to him, through questions and answers. As can be seen from the above, these answers often take the form of anecdotes and reveal the underworld piece by piece through a series of dramatic descriptions. In other instances, the traveller's middle-class naivety is highlighted through the conversations that he has with his guide. While Jarvey explains how poverty drives a lot of young people to prostitution, Dyssord persists in questioning him on the actions of the police in the matter:

– And the police, John? I insisted.

My man absently took a puff. The he gave me a shifty look and said hastily:

– A *finger-post*, that's what they told you I was isn't it?
– A *finger-post*?
– Yes, an informer? Isn't that the reason you asked me that question?
– Not for all the world. That's the first I've heard of it John.
– 'My eye'! I'd be better kitted out if I was doing the *Johnny Darbies* my friend.

Johnny Darbies is a slang word equivalent to cops.

– With a few *james* (pounds), he went on, you easily plug the eye of the most curious detective. Everything in life comes down to 'ginger'.

At home we'd say dough.[28] (87)

Here, the position of the traveller is identifiable with that of his middle-class reader – he insists on knowing why the police are not doing anything about prostitution, he asks to have the slang Jarvey uses explained to him, he inadvertently offends the local man by implying that he is a police informant, and finally he has it revealed to him that the police are easily bribed. Not only, therefore, does the dramatic tension result from the traveller's consistent faux pas and the guide's series of revelations, but the nature of these revelations challenges the integrity of the institutional orders within the city. Through the guide, the masks of the bright city are continually uncovered. Furthermore, it also reveals how Jarvey, as guide and interpreter, essentially becomes an extension of Dyssord's self (the guide acts in the manner of a prosthetic self, enabling Dyssord's sense making processes) so that the traveller achieves self-definition (a sense of his values in the world and their confirmation) through the interpreter's confirmation of these values. As Taylor expresses it, the self cannot be a self on its own, but must coexist with others in complex 'webs of interlocution' (Taylor [1989] 2004, 36). And urban space in particular, with its diversity of class, national and ethnic identities sets up especially dense webs in this respect.

   By extension, Dyssord's relocation of the voice of authority from the middle-class governmental narrative to that of the local inhabitant generates the idea that there is another layer of knowledge, a more authentic layer, to be found in the subterranean locale of the deviant community. This is most evident in Dyssord's narration of his visit to Holloway prison.

3.4   Carceral Spaces and Transparency

In his analysis of the prison Foucault (1975) provides an evocative example of the social logic of order and control, drawing on the seventeenth-century city and the authoritarian practices that ordered urban space in times of plague. The measures enforced by the authorities at periods of infestation severely limited the movement of the city's inhabitants and travellers alike, essentially placing people in quarantine within their homes. Foucault explains how this city is monopolized by the signs of government:

> The plague city, penetrated completely by hierarchy, surveillance, watching, writing, the city immobilized through the functioning of an extensive power which bears down distinctly on each individual body – this is the utopia of the perfectly governed city.[29] (Foucault 1975, 232)

The philosopher sees these systems of quarantine as illustrative of the utopian dreams of any authority, a dream based ultimately on that authority's ability to regulate the movements of its inhabitants to the highest degree possible. In this context, the plague can be conceived as a motif for the organizational principle of disciplinary power; a moment of severe crisis that provides justification (all the more powerful for its being based in Nature) for the erection of controlling measures conditioning the spatial practices of the subject so that these become aligned with the discourses of the dominant. From the nineteenth century onward, this 'disciplinary grid'[30] (Foucault 1975, 232) is made manifest architecturally by buildings such as psychiatric homes, establishments of supervised education and hospitals, the penitentiary, and correction facilities. The latter, notably, is a site where, in certain cases, the panopticon's architectures of surveillance keep the prisoner in check through the real and imagined threat of his permanent visibility. The panopticon was an architectural construction of incarceration, as conceived by English philosopher Jeremy Bentham. Briefly, the structure was organized so that the prison guard could survey each cell without being seen. Operating in similar manner to forms of panoptic visibility, the ideologies of a dominant authority shape the structure of the entire city. Foucault sees the technologies of discipline embodied by the panopticon as illustrative of the nineteenth century's breakaway from darkness as something to be feared, and its simultaneous move toward the fear of exposure. He summarizes this psychosocial tendency in a comparison of the dungeon with the panopticon, 'All in all it inverts the principle of the dungeon, or rather its three functions – to enclose, deprive of light and hide – we keep only the first of these and suppress the others. Light and the gaze of a guard capture better than shadow, which in the end protects. Visibility is a trap' (Foucault 1975, 233–34).[31] The panopticon is expressive of a new kind of violence within society; that of the invisible, but all-seeing, eye. These architectural sites are identified by Foucault as instrumental in grounding normative discourses, and in the erection of binary dualisms according to which power consolidates itself; thus society is architecturally divided into 'mad/sane; dangerous/safe; normal/abnormal' (Foucault 1975, 232).[32]

In Dyssord's account the prison emerges as emblematic of the negative poles of these binaries, at the same time as its association with society's dregs and institutional cruelty make it a tantalizing space for the traveller. In addition to this, it is a space that (at least at this point in time), was considered inappropriate for the average tourist: '– You should not visit English prisons'[33] (43); Dyssord records his friends' warning to him before his departure from Paris. All of these elements combine to further the prison's attraction for the author, but the most important preconception which haunts Dyssord before his visit to Holloway prison is the diary of Oscar Wilde and the image of the suffragette Christabel Pankhurst. Both are representative for Dyssord of the legal institution's misplaced concern for a moral order that results in the incarceration and torture of the individual, all of which is hidden from public view. With Dyssord, the reader first encounters the English prison system through quotations taken from Wilde's *The Ballad of Reading Gaol* (1898),[34] producing an image of the prison as a space of traumatic persecution and government hypocrisy. Pankhurst's case is also given as evidence of institutional dissimulation and short-sightedness – when the suffragettes' cause emerged triumphant, the government erected a statue to her outside Parliament. These initial impressions of Holloway create a degree of tension before the traveller's visit, setting up the traveller to perform as agent in the exposition of governmental dissimulation. However, as MacCannell (1976, 50) explains: 'The becoming public of almost everything – a process that makes all men equal before the attraction – is a necessary part of the integrity of the modern social world'. The traditional social structure that had kept the prison hidden from the view of the public is recomposed by the governmental morality of transparency in the twentieth century, and further, by the tourist network that results from such morality. Clare Birchall confirms this tendency of modernity, saying, 'The ideal of open government and publicity, as one context for transparency, can be traced back (at least) to the rise of representative governments and Enlightenment thinkers such as Kant' (2011, 61). This is a modern ideal of secular, popular democratic government: to provide governance that is intelligible and accessible to the public. Dyssord's dark anticipations are, therefore, thwarted by the relative ease with which he gains access to Holloway.

The dark tourist's preconceptions are broken down through encounter. He expresses his gratitude to the Home Office for allowing him entry, and further, for providing him with governors to guide him, permitting him to taste prison food and giving him access to the inmates' cells. The traveller is initially sceptical towards this attitude of openness, and remarks sardonically: 'Would it be enough to express my gratitude by telling them that if I ever commit an infraction, my preference would be to commit it in London?' (46).[35] Without the difficulty of penetrating the prison, the mystery of this space evaporates, and the traveller is left to rely on his concrete perceptions, rather than imaginary constructs, in order to represent Holloway. The transparency of the space is almost an anticlimax for the dark traveller, then, and he notes that 'their prisons have in fact become models of comfort and hygiene' (46).[36] He proceeds to describe the architecture of the prison and its inner workings in terms antithetical to those he had anticipated, with the result that the impression of Holloway is one of complete transparency (indeed, in terms of its architectural arrangement Holloway is a panoptic structure):

> A brightness, a clinical neatness in the cloistered gardens and rooms we visited. No leprous or sullied walls, with those pictures and rasping letters that often afflict these places where human beings are collected up: schools, barracks, prisons. Everywhere daylight penetrates these workshops through large bay windows and glass roofs. [...] The cells are all the same, in each one the divisions between them are linked by a great gallery which joins them at the centre. The silence, a monastic silence reigns in each one, and only the muted steps of the guards troubles it, or those of the inmates busy with cleaning work.[37] (48, 50)

In display, the prison is reduced to an aesthetic experience for the traveller. Clare Garsten and Monica Lindh de Montoya propose that this level of governmental transparency is inscribed in political and cultural practices that 'not only suggest, but push for, a certain normative order', and they go on to explain that this is a way of organizing the sense of freedom that an individual has in society through their participation 'in the construction of his or her fate and of society-at-large. In such a vision of social life, the transactions between citizens and the state and within the economy must be open and observable in the interests of maintaining a level playing field for all concerned' (2008, 4).

However, and in conclusion, even this apparent display of bright space is renegotiated in the company of Jarvey. On his visit to Wormwood Scrubs prison, the traveller has much the same experience as he does at Holloway. While not all doors are open to him in this male penitentiary, he has the impression that 'after what I've been shown', the rumour of prison torture is, 'somewhat exaggerated' (72).[38] The traveller's naivety is revealed later on, when his guide Jarvey recounts how a friend of his was beaten in the prison in a room called 'The Triangle'. Dyssord disputes the existence of such a room, saying 'they showed me everything [...] that's what they assured me at least' (132–33).[39] To which Jarvey responds:

> You really don't think that after giving you a good impression of English prisons, the governor of one is going to be in a hurry to have you visit the torture room… No, you're dreaming, *old chap!*[40] (133)

Jarvey's revelation that the tourist cannot trust either the official guide, or what is presented to him as reality, confirms the existence of dark space within the city. While initially allowing the reader to identify with Dyssord, as the traveller's naivety is broken down by accession to intimacy with the social community of the East End, the revelation of his gullibility serves to justify the traveller's original suspicion of the bright city.

Birchall, in her discussion of Jacques Derrida's *Glas* (1974), however, reveals the extent to which the idea of the secret underlies all governmental pretence to transparency. For Derrida, implicit in the notion of transparency is the idea that a secret can be exposed and brought to light, in a similar thought process that would suppose a text can be fully understood. Derrida talks about the secret, not as something unknown, but as something that is fundamentally unknowable. This unknowability does not stem from the fact that it is particularly mysterious, but rather from the flaw in our understanding of presence. Texts, people, spaces, events and knowledge are not available to knowledge in the normative way that we suppose them to be. There is always some lack; some potential that exists outside the boundary of what can be discovered. As Birchall puts it, 'in any communication, any expression of knowledge, something is always "held back". What is "held back" is in no way held in a reserve, waiting to be discovered. Rather, there is a singular excess that cannot fully show itself: a non-signifying, non-present remainder' (Birchall 2001, 71). There is, therefore, always an absolute secret in existence at the limits of language, of culture and knowledge. Secrecy is, in this schema, constitutive. Going further then, the discourse of transparency is a discourse of violence, it essentially posits the erasure of the space of the other. Thus, for Birchall, 'Secrecy is always already at work in transparency' (2011, 71).

Returning to Dyssord's encounter with Jarvey in this instance then, the exchange here reveals a kind of radical sphere where the secret becomes the crossroads, across class and culture, where the two men share a common space. Dyssord's lack of knowledge forces him to the realization that all is not what it seems, that appearances cannot be relied upon. That he requires the other in the person of Jarvey to realize this is significant because it evokes a sense of contact across cultures, but also because there is the sense that complete legibility has been troubled. In the end, this ultimately serves within the account to reinforce Dyssord's position as an authentic traveller, and to confirm the existence of a 'secret' London, despite the superficial appearances to the contrary. The account ends with Jarvey's dismissal of the tourist: 'When a stranger comes to London, *old frick*, you show him the fattest Tower guard, he goes off, satisfied, saying: 'They live well along the Thames' (256).[41] Finally, in gaining approval for his distinctive travel practice from Jarvey, Dyssord seems to have achieved his aim – intimate acceptance that proves his authenticity and distinguishes him from the delusions of 'London on parade' / 'Londres de parade' (255).

3.5 Spaces of Quietude: Leroy's Forgotten London

These Alerts and All Clears have the unique power to disorganize the life of every citizen within earshot such as this country has never known before. Sometimes they seem quite irrelevant although one has a pleasant feeling of relief when the All Clear sounds, as though officially we could relax. [...] When the guns and bombs draw near we creep yawning into the pantry, make tea, help Victoria [the baby] suck barley-sugar, and eventually creep back again. One has the impression of all London and its suburbs leading similar lives. Last weekend Bob Kieffer apologized to Victoria on behalf of his generation for this humiliating state of affairs. [...] After the war we shall suffer a spate of information about wreckage, carnage, heroism, and fortitude. Or by then will everyone have grown tired of such tales? (Beardmore [28 August – 3 September 1940] 1984, 77–78)

Peace restores normality to this millennial city: the dawn of joyous days follows those of darkness. If profound changes, born of the world war, have transformed certain aspects of London, the maintenance of strong and nurturing traditions preserves its essential character.[42] (Leroy 1946, 223)

Alfred Leroy's account of London, *Londres et la vie anglaise / London and English Life* (1946), was compiled over the period 1938 to 1945, effectively spanning the duration of World War II.[43] While a reader might be justified in expecting an account of war-time experience in London (as in Charles d'Ydewalle's [1945] *Ici, Londres / Here, London*, for example), what is striking about this book is that the author does not give any immediate account of the war; rather he provides the reader with a guide, 'an initiation' / 'une initiation' (Leroy 1946, 223), to the capital's traditional monuments, historical areas of interest, and notably, to those areas within the city where the traveller can find respite from the rush of metropolitan activity. Little is readily available in biographical terms about Leroy's life. But it is clear that he was an author of renown, having written over 20 volumes – mainly in the field of art history – and having been awarded prizes by the *Académie française* for his books *Madame du Barry* (1942) and *Histoire de la civilisation anglaise* (1965). Leroy was clearly an Anglophile writing books such as *Aux bords de la Tamise* (1946), in which he provides the reader with an exposition on English landscape painting throughout the ages. To conclude this chapter I turn now to focus on Leroy's practice of London, which will form a point of contrast in relation to Dyssord, and also allow us to further our discussion on monumentality and nature in the modern city. Before we do this, in order to situate the absences at play in Leroy's version of what I have termed above 'bright London', and the account's strategies of sense-making it is important to contextualize historically. Some background to the realities of the city in the aftermath of the bombing raids of World War II will allow us to investigate better how Leroy's guide reads as a performed reinstatement of conservative ideals of historical tradition and pastoral repose, and how his narrative suggests a response to the threat to modern value systems as they emerged from World War II.

There had been some bombing in London during World War I, and some tragic loss of life.[44] During World War II, however, the intensity of this destruction increased to levels hitherto unimaginable. London, with its densely packed core, economic centrality and reserve of labour was an obvious and easy target. On 7 September 1940, 'Black Saturday', the Blitz began in London. Daylight and night-time raids caused such intense fires along the Docks at the East End that fire crews from the cities of Birmingham and Nottingham were brought in to assist with the damage. The city was bombarded virtually every night thereafter until an unofficial truce brought tentative peace three months later. By the end of 1940 London had suffered over 13,000 casualties – 40 per cent of the total casualties that the war would eventually inflict on the capital. Other attacks in 1941 caused significant damage – most notably on 19–20 March when the East End was once again set alight, and on 19–20 April when, in terms of weapons tonnage, London suffered the heaviest bombardment of its history (White 2001, 37–45).

In terms of infrastructure the capital proved more resilient than first thought, and the Luftwaffe never came close to completely destroying London. The damage, however, was tremendous. The most affected area was the City, or the metropolitan heart of the capital. Almost every building between Moorgate and Aldersgate Street was levelled. Older buildings suffered the greatest damage, while post-1900 steel-framed structures better withstood the onslaught. White remarks: 'It did not seem much like it at the time, but the Blitz was […] a great modernizer, shifting great swathes of central London and the East End decisively into the twentieth century' (White 2001, 39). At the time, however, the outlook of many was not so resilient. The Anglo-Irish novelist Elizabeth Bowen writes of the eerie silence and stillness that descended on the metropolis:

> London looked like the moon's capital, shallow, cratered, extinct […]. People stayed indoors with a fervour that could be felt: the buildings strained with battened-down life, but not a beam, not a voice, not a note from the radio escaped. Now and then under the streets and buildings the earth rumbled: the Underground sounded loudest at the time. (1945, 173)

The 'fervour that could be felt' affected Greater London and the city centre alike, with the result that the class-based psychic division between the suburb and the City was no longer so easily tenable. The suburbs, which had suffered vilification from the urban core for decades, were transformed in the popular imagination by collectivist ideas, a desire for improvement and a better life, all of which came to represent the values of wartime England and modern morality's ideas of human dignity and community in the twentieth century. Films such as *Mrs Miniver* and *In Which We Serve* from 1942, *This Happy Breed* (1944) and *Brief Encounter* (1945) facilitated this shift in the geographical imagination, which was concretized by the mass exodus of people into the city's neighbouring countryside. Over the war, consecutive series of evacuations brought with them the first drop in inner London's resident population, which fell to 2.3 million in 1941 – a drop of 43 per cent. Even by mid-1945 there were only 2.6 million civilians living in inner London and 6.7 million in the entire city. It was not until 1951 that Greater London approached its pre-war population at 8.2 million, but the inner city, at 3.4 million citizens, was still down 15 per cent on its 1939 census figure (General Register Office [1955] 1956, xiii). The war thus brought to a halt the many centuries of steady growth in London, shaking the image of the city as a great maw swallowing the population of England and drawing its citizens ever nearer to the 'inevitable' urbanization that the narratives of modernity had thus far emphasized.

It was only when the hostilities ceased that Londoners could sit back and take stock of their city. The devastation was enormous – so great in fact that certain bomb craters in the less centralized areas of the city were discernible until the end of the twentieth century. Much of the City's medieval street pattern and densely packed Victorian warehouses and office blocks had been razed to the ground. Acres of housing had been demolished in the East End and dockside areas, but nearly every neighbourhood was scarred by the air raids (Cole and Howard 1956, 370–72). The extent of the effects of the war cannot, however, be gleaned from statistical information alone. In *La Ville en Guerre* (1986), a special edition of the periodical *Autrement*, Éric Sarner hypothesizes that war, and most particularly the destruction of entire cities as was the fate of Hiroshima and Nagasaki in 1945, caused modern society to lose faith in the inevitability of modernist trajectories towards transparency and greater technological progression:

> Let's risk a hypothesis on a moment from which 'transparency' disappeared. A moment: between the end of the Second World War and My-Laï. A place perhaps, completely black, a blackness hitherto unseen, the epicentre of which might be located somewhere between Hiroshima and Nagasaki. […] If anything irreversible happened then to our way of seeing and our imagination, it was that the world contracted and also that many of us became, in the years following, people of big cities and the cities became more than ever before what they had always been: a game of high stakes.[45] (6)

From World War II onward, London could no longer consider itself either impenetrable or independent of other nations for the security of its existence. And while, perhaps, national pride remained solidly intact in the aftermath of victory, the individual experience of the war could not be easily reconciled with imperial ideologies expounding the inevitable might and right of English culture; this culture having found itself under serious threat of extinction. Leroy's account can be read in terms of the attendant anxiety that the war introduced to daily life in the city.

It is amid this ruined urban landscape that Leroy produces his account of London. However, the French traveller's practice of the city does not provide the reader with any concrete impression of the aftermath of the war or the chaos wrought upon the metropolitan landscape; rather the interest of his account lies in its omission of any such information, and its concentration on London's ancient historical monuments and oases of landscaped parks within the city centre.

The legislative frameworks structuring this account are structures that work at an avoidance of the present. This avoidance can be seen in terms of loss, but also it speaks to a need to forget. Augé (1998) sees forgetting as fundamental to the functioning of modern society and its individuals, as well as to the orientation of memory in social space. In *Les Formes de l'oubli* (1998, 75–79) Augé notes three stages involved in the process of forgetting: suspense, return and recommencement. Leroy's representation of the historical and garden areas of the metropolis are suggestive of the above processes and, as we shall see, imply that the monument facilitates a process of forgetting the trauma of the recent past, and serves, therefore, to ward off anxiety about an uncertain future.

Augé names 'suspens' / 'suspense' as one of the figures of forgetting, of which 'the first aim is to find the present by temporarily separating it from the past and the future and more precisely forgetting the future to the extent that this is identified with a return to the past' (1998, 77).[46] In spatial terms, Leroy's (1946) attempt to suspend the past and future temporalities of urban existence in post-war London is made manifest in his attraction to the inner city's parks. These green areas are associated with relief and repose and, correspondingly, London is seen as a city that retains 'refuges against the noise, the hurry, the intrepid rhythm of modern existence' (29).[47] The traveller's orientation towards Hyde

Park is motivated by an intention to suspend all outside influence, 'to go without precise aim [...] to stroll along these noble pathways' (13).[48] Here, the narrative is related in the present tense; a mode of expression that allows for the elimination of all other temporal states, anchoring the description in the immediacy of the current moment, and 'In the end,' Augé tells us, 'it is always in the present tense that forgetting is conjugated'[49] (1998, 78). This present is described in idyllic, pastoral terms. Leroy consistently appropriates the park's landscape to stress the peaceful and harmonious atmosphere of the scene. However, the major function of this space is revealed in the interpretation of it as an area of natural landscape permitting the traveller to forget the existence of the city beyond it. In this account Nature is idealized, not in terms of the picturesque or the sublime, but in the soft, anxiety-free lexicon of the beautiful:

> Hyde Park is not a garden, but a corner of nature, its beautiful views give the impression that nothing limits the horizon. Its trees provide numerous peaceful, solitary retreats; its lawns muffle the walkers' footsteps. Having left behind the feverish life of a capital city, we come upon a place devoid of traffic, a place where isolation is still possible, amid the sky, the foliage and the shadows.[50] (16)

The disassociation of Hyde Park from human influence, presented here as artifice, places it within the realm of an uncontaminated, quixotic, dream-like arena. The emphasis is placed on the absence of the human element – even the lawns absorb the sound of other people's footsteps – although, of course, the use of the word 'lawn' alerts the reader to the extent to which Leroy projects an idealized vision of Nature onto a landscaped area of the city. The significance of Hyde Park lies not, therefore, in its authenticity as a natural space, but in the way in which its careful planning facilitates the imagination's flight into 'pure' nature. Notably, it is a space designed to counteract the metropolitan landscape, and in this light such an imaginary of the green park could not emerge without the antithetical existence of the city. But the question of authenticity is not of concern to Leroy. The problems of industrial civilization and the questions it raises are no longer of any importance here; rather, if the illusion of a natural space facilitates the self's need for peace and repose, then this is sufficient:

> We have the right to break with society, which daily saps our passion, our thoughts, which leaves us without a minute to ourselves, which is the implacable mistress of our lives from the moment we wake up to the moment we go to sleep. [...] The middle of Hyde Park and Kensington Gardens allows for forgetting, moral isolation, things that are unheard of in the modern cities of the continent.[51] (17)

I am using the term 'self' here in the sense emphasized by Taylor where he deploys the term to 'speak of people as selves, meaning that they are beings of the requisite depth and complexity to have an identity' (Taylor [1989] 2004, 32). This is a self, thus, who seeks to make sense of society and, in this way, is oriented in a 'space of questions about the good, that it stand somewhere on these questions' (Taylor [1989] 2004, 32). This is akin to the Heideggerian position that we cannot exist as Dasein without some such orientation in the world, and that what I am as a self in the world is defined around the ways that things become meaningful for me. Here, the interpretive frame which the self uses to articulate its position in the world becomes key in settling the identity in relation to its point in time, space and society. We move, as Taylor puts it, in a space of questions 'as we seek to find an orientation to the good' (Taylor [1989] 2004, 34). In a war-torn landscape such questions become more urgent, and also more collective – the question of meaning and the orientation of European society towards the good is profoundly problematic in the aftermath of total and nuclear war. War in a sense must constitute a disruption to what Pierre Bourdieu terms the 'habitus', 'the ways we are taught to behave, which become unreflecting, second nature to us' (Taylor 2001, 187). A society at war forces an adaptation in the behaviour of social groups, but most notably it forces the self to renegotiate the boundaries of what constitutes the good. The experience of World War I and World War II in Europe destabilized ethical norms of interpersonal relation – society's formulation along an increasingly secularized moral platform of individuals conceived as beings with a natural, equal right to dignity and respect – which, since the Enlightenment, had slowly (and not without struggle) become unreflecting and second nature.

The traveller's strategy in the face of this space of uncertainty is to turn inwards, and to sketch what we might term a 'moral topography' (Taylor [1989] 2004, 111), through engagement with Nature in the city. This 'inwardness' as Taylor identifies it, is particularly constituent of the self in modern society (Taylor 2001, 111). Escape from reality and the simultaneity of the modern city is necessary to the traveller, so that London is strategically positioned, not in terms of the stimulating perspectives that the city provides, but in terms of how well it integrates spaces of repose and reflection that facilitate the illusion of solitude. The crowd is rejected in favour of a return to a space of interior life, where the traveller can expel the contingency of urban existence to dwell within the imaginary safety of his own mental landscape. Leroy's freedom from the devastation is found in the deliberate avoidance of the metropolitan throng. It is, however, only through the implicit presence of the crises-ridden metropolis that the immensity and value of the relief found in isolation emerges. The freedom to be found in forgetting is, therefore, expressed in terms of a flight back to Nature and to the enduring orders of the natural world. The expanse of Hyde Park (350 acres) and the adjacent 275 acres of Kensington Gardens constitute a space larger than the Principality of Monaco, and thus ensure the traveller's physical and sensory distance from the urban landscape. The vastness of the park is not to be underestimated here, in its sensory difference from the noise and smells of the city in ruins, it provides geographical access to an inner moral topography, one that remains intact and faithful to peace, repose and the values of civilized society. In Leroy's account Hyde Park functions to allow external landscape to segue into a topography of order and stability, and the account seems to resonate with symbolism that is all the more intense due to the reader's awareness that this haven constitutes a fragile remnant of order amid the ruin and chaos of central London in 1945. We can identify here a perspective on human nature that echoes what Lionel Trilling calls 'the visionary norm' of 'the noble life' (Trilling 1972, 40), a norm built on the moral values of order, peace, honour and beauty. These are the values attained by Leroy in Hyde Park, whose long history provides the traveller with some reassurance as to the possibility for things to endure.

3.6   Reconstructing London

Propelled by similar motivations, Leroy returns to sites of London's ancient past in a rejection of the consequences of industrial warfare, as a means of reconfirming the durability of the monarchical values of traditional civilization and of recuperating meaning in the ruined city. Augé (1998) points out that 'memory itself needs the process of forgetting: it is necessary to forget the recent past to return to the ancient past' (7).[52] The idea can be reversed: recovery of the ancient past facilitates the process of forgetting the recent past. For Leroy, exploring the ancient past through encounter with the historical monuments representative of England's monarchical and governmental tradition reassures the traveller as to the longevity of the morality and customs of European civilization.

This again leads us into the domain of authenticity, this time with respect to the idea that a culture or nation is built on an assemblage of essential, or core, characteristics, and that these endure across time. This in a sense constitutes a refusal of Time, as it harbours a longing for an essential, static source of meaning. In the context of tourism, John Taylor sees this kind of authenticity to be dependent on the reproduction of a myth of origins. For Taylor, 'tourism sites, objects, images and even people are not simply viewed as contemporaneous productions, or as context dependent and complex things in the present. Instead, they are positioned as signifiers of past events, epochs, or ways of life. In this way, authenticity is equated with the "traditional"' (Taylor 2001, 9).

A crucial stage in returning to the ancient past as a mode of forgetting is, Augé states, the forgetting of the present moment and 'the immediate past with which it tends to be confused – so as to re-establish a continuity with a more ancient past, eliminate the simple past and replace it with the pluperfect' (1998, 76).[53] Rupture with the recent past to return to a more authentic or original state is evident throughout Leroy's text, most notably in his present tense descriptions of buildings that no longer exist at the time of writing. In this use of tense then, Leroy maintains the illusion of the travel account's simultaneity with the present, but this is essentially a return to the past through the present: an attempt to set into motion, therefore, the values of tradition by restoring iconic buildings to the present. For instance, he describes in detail the House of Commons, outlining its architectural layout as well as the paintings hung on its walls:

> The Chamber of Commons is decorated with twelve windows bearing the coat of arms of towns and municipalities; the speaker's seat sits at the northern-most end of the room [...]. Coming out of this room, where so many souvenirs appeal to the imagination, one must cast a glance at *Saint Stephen's Hall*, a former chapel, completely restored in 1834, a grand staircase leads to Westminster Hall.[54] (1946, 140)

At the bottom of the page a footnote to the reader alerts her to the fact that 'the Chamber of Commons was completely destroyed by air raids' (140).[55] Similarly, the oak ceiling of Westminster Hall is lauded as 'one of greatest *existing* wonders of England'[56] (141, my emphasis), while the area of Temple Bar is described as possessing 'the charm of old shields from the encroachment of modern life, it is a place for repose, for strolling, flights of the imagination [...] the activity surrounding it is forgotten amid these old stones, these shady gardens, images summoning fantasies of the XVth century' (141).[57] Again, both eulogies of these places are tempered by footnotes testifying to their demise, with the ceiling joists of Westminster Hall having been burnt during air raids and the Temple ravaged by the war (141).

This technique of conjugating the past in the present and the present in the past perfect tense, suggests the prioritization of the French imperfect tense – the past of London before the war. While the footnotes contribute to book's nostalgic mode.

The traveller's descriptive panegyric of these ruins effectively reconstructs the past as though it were still a reality, and one of the 'must sees' for the tourist reading this account. Drawing the eye downwards to the reality contained in the footnote, therefore, produces a sense of loss, making the main-text description poignant for the effective illusion set up by the piece's grammatical structure. The effect is that the ancient past of London is positioned as the authoritative, legislative reference point for deciphering the city's spiritual reality. This is, given Leroy's Anglophilia, perhaps not surprising. Restoring the buildings through text – or 'architexturally' – is akin here to restoring the traveller's faith in the persistence of the English way of life. Lefebvre points to the necessity of space for maintaining a world-view: 'What is an ideology without a space to which it refers, a space which it describes, whose vocabulary and links it makes use of, and whose code it embodies?'[58] (Lefebvre [1974] 1991, 44). The values of tradition are reconstructed through Leroy's visits to sites such as Hampton Court and Windsor Castle, where monarchs are represented as an impenetrable bastion to safeguard civilization: 'They constitute an incomparable force against dangerous risks, destructive and perilous desires' (1946, 106).[59] He also visits various museums housing artefacts testifying to the cultural status of the English Empire, most notably that of the Imperial Institute Museum:[60]

> The British Empire with its resources, its diverse peoples, its faraway lands, the British Empire in its immensity, but also in its unswerving union, its loyalty, its moral grandeur, an Empire just as it was after centuries of effort and work by the subjects of Queen Victoria, it given to us to see here thanks to the panoramic collections of the Imperial Institute Museum.[61] (201)

This accumulation of the past, on display in the museum, is appropriated as a means of sanctioning the eternal character of English imperialism, and of placing it beyond the contingencies of history. The museum functions for the French traveller as a space where discourses of civilization and imperial security can be perpetuated. Paula Findlen (1989, 60) comments on the importance of the museum for political discursive practice, demonstrating how 'as a repository of past activities, created in the mirror of the present, the museum was above all a dialectical structure which served as a meeting point in which the historical claims of the present were invoked in the memory of the past'. Within the context of Leroy's account, the museum is rather the spatial repository of past activities that furnish the reconstitution of the present in terms of an inevitable victory. Imperialism is represented as a vital and inextinguishable force in the shaping of modern civilization, 'as vital as air and freedom' (202).[62] The museum functions, then, as an occasion for the reinstatement of order, where the ancient past is appropriated in terms that avoid consideration of the recent trauma endured by London. While the museum's artefacts are a result of concrete and cumulative historical processes, the museum is appropriated by the traveller in conciliation with this place's tendency to efface historical complexity and to reconstruct history in conjunction with ideologies that justify the State's existence. In effect, Leroy's practice of the museum serves to neutral-ize the violence of imperialism, and thus participates in the creation of a mythology of the inevitability of England's endurance decided in particular relation to the country's monarchical tradition. Whether this is an attempt to explain the capitulation of France in terms of the country's republican form of government is not clear from the account, although it is certainly a tenable hypothesis as Leroy identifies monarchy as the key to a harmonious and durable civilization, expounding that 'the most just harmony exists, a harmony developed over time, which removes all worry, is beyond all criticism, and any imaginable reform – royalty' (106).[63] This suggests that popular democratic forms of critique lead only to weak government and expose the country to disharmony. It is, furthermore, a statement that denies the complexity and centrality of the English parlia-ment to governmental order in England.

The strategies of forgetting that Leroy deploys permit London to be read, then, from within the confines of the spatiality of tradition and repose. Leroy's London is erected upon a discourse of stability and continuance enabled by the monumentality of the idyllic and the ancient past and facilitates amnesia with regard to the destruction of the recent past:

> Everywhere history solicits the imagination, everywhere it is intimately bound to modern life. We find ourselves in places rich with memories, in places where man has never ceased working, hoping, improving, fighting for the glory of England, for their own wealth. [...] *For centuries, generation has followed generation, and never for a moment has the machine stopped.* [...] A world is summoned up, with every step, a ghost world, of which historians will recount the efforts, the courage, the tenacity, the imperious will.[64] (107, my emphasis)

It is this process of forgetting – emergent here through the textual reconstruction of spaces that might house a perceived set of authentic, enduring values – that ensures the recovery of a sense of integrity and identity necessary to overcome the feeling of loss, resultant from the war, of the innocence of modernity's Enlightenment ideals as well as to suppress the anxiety attendant on urban life in a nuclear age.

Chapter Four

WANDERING GEOMETRY: ORDER AND IDENTITY IN NEW YORK

As Karl Rossmann, a poor boy of sixteen who had been packed off to America by his parents because a servant girl had seduced him and got herself a child by him, stood on the liner slowly entering the harbour of New York, a sudden burst of sunshine seemed to illuminate the Statue of Liberty, so that he saw it in a new light, although he had sighted it long before. The arm with the sword rose up as if newly stretched aloft, and round the figure blew the free winds of heaven.

Kafka [1946] 1962, 3

Manhattan as the product of an unformulated theory, Manhattanism, whose program – to exist in a world totally fabricated by man, i.e., to live inside fantasy – was so ambitious that to be realized, it could never be openly stated.

Koolhaas [1978] 1994, 9

Men go to America to escape from God, from all the prohibitions of history.

Conrad [1998] 1999, 518

The imaginative geographies of twentieth-century New York, a time when the city was considered by many to be the capital of the world (perhaps the last), provide the impetus for discussion in this chapter. While imperialist Europe may have dominated the nineteenth-century's imagination of civilization, in the wake of two world wars, the twentieth century witnessed the dislocation of a geopolitics dominated by European imperialist expansion, and the establishment of a new global political order increasingly dominated by the capitalist market economy and American foreign policy. This shift of power within the West was also fundamental for the establishment of New York City as the pinnacle of what it meant to be modern in terms of Western culture. Modernity, with its attendant discourses of high and low culture, Futurism and nostalgia, internationalism and nationalism, hope and despair, finds an alternative, non-European mode of expression in New York, with the result that throughout the cultural-historical turbulences of the last century, this metropolis has consistently provided a position of difference from which Europe could articulate its modernity.

Western Europe[1] has always been crucial in producing the imaginative geography of New York City and determining its position within a global symbolic order. From Europe's discovery of America onward, one of the processes that scholars identify as fundamental to the European construction of American space is the elimination of chaos and the Otherness of difference through simplification. When Henry Hudson 'discovered' New York in 1609, all previous meanings of this stretch of land were obliterated. In April 1609, Hudson, along with a small crew of English and Dutch seamen, set sail from Amsterdam to cross the Atlantic on board their ship the *Half Moon*. Hudson's skills as a navigator were employed by the Dutch East India Company, who hired him to find a long sought after northern passage to the Orient. On the northward journey the cold was severe, and mutiny threatened the ship's progress. Although the captain had been ordered to return to Holland if no northern route proved possible, Hudson, determined to continue, changed course to the south. Steering along the North American coast, he first entered Chesapeake Bay, followed by Delaware Bay, before sailing up what is now the river into New York Harbour on 11 September 1609. From this moment, the typological landscape of the land mass was determined by Europe. Certeau states that place-naming is a relationship born from the users' lack of place, as he sees it, 'an indication of the relationship that spatial practices entertain with […] absence [of place] is furnished precisely by their manipulation of and with "proper" names' (Certeau 1984, 103). In terms of the European concern to fill in the places on what was for them a blank map, the Native American river, the *Muhheaknuuk* (great waters constantly in motion), became the 'river of the mountains', before becoming the 'Hudson River'. Likewise, *Manhatta* becomes *Manatvs*, which becomes Manhattan, while New Amsterdam gives way to New York. From the onset of Europe's colonization of American space, the conceptual framework for understanding the American Other has been, in the words of the critic Plinio Freire Gomes, an exercise in 'blank variations' (2005, 85). In his analysis of Renaissance cartographic practice, Gomes illustrates how insufficient vocabulary to describe and the inability to map unexplored territories in the 'New World' led to the explosion of Western European horizons for knowledge. Gomes sees the American space as generative of a 'crisis of expression' (96), in that the vast unknown of the American landscape – its cultures, cities, flora and fauna – defied description, and thus undermined conventional European categories for the classification of knowledge. The appellation 'New World' can be interpreted as a means of comprehending the Unknown in European terms; via the adjective 'New' the Unknown is relativized in Eurocentric terms, while Europe in its turn becomes an 'Old World' in the aftermath of America's discovery. Appropriating the continent in terms of its newness essentially reinvents the space as an extension of Western Europe. Leaving blank spaces on the map was consistent, therefore, with an ideological vision of the continent as a *tabula rasa*, and that vision allowed the European West to establish a free, geometrical, and discursive plane via which native America might be stripped of all prior substance (Gomes 2005).[2] As the critic Peter Conrad puts it, 'America was invented in order to save divisive, oppressive Europe from itself', and thus performed as 'a conscience in exile across the ocean' ([1988] 1999, 501). America was the virginal terrain for Europe's regeneration, a model space where all desirable elements for society that were spatially and temporally dispersed across the Old World could be assembled in a single place. According to the architect Rem Koolhass, the earliest representations of New York City by French engraver Jollain were 'an urban science fiction' ([1978] 1994, 15), and the product of a utopian wish for the city to function as a blank conceptual space where Europe could start again. Koolhaas goes on to say:

America is a self-evident invention: a conjuring trick. All the components of the map are European; but kidnapped from their context and transplanted to a mythical island, they are reassembled into an unrecognizable – yet ultimately accurate – new whole: a utopian Europe, the product of compression and density. (15)

New York's prodigious, and hitherto inconceivable, geometric landscape will be examined here as a space where Europe asks the question of what it means to be modern in the twentieth century. While Europe was still recovering from the effects of World War I, the American cultural and economic scene only benefited from the boost that the material demands and unifying ideologies of war provided. We might say that despite the Wall Street Crash of 1929 and the Great Depression, America was never threatened with the loss of its civilization, was never forced to re-evaluate its faith in rationalist progress, in the same way that post-war Europe, and in particular post-Occupation France was. American modernity, therefore, becomes the dominant scene of discourses of progress in the twentieth century. It is the space where Europeans express their anxieties about the loss of past faiths and the possibility of future ones, where they ask what individuality might consist of in a world increasingly powered by machines, and more practically perhaps, how communities might be sustained in an architectural landscape designed for the convenience of the motorcar. And, what effects do post-industrial capitalism and its media intrusion hold in store for the psychological well-being of the individual and society. Moreover, the extremism of this city's architectural dimensions, along with the eclecticism of its social fabric, seem to provoke questions pertaining to humankind's destiny in the widest sense. New York as 'theatre of progress' (Koolhaas [1978] 1994, 12) begs the question of where the human race is headed. For the sky – as the aspirational verticality of the city's skyscrapers might suggest – towards a utopian society based on the meritocratic democracy of the capitalist market? Or for cataclysm – where New York's Promethean architecture becomes legible as Babelesque hubris – towards the inevitable decline predestined for all decadent metropoles, the end of 'traditional' community, and the subjugation of ethnic and historical identities to the categorical efficiency of the metropolitan grid? What is the position of the individual within a system which, through its architectural and cultural expression, seems to urge conformity? These are the identifiable concerns in French encounters with the city, and the paradigms within which New York becomes legible to the outsider. The discursive exploration of the potential shape of modernity that takes place in New York is revealing of a deep emotional investment in the urban landscape that fluctuates between fascination, awe and profound hope on the one hand, and deep-rooted anxiety and a feeling of impending doom on the other. Very often all of the above emotions are identifiable within a single account. One of the concerns of this chapter is to trace the shifting discourses of the French traveller through an engagement with the above questions. In an analysis of travel writing by Paul Morand (1930) and Jean-Paul Sartre (1945), this chapter explores, then, how New York City, as 'theatre of progress', becomes a privileged space for the evolving crises in modern identity over the twentieth century.

Due to the vastness of a topic such as 'modernity', and the richness of the debate contained within the travel texts, I focus here on the traveller's encounter with the geometry of the city's built environment. In giving space to discuss Morand and Sartre, and Perec and Baudrillard (in the next chapter) in some depth, I have had to make choices with regard to the material studied here. New York appears in numerous French travel accounts across the twentieth century. To name a significant few, Georges Duhamel's *Scènes de la vie future* (1930) won the Grand Prix de l'Académie française in its condemnation of consumerism, collectivism and the reverence for technology; Simone de Beauvoir's *L'Amérique au jour le jour* (1954) explores the city using the frameworks of the circadian narrative and notably critique's race relations in the United States through her representation of Harlem; Albert Camus's *Les Pluies de New York* ([1965] 1975) contains similar preoccupations to those of Sartre in placing Nature at the heart of his impressions of the city; meanwhile Edgar Morin and Karel Appel in their bilingual illustrated book, *New York la ville des villes / New York City of Cities* (1984) renders the city's transnational melting pot and draws into relief the presence in New York of extreme wealth alongside extreme poverty. These texts are each fascinating in their own way, my choices have been made out of a concern to deal in relative depth with a few representative texts. Each writer finds his or her pathway through the city, and the twists and turns of these paths merit close attention; in the same way that one would not try to 'say everything' within a discussion of fictional literature, then, I have felt the need to reserve the texts above for closer commentary elsewhere. In addition, in choosing to organize the subsequent chapters around the architectural spaces of representation of the city, I have chosen the texts studied across the next two chapters for the attention they pay to the relationship between the figured city of architects, planners and administrators and the articulation of space as it is lived at a particular historical moment, as well as for the interest which their poetic spatial practices hold for the discussion of modernity that we have been weaving throughout this book.

For the writers discussed, the prodigious geometric patterns of New York are a means of visualizing and practising the city in material terms; moreover the interpretation of the horizontal and vertical orders of the urban landscape is often key to how the American Other is represented. By focusing on the imaginative geographies of New York's geometry that emerge within these travel accounts, this chapter examines how the city's architectural arrangement informs the writer as to their European identity, articulated as a response to American space and to the legislative conceptual frameworks within which America is understood. The gridiron (horizontality) and the skyscraper (verticality) are important discursive structures in the narrative strategies for rendering legible the American other and questions of identity (social and individual), as well as order (architectural synchrony and diachronic historicity) are central to the observations on the city presented here.

4.1   Reading the Grid

The analysis of these travellers' practice of the city's geometry raises the question of how European travellers read and write the city: what hermeneutic codes do they use in order to make New York meaningful, and how do these codes affect the city's representation in the travel journal? Both panoramic and quotidian scenes feature in both of the travel journals analysed here, but the question is to see how these scenes are prioritized and valorized in terms of the writer's overall discourse on New York. A final question might be whether changes in narrative practice of how the grid is appropriated (as real and representational pattern) tell us anything about concerns for French identity as these have evolved over the twentieth century. In seeking to answer these questions, this chapter examines how these travel writers' representations of the city generate discursive physiognomies for New York's architecture and trace discourses of progress articulated through the American urban experience.

For the European within the 'maelstrom' (Berman [1982] 1988), the city that best articulates the vast, frightening and exhilarating change attendant to modernity is New York. Perhaps the fascination, fear and fondness Europe has for the city can be attributed to the considerable role New York has played in the lives of Europeans who left their homeland in search of a place in which to begin again. Perhaps the attraction of New York has more to do with the eclecticism of the city's urbanity, or perhaps it is to do with the city's potential to constitute the Mecca of the American dream. Many reasons single out New York as a city central to Europe's historical identity. For the first time in the history of the West, New York's spatial extremities provided perspectives on the city inconceivable prior to its construction, offering civilization a modern equivalent to the Egyptian pyramids or the Aztec city of Technotitlan. And if, as the geographer Edward Soja (1996, 1) asserts, 'we are becoming increasingly aware that we are, and always have been, intrinsically spatial beings, active participants in the social construction of our embracing spatialities', then New York City may be viewed as a climactic space for the European traveller, its extremities accentuating their sensibility to the social and historical significance of the urban environment and personal and collective identities within it.

In his essay, 'Sémiologie et urbanisme' / 'Semiology and Urbanism' (1967), Barthes comments on the 'objective' impulse inherent in modern conceptualizations and expressions of urban space and sees this impulse as inherently symbolic:

> Scientific geography and modern cartography in particular can be considered are as a kind of obliteration, a censure that objectivity has imposed on meaning (objectivity being a form – like any other – of the imaginary).[3] ([1967] 2002, II: 1277)

New York's gridiron is not an invention of the twentieth-century city. The city acquired its geometric shape early in the nineteenth century when in 1807 Simeon de Witt, Gouveneur Morris and John Rutherford were commissioned to design the model that would determine the 'final and conclusive' conditions for occupancy on Manhattan Island. Four years later, the commissioners proposed the demarcation of 12 avenues running north to south and 155 streets running east to west from north of Canal Street. On the basis of this design the city is now divided into a gridiron pattern of 13 avenues that intersect with 156 streets or 2,028 blocks. Koolhaas sees this cartographic organization as 'a matrix that captures, at the same time, all remaining territory and all future activity on the island' ([1978] 1994, 10). In its outline for the grid's dimensions, the Planning Commission states the reasoning behind its choice of an orthogonal plan:

> That one of the first objects which claimed their attention was the form and manner in which the business should be conducted; that is to say, whether they should confine themselves to rectilinear and rectangular streets, or whether they should adopt some of those supposed

improvements by circles, ovals, and stars, which certainly embellish a plan, whatever may be their effect as to convenience and utility. In considering that subject they could not but bear in mind that a city is to be composed principally of the habitations of men, and that straight-sided and right-angled houses are the most cheap to build and the most convenient to live in. The effect of these plain and simple reflections was decisive. (The Commissioners' plan of New York, 1807, cited in Koolhaas [1978] 1994, 19)

From this statement, it is clear that the Commissioners' plan for New York emphasizes the practical efficiency of the gridiron as a neutral utilitarian structure, and its convenience as a functional mode for organizing the island's real estate and infrastructural layout. However, the gridiron does not remain neutral for long. Indeed, its very neutrality becomes highly pertinent to a conceptualization of humanity's modern identity, and the grid is appropriated as an emblematic structure informing European discursive strategies for comprehending America. As Koolhaas points out, 'the Grid is, above all, a conceptual speculation' ([1978] 1994, 20). Likewise, Lefebvre notes the Western ratio-scientific world-view implicit in this design: 'A classical (Cartesian) rationality thus appears to underpin various spatial distinctions and divisions. […] What is being covered up here is a moral and political order: the specific power that organizes these conditions, with its specific socio-economic allegiance, *seems* to flow directly from the Logos – that is from a "consensual" embrace of the rational' ([1974] 1991, 317).[4] In this scenario, it is in conjunction with early twentieth-century modernist consciousness that the significance of the gridiron as a mappemonde of humanity's schema for experience in the world takes on particular urgency. For modernist architects, the grid epitomized the purity of architectural function, denying ornament and rejecting iconology (Venturi et al. [1972] 1977b, 7). As we shall see, however, the imagination of spatial neutrality takes on its own symbolic status, ensconcing the gridiron in differential discourses of the transcendental on the one hand, and rationalist progress on the other. In the travel texts under discussion here, the imaginative geography of the gridiron is structured through the metaphorical transfer of discourses of rationalization and governmentality onto its orthogonal pattern. Negotiating the gridiron also suggests a negotiation of questions pertaining to possibilities for individual liberty, the development of modern technologies, and extends as far as socio-political discourses on the destiny of humankind.

The discourses investing New York's geometries with such ideological symbolism have recourse to history, and in the past other cultures imparted different meanings to the conjectural pattern of the grid. Across the history of city organization, and with differing motivations behind its choice, the orthogonal grid has consistently been the preferred mode of organization for urban space. Use of the gridiron (or checkerboard) as a blueprint for political structures can be found in both Eastern and Western civilizations. For example, orthogonal design defines the tenth-century city of Suzhou, a city in ancient China. In Suzhou the grid symbolized power, its logic spatially arranging what were intended as unalterable social hierarchies under the Song Dynasty. In colonial Savannah of the early eighteenth century, the gridiron design was adopted as the closest model to mirror the egalitarian ideologies at the heart of democratic society. On this point, however, it is important to point out that the grid was not always so democratically innocent: under the democratic society of the ancient Greek colonies, the grid, rather than assure the egalitarian allotment of property to each citizen, functioned as a way of ensuring the privileged status of the propertied class descendent from the original settlers, and thus of maintaining the social superiority of the territorial aristocracy (Kostof 2001, 99). As Kostof asserts, 'the fact is that egalitarianism is no more natural to gridded patterns than to any other urban form. However noble the original premise, inequities will creep in sooner or later' (100). The grid organizes its citizens visibly and symbolically into a hierarchy according to which social relations are lived out. For Lefebvre, this 'assignment of functions, and the way functions are actually distributed 'on the ground', becomes indistinguishable from the kind of analytical activity that discerns differences' ([1974] 1991, 317).[5] In the case of the Greek colonies, for example, despite the apparent egalitarian block division of its pattern, hierarchical positions become visible through the attachment of value to the various locations within the grid itself.

The reality of urban living invariably distorts the intentions and idealism of 'democratic' design. Typically, differences in the value of various segments within the gridiron pattern are established through a process of gentrification,[6] for which New York's real estate history is an unmatched paradigm. The process can be mapped by the following characteristics. The ordinary citizen gains easy access to urban property in the initial phases of occupancy, when cheap rural land is urbanized through rapid appropriative action and staking out. However, with the flood of immigration to New York in the early and mid-nineteenth century, aristocratic proprietors moved progressively uptown, dissociating themselves from the poorer classes who, in their turn, reappropriated the houses of the upper classes and formed the tenements in downtown Greenwich Village. Likewise, at the other end of Manhattan, black migrant workers entered the city from the West and settled in Harlem, and thus encouraged the movement of the upper classes to the East Side, demonstrating that the realities of demographic movement within the city are as much processes of symbolic concern as they are a product of speculation and economic development.[7]

In spite of the reality of social stratification and locational hierarchies, however, Europe has still traditionally imagined the rectilinear ubiquity of the gridiron pattern in idealist or utopian terms. Since the Renaissance, and in the aftermath of the great epistemological break of the West that was Cartesian rationalism, Europe has found in the geometric simplicity of the grid a spatial model for a uniquely human consciousness based in clear and distinct ideas. Thereafter, its spatiality became associated with the disjunction of consciousness from the irrationality and instinctive corporality that seemed to govern Nature and the natural world. By way of contrast, other architectural structures – circles, ovals and stars – take on oppositional significance in dialectic with the discourses of Renaissance Humanism. For Descartes the grid's spatial arrangement was a potential external conductor of rationalist logic, and, by extension, the geometric simplicity of the gridiron could act as a provisional model of the basic logic within which humans should live. Wishing for the complete freedom of the architect, Descartes ([1637] 1966) advocated a *tabula rasa* approach to urban life. The architect should be free to employ his singular imagination, in conjunction with a rational, coherent mode of thinking in order that a rational, coherent model of urban space might emerge. The philosopher believed this to be essential to the evolution of a logical environment in which man could in his turn become logical. Cartesianism's ideal of a rationalist basis for the construction of human society finds its quintessential expression in the gridiron's outward structure, and attributes to this structure an ontological effectiveness whereby geometric cities engender rational individuals and communities. In Cartesian thought, the singular products of architecture and the global schemas of the urban planner are linked. The emphasis is placed on the urban planner's importance as conceptual organizer of spatial totalities, so that the city is imagined as a coherent schematic whole. This line of thinking configures the urban landscape in the manner of a blueprint. As a result, the structures of city life are conceived of synchronically; as an urban *tabula rasa* constructed according to compositional rules.

Thinking of the city as a composition has two major consequences for the approach to urban space. In the first instance, composition implies that every urban habitat be built for a specific purpose in accordance with the labour and living requirements of each societal order; thus the city responds rationally to its residents. Second, the city is a composition in the sense that it is an active agent in the construction of its inhabitants' spatial and temporal existence within the urban environment: the city conditions the responses of its residents. Through its operational procedures of subdivision, fragmentation, parcelling and allocation, urban space geometrically organizes the cohabitation of men and women in civilization. In other words, the urban plan is not only a visible and immediate frame, but functions also as a mobile network of spatial arrangements generative of specific modes for being in the world (Lefebvre [1974] 1991, 319–20). Adopted as a model for the rationalization of space, the grid is seen to provide Reason's spatial blueprint, and is represented as conducive to the normative evolution of a rational universal consciousness. With its orthogonal repetition and immutable outlining of the city, the gridiron comes to signify a system that seeks the eradication of chaos, or everyday existence, through structure.

The idea of an urban *tabula rasa* takes on special significance for the modernist movement, with perhaps the most influential advocate of urban architectural totalitarianism being Le Corbusier. The architect admitted that while he loved New York, its geometry did not go far enough, and he proposed that the metropolis be razed to the ground so as to build a city in keeping with a singular coherent design. Le Corbusier envisaged skyscrapers designed in a repeatable architectural model, their height being dictated by the buildings' position on the avenues, so as to allow for differing gradients to maximize the level of sun exposure onto the street at all times of the day. The streets' gridiron was merely to be the city's ground level. Between the skyscrapers another orthogonal system of elevated walkways was to be erected, leaving the streets free for the circulation of traffic. Le Corbusier's design sought to maximize architectural control over urban movement, and took as its basis humanist values of transparency and order, transcribing these ideas into an architectural manifesto for modernism. This is totalitarian design in a quite literal sense, and Le Corbusier's principle of simplification and efficiency in total urban design is entirely in keeping with a view of urban life as the extension of a technologically organized world.

Precedents did exist: in the eighteenth century gridiron design was given moral status by the British architect Sir William Chambers, who asserted that 'on a plane where no [im]pediment obliges […] it cannot be supposed that men would go by a crooked line, where they could arrive by a straight one' (Chambers 1773, 36). But it is Le Corbusier (1925) who conceptualizes the design in such a way that it comes to define the aesthetics of early modernism in the twentieth century. This Utopian vision of the city has its roots in nineteenth-century philosophies such as those of Charles Fourier, Henri Saint-Simon and Ebenezer Howard. Le Corbusier expressed his vision in the 'The Contemporary City for Three Million Inhabitants' design, exhibited at the Salon d'Automne in 1922. The design consisted of a city of skyscrapers in a park, where an ordered diagram integrated modern construction techniques, automobiles and aeroplanes, so that Nature and machine coexisted in harmonic union. It was, in effect, the urban extension of the singular architectural project for the Maison Citrohan of the same year. 'Citrohan', a deliberate pun on 'Citroën', showed Le Corbusier's affiliation with Walter Gropius's and J.J.P. Oud's work of the same period, which was also focused on using mass-production processes (similar to the war-time automobile construction revolution of Henry Ford) to solve the housing crises of the post-war years.[8] 'However', as William J. R. Curtis points out, 'the *idea* of mass-production dwelling was as important as the fact, and the Citrohan envisaged a way of life freed from the unnecessary clutter of the customary bourgeois dwelling of the time' (Curtis [1982] 2005, 170–71). This visionary ethos, of a space whose functions had been examined from the ground up and stripped to the bare essentials, whose inhabitants could be free to regard the 'essential joys' of life, space and greenery, was extended to the entire urban environment. In 1925 Le Corbusier's philosophies found expression in his design for the *Exposition des Arts Décoratifs* where the 'Ville Voisine' revealed a scheme for inserting enormous glass skyscrapers into the centre of Paris.

While Le Corbusier adapted the architectural inheritance of the Renaissance and wrote of the city in organic terms, he denied the curvature and meandering of older cities that had grown up in what architects term loosely an 'organic' pattern.[9] Rejecting as anti-humanist the unplanned, sporadic growth of older cities, Le Corbusier equated both the spirit and function of modern urban civilization with the spatial simplicity of the grid's linearity. Much of the legacy of Le Corbusier's philosophy of architecture can be traced to the biological discourses of the nineteenth century, in which new categorizations within human medicine impacted on discursive strategies for understanding the urban environment. Henceforth, one could talk of streets in terms of arteries, squares as the beating heart of the city, gardens as the lungs and so on. By extension, in understanding the metaphors of the human *body* as a machine, one is better equipped to understand Le Corbusier's dictum of the *house* as a machine for living as a discursive appropriation of the new technologies of urban life in humanist terms; the simplification of line and the introduction of geometric order into architecture were addenda to the perfect, integral necessity of the human body. This blend of rationalism and idealism tends, therefore, to see mechanization and rational design as central, positive forces in the creation of a new culture. In order that humans could breathe, walk, live, exist as rational and healthy organisms, the straight line must be reintroduced into the urban environment. All of civilized human beings' needs demanded the geometric pattern of the gridiron:

> A modern city should be lived in straight lines, practically: in the construction of buildings, sewers, canals, roads, footpaths, etc. Circulation requires the straight line. The straight line is healthy too for the soul of cities. The curve is ruinous, difficult and dangerous, it paralyses.
>
> The straight line is present throughout human history, in every human intention, in every human act.[10] (Le Corbusier 1925, 10)

Thus ardour for the geometric is not only functional, it is also a morally driven conceptualization of space, essentially erecting a faith in the straight line as human beings' natural destiny, orienting humanity towards the good. The architect's quest for perennial values in architecture is inseparable therefore, from the quest to reveal the principles of organization integrating human biology, consciousness and social life. The architectural vision that encompassed the entire city in its plan was no less than a vision to design society according to principles that acknowledged industrialization and technological implements (in particular the motorcar) as 'extensions of man' (McLuhan [1964] 2002). Urban design is hereby invested with values of moral and socio-political transcendence. The straight line is human while 'the curved street is the path of donkeys, the straight street the path of men' (Le Corbusier 1925, 10).[11] Thus, the patterns of orthogonal repetition as representations of space that can map rationalist consciousness *into* social space enter European discourses of identity as a civilizing system seeking the human appropriation of the unknown through category and its extension in structure.

4.2 Morand's Guide to Modernity

It is rationality and a modernist's appeal to clarity and category that define Paul Morand's travel journal, *New-York*, published in 1930. A consummate traveller, Morand visits the city at the moment when New York had established itself as horizontal and vertical theatre of progress. The tourist has perhaps never quite lost the colonialist tendency to treat foreign spaces as sites for the expression of their own desires, a *tabula rasa* onto which they can impose their own frames of reference. Within Morand's travel book, the narrative practice of the city is combined with a desire to experience and display the anomalies of urban life in New York, and to legislate for these anomalies in terms of a genealogy of urban development. Appropriated thus, New York emerges as the ultimate urban manifestation of technological progress and as the harbinger of Europe's inevitable future.

The horizontal rationale of New York's gridiron is used by Morand as the formal design both for his physical spatial practice of the city and as a narratological structure for the representational space of the travel journal. From the first page of the book (a map) to the next (the table of contents) the reader is made visually aware of the writer's approach to the city. The account is cartographically structured in its layout and comprised of four major sections. The first three sections correspond to the geographical order of the major zones of Manhattan: 'Downtown', 'Midtown', 'Uptown'.[12] The closing section, entitled 'New York Panorama' / 'Panorama de New-York', constitutes a general philosophical survey, an attempt to 'sum up' the metropolis. In the first three sections, the grid's two-dimensional discipline lends the writing compositional clarity, elucidating the traveller's position for the reader through a narrative logic consistent with the official delineation of the New York space. This cartographic structure allows Morand to control both his own repertoire (his representation observes the cartographic logic of the map diligently) as well as that of the reader, providing the latter with an orderly referential sequence through which the city can be managed and understood. Effectively, *New-York* is framed by the structural representation of an exterior cartographic referent that already exists within a symbolic order, so that the narrative organization of the city suggests a completely transparent relationship between the traveller's representation and that representation's object: New York, inserted within an overall schema designed to facilitate logical comprehension, is appropriated as text. In this, Morand's 'texturology' (Certeau 1984, 93) consists in the transformation of 'the urban *fact* into the *concept* of a city' (Certeau 1984, 94, emphasis in the original).

In terms of structural layout, the journal presents the reader with an official (that is, cartographically controlled) organization that is (more than likely) already familiar. This choice of redefined structure is one of the clues for identifying Morand as a tourist guide. Seeking clarity and familiarity, his text functions in the same way as a guidebook, with geographical order taking precedence over what could be considered a more temporally organized mode of travel writing (such as Simone de Beauvoir's choice, for example, in her travel account, *Amérique au jour le jour* (1947), to arrange the journal as a daily log or diary of impressions). The easy parcelling of the city mimics the guidebook form, with the text clearly divided into the tripartite sections of Downtown, Midtown, and Uptown respectively. Tourists, as Augé has demonstrated, are ritual practitioners of a world that has been familiarized through imagery, repertoires and other technologies of travel like that of the guidebook or timetable. Thus, through the 'tourist's gaze' (Urry 1990), the site is officially designated, its borders geographically delineated, and its temporal existence rendered in terms of an official historical discourse: *space* is constituted as *place* (Certeau [1980] 1990, I: 173). The map and cartographic organization of Morand's journal perform the first of these two operations systematically, with the result that the space of the city is secured visually and with linear textuality in the reader's mind. While Morand does not exclude the everyday, or *space* as it is lived and experienced by him personally, his encounter with New York is always, and explicitly, inserted within the larger discursive framework of the urban tourist, and his consciousness of this position affiliates his travel practice to the tourist's methods for establishing hierarchies of meaning within New York City – Morand is never without his 'excellent guidebook […] always to hand' (Morand 1930, 130).[13] His journey operates as a legislative packaging of the unfamiliar and, furthermore, his tourist tendencies permit him to comprehend New York within a comparative urban framework, whereby tourist practices facilitate synchronic modalities for understanding space in terms that abstract the city from its everyday particularities.

Apart from the guidebook, other frames of reference inform Morand's experience of the city, and are suggestive of an attempt to neutralize any potential for the city to seem strange or upsetting to his European eyes. One of these interpretive frames is history. For our context, history is understood as the official, collective narrative constituting

European interpretations of the past. Morand's account of the city opens with its discovery by European explorers. The tone of the opening pages is both rhetorically and historically hyperbolic:

> Silence.
>
> The last waves of the Atlantic thrust themselves onto the brown and crimson rocks and are torn apart.
>
> A seagull cries.
>
> From each side of the promontory, the tide swells upstream into the estuaries. On the right bank, night begins to cloak the hills. On the left, sets a yellow, sulphurous sun.
>
> America is great, already. With anonymous grandeur; sidereal immensity. Still, folded up like seedlings, these places that will be New York await their birth.[14] (5)

Morand effectively mythologizes the story of New York's discovery through the use of certain narrative strategies. He employs direct speech to relate the Native American's fear and wonder upon first sighting Hudson and his crew. He tells well-known anecdotes of the Dutch purchasing the island from the natives for the equivalent of 24 dollars. It is significant that the traveller recounts these historical versions in the present tense, lending a sense of immediacy and, by implication, authenticity to the representation. In that Morand's travel practice is informed by tourist strategies and, therefore, by an ideological force conditioning spatial practice, his narrative seems to function as a discursive mesh, enveloping the foreign space in familiarity and avoiding confrontation with radical difference. This would suggest that deciphering the city is inherently bound to the operations of marketing and control. As Morand states: 'The pleasure that one feels sitting on a bench in the Battery stems in large part from those first colonial memories' (20).[15]

The risk of defamiliarization and the ontological threat of the other's strangeness are overcome through careful packaging and organization. And the appeal of New York to Morand lies partly in the extent to which its affiliation with European colonial history makes its territory accessible and comprehensible. By dispelling the unknown, the discursive strategies of the guidebook, in tandem with Morand's own travel text, neutralize the potential of any socio-cultural dislocation. Morand denies the unease of temporal fragmentation or spatial disorientation writing through textual strategies – geographical organization, maps and integrated histories – which all combine to assemble a place that is accessible, coherent and transparent. We recall Lynch's assertion that familiarity and, therefore, psychological comfort in the city can be achieved when it conforms to some previously established stereotype:

> An object seen for the first time may be identified and related to not because it is individually familiar but because it conforms to a stereotype already constructed by the observer. (1960, 6)

Furthermore, by dividing urban space both textually and visually into predictable and manageable units, Morand cements his authority as selector of the 'essentials' or 'must sees', purporting a succinct path by which one can frame the entire city. His guidebook provides a key to the city, rituals via which to achieve transparency, by dissecting New

York along previously established, value-laden, lines. From the point of view of the home culture, it is through these strategies that Morand participates in the construction of New York as an integral monument, what Certeau from the 110th floor of the World Trade Centres would famously call 'a wave of verticals' (Certeau 1984, 91). Morand's textual mapping ensures this monument's constant reaffirmation through predictability, and the ritualized appreciation of the tourist's gaze. From the reader's perspective, therefore, Morand's book performs as a point of access to officially sanctioned meanings within the city. In rendering the site legible, Morand reassures himself of its identity and recipro- cally of his own in relation to it. Thus the threat of the unknown is neutralized, and the modern urban landscape never undermines the traveller's frames of reference. We can see this in the way that he has already appropriated the city through a series of associa- tions gleaned from previous metropolitan excursions. Previous travel affords him author- ity and reassures him as to his capacity to understand the foreign space before him:

> If I could penetrate and quickly understand New York, it's because I had ten years of experience overseas behind me [...]. London and New York are one and the same, at a distance of one hundred years; contemporary London is the New York of the Knickerbocker era; which leads me to Washington Square.[16] (1930, 108–9)

By constructing the metropolitan lineage, London–New York, Morand inserts the latter city into a discursive pattern of which he believes he knows the previous format (indeed Morand went on to write a travel account entitled *Londres* in 1933. This pattern ensures the persistence of tourist practices of the city as an affirmation of what one already knows and of what one can be given to expect, so that the newness of the city and its prodigious architectures and alternate spaces for experience never shock, rather New York is predictable in terms of a European urban inheritance.

   In addition, Morand's account furthers this genealogical coherency through the reit- eration of colonial history to the reader, thus representing a controlled set of expecta- tions that the traveller subsequently satisfies, directing the flow of human traffic along the 'supervised' trajectory of the 'beaten track'. The beaten track of the tourist ritualizes and reduces the spatio-temporal complexity of the urban universe, revising New York in accordance with hierarchical principles for the safe, unthreatening practice of the urban space. In that he seeks to guide the reader through the city within the spatio-temporal constraints of the tourist, Morand's journal functions in an exclusionary manner, dispar- aging certain areas of New York that have not entered the accepted discursive repertoire of the European tourist. Thus, he instructs the reader as to the unworthiness of a visit to the less glamorized boroughs on the outskirts of the city saying:

> There is nothing 'touristic' in these suburban areas, they are nothing but monstrous hernias, joined to the main island in 1898: New Jersey, Brooklyn, Queensborough, the Bronx and Richmond form what is called Greater New York.[17] (1930, 260)

Morand implies that his reader should exclude anything not officially historical or con- ventionally picturesque; the everyday life of the city does not merit the attention or time of the tourist and thus social space is essentially precluded here. As appropriated by Morand, New York becomes legible in terms of a series of value-laden 'sites', places of historical interest or cultural importance and, therefore, outside the range of the quotidian world of the city. Defining the city in terms of History places value on those areas already familiar in European narratives of New York, and by extension, devalues the contingencies and ordinariness of the present. The present is filtered through stereotypes that avoid description of individual human agency, exclude hazard and emphasize instead the patterns of the city's generalized and predictable landscape. The colonialist framing of New York as an extension of European society enables the city's ordered and technological landscape to be represented as harbinger of collective societal development.

4.3   The Order of Things

Morand is a tourist at a time on the cusp of the electronic revolution that would alter travel and conceptions of urban space irrevocably. In 1929 the level of technological development shaping urban communities in New York was by no means globally applicable, and the uniqueness of New York for Morand lies in the opportunity it provides to observe the effects of modernity within a space and a society more technologically advanced than any other in the world at that time. It is also of significance that for Morand, New York exists within an urban genealogy; to observe urban society in this metropolis implicates the future of Europe, so that New York becomes a preview of the urban living patterns European cities are destined to mimic. This teleological outlook on global metropolitan development is emphasized through respective references to London and New York as 'mother and daughter' / 'mère et fille' (1930, 109). Genealogy is not only a means to rationally account for the city's development, it also grants this tourist the privileged status of commentator on the prospective future of European urban life. Thus, while the individual encounter features little in Morand's writing, technological and architectural developments that have generated new universal conditions for social interrelations in New York are fascinating to him because they are suggestive of the future that lies in store for the traveller's home culture. The city's attraction lies in its established reputation as a theatre of modernist progress, whose plot consists in 'barbarism giving way to refinement' (Koolhaas [1978] 1994, 15).[18] At this juncture, New York's refinement consists in the revolution of urban space through technological development, and the exploitation of this technology by private and public enterprise in a manner that invariably alters the patterns of human interrelations within the environment. New York's pace, mechanized time, crowds and electric blurring of night and day fascinate the European traveller. Furthermore, the spatio-temporal extremes of the city, and the effect of these on human practices of the city, are expressly sought out by Morand, just as he might seek out an expected landmark.

Morand interprets urban living conditions within New York as omens announcing the end of traditional forms of communal organization. The lynchpins of community and social forms of congregation are profoundly altered by the demands of urban life. The traveller depicts the end of the nuclear family, and sees in the city's frenetic pace the demise of organic rhythms traditionally associated with rural temporality. The demands of the capitalist economy require changes in the structure of everyday life – eating habits, sleeping habits and social habits, are all altered by the technologies of the city. For example, meal times are no longer a family-oriented affair punctuating the working day: 'In New York no goes home in the middle of the day, one eats at work, either in the offices, while working, or in clubs, or cafeterias' (51).[19]

The everyday rhythms of metropolitan life are set by the New York Stock Exchange. The dictates of mechanical time determine the ebb and flow of the urban population; at regular intervals the city becomes the scene of mass movement, the space of that peculiar feature of urban life – the ordered eclecticism of the crowd. 'The final bell' initiates an automatic response: each skyscraper, an 'anthill at work', relinquishes its hold over the worker who, upon departing the 'temple's sanctuary', become part of the buzzing mass on the street (36).[20] And the repetitive nature of this temporal framework means that everyday, at the same time, the street becomes 'a human river' (35), invaded by a 'contorted monster [that] goes up Broadway, floods the Brooklyn Bridge, invades the "L", which is to say the Elevated, an elevated railway, drowns the subterranean space of the subway' (62).[21] Significantly, Morand's position as leisurely tourist affords him the degree of disintegration and distance necessary in order to amass his observations. The traveller remains separated from the crowd all the while the measured, sequential time of the clock enables the metropolis to function almost automatically, translating individual movement into mass movement, which in conjunction with the architectural infrastructures of urban design contribute to the smooth organization of individuals in accordance with the synchronic and diachronic orders of the city:

> The final bell has been rung. The tumult subsides. Straight away, the bosses leave the battlefield, jump onto the still-empty subway where two hours later, ordinary people will, in their turn, avidly read the stocks pages... [...] Night falls. The skyscrapers, these human presses rid themselves of an entire, exhausted civilization. The vertical ordering of individuals gives way now, for the night, to a new horizontal order.[22] (61–62)

Effectively, Morand's account posits New York as a site where a new anthropology of urban life is emerging. The attendant rituals of capitalist urban living are noted as rhythms produced by technological innovations that are constitutive of the collective identity of modern person within the urban environment. Since the nineteenth century, the phenomenon of the crowd has been a trope in urban literature, performing as a metaphorical device to express nostalgia or loss of identity at the hands of the industrial, consumerist machine. However, unlike, for example, Poe's anxiety-ridden short story, 'The Man of the Crowd' (1840), Morand's writing exults in the strangeness and anonymity of this collective movement. He recounts how the nocturnal crowd defies the natural order of day and night by exploiting the new technologies of modern life that alter natural timeframes for activity. Electricity is represented as an inorganic extension of daylight, a ruse to fool people and encourage them to continue their activities, namely consumption, into the hours of darkness. The electric lamp, 'a fascinating machine', hypnotizes 'the tired crowd that has decided not to go home, but to spend its money' (277).[23] Other stimulants also assist in this ruse. The crowd is drunk on caffeine, Cola altering the body's chemical balance so that 'you no longer even think about sleeping. You're drunk, intoxicated, full of fictional well-being' (277).[24] Through this, Morand sets up a discourse whereby the human being becomes the object of the city's mechanisms; no longer master of their physiological rhythms, the city deprives them of self-control and they melt into the synthetic reality of urban stimulants.

These new manifestations of space and time are at once attractive and repellent. The European traveller revels in the aesthetics of urban modernity at the same time that he bemoans the seeming absence of traditional expressions of domestic and social order, such as religion and the family. However, the tourist does not seek out these social enclaves and, in prioritizing the strange and the new, does not have time to venture into those areas of the city where such aspects of life might be observed. In this way, the abstract rationale of the city's narrative and geographical cartography is never threatened by the detail of the everyday. Morand never questions his impressions; his concern is to gather information to present a coherent, panoramic expression of New York, to understand the city's place in terms of a global urban order: as a historical procession that has subsumed the individual in its quest for mechanized progress. Morand's fascination can be understood in terms of the modernist awareness of living in a revolutionary age that had generated explosive upheavals in every dimension of personal, social and political life. This is a visitor who can remember what it is like to live, materially and spiritually, in a world that is not modern at all. London is one hundred years behind this frenzied existence, Paris even more so, and from this inner dichotomy the sense of living in two temporally dislocated worlds is played out towards the end of the travel account, where European modernity is conceived of as the past, and New York emerges as harbinger of a future world order.

The teleological progression of humanity towards its urban destiny is expressed through the traveller's appropriation of the skyscraper's verticality, which functions as the hierarchical determiner of new forms of social stratification. With the upward development of skyscrapers, the geometrical pattern of the city extends vertically. This progression is initially functional: the occurrence of a vertical order for the city expanding as and when material technologies permitted. However, in conjunction with the logic of commercial competition and consumerism, the fight for domination of the sky becomes increasingly symbolic, with technology initiating new modes for understanding cultural power. As Lefebvre sees it, 'verticality and great height have ever been the spatial expression of a potentially violent power' (Lefebvre [1974] 1991, 98).[25] Indeed, in Morand's travel account we find verticality transformed into a representational space where a series of metaphors suggest the transition from an 'organic' human order to an irretrievably mechanized one. First, the technical virtuosity of the skyscraper's height creates new demands on perspective. To look at the top of the skyscraper from ground level Morand must crane his neck; the building's monumental height defies human vision in its 'perspectival exhaustion' (35).[26] Second, the skyscraper is represented as the architectural expression of the city's mechanized time. These edifices dominate the society that conceived them; the skyscrapers are 'human presses' (62), taking possession of their creators and vomiting up 'human matter'[27] (41) at the close of the market.

Yet this architectural intervention in the structural organization of society is possessed of its own sentience for Morand, albeit one that will supersede the human. These structures are represented as extensions of humankind's collective destiny, of progress, suggesting that humans will somehow evolve more vitally through this marriage of humanity and architectural prodigality. These urban anomalies construct their own society, a fraternity of reinforced steel, 'linked by a sympathy among giants' the skyscrapers 'support each other in their attempt to rise' (35).[28] Morand's representation of the skyscraper inserts urban form within a Darwinian discourse of inevitability. He represents these buildings as a natural consequence of progress:

> If they have reached such heights, it is because it was necessary to use the last plots of land on a rock where there were no other options; they rose *naturally*, like the water level of a *river* as it narrows to fit the confinement of its banks.[29] (27, my emphasis)

In Morand's anthropomorphic expression the skyscraper becomes an organic entity, possessed of its own beauty and spirituality:

> The skyscrapers! There are some who are women and others men. […] Anchored in the living flesh of the rock, descending under the ground by four or five floors, bearing in the deepest parts of themselves their vital organs, dynamos, central heating, branded rivets, moored by underground cables, beams of a height to stir the soul, steel pylons, they rise, tremulous with the wonderful ballet of the higher floors.[30] (36–37)

It is this terrible beauty that gives the city 'its futuristic quality'; 'success is the soul of these buildings; they are tabernacles of success' (40).[31] In this Morand once again calls to the future statements by Certeau on the rhetorical power of the former World Trade Centres, 'On this stage of concrete, steel and glass, cut out between two oceans (the Atlantic and the American) by a frigid body of water, the tallest letters in the world compose a gigantic rhetoric of excess in both expenditure and production' (Certeau 1984, 91). A power that in the post-9/11 world of today resonates all the more powerfully and globally. In Morand's 1930 account, the rapture he expresses sets up New York as an inevitable urban model of modernity for the rest of Europe, and exhibits the faith of early modernists in the machine age and the beauty of technology's transformative power:

> Its adventure will become ours. To protect ourselves against the novelties of Broadway is to deny this pre-established order called the future. […] New York is what all cities will be one day: geometric. A simplification of lines, of feelings; the reign of directness. Einstein called it a two-dimensional city.[32] (266, 273–74)

The metropolis thus becomes legible within a series of organic metaphors that merge modernist discourses of purity and rationality with evolutionary discourses of natural selection. Within this schema, to question the sustainability of urban life in the skyscraper city is futile: the destiny of humanity is geometric. Taken together, the poetics and guidebook format of Morand's text reveal the tourist's legislative tendency to reduce space into comprehensive, prescribed units. The narrative is atemporalized via Morand's synchronic cartographic division along the lines of the New York grid. This text appropriates everyday space and wipes out the contingency of such a space by mapping it in terms of the rationalist spatializations of cartography.

4.4   Framing America: Sartre in New York

Fifteen years after Morand, Jean-Paul Sartre's *Situations III* reveals a more politico-aesthetic imagination of the American metropolis wherein New York's space facilitates the articulation of concerns about the effects of modernization and urban rationalization upon individual consciousness. While not touristic in approach, we will see that the Sartrean discursive apparatus, however self-reflexive, remains within the frameworks of legislative negotiation of the Other. Situating the account is, as Sartre would have recognized, essential to analysing the nexus of meaning that emerges in the accounts. In the aftermath of World War II, and the threat to civilization which Nazism and the atomic bomb posed, modernist faith in the inevitable link between technology and progress, nationalist ideologies and human beings' inevitable *aufklärung*, are called into question. Within Sartre's travel account, questions as to the potential for individual freedom within New York's built environment (read by the traveller as conformist ideology made manifest) structure the traveller's representational strategies, and reveal profound anxieties about the influence of governmentality upon the community. Sartre's representation of the city as a 'Ville coloniale' / 'colonial city' problematizes representations of the city as a theatre of progress (the term 'colonial', in this context, implying the unfinished quality of the city) and, through the rejection of New York as the modern capital of the world, belittles utopian – European – dreams of starting afresh in America. In this schema, the American dream is firmly placed within a symbolic order emergent from the material circumstances of history. The idea that New York might somehow provide shelter from the ravages of history is denied by Sartre's imagination of the city's ruination, and by his insertion of the mechanical metropolis into a discourse that emphasizes the forces beyond humanity's control, namely Nature and Time.

   Nevertheless, while Sartre's account seems to legislate for the city in totalizing terms, the representation is also steeped in ambivalence, which results from a hesitation between assuming an objective or subjective position from which to speak. The distinction between legislation for the other, and self-reflexive recognition of subjective limitations blur the lines between the legislative and interpretive modalities of travel writing. Sartre's negotiations are framed by a self-awareness as to the (inherently limited) subjective position and the necessarily oppositional polarity within which his perspectives are formed, awareness of his European value-system conditioning what he identifies as American. The dominant (Jauss [1970] 1986) modes of Sartre's account, however, exhibit an impulse to categorize the signs of city in terms of a generalized opposition between Europe and America, and to present this binary as indicative of the teleological fate of capitalism. While, like Morand, questions of the individual's possibilities for consciousness and freedom preoccupy Sartre's negotiation of urban space, Sartre's representation poses these questions not within the inevitable schema of Morand's urban evolutionary narrative, but from a perspective that suggests the urgent necessity to restore to man a sense of his choice in the matter of progress, and his account demonstrates an anxiety around the pursuit of utopia in a mechanical society that requires mass conventionalization for its existence.

The reportage was written in 1945 after Sartre's much-anticipated visit to the French *émigré* community in New York.[33] The American essays are located in the book alongside other pieces describing life in German-occupied Paris. The surrounding essays elaborate various philosophical viewpoints on topics such as occupation, collaboration and freedom.[34] Within the American essays the geometric purity of American space has none of Morand's modernist enthusiasm.[35] Prior to the outbreak of World War II the effects of the collapse of the American economy in the months preceding the appearance of Morand's *New-York* were felt across the Atlantic and were ultimately to have profound effects on the tentative peace in Europe during the interwar years. Europe could no longer pretend to be immune to the effects of international economic crises and the cultural anxiety produced within such a climate of economic and political uncertainty undermined faith in the invulnerability of American finance. Europeans – from politicians, bankers and industrial magnates to tradesmen and housewives – became conscious of their reliance upon the status quo of Wall Street. The end of World War II secured America's status as a world superpower, relativizing all European powers on this new global stage. Conrad comments that:

> Until 1941, America managed to resist the destructive dialectic of European history. [...] Once America intervened in the war, first in the Pacific after the Japanese attack on Pearl Harbour and later in Europe, a return to unspoiled isolation was impossible. The anxious peace of 1945 left the United States as the custodian of a divided continent. ([1998] 1999, 553)

Along with this new power balance, years of collaboration resulted in a new French consciousness of national identity (Sartre 1949, 65). This is a world which, having realized the implications of the nuclear bomb, must henceforward come to terms with the permanent atomic threat to civilization. The idea that America's fate was ineluctably tied to that of Europe suggests that examination of American society's cultural value-systems became all the more urgent. Sartre pinpoints the contradictions that the dual events of global geopolitical domination and detrimental economic failure produced within the American psyche, and the effect these events had on the urban landscape:

> Without doubt the war revealed to Americans that America was the greatest power in the world. But the era of easy living is over; many economists fear a new crash. So, no more skyscrapers are being built. It seems that they are too difficult to rent out.[36] (123)

As a traveller to a country that has decidedly assumed its position as hub of the Western world, it is unsurprising, perhaps, that Sartre's European representation of New York, delivered in a narrative marked by disdain on the one hand and poignancy on the other, attempts to expose the fragility and vulnerability of the metropolis. The contradiction in Sartre's writing is symptomatic of the contradictions that he finds inherent in urban

America. The 'fall into history' as Conrad ([1998] 1999, 553) puts it entailed often-tragic personal choices between freedom and political engagement. Sartre's representation of the fragile state of world peace at this point in the history is also pertinent to his representation of New York, which is consistently rendered in terms of fragility and vulnerability:

> We believed unquestioningly that peace was the natural state and substance of the Universe, that war was nothing but a temporary glitch on its surface. Today we realize our error: the end of the war, it is nothing but the end of *this* war. [...] The world has become simpler: two giants stand, alone, and refuse to look each other in the eye. [...] Its most significant events warned us of humanity's fragility. So we wished it to end and paid no attention to the manner of that ending. More than one European would have preferred Japan to be invaded, crushed beneath a flood of bombing: but this little bomb which can kill one hundred thousand men, it forces us, suddenly, to face our responsibilities. With the next one, the earth might explode [...]. The community that designates itself guardian of the atomic bomb is above the natural order because it is responsible for this order's life and death.[37] (66–69)

Sartre's 1945 travel account reads as a denial of America as a utopian space, thus a denial of how America had previously existed within the spiritual concoction of national and international myths based on the idea of purity. While Morand's narrative opens with an account of the day of creation, Sartre's American essays are directly preceded by a treatise on Armistice Day whose final lines testify to the desolate isolation facing the individual in the aftermath of world war: 'The war, in ending, left man naked, under no illusions, abandoned to his own devices, having finally understood that he could rely on nothing but himself' (71).[38] It is this realization that marks Sartre's distrust of American society, portrayed as a system that never questions its might or right, a consumer-driven structure that prefers to lull its participants into a sense of domestic sanctity and impenetrability. Faith in the spiritual purity of the American Dream is deliberately questioned and undermined from Sartre's European standpoint. However, in keeping with the tension between the legislative and interpretive positions of the text, the traveller's poetic prose suggests a hesitation between condemnation of the American ideological system and admiration of New York's sweeping architectural expressions. Sartre cannot help but find a spiritual beauty in the skyward-driven perpendiculars of the urban landscape.

4.5   Fragile Homes, Mobile Identities

Throughout Sartre's American essays the grid forms the strategic modality for interpretation of modern urban American as an expression of the spatial and cultural homogenization, and also as the sign of a naive utopian faith in the necessity of the governmental institution as a means to a better future. In his account, Sartre opposes the urban geometry of America to the European realization of place – the unplanned spontaneity of medieval cities and the circularity of Renaissance towns. The latter consists for Sartre in historically rooted conceptions of the home, where the house transcends its status as functional building to assume an organic and spiritual profundity as dwelling space. The foundation of his depiction of the United States hinges on the latter's insertion into an oppositional framework, whereby America performs as a counterpoint to Europe. In this respect, the travel experience is initially a project in comparison, although, as we shall see, the extremities of New York's environment force Sartre to adjust his vision. The associations of European identity with history, permanency, as well as with genealogical and sociological heritage, provide the opposing pole against which Sartre articulates America as a space that is unfinished, primitive and exposed; a space symptomatic of ahistorical utopian desires for control over the contingencies of the natural environment and time. The juxtaposition of American with European space creates a comparative binary in which urban life in America, when placed against the generational lineage of Europeans and their dwelling place, becomes representative of embryonic and even primeval life forms:

> Today the American looks at his city objectively, he never thinks to find it ugly, but he certainly thinks it is old. If it were even older, like ours, he might find a social heritage there, a tradition. We ordinarily live in the homes of our grandfathers. Our streets reflect the customs and the values of past centuries: they subdue the present somewhat. [...] *A city for us, is above all a past; for them, it is first and foremost a future*, what they love about it above all, is that it is not yet everything it could be.[39] (101, my emphasis)

Depicting America as a space unconcerned with the past allows Sartre to engage with the discursive paradox that has consistently informed European travel writers' representations of American space: while in America urban life has reached its most highly developed state in technological terms, attitudes to urban space have more in common with the nomadic and tribal attitudes of 'primitive' societies than with the paradigms for dwelling within which Europeans understand 'civilization'. Travelling across the country, Sartre remarks on the flimsiness of the houses, the generic appearance of the buildings devoid of distinguishing features, laid out monotonously in orthogonal patterns. He contrasts this fragility and sameness with the solidity and individuality of European housing. The insubstantial and prefabricated quality of housing material undermines the idea of home as fixed and localizable in terms of place, leading Sartre to observe that:

> This home, is a collection of objects, furniture, souvenirs that belong to them, that mirror them back to themselves and constitute the internal, living landscape of their accommodation. These are their home. They follow them everywhere, like Aeneas.[40] (96–97)

Sartre announces that the American idea of home as a portable, fragmented set of objects and memories results from a culture of material fragility and equivalence, as he notes that 'the house is the carcass; one abandons it on the least pretext' (97).[41]

As mentioned earlier, this disconnection of the house from the European idea of home – where the memory ascribed to the house has 'an obsessive quality'[42] (Lefebvre [1974] 1991, 120) – is one of the points of departure for legislative representations of American space in primitive terms. One explanation for this could be that American disregard for the physical house flies in the face of a European philosophical tradition which, as exemplified by the writing of Heidegger ([1971] 2005) and Bachelard ([1957]

2001), depicts the house as a dwelling space, and associates this dwelling with an authentic state of being or Dasein; an existential position that posits the house as the base from which being in the world is constructed. The house is fundamental to the European idea of a stable position from which the world can be interpreted and meaningfully lived in. Architects and cultural theorists alike have identified a series of architectural features for a model of the house as basis of stability and sedentary identity (Lyotard 1998; Heidegger ([1971] 2005; Rossi 1982). This house is first and foremost detached, separate and distinct from its neighbours. Its structure is formed of brick or stone – both durable, organic materials. Finally, its primary mode of figurative organization is the square. For Bachelard, in particular, the house has an 'almost ontological dignity'[43] (Lefebvre [1974] 1991, 121) and functions as an absolute space that connects to the material world the representational spaces of the philosopher-poet's dreams of stability. Anthropologists have opposed this latter manifestation with the prevalence of round tents or triangular structures observable in nomadic societies. McLuhan ([1964] 2002) offers an explanation for this structural difference, which he sees as being primarily based in differences between the sensorial priorities separating literate, work-specialized civilizations from tribal, non-literate societies, emphasizing the kinetic, tactile energy at work in circular or triangular structures and contrasting this to the visual closure imminent in square space:

> A tent or wigwam is not an enclosed or visual space. Neither is a cave nor a hole in the ground. These kinds of space – the tent, the wigwam, the igloo, the cave – are not 'enclosed' in the visual sense because they follow dynamic lines of force, like a triangle. When enclosed, or translated into visual space, architecture tends to lose its tactile kinetic pressure. A square is the enclosure of a visual space; that is, it consists of space properties abstracted from manifest tensions. [...] A square moves beyond such kinetic pressures to enclose visual space relations, while depending upon diagonal anchors. This separation of the visual from the direct tactile and kinetic pressure, and its translations into new dwelling places, occurs only when men have learned to practice specialization of their senses, and fragmentation of their work skills. *The square room or house speaks the language of the sedentary specialist, while the round hut or igloo, like the conical wigwam, tells of the integral nomadic ways of food-gathering communities.* (135, my emphasis)

This house, square, materially solid, and detached, is the iconic model for the private being and, as Bachelard ([1957] 2001) posited, for the latent subconscious and mnemonic consciousness of the European individual. However, in America the physical entity of the house reveals how technological advances and the resultant creation of a commodity market causes humanity to revert to the state of a nomad; the interchangeable and the iconic quality of objects arouse nascent combative and primal desire. Commodity culture is read as a sign of primitiveness and this, in turn, enables Sartre to identify the urban practice of the inhabitants as possessing its own traditions and rituals. This primitiveness is based on a tradition of constant destruction, the rituals of which centre around the relentless substitution of one thing for another. Within this technologically advanced society, the house is relegated to the status of commodity. Construction, now taking place at speed, renders the house insignificant as a symbolic dwelling structure ingrained with importance for individual and familial identities: the house is no longer built to last. Within the Sartrean logic, if the home is replaceable, then so too are the identities within its walls.

The material fabric of urban America signifies this substitutability to Sartre, while the colours of the houses become equated with artifice, and the inconsistency of urban design is seen as a sign of incompleteness:

> The brick houses are the colour of dried blood, or else cloyed with paint, smeared in bright yellow, green or crude white. [...] All of these hastily built houses are designed to be hastily demolished, and are remarkably similar to the 'refabricated' houses of Fontana. [...] *And above all nothing is more touching, than the contrast between the formidable power, the abundance of what we call the 'American colossus' and the puny insignificance of these maisonettes that line the largest streets in the world.* But, on reflection, nothing says it better that *America is unfinished*, that its ideas, its projects, its social structure and its cities have a reality that is purely provisional.[44] (102–4, my emphasis)

While this notion of a provisional city was precisely (just over 20 years before) what the Futurist architect Sant'Elia (Martin 2005) lauded as the basis of a new machine culture, Sartre feels only the contradiction between the reality of these fragile structures and the might of American industry and infrastructure. Within this context of interchange and incompletion, McLuhan's ([1964] 2002) theoretical identification of rectangular structures with sedentary living is undermined. In modernist interpretations the square does not necessitate closure, and the temporary nature of modern materials implies an imminent demise that is antithetical to stability. While the visual closure of the house holds the shape of rectangular permanence, according to Sartre this permanence is illusory. The house is not substantiated by either a material or historical identity, and for Sartre these structures attest to an ephemeral culture; a culture that as yet, has no historical identity to speak of. Likewise, the European idea of 'home' provides the contrastive, legislative code for the association of American urban living with movement and transience. American prefabricated design and mass production deprive the home of its distinctness, while the home's mobility is represented as evidence of a tribal lack of roots, and a corresponding disregard for place-based identity. If the 'home' forms part of a repertoire for the grounding of identity, then its mobility and repeatability in America and the ease with which Americans move house suggest to Sartre the malleability of identity. The 'home', as cosmological container of the individual's social identity, is exploded by the constant construction and destruction of the moving landscape of American urban life, and Sartre's European code for interpreting this impermanence renders the house significant of the unfinished nature of spatial, and by extension, cultural identity in America. It can be suggested here that this reveals Sartre's lack of understanding of American values and the cultural investment in the frontier, mobility and the replaceable character of the house as representational of freedom from limitation and open-mindedness as well as signalling a spiritual attachment to the expanse of the American landscape (see Lackey 1997). There is the sense that Sartre considers America to be a society that does not yet know itself, and in the image of the fragile rows of houses lining the biggest highways in the world, the suggestion emerges that America is oblivious to its vulnerability before the inevitabilities of history.

Can life possess substance in such insubstantial surroundings? This is the question that troubles Sartre, whose European eyes do not see the aesthetic of the American house in terms apart from the castellated retreats of Europe, those enduring structures offering a bastion of defence and an unbreachable wall of privacy against the world.[45] However, in the final lines of the essay an alternative viewpoint is presented which, while it once again opposes European urban life to that of America, reverses the poles of appreciation. These towns, while fragile, give out on to the vast expanse of the American landscape and make no attempt to find shelter from this vastness. Unlike the enclosed, defensive structures of Europe, then, these insubstantial urban gatherings are not rooted, but neither are they oppressive:

> But these weightless cities, so similar to Fontana, to the camps of the Far West, reveal another side of the United States: its freedom. Everyone is free here, not to criticize or reform traditions, but to flee from them, to disappear into the desert or another city. These cities are open. Open onto the world, open onto the future. It's this that gives them all their spirit of adventure and, in their disorder, in their ugliness even, a kind of beauty.[46] (110–11)

This about-turn in Sartre's attitude signals his attempt to appreciate the beauty of America. Indeed, it is in contemplating the uprootable towns dotting the expansive American landscape that Sartre's perception of American liberty evolves beyond his European preconceptions. The American town's fragility is also a means of escape, its temporariness a testament to adventure. This recalls the ideology behind Sant'Ellia's *Città Nuova* (1914). This unrealized Futurist city was designed to facilitate transit and velocity, and temporariness was the precise aim. In this vision, people would outlast their cities; each generation would build their metropolis anew. In this way, the spirit of each successive age would not have to be articulated in architecture; nostalgia and tradition would not stagnate the generations of the machine age. More often than not, however, the traveller's philosophical concerns about the effects of consumer society and homogenization, as well as his concern to nuance the notion of freedom within the conventions of American society, motivate his interpretations of the city.

Both mechanization and industrialization, as McLuhan ([1964] 2002) has shown, tend to lead a community towards the cultural homogenization of its population, and in New York this found expression in the schools for 'Americanization', and governmental and consumerist advertising across the radio waves and on the billboards of the city streets. McLuhan has argued that all forms of technology alter societal interrelations and produce new cultural manifestations within society. Following on from this, he opposes our contemporary global electronic age with that of nationalized industrialized societies once predominant in the Anglophone countries of the West, and demonstrates that the mechanical mode of production (associated most readily with the assembly line), requires intense specialization and fragmentation on the part of the members of that society, that is from producers to consumers. Correspondingly, the machine-oriented society requires repetitive behaviour, and necessitates routine and uniformity on the part of those who live in it. Furthermore, products of the machine age generate a demand for the conventional and uniform in consumer goods (McLuhan [1964] 2002). It is this technological and institutional thrust towards homogenization, finding expression in American con-sumerist domestication, which forms the main centre of concern for Sartre, whose anti-essentialist outlook and materialist vision of individual identity motivate his experience and writing of America. Questions of the individual's freedom in such a homogenizing society constitute the main line of inquiry for his interpretation of post-war modernity.

For Sartre, American space, devoid as it is of a past, is comprehensible as a space where identities can be randomly constructed in conjunction with the ideological ideal-ism of the American nation. Sartre identifies the architecture and technologies of mod-ern life as the primary transmitters of national policies that he interprets as seeking the alienation of the individual from their ability to choose their own pathway through life, to attain a position from which to critique and act with freedom. In the streets, 'the walls speak to you' / 'les murs vous parlent' (86), in the factories the owners have installed loud-speakers so as to distract the workers from the fumes and noise of the machinery. And in all of this Sartre identifies a pernicious system of advice:

> In the factories, they've installed loudspeakers everywhere. Their mission is to fight against the isolation of the worker before the object.

> If you walk through this immense naval construction site, on the outskirts of Baltimore, you'll encounter the dispersion of humanity, the grave solitude of workers that we in Europe know well. [...] *But as soon as they put on their helmet, they hear music. And this music is already a form of guidance that slyly insinuates its way into their heads; it is already a well-managed dream.* [...] You will see that the American citizen is well supervised.[47] (79–80, my emphasis)

This passage suggests that Sartre's interest in the factory space is not motivated by con-cerns about the actual experience of the worker, but lies rather in how the factory pro-vides a discursive space where the philosopher can expound his views. Sartre interprets the piped music as indicative of an establishment requiring the docility its workers. The radio's educational content is a strategic method for undermining individual identity through the promotion of collective concerns; the radio is inserted into a macrostruc-tural discourse of what McLuhan ([1964] 2002, 344) terms the radio's 'tribal auditory magic'.

As a phenomenologist, Sartre finds various forms of media legible in terms of a ten-sion between the ideologies of freedom and the freedom of the individual. The mass-produced consumer items of everyday life, the mechanical corkscrew, the fridge and the car, are all interpreted as components contributing to the standardization of society; these apparatus are read as interventions in the identity of individuals that rob them of their specificity and difference:

> The nation walks alongside you, giving you guidance and orders. But it does so softly and is concerned to explain in detail the reasons for its injunction. Not one commandment that is not accompanied by a comment or image to justify it [...]. *In the same way, the American whose reason and liberty is solicited every hour of the day, makes it a point of honour to do what he is told; it is acting like everyone else that he feels himself to be both most rational and patriotic, it is in conforming that he feels the most free.*[48] (79, my emphasis)

In reflecting upon these media Sartre identifies the construction of an interface between the individual and consciousness, whereby personality is subsumed by collective behaviours that reinforce the societal superstructure.[49] American conformity is not an oppressive measure that requires adherence to a particular governmental manifesto; the entire community participates in generating a superstructure encouraging compliance through domesticity. America is a mediated world, but its media do not seek to shake the individual out of their comfort zone in order to promote either national or global revolution, rather Americanization is a 'soft' process; an incantation based on persuasion and subtle indoctrination through the technologies of communication. The schools of Americanization in New York offer courses on sewing, on cooking and even on the 'art' of flirtation. The conformity encouraged by the American system is, therefore, a distinctly domestic one (and for Sartre ideologically motivated). For the phenomenologist it is through an inviting exterior that America seeks to convince its citizens that 'the West is best'. Education seeks not 'to form a man [but] a pure American' (79).[50]

   Within this vision, objects become agents in their own right, performing upon the individual with the effect that they are distanced from their authentic self. Sartre uses the example of his meeting with a French émigré to illustrate the effect of the macrostructure on the individual:

> I met a European man on his way to being integrated the day after my arrival. […] He was born in Paris, and has only lived in America for fifteen years […]. However America already owns half of him […]. I had the impression of witnessing an Ovidian metamorphosis: his face was still too expressive; he had retained that slightly annoying imitation of intelligence that, wherever you go, allows you to identify someone as French. But soon he will be a tree or a rock.[51] (76–77)

In this account, Sartre does not seem so much to encounter a man as an archetype. The meeting leads again to a reflection on the macrostructural forces at work in America, demonstrating the traveller's legislative framework for reading the individuals he meets in schematic consistency with his phenomenological vision, an ideologically motivated exteriority that reinforces a pre-established modality of sense-making; here a man who has not retained the traits of his national affiliation is regarded as a gross simulation. Within the Sartrean narrative, America functions, therefore, as an abstract macrostructural force, and for the author all of America's cultural manifestations consist in the erection of a mythological framework wherein media generate a concrete but simulated reality in order to steer human beings away from the complexities of life and of choice within that life; or in Sartrean language, from their being *pour-soi* towards the simplicity of the system, a form of self-deceit or being *en-soi*, which in the end denies the complexity and plurality of human experience. European value systems remain unchanged and within the context of various conversations between Sartre and Americans the European viewpoint emerges as worldly and above all realistic, while in contrast, the American viewpoint is portrayed as idealistic and naive:

> But above all what you see is this concrete, everyday Reason made manifest in flesh and blood, a Reason you can see. […] One evening an American said to me: 'Well, if international

politics were the affair of reasonable, sane men, wouldn't war cease to exist forever?' The French who were present said that one did not necessarily imply the other and he got angry, 'Go on then, he said indignantly, go and build your cemeteries!' As for myself, I said nothing, discussion between us was impossible: I believe in evil and he doesn't.[52] (82–83)

What emerges from Sartre's narrative is the idea that this is not merely a question of differing world-views but that the American outlook on reality is inherently deluded. In the account of the French-American above, it is through the discourse of the inanimate *en-soi / being-in-itself* that Americans are more widely understood. In this sense, within the terms of his own philosophical system, Sartre performs a kind of bad faith, the other is misrecognized and legislated for in consistence with the author's discursive political position that positions Sartre's rationalized apprehension of America in terms of an ideological schema for understanding global politics. Having said this, if the portrayal of America might be read as a neo-colonialist form of European condescension towards America, it can also be read in terms of nostalgia, a nostalgia for the innocence of the world, for Sartre finds in New York a spectacular beauty that exists nowhere else.

4.6   Wandering Geometry: Located and Lost

The New York gridiron is interpreted in two ways within Sartre's travel account. The traveller's first reaction to the city's geometry is to see it in metaphorical terms relating to his major philosophical dilemma of American conformity versus individuality. The gridiron is an archetype for representing the contradiction that Sartre identifies in America, namely that American individualism must be conceived of as a collective phenomenon: in order for the individual to attain a being that is *pour-soi / for-itself* they must first recognize the way in which their being is in consistent negotiation with the gaze of other sentient beings, possessed also of consciousness. Sartre ignores the everyday diversity and reality of the street to employ the grid as metaphor for this abstracted conception of American life:

> In its length and breadth – flat – New York is most conformist city in the world. This grid, it is New York; the streets resemble each other to the extent that they have not named them, they've been content to assign them, like soldiers, an ID number.[53] (84–85)

Sartre's approach to New York envisages it as the manifestation of an ideological conundrum. The nameless, repetitive structure of the gridiron is portrayed in terms of an army's institutional denial of personality through the obliteration of one's proper name, so that military references attach the gridiron's abstract purity to a form of inhumanity. The nameless streets and the repetitive pattern of the urban landscape, when read in conjunction with Sartre's hermeneutics, are the source of profound anxiety and absurdity: 'among the numerical anonymity of the streets and avenues', the traveller feels that he might 'merely be anyone anywhere' (118).[54] Sartre's representation of the gridiron inserts it within an oppositional symbolic order: unlike in Europe, the numerically ordained streets of New York offer no means of grounding oneself in a symbolic order other than that of an abstract matrix. When the grid is appropriated in such a manner, history, community, and by extension, personality are categorically denied. For Sartre, the unlabelled anonymity of the geometric desecrates his sense of position; an infinitely repeatable situation is an abstract, inauthentic one, and likewise individual difference is subsumed by the serial number.[55]

However, the individual *pour-soi* does exist in America and Sartre interprets American individualism in terms of a paradox. The traveller appropriates the skyscraper as a metaphor to explain what he sees as the particular shape of personal freedom in American society. While the grid is practised as architectural metaphor for conformity, the skyscraper's verticality is interpreted as representational of the individual that emerges from within the system. Looking upwards, the author finds the eclecticism that he has been unable to see in the faces he encounters within the manifold of towers that surround him. The lofty buildings, defying his line of sight, also defy any purist urban totalitarian vision through their differing heights, the eccentricity of their various colours and their diverse architectures borrowed from the medieval, the Moorish, the Renaissance and the modernist styles. This perspective is mapped directly onto American individualism, and supposes the existence of the systematic grid from within which (in opposition to European individualism, which consists for Sartre in a defiance of authoritarian structure) the American individual negotiates in order to achieve a state of collective freedom. The suggestion is that, paradoxically, it is only through the free fallacy of being *pour-autrui*, or being subjected to the objectifying gaze of society and performing one's role to the demands of the system that the individual (in this case through financial gain) ascends to an approximate state of being *pour-soi*:

> Individualism in America, in the fight for life, is above all the passionate aspiration of everyone to be an individual. There are individuals in American like there are skyscrapers; there is Ford, Rockefeller, Hemingway, Roosevelt. They are models and examples.[56] (87)

The buildings are, indeed, as Sartre goes on to recognize, the symbol of individual or corporate wealth. As their existence is the result of economic success, so Sartre feels they are fitting representatives of individualism, perhaps not individualism in its European form, but an individualism that is specifically American.

Sartre's tendency to generalize on the 'American system' invites his being labelled as a neo-colonialist in that his representation suggests a reliance on notions of European depth and authenticity so that an image of America as a superficial, ahistorical and perniciously totalitarian state might emerge. However, while Sartre acknowledges the presence of the ideological framework and its powerful influence, the traveller seems to recognize the urgency in finding spaces where the whole of society is not reduced to the synchronic sameness of the system. In the same way that Sartre sees the American individual as emerging from within a paradox, so too paradox haunts the narrative voice within the Sartrean text. Stereotypes become untenable once the traveller turns his gaze inward and begins to reflect on the limits of his necessarily subjective perspective:

> How can I speak about 135 million Americans? I would have to live ten years here and I will only spend six weeks [...] Some people tell me: 'Stick to the facts!' But which facts? [...] In

making a choice I'll have already predetermined what America is. [...] So, acknowledging my responsibility, I have decided to give myself over to my impressions and my personal constructions. This America, perhaps I am dreaming it. In any case, I will be honest in my dreaming. I will tell it as I've experienced it.[57] (75–76)

There are a number of important points here with regard to the attitude adopted by many twentieth-century travellers at the prospect of speaking on the country visited. First, while we have seen how Sartre's practice of America suggests a generalized and negative interpretation of the city's macrostructural interventions in daily life, such observations become problematic once the traveller reflects on the situatedness of the position from which he speaks. When the traveller turns the phenomenological principle towards himself, he is confronted with the limitations of his own spatio-temporally limited relationship with the American space. When the gaze of the traveller shifts from the American social structure to the American individual, the insufficiencies of abstract generalizations come to light. Thus a tension is created between the objective desire to represent the American space 'truthfully' and the plurality of potential positions from which the author can choose to narrate, this is effectively a tension between the legislative and self-reflexive interpretive modalities for writing travel, wherein the latter necessarily undermines the seeming authority of the textual account.

Furthermore, by reversing the positions of observer and observed, Sartre relativizes the content of his general observations. By placing himself in the situation of the observed, he acknowledges the seductive impulse of the outsider to generalize, contending that while these generalizations may not be false, neither are they entirely true:

As soon as a friend purports to explain our character and clarify our intentions, once he reduces each of our actions to a principle [...] we listen to him, ill at ease, with neither the capacity to deny what he says nor entirely to accept it. Perhaps this construction is true, but from which truth? [...] In the same way, when in Europe, we're presented with a carefully arranged set of notions – melting-pot, puritanism, realism, optimism, etc. – which we are told are the keys to the American character, we feel a certain intellectual satisfaction and we think that, in fact, it must be thus.[58] (125–26)

In acknowledging his discomfort at the anthropological abstractions that an outsider uses to totalize a foreign culture, the traveller recognizes the problems which the outside impulse to comprehend generates and the violent effect this has on the individuality of the other as well as everything else that cannot be included within its systemic categories. However, while he admits the problematic status of his position as observer and acknowledges the ellipses of categorical reasoning in terms of the individual within a culture, Sartre does not entirely relinquish the validity of critiquing America as a cultural system. He overcomes the dilemma of the stereotype by differentiating between the system and the individual, and states that, while in certain instances the individual may confirm the stereotype, nevertheless, through their personal behaviours and lucid self-criticisms, they also potentially undermine it. In this manner, the traveller creates a space for generalized criticism while admitting the failure of such a critique when it comes to the microcosms of the particular. Sartre's narrative therefore expresses a plurality of truths, without abandoning the view that general political and cultural critique may still prove possible.

The latter portion of the travel narrative works to nuance the global statements about American governmental space. Thus, from within the tension created between the self-reflexive critique of a position from which to speak on the one hand, and a more ethical concern to engage in critique of the ideologies of macrostructural America on the other, an unsystematic valorization of lucidity emerges. Through this reflexive, interpretive gaze, the possibility for coherent truths is diminished but a kind of empathy towards the American space emerges to replace the dream of a stable position from which to speak.[59] Throughout Sartre's reportage a profound empathy for his fellow man and woman counterbalances an abhorrence of the system that encloses them, and he acknowledges the complexities and contingencies within that system; contradictions and tensions that mark a space somewhere in between the individual and the society they inhabit:

> There is the respect for science, industry, positivism, the mad passion for gadgets and the black humour of the New Yorker who laughs bitterly at this mechanized society and the hundreds of millions of Americans who everyday stave off their hunger for novelty by reading comics about the amazing adventures of Superman, Wonder Woman and Mandrake the Magician.[60] (129)

The desire to critique America as ideological entity, while acknowledging the contradictions and complexities that also form an essential part of American culture, finds further expression in Sartre's representation of the architectures of the New York urban landscape.

We can suggest that the Sartrean narrative exemplifies the process which Louis Marin terms 'utopian neutralization' (1973). By acknowledging the individuals and cultural contradictions that undermine the homogeneity of the American system, and by figuring urban America as fragile and exposed, there emerges within the narrative an inverse image of the material abundance and ideological might of post-war democratic consumer society in America. From within his representation of the architectures of New York, there emerges an alternative bank of imagery that reverses the modernist figuration of New York as utopian space, to present an increasingly mechanized version of humanity. This imagery is grounded in the natural and temporal presences that override the rational aspirations of the urban geometry. Even within the most prodigious example of human beings' attempt at systematic, architectural control of their environment, the presence of a natural order beyond their powers of mastery makes its presence felt.

In this narrative, the city emerges as a space inseparable from the vast expanses of nature that surround it. The aspirations of New York to constitute the pinnacle of modern civilization are undermined when Sartre records the biological reactions that he has to its extremities. In this way, the beauty of the urban landscape is relocated in terms of the sublime (Burke [1757] 1998), where this is understood as a profoundly paradoxical emotional position wherein awe and acute anxiety exist in equal measure. Thus, rather than attest to humanity's prodigious accomplishments, the city provides proof of the inescapable presence of Nature. Sartre writes of his initial encounter with the metropolis as producing a 'mal de New-York' / 'New York sickness', likening the sensation to a sickness felt when the body is forced to adjust itself biologically to heights, or to air and sea travel. The sickness felt by Sartre upon encountering New York signals the need for a physical adjustment of some kind, similar to that produced when the body enters environments of natural extremes. The adjustment required in this case is one of perspective. Initially the traveller's horizons of expectations, limited by an eye accustomed to the insularity and material assuredness of a European city, is ill-equipped to cope with the scale of New York. Even when this initial feeling of being overwhelmed subsides, and Sartre begins to recognize the particular details of the districts, he never loses the sense that the city is open and exposed to the vast space that surrounds it. The geometry of New York facilitates the gaze's dissolution of immediate, urban detail, so that the eye is drawn in latitudinal directions towards the infinity of the sky's horizon line. In an appreciation of this visceral experience of extending space, the European city appears pathetic:

> These long drawn lines suddenly gave me the feeling of space. Our European cities are built to protect us against space; the houses flock together like sheep. But space lives in New York, animating the city, swelling it. Space, the great open spaces of the steppes and pampas, runs through its arteries like a draught of cold air, separating the inhabitants on the right from those on the left [...] *When you know how to look* the two rows of buildings that, like cliffs, line a great avenue, *you are rewarded*: their mission ends over there, at the end of the avenue, a sliver of sky floats between them.[61] (117, 120, my emphasis)

Thus the city is haunted by an external presence – that of natural space. The sky surrounds New York, 'solitary and pure like a wild beast'[62] (121) and never permits the traveller to forget the external forces that pre-exist human civilization and that will endure after its passing. While these horizon lines induce the traveller to admire the prodigality of this urban space in comparison with the European city's attempt to shield itself from the unpredictability of nature. The sublime of New York, in contrast to the picturesque character of the European city, is characterized by the presence of something beyond the control of the human being that produces conflicting sensations of awe coupled with horror:

> Am I in a city or in the countryside? New York provides no shelter from the violence of nature. It is a city of open skies. Storms flood its streets, so wide, so long, so far to cross when it rains. Hurricanes shake the brick houses and rock the skyscrapers. As though declaring war, the radio solemnly announces these storms. [...] From the end of May, heat hits the city like an atomic bomb. It is Evil. People come up to each other saying: '*It's a murder.*' The trains transport millions of fleeing inhabitants who leave a humid imprint, like a snail, on the seat when they get off. It is not the city that they're fleeing, it is Nature. Even in the depths of my apartment I endure the assault of a hostile, mute, mysterious nature. [...] New York is a colonial town, a campsite. All the hostility, the cruelty of Nature dwells in this city, the most prodigious monument that man ever erected to himself. It is a weightless city, its weightlessness surprises most Europeans. In this enormous malevolent space, in this rocky desert where no vegetation can grow, they've built thousands of brick, wood and concrete houses which all seem on the verge of taking flight.[63] (119–20)

Nature encroaches on the city evidencing the chaotic forces existing beyond its boundaries, exploiting the geometric audacity of the city's design to reveal the delusion of purity inherent in the grid. With the arrival of the New York summer, 'Le Mal' / 'Evil' – allegorical figure of the primitive forces beyond human rationality – descends upon the city. And so Nature triumphs over the presumption of New York's verticality, reducing it to a jungle swarming with insects (119). In this vision, the diabolical capabilities of Nature render the city helpless. Sartre's references are notably biblical; the imagery constructs New York as a modern Babel, this civilization's megalomaniac desire to reach the skies is revealed as futile when a world beyond its control makes its presence known. This is a fragile city at the mercy of a force that can unleash a plague of insects, floods or unbearable heat on its inhabitants. Furthermore, the reference to the climatic heat of New York as an atomic bomb adds a further ideological dimension to the description of the city, inviting the reader to associate New York with the fate of Hiroshima and Nagasaki. The implication painfully and pointedly alludes to a reversal of America's ahistorical purity and the impossibility of its enduring innocence in the midst of a dangerous historical era.

It is precisely this fragility that Sartre finds most beautiful and most liberating. In comparison to the oppressive architecture of Europe, the ephemeral architecture of New York bewitches the observer. Again Sartre's rhetoric is reminiscent of Certeau who describes New York as 'a city composed of paroxysmal places in monumental reliefs' (Certeau 1984, 91). However, unlike Certeau's assertion that 'New York has never learned the art of growing old' (91), for Sartre, New York's architectural dimensions are not read as prodigious examples of modern technological might, rather the city is legible in terms of humanity's inevitable vulnerability, yet poignant aspiration, in the face of forces beyond its control. While, as Sartre acknowledges, the skyscrapers may have been vessels of hope in the 1920s, now the traveller cannot help but envisage their decline, as History will inevitably make itself felt on this continent as it has on his own. The account closes with the portentous lines:

> I walk between the little brick houses, the colour of dried blood. They are younger than European houses, but their fragility makes them appear much older. I see the Empire State Building in the distance, or the Chrysler Building, pointing vainly towards the sky, and I think suddenly that New York is on the verge of acquiring a History and that it already has its ruins.[64] (124)

The utopia of the *terra blanca* is undermined by the insinuation of a future that will inevitably bring ruins of its own. The idealism that the geometric system represents, and the system seeking to uphold it are, in Sartre's eschatological vision, doomed to ruin at the hands of Time and the progression of History. However, these lines reveal a sympathy on Sartre's part towards an America that steps so boldly into the future with optimism and complete self-assurance at its transformative power, without any conception of its vulnerability at the hands of an indeterminable history that might threaten to destroy it at any moment.

From the European discovery of America onward, Western European travel writing on New York is illustrative of paradigms consistent with a world-view as to the attainability of objective knowledge, the possibility of its effective, controlled, and ethi-cally ordered distribution, and its movement toward the universality of rational – or, in other words, design-led – society. The most succinct version of this discourse was, of course, the reformulation in terms relative to Europe of American space as the 'New World'. As Rob Kroes expresses it, 'America is never seen as purely *sui generis*, as constitut-ing an alien entity to be fathomed in terms of an inner logic wholly its own' (1999, 1135). Both the examples of Morand's and Sartre's travel accounts assert the modern tendency to exploit travel as a means to reach the essential, or the core of a culture, a tendency inseparable from travel as the quest for authenticity. And in turn it is this notion of the possibility of an 'authentic' space that conditions the attendant production of alterity in narrative terms. As we have seen above, this quest is bound to the view that there exists an authentic, or collective, version of 'New York' that can then, under the right circumstances, be experienced and contained, decoded and represented. But this vision of a real 'America' hinges quite paradoxically on a system of comparative dyads that traditionally haunt France's ideological battlefields, so that, in looking toward America, French intellectuals have sought to validate or invalidate an identity position built on a conception of Frenchness. Kroes observes that 'reflection on America as a counter-point to European conventions functions within a larger reflection on Europe's history and destiny' (1999, 1135). The representational mode that corresponds to this legislative version of authenticity is metonymical opposition, a reading that moves directly from singularity to a generalized diagnosis of American culture as lacking depth, history and wholeness by comparison with a European symbolic order of historical plenitude. While the cultural contexts framing interpretation change, the ordered schema, or what Soja calls 'the lure of binarism' (1996, 60), consistently enables the travel writer to legislate for the reality of the city as coherent structure, imposing on mobility the stability of narra-tive order. In legislative travel writing on New York, space is constructed as empirically comprehensible in accordance with the relative, historical shifts in ideological location; a framework wherein social space serves as a quantifiable backdrop against which the nar-rative performs its coherence.

Chapter Five

WRITING AROUND THE LINES: INTERPRETIVE TRAVEL WRITING

I confess that in America I saw more than America; I sought the image of democracy itself, with its inclinations, its character, its prejudices and its passions, in order to learn what we have to fear or to hope from its progress.[1]

Tocqueville [1831] 1835, I: xxxvi

why are we telling these stories?
what did we come here to find?
what did we come here to ask?[2]

Perec 1995, 57

So far we have argued that centric perspectives on urban space have their own *poetics*, or formal means of operating, and their own *politics* – a relation, therefore, with social space that invests these perspectives in networks of power. We now move to connect the ethics of this power – its relative exclusions and hierarchies that work at the cognitive, aesthetic and affective levels within social space – to the performance of legibility in literary form, a move that allows us to obtain a view of travel discourse as a means of producing social space. It is time now to ask whether a dominant regime of representation of such discursive appropriations can be challenged, contested or changed and what the poetics of such a counterstrategy might look like. If the paradigms holding together the hegemonic site are order and reduction, then it would seem that what is called for is a 'tactics' (Certeau [1980] 1990, I) of language that destabilizes such a system, a form of mobility that might counter such reductionism. Smethurst puts the question another way when he suggests that 'if we were somehow able to reinstall a proper sense of mobility, and use this against the imposed imperial (and narrative) form in European travel writing, it might help to deconstruct that form' (Kuehn and Smethurst 2008, 2). Such a language could not simply reposition the poles of hierarchy, however, for this, as Henrietta Lidchi (1997) has demonstrated, is to rest within the logic of stereotypical association and fails to get beyond the idealized unified striations of the discursive site.

The question then becomes how to instil 'a proper sense of mobility' into the travel text – a mobility that would, in a negative movement, threaten the discrete components of the legislative mode while also opening out the space of otherness without seeking its closure through legibility. The installation of mobility in textual form, what I have referred to as an interpretive mode of travel, necessarily involves a consciousness and a mistrust of the operations via which legislative meaning comes to establish the integrity of its ordered interiority (see Sennett [1990] 1993). Only from such awareness can Western travel discourse move beyond the representational modality reposing on the subject's presumed privileged access to attributes of sameness and constancy that might be applied universally. Contrary to this presumption, a self-conscious reflexivity potentially destabilizes the subject's integrity by undermining the transparency of sign-object relations, which now becomes a problem rather than an assumption. As Bauman states, 'It has suddenly become clear, that the validity of an aesthetic judgement depends on the "site" from which it has been made and the authority ascribed to that site; that the authority in question is not an inalienable, "natural" property of the site, but something fluctuating with the changing location of the site' (1987, 135). The coherency of the site depends on the transparency of its meaning; however, it is precisely by rendering problematic the legibility of the relationship between the word and the world that an alternative space of mobility and poetic ambivalence is allowed to appear. It is from this perspective that we may read George Perec's and Jean Baudrillard's travel narratives as interpretive dislocations of the hegemonic discursive techniques associated with modern European travel writing.

The potential resistance identified by Smethurst in mobility's deferral of boundaries raises a series of problems, however, for the context of intra-Western travel writing. Not least of these is the philosophical conundrum of how to criticize the totalizing strategies of rationalism without such a criticism, emerging as it does from a site of Western privilege, creating its own elevated totality. I suggest that this development might be characterized by a shift in focus from the simplicity of the outward geometric in a linear sense, towards the complexity of the spaces in-between the lines: from the panoramic of the crowd to the multiplicity of urban identities – the social space which Lefebvre identifies with living (Lefebvre [1974] 2000) – or, in other words, from legislative to interpretive modes of travel. Addressing this shift we turn first to look at the poetics at stake in Perec's *Récits d'Ellis Island: Histoires d'errance et d'espoir* ([1980] 1994), before moving on to engage with Baudrillard's controversial account of 'America' in *Amérique* ([1986] 2000).

5.1   Georges Perec on Ellis Island

Forty years after Sartre, New York acquires its ruin and, consequently, a past in Georges Perec's representation of Ellis Island, a space highly significant in terms of the imaginative geography of New York City in that, from the late nineteenth century until the 1930s it was the governmental immigration outpost, where European migrants were vetted before entry into the United States.[3] For much of the population of New York today, the island forms part of either their first-hand or their ancestral cultural inheritance. The island is significant in terms of European cultural memory too for these same reasons, although, for the European, Ellis marks the point of transition from one life to another rather than any affiliations of heritage: thus the poles of significance for Europe and America are necessarily opposed. Europe as the point of departure (for a variety of reasons, usually negative) is henceforth imagined in terms of the past left behind, while America, as point of arrival, is endowed with hopes for the future, for freedom and betterment. Official historical discourse makes of Ellis a site of positive memorial, a place that forms a bond for many Americans between their current home and their European heritage. This bond was officially articulated by the conversion of the site into a museum in 1976. Thus, while during the most intense years of immigration to the United States from 1892 to 1924 the emigrant was 'regarded pretty much as a species of import' (Pitkin 1975, 169), or more ominously during World War II, 'in the aspect of his potential threat to the national security' (Pitkin 1975, 170), by the sixties the idea of heritage and commemoration determine the island's future. Edward Corsi, an Italian immigrant and Commissioner of Naturalization for Immigration from 1933, gratified those urging for Ellis Island's conversion into a national monument: 'For Ellis Island', he said in a letter to the *New York Times*, 'is more than a piece of real estate. It is an important part of our American heritage. For millions of American families it has been a gateway to a new life of liberty and opportunity' (cited in Pitkin 1975, 185). The museum thus appropriates the past in terms more amenable to the present (see Horne 1984; Hudson 1975; Jordonova 1989; Lumley 1988). In the case of Ellis Island, its conversion to a national monument and museum of immigration affords the authorities the opportunity to recast the emigrant experience on Ellis Island in positive terms.[4] And the tourist, whether a stranger or an immigrant's ancestor, generally practises Ellis in this positivist, orderly way, either as a site of historical information, or one of ancestral pilgrimage and personal confirmation (see Fine 1977 and Pile 2002).

However, Perec's account renders problematic the monument as a site of positive historical inheritance and tourist invention. In articulating the history of Ellis Island, the representational operations at work in Perec's text recognize the institutional character of the island, and question the site of governmental space from the point of view of the violence done to the individual identities that passed through it. This may be seen as part of what Pierre Nora (1997) has identified in the late twentieth century as the movement from a prioritization of *history* towards an emphasis on *memory*. Among other factors, Nora recognizes this turn as emerging from the 'acceleration of history', which Augé (1992) explains in terms of globalization, the technological accessibility of the world, and the media's ability to inform the public of events anywhere in the world. This speeding up of history, Nora claims, renders the future increasingly uncertain, and threatens to erode memory, which he identifies with the collective social imaginary that is passed down through members of a community. In urban society, this threat to memory's destruction imposes on us, Nora argues, a duty to remember, as expressed in the West's obsession with heritage, preservation and the stockpiling of vestiges of the past. Nora posits other factors that contribute to this European awareness of memory's distinction from history. For example, he sees the reinterpretation of the national past as a consequence of the post-de Gaulle era (1997, 2). Finally, he identifies the intellectual collapse of Marxism as signalling the end of the revolutionary idea. Nora argues that the Marxist concept of historical time based on revolutions and informed by notions of rupture is replaced by another concept of time based on a renewed notion of tradition, and on the inscription of that tradition into space via 'les lieux de mémoire' / 'places of memory'.

Perec's travel narrative suggests an oppositional differentiation between memory and historical consciousness, and articulates this opposition through formal narrative tactics within the text. The opening sections of Perec's narrative explore the island as the geographical concentration of diaspora, the historical centre for the dislocation of European identities. The later sections of the book emphasize the intangibility of individual memory, while expressing an urgent desire that this memory be preserved.

Récits d'Ellis Island can be distinguished from the other travel narratives analysed here for the unusual motivations that drive Perec's travel practice. A wider reading of Perec's work reveals the author's preoccupation with space, the question of its representation and its relation to his personal identity. Ellis Island is no different. His journey to Ellis is motivated by his acute imagined attachment to the island depot as a site of personal recognition and recuperation. Interpreting Ellis Island as a space of scission and caesura, a space of equivocal identities in-between a past and a future as yet unattained, constitutes the moment of Perec's identification with the island. Perec distinguishes this interpretation of the island from other possible modes of identification. For example, his fellow traveller, the filmmaker Robert Bober, is also a Jew, and he comes to the island to find links to his past; the island exists for him as part of a series of reference points that constitute his positive, tangible and stable experience of Jewish tradition. Perec recognizes the persistence and positive constitution of Bober's Jewish identity as fundamentally linked to the fact of survival and inheritance: survival of the Holocaust and cultural continuation. He juxtaposes Bober's Jewish identity with his own sense of being a Jew, explaining Bober's identity in positive terms:

> to him, being Jewish means continuing to affirm one's place
> in a tradition, a language, a culture, and
> a community that neither centuries of diaspora
> nor the systematic genocide of the 'final solution'
> succeeded in definitively crushing;
> to him, being Jewish means inheriting and then passing on
> an entire body of customs,
> ways of eating, dancing, and singing, of words,
> tastes, and habits,
> and above all it's the sense of sharing
> these acts and rites with others, regardless of boundaries and
> nationalities, and these shared things become roots,
> it's obvious how essential and fragile they are,
> threatened as always by time and by man.[5] (Perec 1995, 60)

For Perec, however, the island has significance in a manner directly opposed to such a heritage. Memory is not necessarily a positive image of the past, concretely locatable in some actual event or site. Perec's relationship to his Jewish identity is defined against this positive, concrete cultural experience of communal identity as a lack. The trauma of the Holocaust, its cancelling out of the possibility of continuity with the past for many surviving Jews, engendered a lapse or rupture in familial and collective memory. The Holocaust called Jewish identity into question by its annihilation of whole families and entire towns and its legacy ensured that the survivors' identities were now devastatingly linked to the presence of absence within their selfhood. This lack is necessarily different from a process of forgetting or of personal rebellion. Perec was never given the chance

either to forget or to rebel. He has been cut off from the possibility of a cultural com-
monality by the intervention of exterior forces operating beyond his sphere of control.
His cultural identity is a product of historical contingency, and in a very concrete way
is a cultural identity of disinheritance. The trauma of the Holocaust requires a reappraisal of memory and its relationship to the imagination. While memory in all positive
senses of the term can be seen as a movement of time distinguished temporally from the
present, this normally supposes the happening of an exterior event at some time in the
past and its potential to be positively appropriated through a re-enactment of the memories' traces (Ricœur 1988). However, an appraisal of the Jewish experience during the
Holocaust leads to the conclusion that memory is a kind of 'non-time'. In the wake of
the Holocaust's destruction the act of remembering presents the problem of articulating
a rupture in memory, as well as raising questions concerning the limitations of historical
representation. Within Perec's narrative the reader confronts the absence of the personal
event in the past: the absence of inheritance. Perec's identity here is based on the presence of this absence, and is thereby integrally linked to the imagined possibilities of the
past and the possibility of alternative futures. It is the absence of memory that defines his
imagination of the past, and it is in this way that Ellis Island communicates to him and
holds relevance:

> what I find present here
> are in no way landmarks or roots or
> relics
> but their opposite: something shapeless, on the outer edge of
> what is sayable,
> something that might be called closure, or cleavage,
> or severance,
> and that in my mind is linked
> in a most intimate and confused way
> with the very fact of being a Jew.[6] (Perec 1995, 58)

The closest real connection that links Perec to the island is a phantom possibility: Ellis
Island is for him a space of estrangement, but also of probable autobiography, because
it is where his parents might have escaped to had they not been murdered at Auschwitz.
The imagined eventuality that his parents might have left Poland to make a new life in
America and survive the war makes Ellis a floating signifier of the fragility of Perec's
official Jewish heritage. This alternative version of events is the absence that engenders
the traveller's attempt to forge his story/history from the fragments of a childhood that
history ultimately denied him – something he explains in saying: 'I don't have the feeling
that I've forgotten / but that I was never allowed to learn'[7] (1995, 62).

   The travel account is analysed here in terms of how Perec's spatial practices destabilize the monument as geographical and symbolic site of collective identity, to point to the
importance of a more complex, multilayered, mnemonic reality lying beyond the guided
lens or structured language of representation. In terms of writing this space, Perec's particular geo-poetical representation of the island renders problematic the loss of the banal
and the everyday within historical discursive narrative, and this spatial practice generates

another, interpretive modality for the reconstruction of space via the author's return to the trace, or to the site of Ellis as silent ruin. Perec's spatial practice can be equated to that of a rag picker or *bricoleur* (Certeau [1980] 1990, I), an errant wanderer picking up the scraps of the present on his quest for the lost intricacies of everyday memories of the past. According to Benjamin ([1973] 1985), the rag picker is a practitioner of the city concerned to retrieve from obliteration the refuse objects of everyday life and to form a connective relationship with the city in which the urban landscape is interpreted as a kind of temporal palimpsest. In relation to travel, the residual spaces of such an urban landscape fall outside the authoritarian, appropriative gaze of either the planner or tourist. Benjamin talks of the rag picker as someone whom history has disinherited, someone in an 'obscure state of revolt against society' (Benjamin [1973] 1985, 20). Perec's family history and his intangible connection with the ruined landscape of Ellis Island implicate him in the imaginative geography of the island as he conceives of it as a place where identities have been manufactured anew, and where memory is in danger of being processed irrevocably at the hands of monumental history. He is not a detached observer but a traveller interacting with the ruin almost symbiotically, identifying with the silence of the rusty objects, and feeling a responsibility to somehow record the absences to which they attest; those absences that history overlooks. In this way, Perec's travel writing comes to name Ellis as a space of imaginary yet intimate recognition, where the island functions to explore identity in terms of loss, with this loss revealing itself to be as much a part of modern identity as any recordable event, at the same time as the account illustrates the urgency of preserving the memory of such a loss. Therefore, while it is in the midst of the ruins of Second Empire Paris that Benjamin identifies the emergence of the figure of the rag picker, it can also be said that it is when the stability of place becomes problematic, when a locatable heritage and tradition become uncertain, that *errance* or *wandering* becomes a condition of life, and that subsequently it becomes necessary to create meaning for the divested space of the present through the implication of the trace.

The trace's special identity as a sign rests in the potential it has to reunite a causality (included in the physicality of the mark) with a significance (in the notion of a vestige of passing). At the same time, the trace is an indexical marker: it points to the existence of something that it, in itself, does not purport to describe. In *Espèces d'espaces / Species of Space* (1974) Perec invokes his desire for somewhere circumscribable and describable, somewhere invested with memory, an inherited bank of imagery in which to clothe his identity. Yet, 'place', understood in this way, eludes him:

> I really wish there existed stable places
> immobile, intangible, untouched and
> almost
> untouchable, immutable, rooted; places
> that would be references,
> points of departure, sources:
>
> My home country, the cradle of my
> Family, the house where I would be born, the tree
> that I would have watched grow (that my father
> would have planted on the day of my birth), the

attic of my childhood filled with
intact memories
Such places do not exist, and it is
because they don't exist that space
becomes a question, ceases to be self-evident,
cannot be integrated, cannot be
appropriated. Space is a doubt: I
must continually mark it, designate it;
it never belongs to me, is never given to
me, I must go out and conquer it.[8] (135)

This conquest of space is linked to the duty to record. While memory escapes Perec, this does not exclude the possibility that the trace might constitute a means of accessing a space of identity. However, the trace, passive, silent vestige of something past, underlines the problem of representation, not least because it invites the imagination to reconstitute it in narrative terms while never allowing this narrative to base itself on the illusion of a truth-value. The trace's inherent aporia makes it impossible to deny the presence of absence, and, while demanding to be represented, the vestige highlights the narrative distance between the process of *description* (as an account of the absent past-presence it signifies) and the process of *recording*, which registers the trace indexically as it is encountered in the present. To record the trace is to acknowledge the silence inimical to something that is no longer present without attempting to descriptively bypass this absence by creating an illusion of presence. At the same time, however, recording participates in the recovery of the past in so far as recording absence implies that there was something once there. It is this recuperative operation that Perec refers to as *écriture / writing*, a term via which he expresses the importance of writing as a trace of absence, an absence defining his identity, and thus circularly making writing a necessary component of his identity. In *W ou le souvenir d'enfance / W or the memory of childhood* (1975), Perec elucidates the connection between identity, the trace and writing:

I write: I write because we lived together, because I was one among them, a shadow amid their shadows, a body next to their bodies; I write because they left in me their indelible mark and because the trace of that is writing; their memory is dead to writing; writing is the remembrance of their death and the affirmation of my life.[9] (63–64)

Such a writing, which records rather than describes, has the same indexical power as the physical trace: to *evoke* the absence of presence. As Certeau tells us, 'At the beginning of writing, there is loss. What cannot be said – an impossible adequation between presence and the sign – is the postulate of the labour that is constantly beginning anew and that has as it principle a nowhere of identity and a sacrifice of the thing' (Certeau 1984, 194–95). Here, writing – with the void at its heart (the impossibility of presence) – composes a representational space not of history but of the trace, that concave presence of lack that signals the something that once was. Perec's project on Ellis Island is, therefore, to intimate the spaces beyond those that can be named by history, beyond what can be archived, photographed or described in definitive terms: 'their memory is dead to writing'. These, then, are the most banal, everyday of spaces, where identities take shape and gain substance in memories and imaginations that are beyond the grasp of the documentarist. The forms of expression that Perec employs in the travel account operate as traces, and as such allude to the presence of an absent space existent in memory, by highlighting the very deficiency of language to circumscribe such a space. In this way he creates a visceral echo of the past that writing can be used to invoke but never embody.

5.2   Monuments and Non-places

To analyse interpretive travel writing as a dislocation of discursive modes of spatiality requires us first of all to point out the narrative strategies that Perec's writing undermines. In the first instance, Ellis Island communicates in the present day as a heritage site: the building is a monument. The historical monument is a typical tourist attraction whose presence is often justified more by the outsiders who visit it than by the community whom it purports to spatially inscribe in history. Nevertheless, monuments are important markers of shared experience. Their presence attests to some event in the past, and contributes to the persistence of collective memory and history through the imposition of structure and built form on the space of the city, so that memory becomes fundamental to the mental composition of the social space around us. In pragmatic terms, the function of the monument is special for its status as memorial very often delimits it from everyday practices of urban space (Bertho-Lavenir 1997; McClellan 1994). Ellis Island is clearly such a delimited site and functions within specific paradigms in relation to New York City. For example, Ellis Island's status is fundamentally different to the monumentality of New York's skyscrapers. As Koolhaas ([1978] 1994) suggests, the skyscraper demands to be taken seriously as a monument by the virtue of its tremendous verticality, yet skyscrapers are everyday functioning buildings and so their monumentality is integrated into the daily operations of the urban environment. Their presence is ingrained in the quotidian fabric of urban life and its habitual practice in a way that Ellis Island is not. While the skyscraper's size makes its monumentality almost unavoidable, other monuments are invested with significances established through shared cultural experience. To a large extent, this symbolic investment relies on the suppression of the real, sensible experience of space, so that it may be reconstructed as a site of historical signs to be read and interpreted by the community or individual.

The symbolic purity of Ellis Island is remarkable in this regard. The site's situation, an island off the coast of the city that has essentially no other function other than that of historical marker, means that Ellis is a place with a symbolic richness explicit in its exclusivity from function and, since the conversion of the island into a museum in the 1970s, this symbolic exclusivity has been increasingly controlled by official appropriations of the site. As an institution of public exhibition, Ellis Island is instrumental in consolidating discourses of American heritage. In terms of recent anthropological discourse the official designation of Ellis Island as heritage museum can be seen as an attempt to give the site the status of an 'anthropological place' (Augé 1992). As we have seen, Augé, concerned to differentiate between what may be thought of as spaces of postmodernity and more traditional ideas of location, identifies three criteria according to which a space may be

defined as an anthropological place. It will be helpful to revisit these concepts here in relation to Ellis Island. In the first instance, its frontiers must be determined and stable. This
is true for Ellis Island in the present; its boundaries are fixed in terms of their museologi-
cal function, although for Perec this proves problematic when one thinks of Ellis Island
in the past. Second, an anthropological place has a certain historical quality; it is a place
where events take, or have taken, place. This is undeniably the case with regard to Ellis
Island and yet, while being the result of concrete historical processes, the conversion of
the site into a museum means that history is narrated here in accordance with an official
discursive line. The museum also operates according to the State's desire to efface historical complexity, working to reconstruct that history along simpler, more coherent lines. In
effect, the conversion of Ellis, a previously functioning site, into a museum attests to the
outmoded nature of its function. The historicization process distances the present from
the responsibilities of the past and in so doing neutralizes the violence surrounding the
bureaucratic duties executed on the island, participating in the strategies that are essentially creative of state mythologies. Barthes, in commenting on the modality of these
strategies in general terms, explains that:

> In passing from history to nature, the myth performs a short-circuit: it abolishes the complexity
> of human acts, bestowing on them the simplicity of essences, it suppresses all dialectic,
> anything beyond what is immediately visible, it organizes a world without contradictions
> because it is without depth, a world displayed in evidence, it institutes a happy clarity: things
> appear to have significance all by themselves.[10] (1957, 231)

This mythological process is essential to the construction of collective memory, and this
leads us to the final criterion for Augé's (1992) identification of an anthropological place:
this site is integral to the identity of some community, or in other words, it is a social and
cultural space of 'organic' relationships. Explaining the significance of these places in
relation to their mnemonic value, Augé states: 'Anthropological places are indexed, classified and promoted as "places of memory" / "lieux de mémoire" and therein occupy a
circumscribed and specific position' (100).[11] For Augé, then, the anthropological place is
equivalent to a place of memory, and in Augé's conception both of these terms refer to a
type of memory that is officially and collectively sanctioned. For our purposes then, *lieux
de mémoire* can be interpreted as historically bounded sites. In opposition to this, Perec,
will name Ellis Island as a *non-lieu / non-place*, a space (rather than a site) that undermines
official identity discourses and questions the possibility of writing memory.

Perec's motivation for travel presents a challenge to the official history of Ellis
Island as museum and site of organic interrelations. This challenge is expressed by
the travel account's formal structure. A brief outline assists in demonstrating the
polymorphism that Perec's travel writing employs and that deliberately problematizes the circumscription of space. Brought out in manuscript form by French publishing house POL in 1980, *Récits d'Ellis Island* was originally written as a documentary that both Perec and Bober filmed on Ellis Island in 1979. The documentary was
televised by T.F.1 in 1980, and Perec's voice-over was later transcribed into book
form. Already this filmic aspect adds another visual and auditory dimension to the

travel narrative, and while a study of the travel documentary is beyond the scope of this book, it is worth remarking that, in terms of the text, the voice-over in particular encourages the reader's awareness of sensorial qualities in the prose beyond those of its linguistic aspect. Syntax and semantics are imbued with the auditory significances of rhythm and tenor. I shall return to this point when examining Perec's techniques of enumeration. In terms of the written work itself, the travel account is in five sections. The first is entitled 'L'île des larmes' / 'The Island of Tears'. However, the poetry of the section's title is in tension with the narrative form within, which is documentary in style and relates historical information on the island and its institutional importance for European emigrants wishing to enter America between the years 1892 and 1924. As for the second section, once again the title of the piece, 'Description d'un chemin' / 'Description of a Path', is incongruent with the piece's representational form. Essentially, this piece is a poem that employs a multiplicity of literary devices as well as photographs that work together to sabotage the directness of the opening narrative. I shall focus on the first two sections of *Ellis Island*, which are the most relevant to our study.[12] It can be pointed out, however, that the final section of *Ellis Island*, and the basis of the second part of the documentary, consists of a collection of interviews, gathered under the heading 'Mémoires' / 'Memoirs', with those people who passed through Ellis Island upon emigration to America. This part of the representation reveals that Perec and Bober, while feeling their own peculiar connection to the site of Ellis Island, were aware of the importance of preserving the memory of those who had experienced the island depot before it became the historical institution that it is today. Bober sums up the division in their *travail de mémoire / memory work*: 'The initial film documents our rapport with the place, the other is their film, which is to say the testimonies of all those people who will have disappeared in ten years' (Soussan 2002).[13] These interviews are motivated by personal concerns; the interviewees are drawn exclusively from the Italian and Jewish communities because, Perec says, 'these were the groups that were most involved with Ellis Island and because we felt closest to them personally' (1995, 105).[14] Travel writing, therefore, is indelibly linked to a sense of personal identity, but it is also a means via which to question the representation of the past within official discourses. The representation of space is acknowledged here to be conditional and differential, dependent on the personal outlook of those interpreting the island. Bober has come to connect with his heritage, while for Perec this is impossible. It can be said, therefore, that Ellis Island marks both the link and the break-off point between Europe and America, the spatial umbilical cord irrevocably connecting both continents to each other. It is the particularity of the site's status as depot that guides Perec's representation in the opening section of the account.

The representational content of 'The Island of Tears' presents the reader with a historical account of the island's function in the past, wherein emphasis is placed on the *lack* of roots, constant transformation, and movement that the migrant experience embodies, and which for Perec culminates spatially in the edifices of Ellis Island. This narrative undermines the neutrality of the historical process as the author describes how the space incarnated the exile enforced on European identity, and the subsequent loss of this identity to America's assimilative institutions. Insisting upon the destructive and unstable nature of this space renders problematic the status of Ellis Island as an anthropological place. Rather than the present, Perec's travel journal is preoccupied with the space as it was in the past, and from this perspective the island's status as an anthropological place of collective memory and ritualistic commemoration is placed in doubt. Perec sees the island as a non-place: a space of non-definition, of identities in flux, of historical and cultural dislocation. All of these features are determiners in Perec's relationship to his Jewish background, which, as I have said above, rather than being constructed from place-based memories of presence, is instead defined by the absence of these memories: a personality perversely constructed around the lack of place, something Perec will designate as the *non-lieu*.[15] This is to say that, in opposition to fixed, circumscribed or stable spatial identity, the *non-lieu* may be thought of as an interim or in-between space.

In this mode of identification, the traveller shifts his perspective from the present to the past. The effect of such a shift is that the historical boundaries defining the island's significance in terms of the present are disregarded in favour of an emphasis on the governmentality of the island as institution, and the authoritarian contingencies to which the emigrant's identity were subjected in the past. In representing this past, Ellis Island emerges within Perec's narrative as a site that is inherently provisional, where the present is suspended between two modes of being: a past identity forsaken and a future identity as yet unattained. The island is thus the intermediary point between the dream of becoming and the death of what was. Baptized the 'Golden Door' by the emigrants of the time, this island symbolized the passage between two worlds, so that it cannot constitute a real *place* but operates rather as a space of mutability and imposed alteration. It is a space incarnating the idea of being neither here nor there. The idea of passage is encapsulated in the image of the boat:

> but this was not America, not yet,
> only an extension of the boat.
> a remnant of the old world
> where nothing had yet been assured,
> where those who had left
> still hadn't arrived,
> where those who had given up everything
> had so far obtained nothing
> and where there was nothing else to do but wait.[16] (1995, 50)

The effects of this interim space on identity are what motivate Perec's narrative as he describes the institutional processes which each of the emigrants had to endure before being permitted to enter the United States. In the first place, it is no longer possible to define oneself against others who habitually form part of a shared cultural milieu. Without reciprocating reference points, the 'I' becomes fluid and blurred as the migratory experience marks a decontextualization of the emigrant and their culture. The emigrants can no longer define themselves according to others of the same background, but are hitherto confronted with the presence of other cultures. This is represented by the multilingual list of Ellis Island's sobriquet:

tränen insel
wispa lez
island of tears
isola delle lagrime
τονισσιτονζαχδιον
ОСТРОВ СІТЁЗ
ウ「フコ゜ メ「フソフロ ([1980] 1994, 28)

In the 1960s Corsi spoke of Ellis Island as a site for the 'welding of many nationalities' (cited in Pitkin 1975, 186), yet, in the above quotation from *Ellis Island*, the difference between these identities – linguistic isolation as well as the distressing proximity of the alterity of others – is brought to the fore. Coming into contact with other cultural identities is a confrontational process that alters the criteria for self- and collective definition (see Goffman 1959; Levinas [1974] 1991). Ellis Island represents the first spatial marker for this confrontation and point of rupture with the past; from now on, the emigrant will define himself/herself as a man or woman of Polish, Irish or Italian *origin*. The present is brought into referential relation with the past. One's contemporary existence is no longer a simple matter of grounding because assumptions about one's identity can no longer be made. More concretely, the narrative highlights the governmentality that is manifest in this intermediary space.

Unlike the soft, persuasive Americanization process which Sartre observes in the streets of New York, on Ellis Island the power of the institution over the lives of those forced into contact with it is made manifest. Perec uses the metaphor of the factory to convey how the administration intervened directly in the outcome of personal destiny:

Essentially, Ellis Island was a sort of factory for manufacturing Americans, a factory for transforming emigrants into immigrants; an American-style factory, as quick and efficient as a sausage factory in Chicago. You put an Irishman, a Ukrainian Jew, or an Italian from Apulia into one end of the production line and at the other end – after vaccination, disinfection, and examination of his eyes and pockets – an American emerged.[17]

This industrial metaphor suggests the exposure of the individual to the anonymous intervention of the authorities, while the narrative account gives details of how emigrants were herded into queues, required to answer a list of standard questions, made to wait in line for their medical examinations, after which they were visibly categorized in accordance with the doctor's diagnosis by the inscription of chalk letters on their clothes. Upon such categorization, the person was either lucky enough to reach the administrative desk or else was sent back to the ship and returned to the crisis he/she had tried to escape from. The series of formalities, the list of questions and the medical examinations, all suggest the inhumanity of the administrative processes that sought to circumscribe the individual rationally in terms of criteria that took no account of the particular situation of any single person. The machine, it is suggested, demands the external legibility and silence of the individual, so that personal agency is removed and the person is evaluated in terms of a series of indexical markers – their papers, their symptoms – that can be interpreted according to the abstract requirements of the system. Correspondingly, the impossibility of self-assertion is compounded by the presence of architectures of control restricting the possibility for independent movement. Significantly, the text contains reproductions of Lewis Hine's photographs filled with grids, grills and barriers. Individual subjects are photographed against a background of latticed windows (Perec [1980] 1994, 76, 77, 80, 81) suggestive of prison bars. They are surrounded by pole barriers used to direct queues, reminiscent of railings used in cattle markets.

The most extreme expression of the semiotic violence the authorities perform upon the emigrants concerns the process of nomination and the changing of European names to make them sound 'more American', or to simply drop one's name and adopt an American one. In this case, the process of transforming an emigrant into an immigrant finds graphic expression in the civil registers. The proper name is the ultimate signifier, for in a sense it forms the limit of the linguistic code in that beyond it one must resort to gesture so that the object/person be recognized. The proper name is, therefore, embedded in the individual identity of a person, and collectively too, in their heritage and culture. Thus, to assume the power to alter the proper name is to assume jurisdiction over identity. Perec illustrates this nominal mutation in the form of an anecdote. At once amusing and poignant, the author tells us the story of an old Russian Jew who is advised to choose 'a truly American name, one that the immigration authorities would have no difficulty in transcribing' (1995, 19)[18] before presenting himself at the registrar so that the Irish civil servant will have no difficulty in transcribing it. A janitor suggests the name Rockefeller. However, after having spent hours waiting his turn to see the civil officer, when the moment comes to say his new name the Russian has forgotten it and responds in Yiddish: *Schon vergessen*, 'I've already forgotten it'. Perec concludes: 'And so he was registered with the truly American name of John Ferguson' (1995, 19).[19] Thus accident and efficiency cancel out the nominative origin of the individual.

Apart from demonstrating the contingency and manipulation that identities were subjected to upon Ellis Island, Perec's perspective on this anecdote is significant. He concludes the story by saying, 'This story is perhaps too good to be true, but ultimately is hardly matters whether it's true or false' (1995, 20).[20] Upsetting the linearity of the descriptive narrative, this line casts doubt over the historical narrative, suggesting its constructed nature, and sabotaging the reliability of the historical narrator as source of objective truth. Furthermore, it suggests the insignificance of fact when it comes to the subject at hand, which is the loss of identity in the past and the inaccessibility of memory in the present. On the other hand, it also suggests that while the verity of the story does not matter, the act of recuperative recording is nevertheless something of worth. This is borne out by the second part of the travel account to which we now turn.

5.3 Writing Potential Memory

If 'The Island of Tears' gives the reader a historical mesh through which the past of Ellis Island may be interpreted, then 'Description of a Path' suggests the insufficiency of such a history. The poetic devices that Perec employs in this section of the travel narra-tive question the very possibility of describing space in the past, and are suggestive of an endeavour to silence language in favour of a registration of the trace. The questionable nature of a historical language's claim to neutrality is undermined first by the presence of Perec: an authorial presence that challenges the anonymous objective presence tradi-tionally represented by historical narrative. Perec appears in the photographs illustrating this section, and is seen standing amid the debris of the rooms that in the previous pho-tographs showed immigrants awaiting their fate ([1980] 1994, 57). Other images show him sitting at a writing desk, with a pile of rusty lamp-heads in the background. In the narrative also, after pages listing statistical information about the island, Perec's voice jerks the temporality of the representation into the present. In placing himself as inquir-ing subject at the centre of the poem and, furthermore, as a subject who feels personally involved with this place (when, in fact, he has no real grounds to be attached to it), Perec transgresses the boundary of time to expose the constructed nature of the historical site; his subjective presence interfering with the museum's transparency. In describing his own journey, he concludes that every trip to Ellis Island is undertaken on the basis of some personal motivation: 'I doubt that anyone visits Ellis Island by chance these days' (1995, 38).[21] This inserts the intimate attachment of personal memorial in the space as it presently functions.

It would seem that the aim of 'Description of a Path' is to return to the historical reference points disseminated from the beginning of the book in order to destroy and invalidate them. Its opening and closing pages are framed by two lists of statistical infor-mation. In order to give an idea of the impact of such enumeration, it will be helpful to quote from them quite extensively here before analysing their position and effect on the narrative. The opening list appears thus:

> five million emigrants arriving from Italy
> four million emigrants arriving from Ireland
> one million emigrants arriving from Sweden
> six million emigrants arriving from Germany
> three million emigrants arriving from Austria and Hungary.[22] (1995, 23)

There are another eight sentences of a similar pattern completing this list, and it is followed by another page listing the shipping companies, their ports of origin and the names of the ships that transported these Europeans to their American futures. The clos-ing list is as follows:

> four million immigrants came from Ireland
> four hundred thousand immigrants came from Turkey and Armenia
> five million immigrants came from Sicily and Italy
> six million immigrants came from Germany
> four hundred thousand immigrants came from Holland.[23] (1995, 70)

It can be stated, first, that the list encountered on the opening page changes significance as one reads down it and the repetition of its format becomes apparent. In contrast to a numerical list (a strategy, which would convey the same information), the verbally articu-lated numbers are invested with a certain rhythmic and visual weight. The repeated format, with the countries listed changing, is monotonous and seems to emphasize the anonymity of statistical information; the slight difference at the end of each phrase only serving to reinforce the sameness of the rest of the sentence. Adding an auditory dimen-sion, Perec's voice-over with its monotone vocal expression underlines this sameness.

The significance of the lists is further complicated by the presence of a metatext inserted in between both enumerations. The metatext takes the form of questions whereby the author expresses his dissatisfaction at historical data and factual information as means to represent the significance of the island:

how can things be described?
or talked about?
or looked at?
beyond the dry official statistics,
beyond the reassuring drone of stories
that have been told a thousand times
by guides in their Boy Scout hats,
beyond the official display of everyday objects
that have become museum pieces, the stuff of history,
precious vestiges, venerable images,
beyond the artificial calm of these photographs,
fixed forever in their misleading black-and-white obviousness
how can you identify this place?[24] (1995, 39, my emphasis)

Once more, the metatextual plea of Perec raises the problem of description's potential to ever convey reality in its entirety, without fixing a structure, a limited framework of connota-tions upon an event.[25]Representation is never innocent, and more fundamentally, descrip-tion signifies something other than what exists in reality. Perec's consciousness of this aspect of language becomes all the more urgent when one considers the context of his undertaking. Furthermore, the metatext redirects signification, placing it outside the text itself and hint-ing at a meaning to be found beyond what is tangibly present or representable in positive terms. What motivates Perec, and what was consistently his motivation throughout his writ-ing career, is the detail that escapes the structure: the everyday, independent and personal occurrences that seem banal, but which offer a myriad of alternative perspectives on the real. For it is these banalities that are formative of memory, the intimate memories that are absent from Ellis Island in the present, and also, as Perec observes in *Tentative d'épuisement d'un lieu Parisien / An Attempt at Exhausting a Place in Paris* ([1975] 1982), largely ignored by any insti-tutional documentation of a space's meaning. In the opening pages of this work, the author expresses his desire for the intimate and the fleeting and attests to the inadequacy of docu-mentation in the face of the eclecticism of the present moment. Sitting in a café, embarking on a project to list the happenings of the next four hours, Perec illuminates his intention:

A great many of these things, if not most of them, have been described, inventoried, photographed, recorded or catalogued. My aim, rather, in the pages that follow is to describe the rest, the stuff we don't generally notice, the unremarkable stuff, that has no importance, what happens when nothing happens, other than the weather, people, cars and clouds.[26] (Perec, [1975] 1982, 3)

On Ellis Island, the desire to record alluded to above is compounded by Perec's compassion for the trauma endured by the emigrants, and the contingency of their situation in the face of history. It suggests a prioritization of memory over history, revealed in the author's unmasking of the discursive strategies at work in any historical narrative:

> how do you decipher these relics?
> how do you move beyond,
> move behind
>   not rest content with what we're given to see
>   not merely see what we knew we would in advance
> How can you grasp what isn't shown, what wasn't photographed
> or catalogued or restored or staged?
> How do you get back what was plain, trivial, routine,
> what was ordinary and kept happening day after day?[27] (1995, 39)

These ruined vestiges suggest the presence of something other than the stabilized history of the monument would allow. History, which essentially unifies the identity of the past and denies the ambiguity of individual trauma as disruptive, aporetic agency, is placed under suspicion here. And so, rather than affirm Ellis Island's monumental status, the travel writer corrodes this significance to suggest the presence of an alternative reality – all that has not been recorded. While, as Perec points out, the text is insufficient to represent, it can be suggested that the metatext creates an interstice where this everyday, plural and personal memory may be evoked. This intervention in the narrative unity of history's appropriation of the past actively implicates an absence based in the shock of the familiar; the absence of the banal distresses the author so that the traveller's encounter with this debris indicates a latent potentiality, the possibility of a memory beyond its immediate dilapidation. The metatext also suggests the fragility of such an evocation and, ultimately, its impossibility. The remains of past memory are not preserved here, not even spatially, for the ruin of the island reveals the destruction of the past at the hands of time. Perec points out that the work of historical restoration, archiving and describing has also altered the past irrevocably, and in the alteration of the built environment, in its conversion to official memorial, memory becomes incongruous, constituted through converted fragments of the past, cast alongside as yet untouched, original remnants.

There is another concern expressed by Perec that demonstrates his unwillingness, in the face of his desire, to resuscitate the objects, testimonies and photographs around him by assigning individual narratives to them: 'it's pointless wanting to make pictures speak, forcing them to say what they can't' (1995, 43).[28] While Perec may long for the detail of the quotidian past, he accepts the silence of the objects as they appear to him now in the present. Continued reappropriation of the past at the hands of the monument and its revisitation through historical discourse accumulates an alternative meaning for the space, converting it into a stable site for tourist consumption. To describe would be to mutate and, thereby, to participate in entangling these objects with their historical, memorial counterpoint, which in the end removes memory from its origins.

It is not enough to insert doubt within the unified narrative of history, however; the need to record still exists in terms of an urgent desire to make present what is irretrievable and absent from the site. The traces of memory that Perec sees around him in the debris require a literary form that will not impinge by forcing a singular modality upon them. It is here that Perec becomes a rag picker and, once again, he adopts the enumerative method with the intention that the bare listing of all of these objects might work as literary trace and so function as indexical pointer to a signification that must lie beyond the list. This manner of recording uses restraint as a means of shattering the signification of the present and of opening up 'the fullness of the void' (Levinas [1974] 1991, 46),[29] where the absence of memory can return as potentiality to the present:

> for example,
> a large white porcelain double sink,
> with a hand-cranked spin dryer resting in it
> four chairs
> two ironing boards set on thick cast-iron legs,
> one with a rectangular, the other with an oval base.[30] (Perec 1995, 46)

The fullness of this void is suggested when Perec observes that all he can say about these objects today is that they held other significances in the past. The immaculately correlated list of ruined objects and statistics highlights the paucity of language once again and signals a gap between the present and the past that cannot be described in words. It is this very gap that holds the key to the signification that Perec is attempting to evoke here. If, as Dylan Trigg has suggested, 'a memory is a movement of time which is distinguished temporally from the present' (2006, 1), then the list of these discarded objects suggests the passage of time and presents the absence of memory. It would seem that Perec's travail of recollection, of noting these objects, is an attempt to reactivate the narrative potential which these silent objects contain, while his avoidance of descriptive technique leaves them devoid of connotation, all excepting the connotation of that which is absent.

After these interventions, the list of the closing section of the narrative takes on a significance beyond the informative content of its message. First, the structural format of the list recalls the opening enumeration and so establishes an abstract connection between both. Second, this structural similarity makes the difference in the words each list contains more striking: the change from 'emigrants' to 'immigrants' evokes the change in status that has taken place over the course of the Europeans' stay on the island, a change that further suggests a rupture with a previous identity; the emigrant leaving Europe attains a future status as immigrant in America. And this process of identity alteration has not been narrated, but rather suggested, by the lists' mutations. Finally, the narrative distance separating these lists from one another brings the import of the metatext to bear on them both and prevents their transparent interpretation as simple bearers of denotational data. The reader, upon encountering the second list, is forced to reappraise his/her reading of the first, which in light of the author's lament at the insufficiency of their statistical fact to represent a memory of what this place was in the past, potentially nullifies what they contain to imagine a signification beyond the limits of the enumeration: 'rather than simply saying: in thirty years sixteen million emigrants passed through Ellis Island' (1995, 53).[31] The lists implicate what they do not represent, standing for the absence of what they do not and cannot say. Furthermore, the author's deprecation of 'dry official statistics' (1995, 39) is suggestive of a violence contained in this official repossession of the past in statistical terms. The statistics' reprehensible failure lies in their lack of memory, in their neglect of:

> what those sixteen million individual stories were,
> the sixteen million stories, identical and distinct,
> of the men, women, and children driven
> from their native land by famine or poverty,
> or by political, racial, or religious oppression.[32] (1995, 53)

Ultimately, these devices, through their very insignificance, come to signal the absence of meaning from the words present and in so doing set themselves up as traces of a meaning that was once to be found.

In conclusion, Perec's encounter with Ellis Island cannot be separated from his desire to express identity in terms of its precariousness and its intimacy. Perec's narrative techniques of accumulation, metatextual questioning and personal testimony attempt to assemble their own traces, culminating in a poetry of absence, suggesting a memory of what has gone and cannot be refound. Thus, by exploring the virtual nature of the trace, this anti-poetry leaves a weak echo of those who have disappeared in the ruined abandoned rooms of Ellis Island. Perec's account suggests an approach to spatial experience that not only acknowledges the presence of an absent Other, but also implicates language in the reconstruction of place and in the alteration of its meaning. In the attempt to resuscitate the memory of space, the traveller reveals both the architectural and discursive strategies at work in the construction of spatial significances, and likewise, the insufficiency of these strategies to grasp that space's plurality and unstable mobility when it comes to personal experience. In undermining the discursive mesh which shrouds landscape, Perec's narrative casts doubt on whether any representation is adequate and in doing so renders historical landscape problematic through an awareness of what is absent from what is accessible to the traveller in terms of architectural presence or representation. This awareness demands an alternative mode of representation, one that opts out of descriptive tactics in favour of enumerative recording, metatext and personal implication and thus creates its own space by adding another layer of unseen, undocumented agency to the space, intimating the life that was there before its translation and recording. Thus, these listed objects, unadorned and insignificant, assemble to create an indispensable zone of silence, the trace of the absence of meaning, which haunts them and preserves the memory of that which an explicit, historical description would dissimulate and mutilate – that memory's imprint on ruined space and its essential fragility and strangeness.

Certeau has commented on the need to appreciate the practices that fall outside the bounds of governmental space:

> The goal is not to make clearer how the violence of order is transmuted into a disciplinary technology, but rather to bring to light the clandestine forms taken by the dispersed, tactical, and makeshift creativity of groups and individuals already caught in the net of 'discipline.' (1984, xiv–xv)

In light of the events that constitute the subject matter of the travel text, the spatial practices of Perec, both representationally and practically, take on wider importance than that of Perec's autobiographical project. The text intimates the role of memory in the constitution of cultural identities and questions whether the descriptive language of the cultural historian (and, it may be inferred, the anthropologist) can ever represent, let alone comprehend this. For victims of the Holocaust or diaspora, the everyday is not (merely) a matter of finding alternative modes of creativity; it is a matter of life and death. The memory of this everyday is therefore fundamental to the shaping of Western identities in the twentieth century; it is the spectre of these events that Perec attempts to resuscitate here. Where history and architecture fail, *écriture* intervenes in order to preserve vestiges of the traumas behind the construction of America as a Promised Land.

5.4   Interpretive Travel and Ethical Spaces: Jean Baudrillard's *America*

> Long live the Fourth World, the world in which you can say 'Right, utopia has arrived. If you aren't part of it, get lost!,' the world that no longer has the right to surface, the disenfranchised, who have no voice and are condemned to oblivion, thrown out to go off and die their second-class deaths.
>
> Disenfranchising.[33] (Baudrillard [1986] 1988, 112)

In our final journey to the United States we take the strands of space, ethics and literary form to engage again with the shift in travel writing that has been described in this book as a move from legislative to interpretive negotiations of alterity.[34] The focus of this section is Jean Baudrillard's travelogue *Amérique / America* ([1986] 2000). Baudrillard's imaginative geography forms the critical impetus for identification of this shift, via which we explore the interplay of spatial, literary and theoretical dimensions in the text and how this interplay creates an ethical tension between the social space of America – the material lifeworld of everyday contingency – and the poetry of the text's appropriation of that space. This section of the chapter broadens its horizon to the entirety of the American space. The reason for this is that, as we shall see, in the nomadic travel performance of Baudrillard 'place' as locatable and defined becomes an increasingly slippery notion. One space maps onto another, disabling any notion of the real through the act of travel, and it is for this precise quality that the travel account is included here for it allows us to discuss the final question on our agenda, as to the possibility for describing others in the wake of postcolonial theory and the mass proliferation of globalized spaces.

In colonialist and postcolonialist scholarship, especially, postmodern travel writing has been criticized for the 'othering' effects its abstract, textual dislocations potentially perform on the realities of everyday life.[35] Baudrillard's text has been dismissed out of hand as neo-imperialist and symptomatic of what humanist critics such as Christopher Norris (1992) and Denis Dutton (1990) see as postmodernism's narcissistic and eschatological tendencies.[36] To take one example, Baudrillard's depiction of the desert has been accused of raising the spectre of binary modernism, which critics see as proof of postmodernism's failure to allay its nostalgia for transparent sign-object relationships. Finally, the author's abstract locutions run the gauntlet of accusations as to the text's essentialism, its indifference toward minority groups in America, while the authorial voice cannot escape the banner of its white European intellectual inheritance. In attempting to clarify and counter the virulence of such critique, this analysis distinguishes between legislative travel practices, which derive from a will to render legible the social space of the other pertaining to function as a record of knowledge, and interpretive practices of space, which – in binding social space to the hermeneutic – reflexively engage in critiquing the possibility of a transparent record.[37] More particularly, what shall be addressed here is the double movement of Baudrillard's travel writing (and its dual accountability) that one might describe as a simultaneous movement of both content and form across the normative boundaries of liberal moral standards for representing the social space of the other. This movement holds in tension writing's potential to act as a record of the other, while at the same time Baudrillard's adoption of a poetic mapping consisting in irony, hyperbole and aphorism suspends the possibility of this record's standing in for, or representing, the other. Instead of record, what emerges from *America* is the self-reflexive, inverted position of the singular traveller's challenge to the categories by which we might come to know an authentic space that might be called 'America.'

It is from a perspective, which moves away from a concern with the descriptive, strategic modes for reducing the other to legibility that it becomes possible to reread the paradoxical poetry of Baudrillard's *America* as a critique of the legislative impulse to control social space, epitomized here in the exploration of the United States as 'Utopia achieved'. The adoption of a poetic approach to alterity renders problematic the relationship between physical or 'objective' space – the real – and the travel writer's translation of space into representational form. But it is not simply a matter of reinserting the subject into space – through this interpretive poetics the notion of space as an inherently stable entity existing a priori to cultural interference is itself cast into doubt. In a twofold move, therefore, the poetics of Baudrillard's form distorts not only the reader's potential to pretend to engage through this text with the 'real' of America (a potential earnestly pursued, as we have seen in earlier travel writing on New York and London), but further these textual strategies open a space of autocritique of Western value systems that presume the legibility of – and by implication, the possibility for – legislative coherence in social space.

To stay with this notion of 'social space' for a moment, for many critics it is the absence of everyday America that leads them to classify Baudrillard's prose as amoral, 'trite' or 'frivolous' (Dutton 1990; Kaplan 1996). If social space is understood as the arena of interaction, and thus where the travel writer engages in the ethics of relationships with the other, then the substance of Baudrillard's text, in the author's subtraction from the text of a 'deep America of mores and mentalities'[38] (Baudrillard [1986] 1988, 5) would seem to forgo any attempt at ethical exchange.[39] However, when the text is situated within the historical context of European writing on America, and given consideration as a transfigurative critique of Western value systems, we can ask whether it is not possible to see in this text a challenge to Western modes for legislating for the other. It is, I argue here, through the absenting of social life, and its interpretive literary rendering in the travel text, that there emerges a profound moral concern about what happens to social space in the era of the simulacrum. In this reading, Baudrillard's *America* exploits travel, both formally and ontologically, as a means to unravel the distinctions between the everyday and the ideological, while the paradox and amoralism of the text's distancing of American social life suggests a critique of impulses to account universally for that life.

The concern over the 'othering effects' of 'postmodern' travel writing and its seeming expulsion of the 'everyday' stems from the ethical turn in travel studies – a turn that is itself inseparable from the legitimacy crisis of modernist epistemologies in general and the recognition of the discursive hegemonies at play in Western travel narratives. To date, the ethics debate in travel studies has evolved largely in relation to sites of colonialist expansion and postcolonialist aftermaths in an effort to come to terms with the social, political and cultural consequences of racial subjugation and empire. As stated earlier, in the main, the theoretical frameworks for travel studies, therefore, have been elaborated with the colonial and postcolonial contexts in mind. The result is that, along with the burgeoning critical interest in the discourse of travel, there emerges a sense of guilt on the part of the West with respect to its imperial past and a burden of responsibility on the Western writer that makes it difficult to write about travel without ensnaring the text in the discursive apparatus of imperial or neo-imperial forms.

5.5   The Ethics of Form

In the tradition of ethical debate dating back to Immanuel Kant, the paradigms that structure ethical discourse can be divided into two kinds of duty: duty toward oneself and duty toward others (Søltoff 2001). For the travel writers it is the latter that is of primary concern, where this duty toward others consists in their responsibility regarding the textual appropriation of others' social space. But what is this social space? Geographers identity three interwoven aspects at work in the production of what has been termed social space, and these categories are useful for considering the ethical implications of representations of travel. These categories include the cognitive (or knowledge of space), the aesthetic (representations and expressions of space), and the moral (interrelative space). It is to be noted that all three are qualitative in character, and social space is seen to emerge here through consistent negotiation between the ideologies, infrastructures and institutions of the dominant and the contingencies of everyday life. Through its affectation to represent space and its discursive negotiation of alterity, the travel text is actively engaged in the wider production of these cognitive, aesthetic and moral aspects of social space. In that it is engaged in the subjective production of space, travel writing treads a fine line between the obliteration of otherness in terms that reduce difference or, at the other extreme, the estrangement of others through the exoticization of difference.

The appropriation of the continent as 'new' is a reinvention, a wiping of the slate, a vision allowing Western Europe to resolve and order this new space through the establishment of a geometrical and discursive plane via which native America might be stripped of all prior substance (Søltoff 2001). In the earliest travel accounts, America is the virginal terrain for Europe's regeneration, a model space where all desirable elements for society that were spatially and temporally dispersed across the Old World could be assembled in a single place, a blank conceptual space where Europe could start again. In the bid to cope with the unknown and to eliminate the threat which this great other posed to contemporary categories of knowledge, certain key binaries establish themselves as the modes for legislating North America, the most common of which are the poles of old/ new, ideal/pragmatic, history/ahistory, deep/superficial, real/utopia, modernity/primitiveness. In later accounts dating from the modern period, these dichotomies are again mobilized, although often, depending on the traveller's ideological position, the poles are reversed. Kristen Ross, in *Fast Cars, Clean Bodies* (1995), explains this reversal in terms of a shift in the balance of Western powers, and the migration of American consumer culture to French shores. Ross argues that while imperialist France may have dominated the nineteenth century's imagination of civilization, in the wake of two world wars, the surety of such a position was called into question, and France found itself colonized by American Fordism and commodity culture.

The potential resistance identified by Kuehn and Smethurst (2008) in mobility's deferral of boundaries raises a series of problems, however, for the context of intra-Western travel writing. Not least of these is the philosophical conundrum of how to criticize the totalizing strategies of rationalism without such a criticism, emerging as it does from a site of Western privilege, creating its own elevated totality. We have seen how Perec instils a kind of silence into his text through the use of reflexive questioning and repetitive forms, we look now to see how Baudrillard instils mobility within coda of literary form, and what kind of spatial production emerges from such mobility. Nevertheless, the ethical implications of this spatial production engage with the questions of, first, whether or not Baudrillard's literary form, based as it is on mobility and executed through the techniques of paradox, aphorism and hyperbole, erodes the solidity of the Archimedean point, and second, what kind of social space emerges from this form.

In *America*, contrary to restrictive analogy or a claim to authenticity, the reader encounters a reflexive rendition of the journey as a collection of signs, with writing synthesizing these signs along an open-ended trajectory, whereby cognitive and aesthetic spatialities of travel are arrayed in a manner similar to that of discrete cinematic scenes. In this scenario, the American landscape is inseparable from the effect which movement produces in its continuous assemblages of scenes that refuse the contained frames of narrative description, the detail of what Roland Barthes calls *l'effet de réel*, or what Baudrillard refers to here as the 'snapshot':

Nostalgia born of the immensity of the Texan hills and the sirens of New Mexico: gliding down the freeway, smash hits on the Chrysler stereo, heat wave. Snapshots aren't enough. We'd need the whole film of the trip in real time [...] ...not simply for the pleasure of remembering but because the fascination of senseless repetition is already present in the abstraction of the journey.[40] ([1986] 1988, 1)

Contrary to the deep structures identifiable in the legislative mode, here the journey is inscribed in an affective schema: travel does not illuminate or facilitate connection to the real; rather, this mobility is seen as the inauguration of meaninglessness, a meaninglessness that is held up against the representational containers of what Gilles Deleuze and Félix Guattari have called 'the classical book, as noble, signifying, and subjective organic interiority (the strata of the book)' ([1980] 2004, 4). The physical movement described here, the speed of the motorcar, finds its aesthetic equivalent in cinematic form – both of which allow for the removal of social space, the space of others; and the screen becomes the dominant interface between the self and the world. This opening section, then, prepares the reader for the mode of defamiliarization that proliferates in this work, and which is the removal of interaction with the contingencies of social America, the abstraction of 'human-made' space, in favour of a semiotic procession through a series of depthless landscapes. *America* is a cinematic geography of hyperreal spaces, and in distinction from a description narrative accumulation aspiring to the authentic, the text accumulates a hybrid collection of poeticized, interpretive geographies screened in dialogue with a series of theoretical observations that are closer in form to poetry than the systemic reasoning of this sociologist's disciplinary background. Adopting the logic of cinematic form, the entire text moves in a panning gesture from the deserts of Death Valley to the lush college campuses of California, through the streets of New York and along the Los Angeles highways.

To think about this panning gesture in ethical terms, mobility, and in particular, speed, bears association with superficiality, a means of exploiting place that refuses the depth of everyday life in favour of a motion that sweeps across the territory to leave behind a series of spatial impressions. These binaries of fast/slow, superficial/depth have their corresponding traveller types that can be identified respectively in the distinction between tourist and traveller, whereby the former corresponds with the fast and superficial halves of the above dyads. It is Baudrillard's impressionistic mobility that leads Kaplan (1996) to equate him with a 'tourist,' and within this equation to call his long-standing binary opposing Europe to America the reproduction of an 'exhausted paradigm'. However, in distinction from the case of the tourist, where haste functions in tandem with an essentializing discursivity, to confine space to its picture-postcard equivalent, Baudrillard draws on Paul Virilio's ([1980] 1989) notion of speed as a means to achieve disappearance. Unlike traditional formulations of the polarity in which travel (as opposed to tourism) leads somehow to a more authentic experience of place, mobility is adopted in order to displace the notion of an authentic, or real, America. Appropriating Virilio's theorization of speed as an essential factor in post-industrial spatio-temporal experience,[41] Baudrillard adopts the momentum of the motorway as his modus operandi for experiencing 'America' and the semiotic conversion of landscape to sign that this unending circulatory form of travel facilitates. This ontological mode of spatial experience, in its technological distortion of 'organic' movement, finds its literary equivalent in the poetic devices that Baudrillard adopts to disrupt meaning. And this kind of incessant movement facilitates a practice of space that, in its dependence on vacuity for its perpetuation, creates an interface between the moving subject and the world, and when translated into literary form, becomes a means via which language can becomes a form of strategic resistance to the systematization processes of Western value systems.

This abstraction from the 'real' and from meaning is performed through the construction of a series of binary oppositions, framed in terms of what Barry Smart (1993) refers to as 'Baudrillard's fatal comparison' of America and Europe. Established on the common ground of modernity, Europe's attachment to the ideological models for understanding history and progress is contrasted with America's disregard for such models and its pragmatic technological and cultural realization of modernity. Baudrillard's *America* is the realized epitome of Enlightenment models under the sign of reason, unencumbered by the consecutive crises of the self and the state of Europe's long nineteenth century. According to this model, America is the pragmatic realization of the conception of freedom formalized in Europe, but spatially materialized here for Baudrillard in the landscapes of the 'New World': 'For us, in Europe, it was the Revolution of 1789 that set its seal upon us, though it was a different seal, that of History, the State, and Ideology. Politics and history, not the utopian, moral sphere, remain our primal scene' ([1986] 1988, 76).[42]

In this scenario, the language of opposition seems to set up a quantitative measure via which both Europe and America can be judged, while at the same time the capitalization of 'History', 'State' and 'Ideology' alert us to the narrative status of these modern containers of value. Furthermore, as we shall explore further on, the notion of America as utopia introduces the paradoxical trope via which Baudrillard's 'fatal optimism' (Coulter 2008, 146) and an aporetic ethical space become discernible.[43] Poetic paradox intervenes further to dismantle the grounding of the binary model in scientific or quantitative language: 'We are still at the centre, but at the centre of the Old World. They who were a marginal transcendence of that Old World are today its new eccentric centre. Eccentricity is stamped on their birth certificate'[44] (Baudrillard [1986] 1988, 81). The phrase draws on the traditional distinction of 'Old' and 'New', but instead of legislative difference, the juxtaposing of opposites 'eccentric' and 'centre' pushes, in paradoxical equation, at the boundaries of sense. Rather than performing to consolidate either of the social spaces of Europe and America, these poetic formulations of Baudrillard's prose enter to disrupt the potential coherence of this comparison to any type of reality, and it becomes clear that it is this very reality that is strategically being forced toward enigma and disappearance in Baudrillard's travelling:

> I went in search of *astral* America, not social and cultural America, but the America of the empty, absolute freedom of the freeways, not the deep America of mores and mentalities, but the America of desert speed, of motels and mineral surfaces. I looked for it in the speed of the screenplay, in the indifferent reflex of television, in the film of days and nights projected across an empty space, in the marvellously affectless succession of signs, images, faces, and

ritual acts on the road; looked for what was nearest to the nuclear and enucleated universe, a universe which is virtually our own, right down to its European cottages. [...] I knew all about this nuclear form, this future catastrophe when I was still in Paris of course. But to understand it, you have to take to the road, to that travelling which achieves what Virilio calls the aesthetics of disappearance.

For the mental desert form expands before your very eyes, and this is the purified form of social desertification. [...] The inhumanity of our ulterior, asocial, superficial world immediately finds its aesthetic form here, its ecstatic form. For the desert is simply that: an ecstatic critique of culture, an ecstatic form of disappearance.[45] ([1986] 1988, 5)

This quotation serves as an introduction to the myriad of possible ways to approach this text, and the ethical tensions that rest irresolvable in this regard. On the one hand, if we adopt a liberal humanist position, this enigmatic disappearing act can be taken as a dismissal of all interest in the social life of America, an anti-humanist obliteration of the material conditions of everyday life. Read in this way, as an indifference toward the complexities of the historico-social condition of US culture, one could argue, along with Kaplan in *Questions of Travel* (1996), that this emphasis on the aesthetic and ecstatic form removes from view the discourses of minorities and other socially oppressed groups. Kaplan accuses Baudrillard's *America* of reproducing the parameters of 'an exhausted paradigm' – namely, the opposition of a 'deep' Europe to a 'superficial' America – stating that this metaphysical binary is exploited by Baudrillard to the detriment of minority discourses emerging from the female, black or immigrant communities. The problem with this reading, however, is that the very taking of a position with regard to a 'description' of the realities of social oppression would reinstate the paradigms of resolution that the entirety of Baudrillard's later writings works to avoid.

As an entry point into the difficult ethical conundrums of Baudrillard's refusal of the social, it is worthwhile taking a brief moment to situate *America* within the broader concerns of Baudrillard's conception of the 'real.' From *L'Échange symbolique de la mort / Symbolic Exchange and Death* (1976) onward, Baudrillard's writing abandons the scientific apparatus of sociology and introduces a poetic, interpretive quality to his prose, a poetic quality that, drawing on the reversibilities of Friedrich Hölderlin, Baudrillard develops as a twofold strategy. On the one hand, interpretive travelling is mobilized as a challenge to the legislative language of theory that remains within the systemic project of the Enlightenment and that even in its dispensation of myths remains, nevertheless, attached to the vision of a perfectible world. Rather than describe, the traveller seeks to defamiliarize the world in order to bring to light the unintelligibility and terroristic character of this belief that all can be rendered familiar. Through the language of enigma, the silent communications of juxtaposition, contradiction, irony and hyperbole, is intimated the interpretive complexity of the world. On the other hand, Baudrillard's work poeticizes the legislative language of theory, and in doing so interrupts the discursive operations that tend toward hegemony and the clarification of social space. It is this 'perfect world' that Baudrillard seeks to inveigle with enigmatic prose, and it is this entire project of perfection, the West's belief in technoscientific perfection of social life, described elsewhere by the author as 'fullness', that is collapsed here onto the cognitive, aesthetic and ethical landscapes of America (Baudrillard 1993a, 38). *America* adopts the interpretive modes of aphorism, parataxis, parable, paradox, enigma, ellipsis and tropes of all kinds in an effort to coax the sociological inferential diagrams of dialectic and logic to the limits of sense. The potential of travel discourse to become a tool in the ideological hegemonies of the West, and an arm in its most favoured instrument of domination – modern science – is overturned here as Baudrillard sets off in search of 'astral America' / 'Amérique sidérale'. Landscapes flash past, elaborated through a poetics of mobility in which travel becomes not only an ontological mode of movement but also a poetic mode of experience. 'Astral America' is the real-and-imagined site, what Soja (1996) would describe as a 'third-space,' from which to undermine legislative modalities and their concomitant production of the West as universal sign. This landscape, then, must be understood as a real-and-fictional ground for a strategic game of resistance to both the stabilizing force of legislative language and 'the perfect crime' – Baudrillard's term to describe the West's efforts to bring about perfection, and epitomized in the book by the 'paradisic and inward-looking illusion' of California's university campuses. The emphatic modulations of the term *America* work to distance the attainability of an 'authentic' space: 'For me there is no truth of America'; 'America is neither dream nor reality'; 'America is a giant hologram' ([1986] 1988, 29–30).[46] This fictional terrain provides the basis for the 'mutual volatilization of the status of the thing and discourse' (Baudrillard 1993b, 235), and it is from the fictional ground that the affective, ethical concerns of Baudrillard's writing emerge.

5.6 Without Grounds

In this light, the comparison between Europe and America, rather than work toward the production of a discrete reality that can be represented in European terms, induces these binaries to expose ironically the quantitative simplicities of their own reduction. The binaries of Europe and America as respectively historical/ahistorical, cultural/acultural and idealist/pragmatic are reproduced here, but this is not a simple combination designed to render either space more legible. Instead these legislative simplifications are complicated by an interpretive poetics that successively strips statements of their comprehensive tendencies so as to harness these binaries toward an implied critique of those same legislative tendencies. In the section 'Utopia Achieved', for example, Baudrillard discusses the differences between American and French multiculturalism. He begins by drastically simplifying the postcolonial situation in France, stating, 'All that happened was a transferring of the colonial situation back to the metropolis, out of its original context' (82).[47] As an abstract locution, this statement denies history and singularity in its neat erasure of the complexities of intercultural crossing in the postcolonial situation. Language obliterates difference here as it easily maps one complexity onto another and so refuses the identity of either. Similarly, in discussing American multiracialism the author talks of an 'intensity born of rivalry' that creates a 'converging energy', a 'complicity' (82) between races, which at the same time is marked by violence and banality. This generality rests on the juxtaposition of contradictory values, just as it emerges in relation to an equally paradoxical contrast with French colonialism, and all are merged here in an ambivalence that refuses analytical rationalization. Baudrillard lauds the lack of racism in America, for example, while his heteroclite combinations tempt the reader to condemn as racist the poetic rendering of such a complex object as human interrelations. At the next turn, however, Baudrillard warns against the notion of universally legislating for culture, which when 'abstractly formalized ... devours singularity just as rapidly as revolution devours its children' (83).[48] This statement not only removes the ground from beneath these other comparative strands but also, through its poetic transfer of revolution as a cannibalistic metaphor for universalism, renders logical response redundant. No sooner has the traveller teased the reader with an easy maxim than he speeds on to provide another aphorism that invalidates the first. The practices of this text, rather than producing knowledge, thus exploit the corrosive qualities of irony and the ellipsis of aphorism to short-circuit meaning.

Nonsense exploits the tangibility of the binary, but it also contains within it the germ of consciousness, and an awareness of the mechanistic means via which systems of representation work to determine meaning for social space. While this self-reflexivity works to draw attention to language, it also intervenes in social space in the form of hyperbolic cultural critique. The defamiliarization of the world enacted through travel writing as poetry seems to perform in terms of a strategic response to the full emptiness of social life under the sign of the consumerist West. In a twofold operation, movement displaces the ground of authenticity, while poetry encroaches upon the linear trajectories of prosaic language. Baudrillard clarifies his project elsewhere, noting that 'to escape fullness you have to create voids between spaces so that there can be collisions and short-circuits' (38). These voids are created in response to a 'real' that can no longer be understood in separation from its image, the meaning of social life is inseparable from its myths, and for Baudrillard a language that seeks to clarify the world merely demonstrates the power of the idea of perfection: 'For reality asks nothing other than to submit itself to hypotheses. And it confirms them all. That, indeed, is its true ruse and vengeance' (Baudrillard 1999, 99). Precisely what is problematic in terms of reading *America* as an authentic search for America is that, as Mike Davis ([1990] 1992) points out, American space cannot be dissociated from its cinematic or simulated aspects.[49] In the same way that the quest for '*the* social' cannot resist the legislative patterns of theoretical language, this space cannot be extracted from the regimes of discursive tradition that have consistently appropriated it as the best and worst that Western civilization has to offer.[50]

And so travelling America is, of necessity, a travelling through the discursive terrain of the simulacrum, which Baudrillard elaborates elsewhere as the replacement of reality with the signs of reality, where the object always already enters the world as sign. In the culture of the media-saturated West, where the sign operates not in relation to any external reference but according to its own logic, to disguise the lack of the real, what we perceive as real is always at the same time the confirmation of a hypothesis. In this scenario, social space is no longer regulated by any kind of symbolic exchange that would order relations according to some transcendental 'other' that would guarantee meaning; rather, what we are faced with is a system of sign-for-sign exchange, where the sign generates value within the logic of its own self-enclosed circulation. As Baudrillard describes it, 'Everything is destined to reappear as simulation. Landscapes as photography, women as the sexual scenario, thoughts as writing, terrorism as fashion and the media, events as television. Things seem only to exist by virtue of this strange destiny. You wonder whether the world itself isn't just here to serve as advertising copy in some other world' (32).[51]

America, then, if we are not to dismiss Baudrillard's 'othering' out of hand, must be read as a 'fiction about a powerful fiction' (Coulter 2008, 152), and the West understood here as a space entangled in the successive ravelling and unravelling of its own universalizing myths, which are the ironic bind of its community. In *America*, where 'the cinema is all around you outside, all over the city'[52] (56), the production of social space of America is inseparable from media-saturated representations of social space. In terms of an ethical ground, therefore, what Baudrillard fictionalizes in America is the morality of neoliberalism and a systemic ideology that must expunge all that does not marry well with it. The 'powerful myth' that Baudrillard engages is Ronald Reagan's vision of America, in which Cold War anti-communist rhetoric is collapsed into the perceived threat to the mythologies of American individualism. It is in the sections of the book 'Utopia Achieved' / 'Utopie Réalisée' and 'The End of US Power' / 'La Fin de la puissance' that Baudrillard's poetic travelling confronts the tyranny of systemic meaning, and paradox works to close down meaning in a strategy to undermine a value system that, in its efforts to eradicate evil from the world, must become itself terroristic. Rather than prescribe an alternative position, Baudrillard merely asks us to consider what complete security, efficiency, and legibility would look like: '[W]hat kind of a state would be capable of dissuading and annihilating all terrorism in the bud...? It would have to arm itself with such terrorism and generalize terror on every level. If this is the price of security, is everybody deep down dreaming of this?' (Baudrillard, 1990, 22). The consequence of such values result in 'Utopia Achieved': this paradoxical conundrum, the placement of 'no place', and how Baudrillard refers to the inexplicable persistence of a 'moral hysteresis' in a society as diverse and secular as the United States.

5.7 The Perfect Crime

The full paradoxical weight of this semantic antagonism can be read in relation to Thomas More's *Utopia* ([1516] 2003), the famous depiction of an island whose coordinates fail to be heard in the moment of a sneeze, on which evil is avoided and crime prevented. In More's account, of course, the meaning of u-topia, no-place, places this perfect society within the realm of the ungraspable. Utopia must remain self-contained if it is to remain pure, and evil cannot be tolerated if it is to remain good; in More's account criminals become slaves to the Utopians. In Baudrillard's appellation of American as 'Utopia Achieved', perfection is made to clash with material realization through the confrontation of two antonymic signifiers. The resulting paradox performs within Baudrillard's much-used technique of reversibility, which can be seen as a form of poetic resolution to the determinism of the concept and the exclusionary operations it necessitates. Transferring utopia to the scene of modernity equates it with the modern belief – persistent in the early years of Reagan's presidency – in the West as the centre of civilization, and in its rightfulness as the absolute model for the rest of the world. 'The miraculous premise of a utopia made reality'[53] (77) is built on the belief in the universality of Western systems, technical and human.

> The Americans are not wrong in their idyllic conviction that they are at the centre of the world, the supreme power, the absolute model for everyone. And this conviction is not so much founded on natural resources, technologies, and arms, as on the miraculous premise of a utopia made reality, of a society which, with a directness we might judge unbearable, is built on the idea that it is the realization of everything the others have dreamt of – justice, plenty, rule of law, wealth, freedom: it knows this, it believes in it, and in the end, the others have come to believe in it too.[54] (77)

But the clarity of these value systems, inscribed in the West's increased technoscientific efforts to bring about perfection and the correspondent belief in the attainability of complete order necessitates the exclusion of all that is other to it. In many of Baudrillard's books the brutality of perfection is expressed through a reversal of Hölderlin's ([1803] 1990) famous maxim, 'Where there is danger some Salvation grows there too' (39). For our period, Baudrillard notes, the poles must be reversed because in the face of the Western legislative tendencies toward security, prevention and immunity, or 'the fatal excess of positivity' (Baudrillard 1994, 49), we can no longer tolerate to be victims of fate or danger. What this excess is in danger of losing, however, is alterity and singularity, and so Baudrillard's reformulation reads, 'But where what saves grows, there also grows danger' (Baudrillard 2000, 80–81). It is the notion of an excess of reality, security and efficiency that Baudrillard equates here to an achieved utopia. And this legislative world is necessarily a pitiless universe:

> If utopia has already been achieved, then unhappiness does not exist, the poor are no longer credible. If America is resuscitated, then the massacre of the Indians did not happen, Vietnam did not happen. [...] The have-nots will be condemned to oblivion, to abandonment, to disappearance pure and simple. This is 'must exit' logic: 'poor people must exit'.[55] (111)

The ultimatum issued in the name of wealth and efficiency wipes them off the map. And rightly so, since they show such bad taste as to deviate from the general consensus.

It is here that Tocqueville's discursive appropriation of America as the supreme example of a 'people' governed by a moral rather than a political outlook reveals its own reductive consequence. For it is within this logic that the obliteration of Native American culture can be understood as a 'natural' result of the progression of a society toward democracy. However, as Baudrillard ([1986] 1988) points out, Tocqueville never draws these two strands of history together; the purity of the concept necessitates the expulsion of its material consequence, and the linearity of language can allow these two facets – the theoretical and the empirical – to remain at a distance from each other, 'as if good and evil had developed separately' (88).[56]

In conclusion, Baudrillard's hyperbolic extension of social space to the realm of Utopia can be read as a poetic attempt to resist the banality of Western universalism. His writing is an effort conceived within the fatal optimism that 'the more the hegemony of the global consensus is reinforced, the greater the risk, or chances it will collapse' (Baudrillard 1995b, 86). Baudrillard's 'othering' is travel conceived as a poetic, interpretive reversal of the perfect crime of legibility, pushing language to the limit of hypothesis, so as to challenge theoretical systematization through the introduction of fiction into the containers of that system. *America* is an interpretive ground that in its accumulation of the othering effects of poetry opens itself out to moral criticism but at the same time silently points to a profound concern with how the idealization of social space, its quantification and marriage to legislative language, conspires toward the eradication of difference and alterity. It is an ironic performance of space as both real and imagined, then, an irony that tyrannically judges American culture as 'banal' at the same time as it exhibits its complicity in this tyranny. Baudrillard's amoral, bombastic judgements open onto a reflexive space without offering an alternative model or an idea of social justice that would replace the simulacra that encroach on social space. But, paradox is at the heart of any attempt by a Western travel writer to form a coherent ethical model via which to approach alterity, for a coherent ethics would necessarily redefine the legislative ground. Baudrillard's travelling, in its conceptual acrobatics, performs ambivalence as a mode of resistance against the epistemological categories of legislative frameworks, to open onto an aporetic ethical ground. This ground emanates from the interpretive reflexivity of the text's literary form, a form that in its negotiation of America as utopia realized reveals all the more those exclusions, beyond 'the interiorized space of language' (1993b) that such paradox elides.

Finally, there is no doubt that power remains in circulation throughout Baudrillard's text. But this power is not holistic or integral; it is not the power of imperial certainty, but the poetic agency that through its aphoristic mobility threatens the logic of mapping language onto social space, and reengages aesthetics in modalities of resistance. In this case we might conceive of how literary form might *perform* an engagement with alterity rather than work to estrange it. This is a way of thinking that challenges us to consider what Bhabha describes as 'a theoretical position that does not set up a theory-practice polarity' ([1994] 2010, 257). In this light, Baudrillard's defamiliarization of America can be seen to recognize the problem of obtaining to a language or to a position from which to speak about the realities of social space. In an interview with Slyvère Lotringer, he qualifies the relationship between theoretical appropriation and objective reality, saying, 'As long as you consider that there is such a thing as a real world, theory has a place, let's say a dialectical position, for the sake of argument. The theory and reality can be exchanged at some point – and that's ideality… But I hold no position on reality… The real is not an objective status of things, it is the point at which theory can do nothing.' (Baudrillard and Lotringer 1986, 140–41) Baudrillard's travelling opens out onto the ground of otherness, and on this affective ground there shifts restlessly the fiction and aporia that if we are not to confine, control or reduce it can poetically shape ethical correspondence with the world.

CONCLUSION

In this book I have been preoccupied with the question of modernity, with the challenges Western modernity poses to the subject's sense of their place in the world, and to the expression of these challenges in relation to the great capitals of the modern era, London and New York. Taylor tells us that 'from the beginning, the number one problem of modern social science has been modernity itself: that historically unprecedented amalgam of new practices and institutional forms (science, technology, industrial production, urbanization), of new ways of living (individualism, secularization, instrumental rationality); and of new forms of malaise (alienation, meaninglessness, a sense of impending social dissolution)' (Taylor 2004, 1). In analysing the travel writing of authors as far apart in time as Jules Janin and Jean Baudrillard we have seen that despite – or rather because of – the vastly different senses which they lend to modernity, travel writing engages us with all of the problems Taylor identifies through its activation of a differential space, wherein the understanding of the self as an agent in relation to others emerges with intensity. More than this, however, it is not only the self but also social, national and transnational identities that are challenged by the encounter with difference in the modern Western city.

We began by asking the question: 'What is a city?' and, through our reading of French travel accounts across the nineteenth and twentieth centuries, have sought to show how the answer to this question is necessarily multiple, wrought anew time and again by the spatial practices of travellers across urban space and time. In this, the idea of space as an empty container or '*neutral* medium into which disjointed things, people and habitats might be introduced' (Lefebvre [1974] 1991, 308) is necessarily renounced. The traveller, as a practitioner of space, demonstrates very clearly the extent to which the figured city is always under pressure from the representational spaces of those who walk its streets and formulate meaning for their experiences through the nexus of alterity.

Taking the long view, we identified a shift in the material and poetic frameworks for obtaining to meaning, referring to a movement from *legislative* to *interpretive* modes of travel. As we have seen, travellers often attempt to articulate the city's difference by constructing oppositional poles: self/other, home/abroad, past/future, history/experience, sign/object and Europe/America. Within the legislative grid, the city is appropriated using pre-established modes of reference that ground the city's Other within the referential categories of the Same. Legislative modes of travel, then, manifest a degree of interpretation, but this level of signification is stabilized within authoritative, non-reflexive aesthetic coda so that coherent meaning might be produced. This is a position rooted in modern means for making sense of society and so establishing 'naturalized' and 'necessary' relations between members of that society and their others. This legislative episteme, I argued, was the equivalent to a faith in the possibility for transparency of social and transnational relations, retaining an optimism about the possibility (at least) of controlling meaning. At the root of this idea, there seems to lay a sense of the stability and integrity of the self as a clearly defined position against which it can contain the other within its own epistemological limits for knowing the world. Effectively, what we see here is the traveller's representational space adhering to a singular idea of meaning, a mode of moving from the particular to the general without necessarily questioning the validity or possibility of this transition. In this mode, the traveller legislates for the signs of difference, moving through the city as a way of staying still, rendering the other transparent and thus ensuring the legibility of urban identities.

The travel accounts of Jules Janin and Jules Vallès, examined in the second chapter, revealed the extent to which French meanings for London in the nineteenth century were motivated by oppositional political frameworks. In these accounts, the political climate of contemporary France informed the imaginative geographies of the traveller, wherein understandings of what society ought to constitute and the role of the people therein, shaped these travellers' mediation of the city. With its meanings effectively rooted in French soil, the representational spaces of these travel writers saw London emerge as an alternative space for the articulation of two powerful and competing strands of political idealism around the 1789 Revolution and the 1871 Commune respectively. If, as Lamizet suggests, 'the city does not exist symbolically for its inhabitants until they are able to activate it: to make it exist in their imaginations, in their language, in their creation'[1] (Lamizet 2002, 213), then the existence of London is inherently double for the French traveller, moving across the nexus of cultural political spaces which travel engenders. Both Janin and Vallès, I have argued, *legislate* for difference in the way that their accounts frame London in opposition to the architectural and social spaces of France. However, we see here that Bauman's idea of the legislator, as someone rooted in a ratio-scientific, and bureaucratic mode of viewing the world, will only take us so far. The legislative mode of viewing which these travellers enact also demonstrates the extent to which the social imaginary of Western modernity emerges from within a range of complex negotiations of traditional, 'premodern' ideas that are still informed, one the one hand, by a providential way of being-in-the world (in the case of Janin), and on the other hand, by a socialist anarchist ideal ensconced in a culturally biased way of viewing the *peuple* of France as superior to the people of England. The contradictions which these respective positions seem to pose reanimate our idea of modernity and activate the multiple positions from which meaning in the city can be approached. Modernity is not a seamless flow, then, but a nexus of cultural, political, social and individual differences that negotiate one another in the quest to make sense of their position in the world.

In the next chapter, examining the work of two lesser-known writers, Jacques Dyssord and Alfred Leroy, we saw the extent to which the authenticity of experience becomes problematic in the urban travel account. For Dyssord, the search for authenticity is the primary motivation, and is constructed along the paradigmatic axis of bright and dark spaces. The former, for Dyssord, become associated with the institutional bourgeois capitalist spaces of the West End of London's urban landscape. By avoiding these and against all advice venturing into the East End of the 'secret' city, Dyssord attempts to make contact with the urban working classes, whom he associates with 'truth' and who provide him with access to an alternative social space within which he comes to reveal London. In this account, the legislative framework is worked out in accordance with the traveller's desire for transparency of the other and in the faith that he is not like other tourists. The 'dark tourism' of Dyssord is performed with a faith in the transparency of the relations between the objects he encounters and their meaning. Therefore, while we witness the potential for Dyssord's use of linguistic difference in his non-translation of certain slang words, we see this to be another ruse to confirm the authenticity of the experience for his reader. In a second movement, this chapter examined the theme of authenticity from a slightly different perspective in relation to Leroy. Leroy's London is essentially an imprint of an earlier, pre-war city. The authentic is not to be found in the reality of the bombed urban landscape, but in the serene, 'natural' spaces of Hyde Park where the traveller can move 'inward' to an imaginative geography of England that holds tradition and English civilization to be transcendent. This is a lens that shapes the other's reality in accordance with a projected ideal of their (supposedly) eternal character, and which is achieved through writing in the present tense about buildings which no longer exist. Thus Leroy leads the reader through an architectural projection of the features he attributes to the unchanging and heroic English character.

The social, historical and cultural issues raised through Morand and Sartre's negotiation of modern New York demonstrate collective concerns that resonate with our contemporary, globalized urban universe. Morand's representational space emerges as a cartographic transposition of the city, so that it is diagrammatically framed. In a similar way, time is mapped onto the city in terms of its history, but also in terms of its position within a genealogy of urban modernity. In this account, the teleological view of modernity is particularly prevalent, as is the desire to impose a singular model across its expression. Morand, in this way, constructs New York as the paradigm for all future expressions of urban modernity throughout the world. From Morand we moved to Sartre, and with this account in 1945 the issue of the future of humankind was also of clear concern to the traveller. Here, however, the stereotypes of New York as proof of human beings' technological and democratic progression are consistently refuted. New York for Sartre is a fragile, futile attempt on the part of humans to deny the vastness and power of Nature to intervene and destroy this illusion. Sartre's account revealed the emergent tension in legislating for difference. Here, through the author's acknowledgement of the limitations of his own subjectivity, the essays reveal one of the key preoccupations of travel writers in the latter half of the twentieth century; namely, how to find a position from which to speak about the other.

The representational mode that corresponds to this legislative version of authenticity is metonymical opposition, a reading that moves directly from singularity to a generalized diagnosis of the other. Thus, while the cultural and temporal contexts framing interpretation change, the ordered schema, or what Soja calls 'the lure of binarism' (1996, 60), consistently enables the travel writer to legislate for the reality of the city as coherent structure, imposing on mobility the stability of narrative description. The coherence within the legislative framework is problematized, however, once the author reflects metatextually on the possibility of writing difference.

As we saw in relation to Perec's and Baudrillard's spatial practice, reflections on the nature of interpretation destabilize the ground on which such binaries operate, so that in effect we move from a strategy of narrative legibility to a tactics of representational spaces that push at the boundaries of language. In these texts, it is the grid of language itself that is problematized through poetic tactical responses to the radicality of the Other's difference. Perec's *Ellis Island* intimates silence in between the lines of the historical narrative of the monument, and through enumeration and metatext carves a space for absence – the absence, namely, of the migrants' quotidian experiences, hardships and personal stories. This absence is inherent also to the writer's identity and to the void at the heart of his experience of Jewishness, to the loss of his parents during the Holocaust, and his relationship to this past as a form of potential memory in American space. Baudrillard's poetics lead the reader through America as a space of paradox, hyperbole and irony in a critique of the legislative impulse to control social space, an impulse that Baudrillard identifies as inherent to the neoliberal capitalist project of Reaganism. The author's adoption of these poetic tactics ultimately renders problematic the relationship between notions of material, or 'objective' space (the real), and the travel writer's translation of America into representational form. I argued that through this interpretive poetics, the notion of space as an inherently stable entity existing a priori to cultural interference is itself rendered untenable, and that Baudrillard's poetics distorts not only the reader's potential to pretend to engage through this text with the 'real' of America, but that these tactics open a space of autocritique of Western value systems that presume the legibility of – and by implication, the possibility for – legislative coherence in social space. Travel performed in this way enables a position of reflexivity where modalities of interpretation are highlighted, and opens out a critical mode of understanding the self as an interwoven extension of the other, where monadic conceptions of identity as stable or inflexible collapse. The interpretive mode of travel, then, involves a consciousness of the operations via which meaning is produced – an awareness of the structures that produce the illusion of social and spatial cohesion. Here, the 'traditional' transparency of the urban sign is recognized to be problematic. When, through the poetic operations of the text, the arbitrary connection between the sign and its object is revealed, the otherness of American space is not resolved but recognized. In the interpretive scenario, then, travel becomes a means of exploration through poetic dislocation, where alterity insinuates itself into the textual apparatus to engage with difference on a level that acknowledges and accentuates the constructed – and by implication, the deconstructable – nature of identities. This difference in repetition and repetition in difference concedes the contingency, rather than the coherency, of identities, facilitating an understanding of urban identities as mutually constructed through encounter. When the elements and processes that provide the frameworks for meaning are exposed, the possibility of stabilizing the space of the other becomes unworkable. To recognize culture as an assemblage (Deleuze and Guattari 1980) of interweaving sensible interactions and experiences is to reveal the contingency of the symbolic composition of institutional systems, orderly representations of space and articulates a cultural narrative of modernity within the malleable and arbitrary strata of imagined geographies: a contingency that necessarily opens onto the possibility for changes – of minds, identities, politics and their practices.

This recognition of the fractal dimension of human encounter in urban spaces promotes questions with regard to the ethics of travel writing. Thus we can identify a reorientation of the traveller's objective – away from a making sense of city in relation to some Kantian noumenal reality – towards an exposition of the processes of construction and/ or destruction of sense. How, when we are cognizant of the difference in cultural codes for understanding the world, can we find a position from which to speak? I would argue that this can never be a singular position, and interpretive travel writing demonstrates the potential for poetics, or *writing* (Perec 1975), to occupy a simultaneous multiplicity of spaces that harnesses movement as a means of mobilizing and multiplying meaning, presenting a critique at the same time as it performs modernity as a series of potential alterities.

In this prismatic scenario, living in and through simulation need not necessarily entail the end of aesthetic practice as a real indicator of human ideas or emotions. Despite the increasing surveillance of cities and the progressive homogeneity of the urban landscape, we find, nevertheless, new forms of interpretive expression; street artists, *parkour* practitioners and urban interventionists, to name but a few, have all emerged as creators of new mobilities that critically engage with the global city. The result is that awareness of the constructed nature of our urban reality engenders ever-evolving, alternative critical and creative forms of movement in and through the city. Cities have always been as much imagined as lived and, perhaps now more than ever, the global city demands new imaginative tactics for its sustainability as a human as well as a built environment. For, if the city and the evolution of its imaginative geography are worthy of attention, it is precisely because Western urban space presents us with the urgent necessity to define a relationship between the theoretical and the practical; between the ideals of urban planners, the spatial designation of social life, and government notions of citizenship, on the one hand, and the uses, practices and enunciations through which people negotiate these orders, on the other. The relevance of narratives of mobility – from migrants to travellers to commuters – to discovering the potential for intervention in the figured city has never been greater. To interrogate urban space and urban practices is, in the end, to ask a double-edged question about the existence of the city, the status of the imagination and the material implications of representational practice at a time when the urban fabric threatens to sprawl into insignificance. The emergence of the human environment as that of a globalized urban lifeworld calls on us, therefore, to invent better means for negotiating simultaneously local, national and transnational spaces while finding ways to recognize the alterities inherent in ourselves – and others – through these encounters.

NOTES

Introduction: Approaching the City

1 'Toute ville est de rencontres, de contacts et d'échanges. Toute ville est de hasards et d'organisations, d'ordres et de désordres, de chaos et de réorganisations dans un flux imperceptible de mutations internes. Toute ville est un complexe vivant.' Unless otherwise stated, all translations throughout the volume are mine.

2 Tout récit est un récit de voyage, – une pratique de l'espace. A ce titre, il intéresse les tactiques quotidiennes, il en fait partie [...]. Ces aventures narrées, qui tout à la fois produisent des géographies d'actions et dérivent dans les lieux communs d'un ordre, ne constituent pas seulement un 'supplément' aux énonciations piétonnières et aux rhétoriques cheminatoires. Elles ne se contentent pas de les déplacer et transposer dans le champ du langage. En fait, elles organisent les marches. Elles font le voyage, avant ou pendant que les pieds l'exécutent. (Certeau [1980] 1990, 171). All subsequent citations in French refer to this second edition of *L'Invention du quotidien*, originally published in 1980.

3 See for instance, Agnew 1984; Anderson 2009; Augé 1994; Barthes [1967] 2002; Bull 2000; Castells 1977; Gunn and Morris 2001; Harvey 1989; Highmore 2005; Jacobs [1961] 1962, Lepoutre 1997; Lynch 1960.

4 The terminology used throughout is appropriated from Henri Lefebvre's (1974) work on urban space. The useful differentiation between spaces of representation and representations of space is taken from *La Production de l'espace*. A fuller discussion of Lefebvre's theory and its appropriateness for the study undertaken here takes place in the next chapter.

5 For explorations from the ethnological, sociological and semiotic perspectives see: Lepoutre 1997; Ligget and Perry 1995; Lash and Urry 1994; Laborit 1971; Kostof 2001; Jeudy 2003; Highmore 2005; Harvey 1985, 1989, and Sennett 1996.

6 'la ville n'est pas une chose ni ne se laisse réduire à une substance'.

7 The first known use of the term 'urbanism' is Camillo Sitte's ([1889] 1965) book *City Planning according to Artistic Principles*, first published as *Der Städtebau nach seinen künstlerischen Grundsätzen* in 1889. Sitte's work, still cited today, sought to establish a set of principles for urban design that moved away from the functionalist considerations of the gridiron, radial and triangular systems of urban planning and emphasized the artistic value of the individual street or plaza over the mathematical system. See Sitte ([1889] 1965, 91–104).

8 Important work has been carried out in French travel studies which tempers the Anglophone emphasis. A pioneer in the field, Charles Forsdick's (2003, 2005 and 2006) theoretical work on travel writing has informed my thinking here. Another significant text in the field is C.W. Thompson's *French Romantic Travel Writing* (2011) which constitutes a near exhaustive study of the evolution in poetics of French Romantic travel writing up to 1850. Margaret Topping is also an influential thinker on the imbrication of travel, the senses and space. See Topping (2004).

9 See, for instance, Budford 1997; Capetti 1993; Humphreys 2002; Kelley 1996; Lehan 1998; Rotella 1998, Scherpe and Roetzel 1992–93; Steve 2003; Timms 1985; Twying 1998; Wallock and Sharpe [1983] 1987, and Wright and Kaplan 2003.

10 Hagen Schulz-Forberg has published significant work in the field of urban European travel writing however. His books include *London – Berlin: Authenticity, Modern and the Metropolis in Urban Travel Writing from 1851 to 1939* (2006), which has been an important reference point for my work. In difference to Schulz-Forberg this book focuses on a limited number of specifically French writers and engages in a more emphatic manner with the significance of aesthetic form in the urban travel journal.

11 See, for example, Merleau-Ponty ([1945] 2001).

12 'L'art de "tourner" des phrases a pour équivalent un art de tourner des parcours.'

13 'la conscience symbolique' / 'la conscience paradigmatique' / 'la conscience syntagmatique'. These modes of apprehension are interpreted by the linguist Giulio Ciro Lepschy (1970, 3–4): 'A sign is in contrast with other signs which come before and after it in a sentence. It has with the preceding and following signs a syntagmatic relationship. This is a relationship *in praesentia*, i.e. between elements (the sign in question, and the preceding and following ones) which are all present in the message. But a sign is also opposed to other signs not because they are in the message but because they belong to the language; it is associated (through similarity or difference) with these other signs, it has with them an associative relationship. This is a relationship *in absentia*, i.e. between the element in question which is there, and other elements which are not there in that particular message.'

14 'Rien ne permet d'affirmer que ce problème d'objet empirique réel, de représentativité, se pose différemment dans un grand royaume africain et dans une entreprise de la banlieue parisienne.'

15 See Thomas Robert Malthus (1803); Charles Booth (1889, 1891) and Friedrich Engels ([1844] 1993). One of the first and seminal articulations of urban life as productive of a certain type of 'personality' or identity is Georg Simmel's 1903 essay, 'The Metropolis and Mental Life'.

16 Owing to ambiguities in the census and a change in methods for classifying what counted as 'urban' during the period, one must be wary of the accuracy of the figures. Nevertheless, demographic experts concur that from the watershed of the census onward, the rate of migration from rural to urban heartlands increased dramatically, with London being generally seen as the most populated city in the Western hemisphere.

17 The population of London in 1851 is recorded as 2,651,939, Paris reached two million in 1877–78, while New York lagged behind with a population of about one and a half million recorded in 1871. These figures are taken from J.T. Coppock ([1976] 2011, 295–373).

18 See Poe's 'A Descent into the Maelstrom' ([1841] 1966). Essentially a tale of anxiety in the face of the sublime, Poe's maelstrom is often interpreted as a metaphor for modern life.

19 'les espaces de représentation' ([1974] 2000, 49).

20 For detailed studies of the importance of travel to Western epistemologies see Rojek and Urry 1997b; Clarke 1999; Hulme and Youngs 2002; Hooper and Youngs 2004; Scott 2004.

21 Statistical data helps bring this point into view. The population of Greater Tokyo, for example, is over 30 million. In 1950, 44 per cent of Americans lived on farms, by 1990 the figure had halved to around 23 per cent. This process is continuing. Some cities of South America, Asia and Africa, when one includes the shantytown peripheries, have populations of 15, 20 and 30 million inhabitants. The imagination and experience of non-Western urban worlds has already impacted on the West in the form of mass migration and, more specifically, on the conceptual practices of contemporary architects and the rapid pace at which cities continue to expand, ensuring that its cities will play a major role in determining the future of the globalized world.

22 'un innumérable de singularités'.

23 'les représentations de l'espace' / 'les espaces de représentation' (Lefebvre [1974] 2000, 48–49).

24 The term is appropriated (and adapted in the next chapter) from the Underground Electric Railway Company's 1924 poster campaign for the London Underground, and the poster, 'Brightest London is best reached by Underground', by Horace Taylor.

1. Producing the City

1 'La ville est à la fois territoire et population, cadre matériel et unité de vie collective, configuration d'objets physiques et nœud de relations entre sujets sociaux.'

2 'habitat'; 'habiter'.

3 'Un "être humain" n'a pas devant lui, autour de lui, l'espace social – celui de sa société – comme un tableau, comme un spectacle ou un miroir. Il sait qu'il a un espace et qu'il *est* dans cet espace. Il n'a pas seulement une vision, une contemplation, un spectacle; il agit, il se situe dans l'espace, partie prenante. A ce titre, il se situe dans une série d'enveloppes qui s'impliquent les unes les autres; leur suite explique la pratique sociale' (Lefebvre [1974] 2000, 339).

4 'La thèse d'un milieu spatiale inerte, où les gens et choses, actes et situations, n'auraient qu'à se loger, correspond à un schéma cartésien (la chose étendue comme "objet" de pense) devenu au cours des âges "sens commun" et "culture". L'espace mental élaboré (par les philosophes et les épistémologues) se constitue en lieu transparent – en milieu logique. La réflexion dès lors croit atteindre l'espace social; mais celui-ci est le siège d'une pratique qui ne consiste pas seulement en l'application de concepts. Elle est aussi méconnaissance, aveuglement, épreuve vécue' (Lefebvre [1974] 2000, 342).

5 'Un lieu est donc une configuration instantanée de positions. Il implique une indication de stabilité' (Certeau [1980] 1990, 173).

6 'La loi du "propre" y règne: les éléments considérés sont les uns *à côté des autres, chacun situé en un endroit "propre" et distinct qu'il définit*' (Certeau [1980] 1990, 173).

7 Tim Cresswell, Doreen Massey, David Harvey and Edward Soja have been among the most influential in the cultural geographical reformulation of the idea of 'place'.

8 'Il y a *espace* dès qu'on prend en considération des vecteurs de direction, des quantités de vitesse et la variable de temps' (Certeau [1980] 1990, 173).

9 'Est l'espace l'effet produit par les opérations qui l'orientent, le circonstancient, le temporalisent et l'amènent à fonctionner en unité polyvalente de programmes conflictuels ou de proximités contractuelles.' (Certeau [1980] 1990, 173)

10 'En somme, *l'espace est un lieu pratiqué*' (Certeau [1980] 1990, 173).

11 'Ainsi la rue géométriquement définie par un urbanisme est transformée en espace par des marcheurs. De même, la lecture est l'espace produit par la pratique du lieu que constitue un système de signes – un écrit' (Certeau [1980] 1990, 173).

12 'L'image de leur organisation d'ensemble était facilement accessible à tous, leur régularité étant de l'ordre d'une topologie emblématique, schématique mais orchestrant, sans dissensions particulières, la coordination des tâches.'

13 'L'architecture naît en Occident, à la Renaissance, au moment où la ville médiévale voit son ordre consensuel disloqué par le développement d'une économie capitaliste qui va modifier la structure sociale et la place des groupes sociaux dans l'espace, surtout par les différences de rapports que chacun d'eux entretient avec la localisation de ses activités.'

14 'Le postulat du départ est que la ville doit être pensée en tant qu'organisation *systématique multidimensionnelle* où l'on retrouve, articulées et indissociables, toutes les dimensions de la société, à savoir les dimensions temporelle, sociale (le groupe des individus), individuelle (l'individu, en tant que plus petite unité complexe de la société, et ses logiques), économique, politique, spatiale. L'espace y joue le rôle particulier et éminent de rendre *visibles* les *composants* de cette organisation et les *principes* et *modalités* de leurs combinaisons. Il convertit en signes sensibles, en formes, en structures, bref en agencements matériels – à la fois infinis dans le détail de leur facture et assez simples et limités en nombre, considérés d'un point de vue général – et idéels – *via* les récits et les figures que mettent en scène les idéologies spatiales – l'ordre et les logiques de l'urbain.'

15 'est fondamental dans toute forme de vie communautaire'.

16 'Nous ne vivons pas dans une sorte de vide, à l'intérieur duquel on pourrait situer des individus et des choses. Nous ne vivons pas à l'intérieur d'un vide qui se colorerait de

différents chatoiements, nous vivons à l'intérieur d'un ensemble de relations qui définissent des emplacements irréductibles les uns aux autres [...]'.

17 '*Les représentations de l'espace*, liées aux rapports de production, à l'"ordre" qu'ils imposent et par là, à des connaissances, à des signes, à des codes, à des relations "frontales"' (Lefebvre [1974] 2000, 43).

18 '*Les espaces de représentation*, c'est-à-dire l'espace *vécu* à travers les images et symboles qui l'accompagnent, donc espace des "habitants", des "usagers", mais aussi de certains artistes [...]. C'est l'espace dominé, donc subi, que tente de modifier et d'approprier l'imagination' (Lefebvre [1974] 2000, 49).

19 I am referring here to the title of the English translation of *Les Mots et les Choses* (1966).

20 'l'habitant symbolique'.

21 'L'espace géométrique des urbanistes et des architectes semble valoir comme le 'sens propre' construit par les grammairiens et les linguistes en vue de disposer d'un niveau normal et normatif auquel référer les dérives du 'figuré.'

22 'des sociétés disciplinaires'.

23 'procèdent à l'organisation des grands milieux d'enfermement'.

24 'les *sociétés de contrôle*'.

25 'Les enfermements sont des *moules*, des moulages distincts, mais les contrôles sont une *modulation*, comme un moulage auto-déformant qui changerait continûment, d'un instant à l'autre, ou comme un tamis dont les mailles changeraient d'un point à un autre.'

26 In difference to other philosophers and cultural theorists, for Virilio it is speed – and not class or wealth – that performs as the primary force shaping human civilisation.

27 'Le développement des hautes vitesses,' according to Virilio, 'aboutirait à la disparition de la conscience en tant que perception directe des phénomènes qui nous renseignent sur notre propre existence'.

28 'Mais à ces appareils producteurs d'un espace disciplinaire quelles *pratiques de l'espace* correspondent, du côté où l'on joue (avec) la discipline?'

29 'la production d'un espace *propre*'

30 'la substitution d'un *non-temps*, ou d'un système synchronique, aux résistances insaisissables et têtues des traditions'.

31 'la création d'un *sujet universel* et anonyme qui est la ville même'.

32 'La spatialisation du discours savant'.

33 'mutation moderne du temps en espace contrôlable,' saying that 'incessamment, l'écriture scientifique, constitution d'un lieu propre, ramène le temps, ce fugitif, à la normalité d'un système observable et lisible.'

34 'ouvre des absences dans le continuum spatial,' according to Certeau, 'et n'en retient que des morceaux choisis, voire des reliques'.

35 For classic studies, see for instance: Augé 1986; Hannerz 1983; Lepoutre 1997; Castells 1977; Grafmeyer 1994; Certeau [1980] 1990; Lefebvre [1974] 1999; Damisch 1996; Laborit 1971; Sansot 1996; Stierle 2001; Bachelard [1957] 2001.

36 'La maison est notre coin du monde. Elle est – on l'a souvent dit – notre premier univers. Elle est vraiment un cosmos [...]. Ainsi la maison ne se vit pas seulement au jour le jour, sur le fil d'une histoire, dans le récit de notre histoire. Par les songes, les diverses demeures de notre vie se compénètrent et gardent les trésors des jours anciens [...]. Les souvenirs du monde extérieur n'auront jamais la même tonalité que les souvenirs de la maison. [...] La maison, dans la vie de l'homme, évince des contingences, elle multiplie ses conseils de continuité. Sans elle, l'homme serait un être dispersé.'

37 The notion of home, with the symbolic stability and integration implied by this word, is not unproblematic for contemporary writers on the city. Jean-François Lyotard, writing of the *domus* as a space of community, 'repeated domestication', and collective memory, sees the development of the megalopolis as a negation of such domestic rhythms. These issues shall be explored further in the chapter 'Wandering Geometry'. See Lyotard (1998).

38 Although, it must be pointed out that the concept of 'home' as a stable entity becomes increasingly problematic throughout the course of the twentieth century, and its disintegration continues to concern theorists and artists alike.

39 This debate extends to the question of travel, problems of definition and interpretation regarding travel writing, travel literature, travel journal, etc., and importantly the determination of critical boundaries for the field of Travel Studies as an academic sphere of research. For further reading, the most notable among scholars engaged in this debate in terms of academic implications are Jan Borm (2000), James M. Buzard (2002), Mary Baine Campbell (1988, 1999), Joan Pau Rubiés (2002) and Tim Youngs (1994).

40 An example of this transformative semiotic in the religious imagination can be found in the text of a Bordeaux pilgrim. Known as the *Itinterarium Burdigalense*, in this extract what would probably have constituted a simple, functional well for the Roman inhabitant becomes an indexical marker, a geographical testimony of Biblical significance. The pilgrim writes: 'A mile from here (Mt Gerizim) is the place called Sychar, where the Samaritan woman went down to draw water, at the very place where Jacob dug the well, and our Lord Jesus spoke with her. Some plane trees are there, planted by Jacob, and there is a bath which takes water from this well' (cited in Elsner and Rubiés (1999, 16)).

41 From the fourth century onward the cult of relics and saints was encouraged to make pilgrimage more locally feasible. On a symbolic level, remains of the saints or tokens pertaining to Christ's life functioned on a similar plane to the sacred geography of the Holy City, lending authenticity via His tangible presence. Narratives grew up locally, Christ's sacred authority being confirmed by the higher clergy and thus giving the allure of a direct link to the spiritual world. On a commercial level the cult of relics was an early forerunner of the souvenir industry. Pilgrims were concerned, therefore, to visit these sites in order to gain speedier passage to Heaven but also to purchase some evidence of their visit. Shop-owners, hoteliers and ship owners all benefited from the pilgrim's need to possess an object, a sign of presence at the site. See Hopper (2002).

42 'un ensemble hiérarchisé de lieux'.

43 Pilgrimage was crucial in establishing Jerusalem as the literal and allegorical centre of the Judaeo-Christian world. This obsession for a centre is evident in the religious cartography emanating from the teaching of the Christian fathers. They introduced a map with a symbolic T-O structure ordering the world according to three divisions, with Asia taking the top half of the circle, and Europe and Africa occupying the lower quarters. Jerusalem was placed at the centre of the map. This cartographic design entered into frequent use from the eleventh century onward, consolidating Jerusalem's empirical status as centre of the world. The city was essentially the meeting point of historical identity, geographical locus and intangible sacred. And, as a pilgrim, the medieval traveller could recognize in the urban site the sacred signs of the evangelical order and historical design. See D. French (1992).

44 For an analysis of this work with respect to Chateaubriand's semiological encounter with the Judean desert, see David Scott's chapter 'Signs in the desert' in Scott (2004, 137–60).

45 'supposait toujours des signes qui lui étaient antérieurs: de sorte que la connaissance se logeait tout entière dans la béance d'un signe découvert ou affirmé ou secrètement transmis. Elle [la divination] avait pour tâche de relever un langage préalable réparti par Dieu dans le monde; c'est en ce sens que par une implication essentielle elle devinait, et elle devinait du *divin.*'

46 It is not surprising, then, that the crusades developed from pilgrimage as a way of controlling the centre of the Christian universe. The tension between the militaristic and religious bents of the Christian mindset was overcome on the first crusade of 1095 by Pope Urban's specification that it was a collective pilgrimage (albeit one addressed to the armed knights of Christendom). After Saladin's reconquest of Jerusalem in 1187, the Christians' consistent failures to recapture the city led to the formation of the idea of the centre as an unattainable ideal. The loss of the

Holy City to the Muslim infidel produced a crisis in the West which expressed itself in terms of moral doubt: if Saladin had managed to depose the rightful inheritors of the city, then it was due to the Christian's moral degradation subsequent to his initial success. Up to this point the clear superiority of Muslim civilization in terms of worldly cultural sophistication had never posed a threat to Christianity's spiritual authority. This negative contact with the Other is among the first documented doubt that can be detected with regard to the invulnerability of Christian morals. William of Tyre (1130–1186), Latin historian of the Crusades, framed his reflections on Saladin's conquest with a terminology explicit in placing the blame on the decline in Western morality: 'In the place of our parents', writes William, 'who were religious men and fearful of God, have been born the sons of perdition [...] it is only according to justice and their sins that the Lord, as if provoked to anger, withdraws his Grace. These men are the men of the current century, and especially from the orient. Anyone who attempted to trace their habits with a diligent pen, or rather to portray the monstrosity of their vices would succumb under the immensity of the material and would turn to satire rather than persist in the writing of history' (cited in Elsner and Rubiés 1999, 25–26).

47 Richard Lassels, a five-time traveller to Italy between 1637 and 1668, appears to have been the first to use the term in English. In his *An Italian Voyage* (1670) he recommends that young gentlemen embark upon a 'Grand Tour of France and the Giro of Italy'.

48 For an analysis of changes in the destinations of the Grand Tourists, see Hibbert (1987).

49 While Brewer is referring specifically to the English on tour, the idea of Europe as a cultural haul also has political and cultural significance for late eighteenth- and early nineteenth-century France, when Napoleon embarked upon his conquest of the continent.

50 The replacement was never total, with many French writers, such as Flaubert and Stendhal still favouring sunnier climes.

51 In his *Discours sur les sciences et les arts*, Rousseau identifies the palaces of Europe with falsity of appearance and civilized society's vice. He opposes these to the simple dwellings of 'primitive' man:

> We cannot reflect on the morality of mankind without contemplating with pleasure the picture of the simplicity which prevailed in earlier time. This image may be justly compared to a beautiful coast, adorned only with the hands of nature; towards which our eyes are constantly turned, and which we see receding with regret. While men were innocent and virtuous and loved to have the gods for witnesses to their actions, they dwelt together in the same huts; but when they became vicious, they grew tired of such inconvenient onlookers, and banished them to magnificent temples. Finally, they expelled their deities even from these, in order to dwell there themselves; or at least the temples of the gods were no longer more magnificent than the palaces of the citizens. This was the height of degeneracy; nor could vice ever be carried to greater lengths than when it was seen, supported, as it were, at the doors of the great, on columns of marble, and graven on Corinthian capitals. (Rousseau [1750] 1923, 145) / 'On ne peut réfléchir sur les mœurs, qu'on ne se plaise à se rappeler l'image de la simplicité des premiers temps. C'est un beau rivage, paré des seules mains de la nature, vers lequel on tourne incessamment les yeux, et dont on se sent éloigner à regret. Quand les hommes innocents et vertueux aimaient à avoir les dieux pour témoins de leurs actions, ils habitaient ensemble sous les mêmes cabanes; mais bientôt devenus méchants, ils se lassèrent de ces incommodes spectateurs et les reléguèrent dans des temples magnifiques. Ils les en chassèrent enfin pour s'y établir eux-mêmes, ou du moins les temples des dieux ne se distinguèrent plus des maisons des citoyens. Ce fut alors le comble de la dépravation; et les vices ne furent jamais poussés plus loin que quand on les vit, pour ainsi dire, soutenus à l'entrée des palais des Grands sur des colonnes de marbre, et gravés sur des chapiteaux corinthiens' (Rousseau [1750] 2011, 20–21).

52 Certain urban sociologists, notably American Georg Simmel (1903), would contradict the positive light I have conveyed on the urban quotidian. For Simmel the city is responsible for

the eradication of intimacy and the creation of a 'blasé attitude' typical of 'metropolitan individuality' that renders the urban dweller more rationalistic, less emotional and, one might say, less alive than his rural counterparts. As Simmel says in *The Metropolis and Mental Life* (1903): 'The calculating exactness of practical life which has resulted from a money economy corresponds to the ideal of natural science, namely that of transforming the world into an arithmetical problem and of fixing every one of its parts in a mathematical formula' (Simmel [1903] 2002, 13).

53 'le kaléidoscope illusoire du tourisme'.

54 This is a term used by Kenneth White and cited by Urbain (2000), whose essay is a critique of White's hypothesis.

55 Urbain highlights the problems in equating travel with the realities of nomadic life, noting that the distinction between movement and dwelling is not as definite in reality as White's theory supposes. In a critique of White's use of the term nomad, he says: 'Nomads, people of fixed boundaries and itineraries, whose lives depend on repetition, are at home in mobility and dwell in this state. In their movement, they neither leave nor change their surroundings. They do not wander or roam: they dwell' (Urbain, 2000, 150).

56 I refer to the *flâneur* in the third person masculine, for, as Deborah L. Parsons (2000) points out, this mode of urban experience was, largely, a masculine one.

57 While there is more to say here, I do not treat of women travel writers in this book – feeling that this would require a study of its own that would elaborate on gender in a sustained way. However, an important work on female presence in the city is Deborah L. Parson's *Streetwalking the Metropolis: Women, the City and Modernity* (2000).

58 '*L'espace commence ainsi, avec seulement des mots, des signes tracés sur la page blanche.*'

59 I explore the notion of authenticity – a complex term that requires unpacking – in the context of the specific accounts analysed in subsequent chapters.

60 'le mélange ou le mépris des genres est un genre parmi d'autres'

61 'l'introduction de la notion de dominante qui organise le système d'une œuvre complexe permet de transformer en catégorie méthodiquement productive ce qu'on appelait le 'mélange des genres'

62 Borm uses the term *travel writing* in a more general way, as a synonym of *travel literature* or the *literature of travel*, to describe 'texts whose main theme is travel' and, therefore, the term *travel writing* allows for the inclusion of fiction and non-fiction in its usage (Borm 2004, 19). Borm is categorical in his use of *travel book* or *travelogue* as terms referring specifically to accounts where the non-fictive can be considered dominant.

63 Genette asks the question: 'But has there ever been a pure fiction? Or a pure non-fiction? The response in both cases is clearly negative.' / 'Mais exista-t-il jamais une pure fiction? Et une pure non-fiction? La réponse est évidemment négative dans les deux cas' (Genette 1983, 11).

64 Augé (1992) considers this tension in terms of an 'altérité intime' / 'intimate alterity' by which he means that absolute individuality is unthinkable given societal influences and familial genealogy and yet the individual is involved in these processes of construction.

65 'Le jeu est un thème qui est très souvent souligné dans les enquêtes sur le centre [ville]; il y a en France une série d'enquêtes concernant l'attrait exercé par Paris sur sa banlieue, et on a observé à travers ces enquêtes que Paris en tant que centre, pour la périphérie, était toujours vécu sémantiquement comme *le lieu privilégié où est l'autre et où nous-mêmes sommes l'autre*, comme le lieu où l'on joue'.

66 In *Argonauts of the Western Pacific* (1961), the ethnographer Malinowski celebrates the dawn of professional, scientific ethnography, implying falsehood in the representation of the other by less specialized genres – such as the travel journal.

67 'L'activité de l'ethnologue de terrain est dès le départ une activité d'arpenteur du social, de manieur d'échelles, de comparatiste au petit pied: il bricole un univers significatif, au besoin en explorant, par enquêtes rapides, des univers intermédiaires, ou en consultant, en historien, les documents utilisables. Il essaie, pour lui-même et pour les autres, de savoir de qui il peut prétendre parler quand il parle de ceux à qui il a parlé.'

68 In view of this debate over the possibility of writing the other, Clifford (1986) has suggested a view of ethnography (and this can be applied to travel writing too) as allegory, as a positive means of recognizing the 'fact that realistic portraits, to the extent that they are "convincing" or "rich," are extended metaphors, patterns of associations that point to coherent (theoretical, esthetic, moral) additional meanings. Allegory (more strongly than "interpretation") calls to mind the poetic, traditional, cosmological nature of such writing processes' (100).

69 'du coup par coup' (Certeau [1980] 1990, 61).

2. Urban Oppositions: Producing French Space in Nineteenth-Century London

1 'Ah! Que de fer, ah! Que de cuivre et d'acier, et que de roues et de rouages, que de machines infatigables et de chevaux invisibles! Que d'événémens, combien de miracles, quel avenir!'

2 'l'espace de la modernité [...] se décèlent ces tendances' (Lefebvre [1974] 2000, 146).

3 'l'espace global' (Lefebvre [1974] 2000, 148).

4 French travel writers were fond of labelling London the modern Babylon. See for instance, chapter 4 of Louis Enault's *Angleterre, Ecosse, Irlande: Voyage pittoresque* (1859) and Fernand de Jupilles's *La Moderne Babylone: Londres et les Anglais* (1886).

5 In 1801 the census listed the total population of London at 864, 845. By 1851, that number had risen to 2,362, 236.

6 In terms of foreign migrants to London, the British National Archives' collection of the records of nineteenth-century immigrants reveals that more than 7,000 people applied to become British citizens over the period 1844 to 1871 under the 1844 Naturalization Act. This includes a mix of people from all over the world, including a large proportion from French and German states, as well as other mainland European countries. Most of these people settled in London and established communities. See '19th-Century Immigrants' Records Released Online', *The National Archives*, last modified 8 May 2013, http://www.nationalarchives.gov.uk/news/840.htm.

7 I am using the word after Foucault's ([1967] 2001) definition of heterotopias as places and spaces that operate outside the purview of dominant normative modes of spatial inclusion and exclusion. These non-hegemonic spaces are, therefore, 'misaligned' with respect to everyday space.

8 Throughout the Middle Ages, Messina, for example, was the most significant point of departure for knights on their way to the Crusades.

9 'Ici l'on parle mille langues, comme dans la Tour de Babel.'

10 'un ensemble complexe de rapports commerciaux et de réseaux de communication' (Lefebvre [1974] 2000, 133).

11 For an exploration of Jacobin concepts of masculinity and heroism, see Annie Jourdan's 'Robespierre and Revolutionary Heroism' in Haydon and Doyle (1999); Lynn Hunt's 'Male virtue and Republican Motherhood' in Baker (1988) and Miguel Abensour's chapter on Saint-Just, 'Saint-Just and the Problem of Heroism' in Fehér (1990).

12 For contemporary English commentaries on these contrasts, see Marshall 1884; Mayhew and Binny 1862; Barnett 1888.

13 See for instance Tristan ([1840] 1978); Blanqui (1851); Chevalier (1851); Blanc ([1861–1865] 2001); Jupilles (1866); Taine ([1872] 1923); Énault ([1875] 1984); Vasili (1885); Gavard (1895) and Cahen ([1908] 1909).

14 Baudrillard, in *For a Critique of the Political Economy of the Sign* ([1972] 1981, 29), writes, 'Far from the primary status of an object being a pragmatic one, it is the sign exchange value which is fundamental – use-value is often no more than a practical guarantee (or even a rationalization pure and simple). Such, in its paradoxical form, is the only correct sociological hypotheses.'

15 Between 1789 and 1900, France had the following different governments: Constitutional Monarchy under Louis XVI (1789–1792); the First Republic (1792–1804); First Empire

under Napoleon I (1804–1814/1815); Bourbon Restoration under Louis XVIII and Charles X (1814/1815– 830); July Monarchy under Louis Philippe d'Orléans (1830–1848); Second Republic under Louis-Napoleon Bonaparte (1848–1852); Second Empire under Louis-Napoléon Bonaparte (Napoleon III) (1852–1870); The Paris Commune (1871) and the Third Republic (1870 –1940).

16 Effectively, 'the people', although the English translation does not bear the same mythological weight as the French word.

17 L'apogée des 'relations' de Londres avec l'industrie fut sans conteste la Grande Exposition de 1851. Première rencontre des Londoniens avec toutes les facettes de l'industrie, elle fut également la première rencontre avec les produits et les hommes du reste du monde. Son organisation provoqua des remous, mais elle fit venir à Londres un nombre considérable de visiteurs: un peu plus de six millions, chiffre que bien des manifestations internationales d'aujourd'hui pourraient envier.'

18 'de faire connaître au monde industriel la part qui revient souvent à notre nation dans ces inventions nouvelles, dans ces merveilles de l'art ou de la mécanique que le palais d'*Hyde Park* étale à tous les yeux. […] Ainsi telle statue, tel bijou, tel meuble, telle pièce de soie, qu'on voit figurer sur la partie anglaise de catalogue, le dessin, l'exécution, en reviennent peut-être a des artistes, à des ouvriers français engagés a haut prix par l'Angleterre.'

19 'N'oubliez jamais, ami lecteur, que la pensée de l'Exposition universelle est née en France'.

20 'la nuit se passa ainsi à causer, chacun de son art, et sans un mot de politique'.

21 'Voilà enfin une émeute qui mérite à la fois les contemplations de la terre et les sourires de là-haut! En voilà des révolutions excellentes, dignes de nos sympathies et de nos respects! On se bat avec les armes les plus courtoises. On dresse, l'un contre l'autre, des barricades de chefs-d'œuvre; on n'entend retenir, dans ces peuples en travail, que le bruit du marteau frappant sur l'enclume, ou le gémissement de la vapeur, attelée à son char enflammé. Écoutez! Ce bruit pareil au canon qui renverse les villes, c'est le bruit des métiers qui se fait entendre d'un bout du monde à l'autre; c'est l'effort généreux des grandes nations qui ne veulent pas être vaincues dans cette lutte immense. Regardez! Tout au loin, sur tous les chemins, dans tous les sentiers, à travers les océans et les mers, du nord au midi, du lever au couchant, par les montagnes et les abîmes, par le soleil et par les glaces, du sein des chartes et du pied des trônes absolus, de la sueur blanche et de la sueur noire […] vous voyez surgir des armées de travailleurs, occupés à nourrir, à parer, à défendre, à protéger, à agrandir, à illustrer ce monde voué aux disputes, ce monde livré au hasard, ce monde abandonné si longtemps aux lâches théories, aux évangiles incendiaires, aux évangélistes oisifs, aux prédicateurs vagabonds, aux misérables qui voudraient changer ces outils en poignards, ces flammes laborieuses en torches avides, ces ouvriers en émeutiers. Lâches flatteurs des plus viles passions des cœurs ignorans, laissez-les faire, ils vont faire de ces espérances, de ces gloires, de ces contentemens, autant de calomnies, de blasphèmes, de parjures, de menaces, de conspirations!'

22 'on se sent pris de cette angoisse sérieuse qui s'empare de l'âme humaine à l'approche de quelque événement considérable'.

23 See Victoria's comments on the Great Exhibition in the editorial of the *Westminster Review* 126 (1886): 29–30.

24 Cited in Armstrong (2008, 152). Lothar Bucher's words were first quoted by Sigfried Giedion in *Space, Time and Architecture* (1967, 253–4).

25 In terms of cultural discourse, criticism of the Exhibition among contemporaries on the event illustrates the problem with the generalized theory of the Panopticon. For example, before the Exhibition, the Home Office was inundated with letters expressing paranoia (perhaps in the aftermath of 1848) at the oncoming barrage of foreigners. On this see Wilson ([2003] 2006, 143). John Ruskin (1854) also remained unimpressed with the event, criticizing the hypocrisy of an Empire that put international treasures on display in furtherance of its own imperial image, while 'Venetian masterpieces were rotting at Venice in the rain, for want of a roof

to cover them' (cited in Beaver 1999, 59). Furthermore, Charles Babbage, mathematician, scientist and engineer, criticized the arrangement of the displays at the Exhibition, arguing that they gave little attention to scientific invention while prioritizing frivolities such as children's toys (Babbage 1851, v–vi).

26 'Je voudrais en vain vous décrire ce bruit, ce tumulte, ces cris, cet empressement, cette activité, ce zèle. À la tour de Babel on parlait autant de langues différentes, on était loin de s'entendre aussi bien. Pas de rivalités entres ces nations diverses, et chacune au contraire, de s'entr'aider de son mieux! Tout le jour la maison est ouverte aux visiteurs, et les curieux, mêlés aux hommes qui travaillent, ne gênent rien et personne. Les policemen prêtent la main à l'étranger […]. On cloue, on décloue, on déploie, on attache, on ajuste, on tend, on peint, on frotte, on polit, on imprime, on écrit des étiquettes, on se hâte!'

27 'Ces sentimens d'un vrai peuple, ils nous étonnent aujourd'hui […] nous autres Français qui avons donné l'éveil à toutes les royautés de ce monde, et qui ne séparions jadis, ces deux forces: Dieu et le roi! – Toujours est-il que cette fête d'aujourd'hui manquerait de sa solennité et de sa grandeur, si elle n'était pas présidée par la reine; que personne ne se fierait à ce pâle soleil, si l'on n'avait pas la conscience que le soleil obéit à la reine, et que pas une voix assez haute ne se rencontrerait pour dire aux peuples de l'univers: *Peuples la lutte est ouverte!*'

28 This is a Greek term coming from the word 'ευ' meaning 'good' or 'well', and 'τόττος' meaning 'place'. It is different, therefore, from the term 'u-topia' in that it suggests a place that is 'perfect' but not 'fictional'. Its trace is contained in the word 'u-topia', however, where 'ου' meaning 'non' and 'ευ' are doubly present in the prefix to 'place'. 'U-topia' thus contains an idea of the 'ought', while 'eu-topia' suggests what 'is'. Janin's idealization of his immediate experience in London contains none of the irony of a u-topic account. See Marin (1973) for a thorough theoretical introduction to the concept of utopia.

29 For example in writing of the London weather and seeing the huge glass structure in the rain, Janin writes '*Quam juvat immites ventos audire*' [What joy to hear the raging winds as I lie there], a citation from the Roman poet Tibullus (*Elegies* I.1 verses 45–46) and also cited by Chateaubriand in *Mémoires d'outre-tombe* where the author describes adolescence as 'une révolution dans ma personne' (Chateaubriand, [1847] 1992, II, 4).

30 'il n'y qu'une façon légitime d'étudier et de comprendre la ville où nous conduit notre fantaisie. Acceptez-la comme elle se montre à vous.'

31 'Que dit Shakespeare en parlant de la vieille Angleterre? *Un nid de cygne au milieu d'un vaste étang!* – Que dit un ancien poète, en parlant de cette ville de Londres remplie de *Babyloniens* et de *Babyloniennes*, qu'il voue au feu éternel? 'Une énorme masse de briques, de fumée et de navires; une ville enfumée et sale, perdue au milieu d'une forêt de mâts; solitude semée de pointes aiguës, coupole gigantesque pareille à la calotte d'un fou!' De ces deux images quelle est la vraie?'

32 The citation is from Act 3 Sc 4 of *Cymbeline* and reads,
　　IMOGEN:
　　'Where then
　　　　Hath Britain all the sun that shines? Day, night,
　　　　Are they not but in Britain? I' the world's volume
　　　　Our Britain seems as of it, but not in't;
　　　　In a great pool a swan's nest: prithee, think
　　　　There's livers out of Britain'.

33 This is a reference from François-René de Chateaubriand's (1836) 'Shakespeare' first published in *Revue de deux mondes*. The essay later appeared in the volume *Essai sur la littérature anglaise* contained in the Dufour edition of Chateaubriand's complete works (1852).

34 Edition consulted contained in Byron, Scott and Moore ([1819–1824] 1859). The original verse reads:
　　'A mighty mass of brick and smoke and shipping,
　　Dirty and dusky, but as wide as eye

Can reach; with here and there a sail just skipping
In sight, then lost amidst the forestry
Of masts; a wilderness of steeples peeping
On tiptoe through their sea-coal canopy;
A huge dun cupola, like a fool's-cap crown
On a fool's head, – and there is London town' (710).

35 'vous découvrez une prodigieuse allée de mâts de vaisseaux qui se prolonge à l'infini, un inextricable fouillis d'agrès [...] de cordages, à faire honte pour la densité de l'enlacement, aux lianes les plus chevelues d'une forêt vierge d'Amérique.'

36 'l'on apercevra un fouillis de mâts, de cordages [...] plus compliqué qu'une forêt vierge d'Amérique'.

37 'Ces Anglais se respectent et s'adorent, à genoux, dans la personne de leur reine! Ils la contemplent du même œil qu'ils contempleraient leur propre image'.

38 See Benedict Anderson ([1983] 2003). Anderson uses this term as a methodological tool for understanding the development of the concept of the nation and nationalism. While it is true that Queen Victoria's claim to the throne was based on the grace of God, the constitutional nature of her position and concerns for the popularity of the monarchy in the minds of the British people make this term equally applicable here. On the Victorian monarchy's consciousness of its public image, see Wilson ([2003] 2006, 123–51).

39 'mal penser, ou mal parler de la reine [...] ils [les Anglais] se compareraient à un homme libre qui va se souffleter sur son propre visage!'

40 In an effort to integrate machinery within the artistic grandeur of the display, rather than arrange it in rows, it was decorated with bright colours and ornaments and placed in architectural frames. In his essay 'Paris: Capital of the Nineteenth Century', Benjamin sees this as a wider sociopolitical tendency of the age, referring to the 'inclination noticeable again and again in the nineteenth century to ennoble technical necessities by artistic aims' (1969, 171).

41 This is important, particularly if one conceives of the public as process, a social body in formation rather than a static entity, as Mary Poovey has convincingly argued. See Mary Poovey (1995).

42 Biographical information is taken from Alexandre Piedagnel's study *Jules Janin*(Piedagnel [1876] 1884).

43 'Vous n'aimez pas la vérité [...] ni le mètre, ni la rime, tout cela exige qu'on prenne trop de soins pour l'obtenir'.

44 'Il n'y a de vrais Parisiens en ce monde que les Parisiens qui ne sont pas nés à Paris. [...] Le Parisien de Paris est assez volontiers, contrefait, malsain, idiot et niais à faire plaisir. [...] Le Parisien de Paris est la dupe de la ville dans laquelle il est né; [...] c'est lui qui l'éclaire, c'est lui qui la répare, c'est lui qui remplit les prisons [...] qui ensanglante la grève.'

45 This is not to say of course that lines of generational and hereditary identities are always disrupted by such socio-cultural networks. But rather than land, cultural as well as monetary capital becomes the basis of the generational passing down social influence and power in urban societies.

46 The Orléanists were a right-wing faction that emerged after the French Revolution. Louis-Philippe d'Orléans acceded to the throne after the Bourbon monarch, Charles X, was overthrown. Louis-Philippe's reign was marked by compromise and weakness, and the period is generally seen as a transitional moment in French history, dominated by the bourgeoisie and conservative doctrine in economic and foreign policy. The king's popularity waned dramatically over the years and the royal family went into exile in Surrey in England after the revolution of 1848 brought Louis Napoleon to power as the head of the Second Republic.

47 'Et pourtant, voici dans ma vie (à Londres!) un dimanche qui sera honoré par moi, comme le jour le plus rempli de mes jours; j'en veux faire un monument de marbre, une apothéose d'airain, pour le placer sur le tombeau de mes beaux dimanches envolés, et celui-là désormais me consolera de tous les jours que j'ai perdus.'

48 'roi qui n'est plus'.

49 'mon *premier devoir*, et mon plus vif *penchant* et toutes mes *obéissances*, et *tous mes respects*, à peine à Londres, devaient me *pousser* à Claremont.'

50 'Tout était fête et joie en ce moment, où le soleil (il est rare) éclairait de son vif rayon tant de petits pieds et de robes printanières circulant sur le gazon […]. [C]es lis de France éclatant soudain dans ce gazon anglais, la perte récente de la fille du vieux roi, qui fut le roi de notre âge mûr et notre dernier rempart contre les viles passions qui nous perdent et qui nous tuent.'

51 'O reine auguste! Elle est restée, et elle sera jusqu'à la fin, notre reine! Chacun l'a saluée à son passage! Tous les fronts s'inclinaient devant cette majesté bienveillante et devant ce courage plus qu'humain! On dit cependant que dans la foule, une ou deux voix enrouées par le gin ont voulu murmurer quelques couplets de *la Marseillaise*! L'indignation les a fait taire et le mépris les a châtiées.'

52 Throughout the account, the industrial and democratic politics of the present are described as modes of life that will not endure or leave any lasting historical impression on future generations.

53 'cette grandeur oubliée: la majesté! cette force divine, le respect!'.

54 'en silence, cherchant les traces royales, sur les sables, sur les gazons'.

55 'Quant à moi, j'accepte volontiers le *nid de cygnes au milieu d'un vaste étang*. Je ne vais pas m'amuser (à quoi bien?) à retrouver la ville sale et enfumée […]'.

56 'au milieu de cette forêt de mâts'.

57 'Laissons, Messieurs, laissons aux sauveurs futurs de l'humanité, aux évangélistes modernes, aux *Christs* vagabonds, le soin et le souci de crier contre Babylone; un voyageur qui passe n'a pas le droit de s'arrêter et de prêcher à tous les carrefours.'

58 [A]llez plutôt sur la rive poétique et cherchez les traces heureuses. […] Oui et celui-là qui sait se souvenir, trouvera un grand charme à parcourir les bords heureux de cette fraîche Tamise […]. En toute chose, croyez-moi mes camarades, allez à ce qui est beau, à ce qui est bon et grand; méfiez-vous de l'ironie et du paradoxe, et quand vous passez sous ces vieux hêtres, témoins et confidens de tant d'illustres amours, n'allez pas demander au vieil arbre, combien de gens se sont pendus à ses branches.'

59 By which I refer to travellers who purposefully seek out those areas of the city that have escaped gentrification or beautification, and in particular those areas that counteract the monumental image of the city.

60 '[L]a plupart de nos humoristes, […] à peine à Londres, n'ont rien de plus pressé que de descendre dans ces caveaux du péché et de la nuit, afin de voir, par leurs yeux, comment les chiens aboient quand la justice boite auprès d'eux! Naturellement, tous les bons instincts des écrivains français, de ces hommes qui sont l'honneur même, se soulèvent de dégoût et d'horreur […] et naturellement, cette indignation passée, toute vive, dans les premières pages françaises, où il est parlé de Londres et de l'Angleterre! Est-ce une chose juste, cependant, de s'en aller, du premier bond, dans ces gémonies, pour en tirer des conclusions contre un gouvernement, assez fort pour mépriser ces invectives, et qui, d'un pied dédaigneux, écraserait cette parodie souterraine, si elles lui causaient le moindre trouble?'

61 'Après trois semaines de séjour à Londres, je m'aperçus que pour pouvoir parler de l'Angleterre, il fallait y passer dix ans. – Je regardais et je ne voyais pas; j'écoutais et n'entendais pas: je n'aime à parler que de ce que j'ai entendu et vu. Je me moquai de moi-même et repassai la mer.'

62 For example, Charles Booth devoted his life to the task of accumulating knowledge on the city. His study of the industrial, social and cultural life of the city began in 1886. He spent 17 years and 17 volumes on the task. By the time Booth had finished his survey, however, the city had grown in population and area. Booth's study, nevertheless, remains a key text for understanding the London of his time, as well as for gaining insight into the dilemmas that the industrial city poses in terms of constructing a methodology via which to appraise the consistently mobile urban landscape. See Booth (1889, 1891).

63 'Je n'ai point le douloureux honneur de partir proscrit, rien ne m'oblige au rôle d'exilé.'

64 'ce serait le premier livre impartial sur l'Angleterre. Tous ont menti jusqu'ici depuis Esquiros jusqu'à Taine. Mettons qu'ils se sont trompés.'

65 'écrire Londres, c'est aussi (surtout) essayer de penser la France, celle de la mémoire mais aussi celle qu'a fait naître le choc de la Commune'.

66 'Qui est l'exilé? C'est celui qui interprète sa vie à l'étranger comme une expérience de non-appartenance à son milieu, et qui la chérit pour cette raison même. L'exilé s'intéresse à sa propre vie, voire à son propre peuple; mais il s'est aperçu que, pour favoriser cet intérêt, il valait mieux habiter à l'étranger, là où n''appartient' pas; il est étranger de façon non plus provisoire mais définitive. [L'exil] n'est certainement pas une découverte des autres.'

67 'Ah! ce n'est pas la rue de France! – cette rue bavarde et joyeuse, où l'on s'aborde à tout instant, où l'on s'arrête à tout propos. On suit les femmes, on blague les hommes; il y a du tapage, des rires, des rayons et des éclairs; il y a des pétillements d'ironie, une odeur de plaisir, des souvenirs de poudre.

La rue à Londres est ou énorme et vide, – muette alors comme un alignement de tombeaux – ou bourrée de viande humaine, encombrée de chariots, pleine à faire reculer les murs, bruyante comme la levée d'un camp et le torrent d'une déroute. Mais ce sont des bruits sourds, un grondement d'usine, le tumulte animal – point une explosion de vie et de passion.'

68 'les peuples à cerveau puissant ont, chaque quart de siècle, de ces apoplexies qu'on nomme des révoltes'.

69 'Qu'on en fasse son deuil! La vie de Londres doit être monotone et grise, désolée, aux heures où le Peuple a quitté le champ de bataille – le Peuple, seul grand dans son anonymat fait de ceux qui courent ou qui rampent vers le pain [...], mais, comme nous sommes dans le pays de l'égoïsme, du flegme, de l'inconfortable et de l'ennui, quand il n'y a pas le brouhaha du travail, il n'y a plus que le cri du vice: du vice plat, lourd, qui hurle dans les assommoirs ou vomit dans les coins.'

70 'leur vertu, c'est ce qu'on appelle notre vice à nous, c'est l'amour féroce du drapeau, la fierté d'être Anglais, c'est le 'chauvinisme' affreux et héroïque. [...] Ils sont capables de tout, au nom de la nation.'

71 'En se baisant, il [le pauvre] montrera qu'il est un homme à des ladies qui le verront bien; mais les ladies vont grossir la foule des meetings philanthropiques, et, en rentrant, elles se mettront à faire des caleçons pour les sauvages – sans oser dire 'caleçon', elles ne prononcent pas le mot, c'est *shocking*. Tout à l'heure, elles coudoyaient pourtant, sans rougir, un homme que la pauvreté faisait obscène.'

72 'L'Anglais me fait horreur... Quels perfides tous ces lords et ces conservateurs et ces libéraux'.

73 For further biographical detail on Vallès, see Designi (1999); Gauthier (1945) and Redfern (1992). For a more general analysis of the *émigré* community in London during the period, see Bensimon (2003) and Freitag (2003).

74 'c'est le fond de la nation que nous voulons étudier'.

75 'Il n'y a pas de tables de nuit! *Il n'y en a pas!*

Oh! Je sais bien que l'on criera au mensonge! Le rôle de l'observateur a ses périls [...]. On dira que je calomnie gratuitement un peuple, que je prends une revanche déloyale de Waterloo. On dira ce qu'on voudra. Je crois de mon devoir d'avertir mes contemporains, je les avertis. *Il n'y a pas de tables de nuit.* [...] Moi, proscrit, je me range cette fois du côté des proscripteurs, et j'applaudis à exil de ce réceptacle indécent.'

76 'La richesse de la grande armoire, l'héritage plié sur les rayons de chêne, des douzaines de draps et de nappes qui sont la fortune des plus simples et l'honneur même des paysannes dans les plus modestes maisons de France. Ils [les Anglais] n'ont pas le culte de la toile, le respect des saintes lessives, la religion des pyramides bâties par les mains couturées des aïeules et qui racontent tout un passé de travail.'

77 'Leur visage reste sec comme la tête du nageur qui a parié de ne pas mouiller ses cheveux; et leur front est impénétrable comme le bonnet goudronné de leurs marins.'

78 'l'âme de cette nation dure'; 'la qualité dominante des Anglais'.

79 Clothing and footwear manufacture moved to the provinces from the 1860s. The emergence of the sweatshop was capital's response to such competition and the attempt to reduce London's overheads to a minimum. The shipbuilding industry also declined dramatically during the 1860s, as did the silk and tanning industries (Stedman Jones 1971, 23–4).

80 'Nous sommes nés pour être dupes et victimes, nous qui sommes de tempérament, d'allure, de cœur, avec les blousiers.'

81 'Le gueux de France ne peut donner une idée du gueux de Londres! Il y a bien chez nous, le mendiant, avec sa face grasse à un moine chassé du couvent, ou, avec son crâne chauve et sa barbe grise, à un saint tombé en enfance; mais c'est un métier, celui de mendiant, presque une mission, et il est même un peu sorcier. Il a ses rations de soupe, ses relais de viande. […] Le pauvre de Londres n'est pas le même. […] Certains m'ont rappelé ces prisonniers que, sur les routes, les gendarmes ramènent de brigade en brigade; qui vont entre les deux chevaux noirs, attachés à la selle; […] et ils voyagent ainsi, la nuit, le jour, jusqu'à ce que la prison les recueille. Tels les affamés anglais!'

82 '[c]'est d'instinct, *dans le sang*, dans ce sang qui ne coule pas comme le sang Latin avec des reflets pourprés au soleil […] mais qui s'extravase sous le coup de poing ou sous le bonnet du pendu, dans le ring ou à la potence.'

83 'Or, le visiteur, qui va de la cave au grenier, voit mieux la prison que le détenu qui rêve dans sa cage, le front contre les barreaux.'

84 'Gardé par des grilles, hérissé de crocs, protégé autant qu'une boulangerie contre les famines de 93, ce *home* et ce foyer! Entre la façade et le trottoir, bâille un hiatus sale, un creux profond, un trou grillé, comme pour mettre un loup. Partout du fer noir ou des pierres d'un gris de tombe, semblables aux ossements lavés par la pluie. Au haut des marches, visage de bois d'une porte qui ressemble à celle d'une prison ou d'un couvent.'

85 'Où aller quand la Cité a rentré ses griffes, fermé sa gueule, éteint ses yeux […]; quand le tumulte a cessé dans le camp des mercenaires et des marchands?'

86 'Il est tard, c'est le soir'; 'mais le jour, c'est de même; c'est toujours ainsi.'

87 'ce qu'ils appellent le soleil'; 'il [le soleil] ne forcera pas les serrures!'

88 'pays hostile, race murée!'

89 'Quelle sinistre impression donnent ces rangées de bâtisses, rongées par le brouillard et par la pluie! Quand les maisons à Londres n'ont pas le reflet lugubre d'un linceul sali, elles ont la couleur […] du bois de justice – des tons de prison ou d'échafaud. C'est affreux! je ne m'en dédis pas: on dirait un peuple de maudits ou de détenus.'

90 'En Angleterre, on n'entend rien dans le calme horrible du dimanche. C'est le silence, sans un bruit qui le raye ou le hache […] l'écrasement d'un peuple par une caste […]. Tout est fermé par ordre'.

91 'Vous souvenez-vous, aux heures tragiques de Paris, comme certaines rues étaient désertes, muettes, profondes?…'

92 'Ils vont, ils viennent comme des *pistons* de machines, ils passent comme […] comme des trains se croisent; ils ne se disent jamais qu'un mot: 'Jolie matinée…Vilain temps' suivant qu'il fait beau ou mauvais – et ils reprennent leur fonction, court, droit et dru. Allez le piston!'

93 'À sa source, la rivière est claire […] ici, elle est trouble et vile comme si l'on avait lavé dedans toute la vaisselle d'une armée […] une rivière longée par une bataille, et dont le lit serait fait de charbon pétri de sang.'

94 In Sartre's representation of New York, analysed in chapter 3, Nature is also portrayed as the modern city's antithesis. In Vallès's account Nature is mourned, the city has dispelled its presence, whereas in Sartre's account Nature returns to threaten the city.

95 'Le flot a des reflets jaunâtres comme de l'or brut'.

96 '[q]ui y tombe y reste'.

97 'Elle [la Tamise] a aussi l'épaisseur de la bière, et l'on ne voit jamais des maisons laver gaiement leur tête, ni des arbres danser en zigzags dans un coin de Tamise, comme on voit des bouts de campagne et de ville dans le miroir vert du Rhône ou le miroir bleu de la Loire!'

98 N'y a-t-il pas mille cheminées qui jettent leurs vapeurs impures vers la nue, en boucles lourdes, en nattes épaisses; c'est la couleur sombre de la rivière, c'est la chevelure triste de la Tamise – du vieux père Tamise: *Old father Thames*. J'ai vu une tête sculptée dans la pierre, l'œil mort, les moustaches tombantes comme des herbes trempées d'eau […]. 'C'est le vieux père Tamise!' m'a dit avec fierté un Anglais.'

99 'la chair brûlée'.

100 'Cette eau ne reflète rien: elle est comme le visage des Anglais.'

101 'Ce n'est pas sans tristesse que l'on quitte cette cité triste. Je jetai sur Londres enfumé et lugubre un regard de reconnaissance joyeux et clair en me rappelant l'hospitalité qu'avaient reçue les Français proscrits – dont on n'aimait pas les idées et dont on redoutait le drapeau. J'ôtai mon chapeau devant la Ville noire, pour remercier ce peuple, qui n'a jamais médit la Reine, de m'avoir appris à moi, d'un pays républicain, ce que c'était la liberté.'

3. Revealing and Reconstructing London

1 Jones, Richard. 2008. 'The Secret City' *Walks of London Website*. Online: http://www.walksoflondon.co.uk/29/index.shtml (accessed 4 November 2014).

2 Bibliographical information on Alfred Leroy is, at the time of writing, relatively scarce. The catalogue of the Bibliothèque Nationale de France (BNF) lists the author's year of birth but does not give any indication as to when he died.

3 'Il fétiche l'abstraction, norme impose. Il détache la forme pure de son impur contenu, le temps-vécu, le temps quotidien, celui du corps, de leur épaisseur opaque, de leur chaleur, de leur vie et de leur mort' (Lefebvre [1974] 2000, 116).

4 'La "lisibilité–visibilité–intelligibilité"' (Lefebvre [1974] 2000, 115).

5 'Un espace determine donc cloisonné accepte ceci et rejette cela […]. Il affirme, nie, dénie' (Lefebvre [1974] 2000, 118).

6 Arianna Drumond, 2103, 'Contextualizing Authenticity in Tourism: An Examination of Postmodern Tourism Theory.' *Cultural Hybridity: Remix and Dialogic Culture* (blog), 14 December, https://blogs.commons.georgetown.edu/cctp-725-fall2013/2013/12/14/contextualizing-authenticity-in-tourism-an-examination-of-postmodern-tourism-theory/.

7 'Authentic', *Online Etymological Dictionary*, last accessed 23 August 2015, http://www.etymonline.com/index.php?term=authentic

8 'En dehors de leur club, de leur cricket et de leur business, ils ne connaissent rien ou ne veulent rien connaître ce qui revient au même. À les entendre, Londres, depuis la guerre, serait devenue une ville modèle. Les chômeurs? Des paresseux pour lesquels on se ruine. Les *slums*? Nettoyés. De belles maisons municipales s'élèvent à leur place. Que dis-je, des maisons? Des palais, où les pauvres gens nagent dans le confort. La prostitution? Inexistante, si ce n'est, toutefois, dans le quartier français, le Soho, où […] les Français que l'on rencontre peuvent se compter sur les doigts. Bref, je n'avais plus à souhaiter le paradis, je m'y trouvais, depuis que j'avais posé le pied sur le quai de la gare Victoria. 'Voire', eûtdit Panurge. Je fiscomme Panurge.'

9 For a detailed analysis of the debates surrounding the 'social service state', see Donald Read's chapter on the subject, 'The Introduction of the "Social Service State"' (Read 1972, 151–93).

10 For more in-depth analyses on this period see Read (1972), Robbins ([1983] 1997, 3–168), Hoggart and Green (1991, 8–33), Inwood (2006, 457–65), Wilson ([2003] 2006) and Sutcliffe (2006, 157–77).

11 'autrement que par ouï-dire, les bas fonds de Londres'; 'de me pencher à mon tour sur ce peuple de l'abîme'.

12 The work of Booth (1889) helped contemporaries to nuance the myths around the East End by examining the 'life' as well as the 'labour' of the people, which, despite his objectivity in statistical matters, reveals sympathy and empathetic observation where the working classes are concerned. Furthermore, Booth refrained from the standard moral condemnations of the

urban poor, and his book gave publicity to the community through analysis of its theatres, music halls, public houses and Sunday debates in Victoria Park.

13 Morrison (1889, 34) summed up both stereotypes, mocking the image of the ghetto, 'the catacombs of London – darker, more tortuous, and more dangerous than those of Rome, and supersaturated with foul life' and outcast London, 'black, nasty still, a wilderness of crazy dens into which pallid wastrels crawl to die.'

14 In the twentieth century, this traditional conception is rearticulated by the Surrealists and the Dadaists as a response to the new social and architectural manifestations of the welfare state, empire, and the development of Modernist idealist forms of expression (such as the early Le Corbusier, Bauhaus or Sant'Elia).

15 'Le West-End, quartier de l'Ouest, aux avenues bordées de riches résidences, aux parcs féeriques avoisinant les *slums*les plus sordides. Le quartier de l'Est, l'East-End, passant de la friperie de Whitechapel à la désolation de Poplars où des gosses rachitiques respirent dans des sous-sols un air visqueux sursaturé de suie et de charbon, tandis que déambulent, par les rues mornes, de lamentables groupes de chômeurs.'

16 'Aimez-vous la vérité?'

17 la pêche à laquelle je me livre m'a fait connaître bien des vilaines *places*. Ce ne sont pas celles où les interprètes amènent les touristes…'

18 'J'aime la vérité' […] en le regardant bien dans les yeux'.

19 I define the 'touristee' as the person inhabiting or working in the place that the tourist visits.

20 'C'est lui qui a en charge la transmission du discours destiné à donner un sens au lieu'.

21 'On n'a pas idée de faire pauser un honnête gentleman comme le fit l'étrange personnage avec qui j'avais rendez-vous'.

22 'Quand je lui exprimais mon intention de visiter en sa compagnie ces slums indésirables, elle *se défila*. En bonne Anglaise qu'elle était, je la vis *se retrancherderrière* les décisions de son Comité. Je connus par là que la *pénétration* psychologique n'est pas le fort des filles d'Ève habitant de l'autre côté de la Manche. Car ces endroits qu'elle me *cachait*, tel le slum de Chadwick, avec une *pudeur* offensée, elle aurait dû se douter que je n'aurais de cesse que je ne les eusse visités. Aussi bien avait-elle tort de s'alarmer à ce point. Westminister n'est pas pire qu'Edgware Road, Paddington et autres lieux qui semblent *un ulcère répugnant sur le beau visage de Londres*.'

23 'L'homme-de-Londres-qui-parle-le-mieux-le slang'.

24 'Cette qualité [de langage] n'était pas faite, loin de là, pour me déplaire. J'ai toujours aimé l'argot et ceux qui le parlent. Il y a plus de poésie en eux que dans un docteur en Sorbonne.'

25 'Donc, continua John Jarvey, en tirant sur sa pipe, bien des gens qui ont 'pris la fièvre du chanvre' (ont été pendus) ou sont allés, si vous le préférez, 'garder les moutons au clair de lune' sont des victimes de *John Barleycorn* (du whisky) ou de *Old Tom* (du gin). […] Ne faites pas attention aux gens qui nous entourent, *The Crown* (la Couronne) est une 'place' qui n'est pas pour vous. Je connais un autre pub où je vais quelquefois, *Horse and Groom* (le cheval et le groom), où vous auriez trouvé une excellente compagnie.'

26 'Mon intention étant de connaître, autrement que par ouï dire, les bas-fonds de Londres, de me pencher à mon tour sur ce peuple de l'abîme.

27 – Qui sont ces deux hommes assis à cette petite table, John? Le vieux à chapeau melon et le tout jeune en casquette. Il me poussa le coude et cracha à ses pieds. – Le jeune? Un *fribbler*. Regardez ses lèvres trop rouges et son air efféminé. Il n'y a pas à s'y tromper. L'autre un trafiquant d'hommes. On en est inondé dans le quartier, ainsi qu'à Paddington, de ces commerçants sans patente.

28 Et la police, John? insistai-je.
     Mon homme tira une bouffée, l'air absent. Puis, me regardant en dessous, il me dit précipitamment:
     • Un *finger-post*, voilà ce qu'on vous a raconté que j'étais n'est-ce pas?
     • Un *finger-post*?
     • Oui, un indicateur? Et c'est pour cela que vous me posez cette question?

- Pas le moins du monde. C'est la première nouvelle, John.
- 'Mon œil'! Je serais autrement 'rembourré', si je faisais de *Johnny Darbies*, mon ami.
Johnny Darbies est un terme de *slang* équivalent à flics.
  - Avec quelques *james* (livres), poursuivit-il, on a vite fait de 'boucher' l'œil du détective le plus curieux. Tout, dans la vie, est une question de 'gingembre'.
Chez nous, nous dirions de pognon.'

29 'La ville pestiférée, toute traversée de hiérarchie, de surveillance, de regard, d'écriture, la ville immobilisée dans le fonctionnement d'un pouvoir extensif qui porte de façon distincte sur tous les corps individuels – c'est l'utopie de la cité parfaitement gouvernée.'

30 'quadrillage disciplinaire'.

31 'En somme on inverse le principe du cachot; ou plutôt de ses trois fonctions – enfermer, priver de lumière et cacher – on ne garde que la première et on supprime les deux autres. La pleine lumière et le regard d'un surveillant captent mieux que l'ombre, qui finalement protégeait. La visibilité est un piège.'

32 'fou/non-fou; dangereux/inoffensif; normal/anormal'.

33 – Vous ne visiterez pas les prisons anglaises'.

34 Wilde was imprisoned in Holloway during his remand for trial and was later moved from Reading Gaol the night before his release so as not to attract crowds. See (1897) 'Oscar Wilde Released', *The New York Times*, 20 May 1897, 7.

35 'Sera-ce leur exprimer suffisamment ma reconnaissance que de leur dire que, si jamais il m'arrive de commettre un délit, c'est à Londres de préférence que je le commettrai?'

36 'Leurs prisons sont devenues, en effet, des modèles de confort et d'hygiène'.

37 'Une clarté, une netteté de clinique dans les cloîtres et dans les pièces traversées. Pas de ces murs lépreux ou souillés, de ces peintures et papiers éraillés qui sont si souvent affligeants dans les endroits où se trouvent réunis des êtres humains: lycées, casernes, prisons. La lumière et le jour entrent de partout dans les ateliers par de larges baies et des verrières. […] Les cellules se succèdent toutes pareilles, dans chacune des divisions reliées entre elles par une grande galerie qui les traverse en leur partie centrale. Le silence, un silence monacal, règne dans celles-ci que ne trouble que le pas feutré des surveillantes, ou celui des détenues employées à des travaux de nettoyage.'

38 'd'après ce qu'il m'a été donné de voir' / '[…] quelque peu poussée au noir'.

39 'l'on m'a tout fait visiter […] on me l'a assuré, du moins'.

40 'Vous ne pensez tout de même pas qu'ayant à vous donner une bonne idée des prisons anglaises, M. le gouverneur de celle-ci allait s'empresser de vous faire visiter la salle de torture…Non, mais vous rêvez, *oldchap!*'

41 'Quand il vient un étranger à Londres, *oldfrick*, on lui montre le garde de la Tour le plus gras, et il s'en va, satisfait, en disant: 'Il fait bon vivre au bord de la Tamise.''

42 'La paix donne à nouveau à la cité millénaire son aspect habituel; l'aube de jours heureux succède aux ténèbres. Si de profonds changements, nés de la guerre mondiale, transforment certains aspects de Londres, le maintien de fortes et bienfaisantes traditions lui conserveront ses caractères essentiels.'

43 At the time of writing, there is little information on Alfred Leroy easily available. He was an arthistorian and published works such as *Histoire de la Peinture anglaise* (800–1939), *Histoire de la Peinture française au Moyen Âge et à la Renaissance* and *Histoire de la Peinture française* (1800–1933) with Éditions Albin Michel. The latter work won the Prix quinquennal Jeanbernat, the Prix Thorlet and the Prix Bordin de l'Académie des Beaux-Arts.

44 For example, in the East End in June 1917, 158 people were killed, 18 of them children, during a daylight raid. Over the course of that war some 600 died from bombs directed at the capital.

45 'Risquons l'hypothèse d'un moment à partir de quoi la 'transparence' n'est plus. Un moment: entre la fin de la Seconde Guerre mondiale et My-Laï. Un lieu peut-être, tout noir et d'un noir inédit, dont l'épicentre se trouverait quelque part entre Hiroshima et Nagasaki. […] Si quelque

chose se passe alors d'irréversible dans notre regard et notre imaginaire c'est que le monde rétrécit, c'est aussi que nous devenons, pour beaucoup, dans les années qui suivent, des gens dans les grandes villes, et que les villes deviennent plus gravement que jamais, ce qu'elles ont toujours été: de fabuleux enjeux.'

46 'l'ambition première est de retrouver le présent en le coupant provisoirement du passé et du futur, et plus précisément, en oubliant le futur pour autant que celui-ci s'identifie au retour du passé.'

47 'des refuges contre le bruit, l'animation, le rythme trépidant de l'existence moderne'.

48 'd'aller sans but précis […] de flâner à travers les nobles allées'.

49 'C'est toujours au présent, finalement, qui se conjugue l'oubli.'

50 'Hyde Park n'est pas un jardin, mais un coin de nature; ses belles perspectives donnent l'impression que rien ne limite l'horizon; ses arbres offrent d'innombrables retraites paisibles et solitaires; ses gazons étouffent la marche des promeneurs. Ayant quitté la vie fiévreuse d'une capitale, nous y abordons un lieu en partie exempt de circulation, un lieu où l'isolement demeure possible entre le ciel, les verdures et les ombrages.'

51 'Nous avons le droit de rompre avec la société, qui absorbe quotidiennement nos volontés, nos pensées, qui ne nous laisse aucune minute avec nous-même, qui, de notre réveil à notre coucher s'installe en maîtresse dans notre vie. […] Le centre de Hyde Park et de Kensington Gardens permet l'oubli, l'isolement moral, choses inconnues dans les cités modernes du continent.'

52 'La mémoire elle-même a besoin de l'oubli: il faut oublier le passé récent pour retrouver le passé ancien.'

53 'le passé immédiat avec lequel il tend à se confondre – pour rétablir une continuité avec le passé plus ancien, éliminer le passé 'composé' au profit d'un passé 'simple'.'

54 'La Chambre de Communes s'orne de douze fenêtres avec les armoires des villes et communes; le siège du speaker s'élève à l'extrémité nord de la salle […]. En sortant de cette pièce, où tant de souvenirs sollicitent l'imagination, il faut jeter un coup d'œil au *Saint Stephen's Hall*, ancienne chapelle, totalement restaurée en 1834; un large escalier conduit à Westminster Hall.'

55 'La Chambre de Communes a été entièrement détruite par les raids aériens'.

56 'une des plus grandes merveilles *existant* en Angleterre'.

57 'le charme des aspects anciens soustraits à tout empiètement de la vie moderne, il est un lieu pour le recueillement, la flânerie, les jeux de l'imagination […] l'activité environnante s'oublie au milieu de vieilles pierres, des jardins ombreux, des images où s'inscrivent la fantaisie du XVe siècle.'

58 'Qu'est-ce qu'une idéologie sans un espace auquel elle se réfère, qu'elle décrit, dont elle utilise le vocabulaire et les connexions, dont elle contient le code?' (Lefebvre [1974] 2000, 55).

59 'Ils constituent une force incomparable contre les aventures dangereuses, les désirs nuisibles et périlleux'.

60 The Imperial Institute was established in 1887 as a result of the Colonial and Indian exhibition of 1886 to promote research that would benefit the Empire. From 1893 the Imperial Institute was located in a building on Exhibition Row, South Kensington. The 85-metre Queen's tower on Exhibition Road is now the last remaining part of the Imperial Institute; the remainder was demolished in the 1950s and 1960s to make way for Imperial College. There were three copper-roofed Renaissance-style towers in the original building, but only one still stands.

61 'L'Empire britannique avec ses ressources, ses peuples divers, ses contrées lointaines, l'Empire britannique et son immensité, mais aussi dans son union indéfectible, dans son loyalisme, dans sa grandeur morale, l'Empire tel que le réaliseront après les siècles d'efforts et de travail les sujets de la reine Victoria, nous est présenté dans une vue panoramique grâce aux collections de l'Imperial Institute Museum.'

62 'aussi nécessaire que l'air et la liberté'.

63 'L'harmonie la plus juste existe, une harmonie lentement élaborée qui ôte toutes les préoccupations, place au-dessus de toute critique, de toute réforme possible, les souverains'.

64 'Partout l'histoire sollicite l'imagination, partout elle s'unit intimement à la vie moderne. Nous sommes ici en des lieux riches en souvenirs, en de lieux où l'homme n'a cessé de travailler,

d'espérer, de s'enrichir, de lutter pour la grandeur de l'Angleterre, pour sa propre opulence. [...] *Depuis des siècles des générations ont succédé à d'autres générations, et jamais, un seul instant, la machine ne s'est arrêtée.* [...] Un monde se lève, à chaque pas, un monde fantôme, dont les historiens nous disent les efforts, le courage, la ténacité, l'impérieuse volonté.'

4. Wandering Geometry: Order and Identity in New York

1 In this chapter, the word 'Europe' is used to refer mainly to Western Europe and the countries which colonized Northern America during the 'Age of Discovery'.

2 During the period of the Great Discoveries, cartographic practice was also undergoing extensive change. As a result of Florentine connections with Constantinople in the early fifteenth century, Ptolemy's *Geography* arrived in Europe. Over the next few decades the book, which proposed the representation of landscape according to a mathematical method, attracted the attention of scholars all over Europe. The representation of space in terms of a geometric projection generated a different understanding of space with important scientific and political effects. First, it offered a way of coping with the amount of information being accumulated by the explorers, missionaries and other travellers. Second, it overcame the restrictions of medieval charts, which had omitted regions outside the *oikoumene*. Essentially, the adoption of Ptolemaic cartographic principles neutralized space, for each point on any given landscape was set into a homogenous grid of coordinates, and so maps had to respect proportion and include everything. This also abolished the separation of the 'centre' from the 'periphery'. All areas, including those yet to be explored, were part of the same whole.

3 'La géographie scientifique et surtout la cartographie moderne peuvent être considérées comme une sorte d'oblitération, de censure que l'objectivité a imposé à la signification (objectivité qui est une forme comme une autre de l'imaginaire.'

4 'Une rationalité classique (cartésienne) s'attache apparemment aux distinctions et découpages administratifs de l'espace. [...] Ce qui recouvre en fait un ordre moral et politique; une puissance agençant ces conditions, une appartenance socio-économique, paraît provenir en droite ligne du Logos, c'est-à-dire d'un "consensus" au rationnel' (Lefebvre [1974] 2000, 365–66).

5 'La répartition des fonctions, accompagnée de leur projection disperse "sur le terrain", se confond avec l'activité analytique qui tient compte des différences' (Lefebvre [1974] 2000, 366).

6 'Gentrification' is the term used by urban sociologists to refer to changes in the housing stock and social organization of urban centres. Scholarly debate has identified economic and cultural factors as equally important to the redistribution of a city's population and the development or decline of specific urban sites. Gentrification is identified by Mike Savage et al. (2003, 87–88) as arising out of the combination of four processes:

　　1 The resettlement and social concentration entailing the displacement of one group of residents with another of higher social status;

　　2 Transformation in the built environment exhibiting some distinctive aesthetic features and the emergence of new local services;

　　3 The gathering together of persons with a putatively shared culture and lifestyle, or at least with shared, class-related, consumer preferences;

　　4 Economic reordering of property values, a commercial opportunity for the construction industry, and often an extension of the system of the private ownership of domestic property.

7 For a discussion of demographics, real estate and symbolic investment in the architectural landscape of the city in the latter half of the nineteenth century see Mona Domosh (1996).

8 The design itself is what we consider today as characteristic of Le Corbusier: a white box on stilts with a flat roof, planar, rectangular windows of industrial design, a double-height living room behind a huge studio window. Halfway up, and on top, were terraces. The building was

actually made of concrete, which meant that the interior spaces could be uninterrupted, but also that much of it would have to be constructed on site.

9 In architectural theory this refers to medieval cities that had grown up haphazardly around pre-existing castles or manor houses, or that emerged unplanned as a consequence of increased trade around estuaries or other centres of commerce.

10 Or, une ville moderne vit de droite, pratiquement; construction des immeubles, des égouts, des canalisations, des chaussées, des trottoirs, etc. La circulation exige la droite. La droite est saine aussi à l'âme des villes. La courbe est ruineuse, difficile et dangereuse; elle paralyse.

La droite est dans toute l'histoire humaine, dans toute l'intention humaine, dans tout acte humain.

11 'la rue courbe est le chemin des ânes, la rue droite est le chemin des hommes'.

12 'la ville basse', 'la ville moyenne', and 'la ville haute'.

13 'excellent guide […] toujours à la main'.

14 'Silence.

Les dernières vagues atlantiques se jettent sur une pointe de rochers brun pourpre et s'y déchirent.

Un cri de mouette.

De chaque côté du promontoire, la marée gonfle et remonte les estuaires. À droite, la nuit commence à cacher les collines. À gauche, descend un soleil jaune soufre.

L'Amérique est grande, déjà. D'une grandeur anonyme, d'une immensité sidérale. Immobile, repliés sur eux-mêmes comme un germe, ces lieux qui seront New-York [sic] attendent de naître.'

15 'Le plaisir que l'on retrouve à venir s'asseoir sur un des bancs de la Batterie est fait en grande partie de ces premiers souvenirs coloniaux.'

16 'Si j'ai pu pénétrer et comprendre vite New-York, c'est que, derrière moi, j'avais dix années d'Outre-Manche […]. Londres et New-York sont une même chose, à cent ans de distance; le Londres actuel, c'est le New-York de l'époque knickerbocker; ce qui me ramène à Washington Square.'

17 'Il n'y a rien dans ces étendues suburbaines de 'touristique'; ce ne sont que de monstrueuses hernies, réunies à l'île centrale depuis 1898: New Jersey, Brooklyn, Queensborough, le Bronx et Richmond forment ce qu'on appelle le plus grand New-York.'

18 Koolhaas (1994) also notes that what is considered refined or civilized at one moment can be deigned barbaric the next, and, as we shall see in relation to Sartre and Baudrillard, discourses on America often mobilize both oppositions of the primitive and the civilized to describe aspects of the same space.

19 'À New-York, personne ne rentre chez soi au milieu de la journée: on mange sur place, soit dans les bureaux, tout en travaillant, soit dans les clubs, soit dans les *cafeterias*.'

20 'Le coup de gong final'; 'fourmilière en travail'; 'sanctuaire du temple'.

21 'un fleuve humain'; 'monstre compressible [qui] remonte Broadway, inonde Brooklyn Bridge, envahit le 'L', c'est-à-dire l'*Elevated*, le chemin de fer aérien, noie les souterrains du métro.'

22 'Le coup de gong final retentit. Le tumulte s'apaise. Aussitôt, les grands chefs quittent le champ de bataille, sautent dans le métro encore vide où, deux heures plus tard, à leur tour les gens de la rue liront avidement la page des chiffres… […] Le soir tombe. Les gratte-ciel, ces pressoirs à hommes, se vident de toute une humanité fatiguée. Le classement vertical des individus va faire place maintenant, pour la nuit, à un nouveau rangement horizontal.'

23 'une machine à fasciner'; 'cette foule fatiguée, décidée à ne pas rentrer chez elle, à dépenser son argent.'

24 'on ne pense même plus à dormir. On est enivré, intoxiqué, empli du bien-être fictive.'

25 'Le vertical et la hauteur manifestèrent toujours spatialement la présence d'un pouvoir capable de violence' (Lefebvre [1974] 2000, 117).

26 'épuisement des perspectives'.

27 'cette matière humaine'.

28 'liés par une sympathie des géants'; 'se soutiennent pour s'aider à monter'.

29 'S'ils ont monté à de telles hauteurs, c'est qu'il fallait utiliser les dernières parcelles d'un roc qui allait faire défaut; ils sont élevés *naturellement*, comme le niveau d'un *fleuve* à mesure qu'il se rétrécit dans l'encaissement de ses rives.'

30 'Les gratte-ciel! Il y en a qui sont des femmes et d'autres des hommes. […] Ancrés dans la chair vive du roc, descendant sous terre de quatre ou cinq étages, portant au plus profond d'eux-mêmes leurs organes essentiels, dynamos, chauffage central, rivetés au fer rouge, amarrés par des câbles souterrains, des poutrelles à grande hauteur d'âme, des pylônes d'acier, ils s'élèvent, tout vibrants du ballant formidable des étages supérieurs.'

31 'son aspect de demain'; 'l'âme de ces édifices, c'est le succès; ils sont les tabernacles de la réussite'.

32 'Son aventure sera la nôtre. Nous défendre contre les nouveautés de Broadway, c'est refuser cet ordre préétabli qui se nomme l'avenir. […] New York est ce que seront demain toutes les villes: géométriques. Simplification des lignes, des sentiments, *règne du direct*. Cité à deux dimensions, a dit Einstein.'

33 For a comprehensive study of the French *émigré* scene in New York during WWII, see Jeffrey Mehlman (2000).

34 The first section of the book is comprised of the essays, 'La République du Silence' / 'The Republic of Silence' (11–14), 'Paris sous l'Occupation' / 'Paris under the Occupation' (15–42), 'Qu'est-ce qu'un collaborateur?' / 'What is a collaborator?' (43–62) and 'Fin de la Guerre' / 'The End of the War' (63–71).

35 Sartre, who visited America for the first time during the final months of the war, also published two somewhat scathing newspaper articles in which he claimed that perhaps he was not the exemplary *résistant* the Americans took him for. See Sartre (1945).

36 'Sans aucun doute la guerre a révélé aux Américains que l'Amérique était la plus grande puissance du monde. Mais l'ère de la vie facile est passée; de nombreux économistes redoutent une nouvelle crise. Aussi ne construit-on plus de gratte-ciel. Il paraît qu'ils sont trop difficiles à louer.'

37 'Nous avons cru sans prévue que la paix était l'état naturel et la substance de l'Univers, que la guerre n'était qu'une agitation temporaire de sa surface. Aujourd'hui nous reconnaissons notre erreur: la fin de la guerre, c'est tout simplement la fin de *cette* guerre. […] Le monde est simplifié: deux géants se dressent, seuls, et ne se regardent pas d'un bon œil. […] Ses ultimes moments ont été pour nous avertir de la fragilité humaine. Aussi aimons-nous qu'elle finisse mais non pas la façon dont elle finit. Plus d'un Européen eût préféré que le Japon fût envahi, écrasé sous les bombardements de la flotte: mais cette petite bombe qui peut tuer cent mille hommes d'un coup et qui, demain, en tuera deux millions, elle nous met tout à coup en face de nos responsabilités. À la prochaine la terre peut sauter […]. La communauté qui s'est faite gardienne de la bombe atomique est au-dessus du règne naturel car elle est responsable de sa vie et de sa mort.'

38 'La guerre, en mourant, laisse l'homme nu, sans illusion, abandonné à ses propres forces, ayant enfin compris qu'il n'a plus à compter que sur lui.'

39 'Aujourd'hui l'Américain regarde sa ville avec objectivité: il ne songe pas à la trouver laide, mais il pense qu'elle est bien vieille. Si elle était encore plus vieille, comme sont les nôtres, il pourrait y retrouver un passé social, une tradition. Nous vivons ordinairement dans les demeures de nos grands-pères. Nos rues reflètent les usages et les mœurs de nos siècles passés; elles tamisent un peu le présent. […] *Une ville, pour nous, c'est surtout un passé; pour eux, c'est d'abord un avenir*, ce qu'ils aiment en elle, c'est tout ce qu'elle n'est pas encore et tout ce qu'elle peut être.'

40 'Ce home, c'est l'ensemble des objets, meubles, photos, souvenirs, qui leur appartiennent, qui leur renvoient leur image et qui constituent le paysage intérieur et vivant de leur logement. Ce sont leurs pénates. Ils les traînent partout, comme Enée.'

41 'La 'house' c'est la carcasse: on l'abandonne sous le moindre prétexte.'

42 'ce souvenir obsède' (Lefebvre [1974] 2000, 143).

43 'une dignité presque ontologique' (Lefebvre [1974] 2000, 143).

44 'Les maisons de briques sont couleur de sang séché ou, au contraire, peinturlurées, barbouillées de jaune vif, de vert ou de blanc cru. […] Toutes ces demeures hâtivement construites et faites à dessein pour être hâtivement démolies se rapprochent singulièrement, comme on voit, des 'prefabricated houses' de Fontana. […] *Et rien n'est plus saisissant, d'abord, que le contraste entre la formidable puissance, l'abondance de ce qu'on nomme le 'colosse américain' et l'insignifiance chétive de ces maisonnettes qui bordent les routes les plus larges du monde.* Mais rien ne marque mieux, à la réflexion, que *l'Amérique n'est pasfaite,* que ses idées, ses projets, sa structure sociale et ses villes n'ont qu'une réalité strictement provisoire.'

45 The idea that the house should not close off the world but rather open the individual out to it was the major motivating factor behind modernist housing design (see Kwinter 2001; Kostof 2004 and Raymond 1984). In this architectural vision, all spatial relations were optional: flat roofs might serve as an extra floor, open-plan interiors elided walls, with reversible panels the interior of the house was no longer a fixed entity, but adjustable. In direct contravention to the ideologies motivating nineteenth-century construction, modernists devised vast windows that sought to remove the opposition between interior and exterior, and replaced the staircase, which had hitherto preserved social hierarchies, with ramps that allowed the inhabitant to move imperceptibly from floor to floor.

46 'Mais ces villes légères, si semblables encore à Fontana, aux campements du Far-West, montrent l'autre face des États-Unis: leur liberté. Chacun est libre, ici, non de critiquer ou de réformer les mœurs, mais de les fuir, de s'en aller dans le désert ou dans une autre ville. Les villes sont ouvertes. Ouvertes sur le monde, ouvertes sur l'avenir. C'est ce qui leur donne à toutes un air aventureux et, dans leur désordre, dans leur laideur même, une sorte d'émouvante beauté.'

47 'Dans les usines, on a installé des haut-parleurs partout. Ils ont mission de lutter contre l'isolement de l'ouvrier en face de la matière. Si vous parcourez cet immense chantier naval, aux environs de Baltimore, vous retrouvez d'abord cette dispersion humaine, cette grande solitude des travailleurs que nous connaissons bien en Europe […]. *Mais, dès qu'ils mettent leur casque, ils peuvent entendre la musique. Et la musique, c'est déjà un conseil qui s'insinue sournoisement en eux, c'est déjà un rêve dirigé.* […] Vous voyez que le citoyen américain est bien encadré.'

48 'La nation marche avec vous, elle vous donne des conseils et des ordres. Mais elle le fait à mi-voix et elle a souci d'expliquer minutieusement son injonction: pas un commandement qui ne s'accompagne d'un bref commentaire ou d'une image justificative […]. Soignez votre visage pour *son* retour; achetez de la crème X) ou de la propagande en faveur des War Bonds. […] *De la même façon l'Américain, dont on sollicite, à toute heure du jour, la raison et la liberté, met son point d'honneur à faire ce qu'on lui demande: c'est en agissant comme tout le monde qu'il se sent à la fois le plus raisonnable et le plus national, c'est en se montrant le plus conformiste qu'il se sent le plus libre.'*

49 Sartre is concerned to understand how the 'frame' of American life differs from the explicitly oppressive mechanisms of totalitarian regimes. He does this within a comparative framework, comparing the exclusively nationalist messages of the Fascist propaganda machine with the American appeal to universal Reason and Liberty.

50 'de former un homme [mais] un américain pur'.

51 'J'ai rencontré un Européen en voie de fusion dès le lendemain de mon arrivée. […] Il est né à Paris, n'habite l'Amérique que depuis quinze ans […]. Pourtant l'Amérique le possède déjà jusqu'à moitié […]. J'avais l'impression d'assister à une métamorphose d'Ovide: le visage de cet homme est encore trop expressif, il a gardé ce mimétisme un peu agaçant de l'intelligence qui fait reconnaître partout une tête française. Mais bientôt il sera arbre ou rocher.'

52 'Mais surtout il y a cette présence concrète, quotidienne, d'une Raison de chair et d'os, d'une Raison qu'on voit. […] Un Américain me disait un soir: 'Enfin, si la politique internationale était l'affaire d'hommes raisonnables et sains, est-ce que la guerre ne serait pas supprimée pour toujours?' Des Français qui étaient présents lui dirent que la chose n'allait pas de soi et il se fâcha. 'Allez, leur dit-il, avec un mépris indigné, allez construire des cimetières!' Pour moi, je ne dis rien, la discussion entre nous n'était pas possible: je crois au mal et il n'y croit pas.'

53 'Prise dans sa longueur et dans sa largeur – à plat – New-York est la ville la plus conformiste du monde […]. Ce quadrillage, c'est New-York: les rues se ressemblent tant qu'on ne leur a pas donné de nom, on s'est borné à leur assigner, comme aux soldats, un numéro matricule.'

54 'dans l'anonymat numérique des rues et des avenues' / "simplement n'importe qui n'importe où'.

55 Berman ([1982] 1988) points out that this feeling of anxiety and its accompanying vision of the masses as hollow men under the control of the machine is 'a familiar twentieth-century refrain, shared by those who love the modern world and those who hate it: modernity is constituted by its machines, of which modern men and women are merely mechanical reproductions' (29).

56 'Ainsi l'individualisme en Amérique, dans la lutte pour la vie, est surtout l'aspiration passionnée de chacun vers l'état d'individu. Il y a des individus comme il y a des gratte-ciel en Amérique, il y a Ford, il y a Rockefeller, il y a Hemingway, il y a Roosevelt. Ils sont des modèles et des exemples.'

57 'Comment parler sur 135 millions d'Américains? Il faudrait avoir vécu dix ans ici et nous y passerons six semaines […]. Les uns nous disent: 'Tenez-vous-en aux faits!' Mais quels faits? […] Si je choisis, je décide déjà de ce qui est l'Amérique. […] Je décide donc de livrer mes impressions et mes constructions personnelles, sous ma propre responsabilité. Cette Amérique peut-être que je la rêve. En tout cas, je serai honnête avec mon rêve: je l'exposerai tel que je le fais.'

58 'Lorsqu'un ami prétend expliquer notre caractère et démêler nos intentions, lorsqu'il rapporte chacun de nos actes à des principes […] nous l'écoutons, mal à notre aise, sans pouvoir nier ce qu'il dit, ni tout à fait l'accepter. Peut-être la construction est vraie mais de quelle vérité? […] Pareillement lorsqu'on nous présente, en Europe, un soigneux agencement de ces notions – melting-pot, puritanisme, réalisme, optimisme, etc. – dont on nous dit qu'elles sont les clés du caractère américain, nous ressentons une certaine satisfaction intellectuelle et nous pensons qu'en effet cela doit être ainsi.'

59 Sartre's (1949) valorization of lucidity is reflected in his representation of the worry that Americans have about their own conformity and their concern to be more American than their neighbour. The self-awareness of one particular man he meets is cited: 'The truth is that every one of us is eaten up at the thought of being less American than his neighbour' / 'La vérité, c'est que chacun de nous est rongé par la peur d'être moins américain que son voisin.' (130)

60 'Il y a le respect de la science, de l'industrie, le positivisme, l'amour maniaque des 'gadgets' et il y a l'humour sombre de 'New-Yorker' qui se moque amèrement de la civilisation mécanique et ces cent millions d'Américains qui trompent chaque jour leur besoin de merveilleux, en lisant dans les *Comics*, les aventures invraisemblables de Superman, de Wonderwoman et de Mandrake le magicien.'

61 'Ces longues lignes tirées au cordeau m'ont donné soudain la sensation de l'espace. Nos villes d'Europe sont construites pour nous protéger contre lui: les maisons s'y groupent comme des moutons. Mais l'espace traverse New-York, l'anime, le dilate. L'espace, le grand espace vide des steppes et des pampas, coule dans ses artères comme un courant d'air froid, séparant les riverains de droite des riverains de gauche […]. *Quand on sait regarder* les deux rangées d'immeubles qui, comme des falaises, bordent une grande artère, *on est récompensé*: leur mission s'achève là-bas, au bout de l'avenue, un lambeau de ciel flotte entre elles.'

62 'solitaire et pur comme une bête sauvage.'

63 'Suis-je perdu dans une cité ou dans la nature? Contre la violence de la nature New-York n'est pas une protection. C'est une ville à ciel ouvert. Les orages inondent ses rues si larges, si longues à traverser quand il pleut. Les ouragans secouent les maisons de briques et balancent les gratte-ciel. La radio les annonce solennellement comme des déclarations de guerre. […] Dès la fin de mai, la chaleur s'abat sur la ville comme une bombe atomique. C'est le Mal. Les gens s'abordent en se disant: '*It's a murder.*' Les trains emportent des millions de citadins qui fuient et qui laissent, lorsqu'ils descendent, une trace humide sur la banquette, comme les escargots. Ce n'est pas la ville qu'ils fuient, c'est la Nature. Jusque dans les profondeurs de mon appartement, je subis les assauts d'une nature hostile, sourde, mystérieuse. […] New-York est une ville coloniale, un terrain de camping. Toute l'hostilité, toute la cruauté de la Nature sont présentes dans cette cité, le monument le plus prodigieux que l'homme se soit jamais élevé

à soi-même. C'est une ville légère; son manque de poids surprend la plupart des Européens. Dans cet espace immense et malveillant, dans ce désert de roc qui ne tolère aucune végétation, on a construit des milliers de maisons en briques, en bois ou en en ciment armé qui semblent toutes, sur le point de s'envoler.'

64 'Je marche entre les petites maisons de briques, couleur de sang séchée. Elles sont plus jeunes que les maisons d'Europe, mais leur fragilité les fait paraître bien plus vieilles. Je vois au loin l'Empire State Building, ou le Chrysler Building, qui pointent vainement vers le ciel, et je songe soudain que New-York est sur le point d'acquérir une Histoire et qu'il a déjà ses ruines.'

5. Writing around the Lines: Interpretive Travel Writing

1 'J'avoue que dans l'Amérique j'ai vu plus que l'Amérique; j'y ai cherché une image de la démocratie elle-même, de ses penchants, de son caractère, de ses préjugéa, de ses passions; j'ai voulu la connaître, ne fût-ce que pour savoir du moins ce que nous devions espérer ou craindre d'elle' (Toqueville [1831] 1848, I: 22).

2 English Translations of Perec's *Ellis Island* are taken from the translation by Harry Mathews (Perec 1995).
   'Pourquoi racontons-nous ces histoires?
   que sommes-nous venus chercher ici?
   que sommes-nous venus demander' (Perec [1980] 1994, 55).

3 The highest concentration of emigrants arrived on Ellis Island between the years 1892 to 1924. During this period almost sixteen million people passed through the island's federal checkpoint; that is, five or six thousand per day. Seventy per cent of all immigrants from Europe passed through New York. From 1914 onward, European emigration began to subside due to the outbreak of war as well as due to measures enacted by the American Congress, such as the Literacy Act (1917) and the introduction of quotas that made it almost impossible for the destitute of Europe (who had constituted the majority of the migrant population) to gain entry to the United States. In 1924 immigration procedures were delegated to European consulates, and Ellis Island was demoted to a detention centre that dealt exclusively with those whose situation was irregular. Throughout World War II it was used as a prison camp for those suspected of anti-American activities and housed Italian fascists, pro-Nazi Germans, Communists or those suspected of Communism. Ellis was definitively closed in 1954 before being converted into the museum we know it as today. Perec's writing adds a human dimension to these statistics: '2% of emigrants were simply sent back to Europe from Ellis Island. This means two hundred and fifty thousand people however. And from 1892 to 1924 there were three thousand suicides on Ellis Island.' / '2% d'émigrants seulement furent refoulés d'Ellis Island. Cela représente pourtant deux cent cinquante mille personnes. Et de 1892 à 1924, il y a eut trois mille suicides sur Ellis Island' (Perec [1980] 1994, 18).

4 Debate over the Island's humanitarian status was on going throughout the years of intense immigration and up until the island's foundation as a national monument. Depending on the perspective taken, the American authorities emerge as taskmasters or benevolent liberators of a ravaged Europe. In their *Monthly Review* of 1949, the Immigration and Naturalization Service defended their activities on the island: 'Ellis Island, in the Harbor of New York City, is used solely as a detention and deportation center by the U.S. Immigration Service. Once a general reception center for all aliens entering the United States, it has not been used for this purpose for thirty years. No immigrant or visitor whose passport and entry papers are in order now goes to the island. More than 99 percent of all immigrants and visitors arrive with documents and papers in order' (cited in Pitkin 1975, 171). This suggests that the Service recognized that the public's image of the island as depot was largely a negative one, while they also seem concerned to distance their present use of the island from that of the past. In 1962 the Communist *Daily Worker* referred to Ellis Island as 'America's first concentration camp' (cited in Pitkin 1975, 171).

5 'être juif, pour lui, c'est continuer à s'insérer
        dans une tradition, une langue, une culture, une
        communauté que ni les siècles de la diaspora ni
        le génocide systématique de la 'solution finale'
        n'ont réussi à définitivement broyer;
        être juif, pour lui, c'est avoir reçu, pour le transmettre
        à son tour, tout un ensemble de coutumes, de
        manières de manger, de danser, de chanter, des mots,
        des goûts, des habitudes,
        et c'est surtout avoir le sentiment de partager ces
        gestes et ces rites avec d'autres, au-delà des
        frontières et des nationalités, partager ces choses
        devenues racines, tout en sachant à chaque instant
        qu'elles sont en même temps fragiles et essentielles,
        menacées par le temps et par les hommes' (Perec [1980] 1994, 60).

6 'ce qui pour moi se trouve ici
        ce ne sont en rien des repères, des racines ou des
        traces,
        mais le contraire: quelque chose d'informe, à la
        limite du dicible,
        quelque chose que je peux nommer clôture, ou scission,
        ou coupure,
        et qui est pour moi très intimement et très confusément
        lié au fait même d'être juif' (Perec [1980] 1994, 56).

7 'Je n'ai pas le sentiment d'avoir oublié, mais celui de n'avoir jamais pu apprendre' ([1980]
   1994, 60).

8 'J'aimerais bien qu'il existe des lieux stables
        immobiles, intangibles, intouchés et
        presque
        intouchables, immuables, enracinés; des
        lieux qui seraient des références, des
        points de départ, des sources:
        Mon pays natal, le berceau de ma
        Famille, la maison où je serais né, l'arbre
        que j'aurais vu grandir (que mon père
        aurait planté le jour de ma naissance), le
        grenier de mon enfance empli de
        souvenirs intacts…
        De tels lieux n'existent pas, et c'est
        parce qu'ils n'existent pas que l'espace
        devient question, cesse d'être évidence,
        cesse d'être incorporé, cesse d'être
        approprié. L'espace est un doute: il me
        faut sans cesse le marquer, le désigner;
        il n'est jamais à moi, il ne m'est jamais
        donné, il faut que j'en fasse la conquête.'

9 'J'écris: j'écris parce que nous avons vécu ensemble, parce que j'ai été un parmi eux, ombre
   au milieu de leurs ombres, corps près de leur corps; j'écris parce qu'ils ont laissé en moi leur
   marque indélébile et que la trace en est l'écriture: leur souvenir est mort à l'écriture; l'écriture
   est le souvenir de leur mort et l'affirmation de ma vie.'

10 'En passant de l'histoire à la nature, le mythe fait une économie: il abolit la complexité des
   actes humains, leur donne la simplicité des essences, il supprime toute dialectique, toute

remontée au-delà du visible immédiat, il organise un monde sans contradictions parce que sans profondeur, un monde étalé dans l'évidence, il fonde une clarté heureuse: les choses ont l'air de signifier toutes seules.'

11 'Les Lieux anthropologiques [sont] répertoriés, classés et promus 'lieux de mémoire' [et] y occupant une place circonscrite et spécifique.'

12 However, it is important to acknowledge the richness of levels of representational activity which this travel narrative employs. 'Description of a Path' is followed by a collection of photographs, entitled 'Album'. Among the images are photographs taken by Lewis Hine, famous for his portraits of American life at the beginning of the twentieth century. The photographs precede the section, 'Repérages' / 'Land Marks'. The purpose of this piece of the work, Perec informs the reader, is to give a sense of the confusion and uncertainty that Bober and he felt upon undertaking their project. Neither of them had ever visited New York prior to 1978, and their only prior contact with Ellis Island had been some old photographs. The first task as they saw it was to lend substance to this abstraction and to prepare for the filmmaking process by making contact with the dozen or so people whose names they had been given. Upon arrival this list seems to provide the inspiration for the enumeration of the burgeoning realities accumulated as soon as the city became an entity involved in the everyday existence of these two foreigners. 'Repérages' consists of lists with titles such as 'Gens que nous avons vus' / 'People we saw', 'Gens que nous n'avons pas vu, mais que nous aurions dû, ou aimé voir' / 'People we didn't see, but should have or would have liked to have seen', 'Lieux' / 'Places', 'Nourritures' / 'Food'. Similar to the lists of 'Description d'un chemin', the sequencing of words like suggests a myriad of experiences behind each entry, so that every word stands in for an entire event, perhaps all the more conspicuous because of its absence. This section of the account is particularly reminiscent of *Espèces d'espaces* (1974), in which the author delimits the tensions between the metonymical experience of the everyday and the larger metaphorical consciousness one forms of space. In this work, these spaces range from the subject's bed, to the neighbourhood, to the conception of one's place in the universe.

13 'Le premier film est notre rapport au lieu, l'autre est leur film, c'est-à-dire des témoignages de tous ces gens qui auront disparu dans dix ans, leurs souvenirs.'

14 'c'était d'elles que, personnellement, nous nous sentions les plus proches' ([1980] 1994, 103).

15 Translated respectively from the French, '*non-lieu*' / 'non-place' and 'nulle part' / 'nowhere', the English loses some of the richness associated with the word '*non-lieu*', which in recent French ethnographical research has come to be used as an alternative term for 'u-topia'. See Augé (1992).

16 'Mais ce n'était pas encore l'Amérique
    seulement un prolongement de bateau
    un débris de la vieille Europe
    où rien encore n'étais acquis,
    où ceux qui étaient partis
    n'étaient pas encore arrivés,
    où ceux qui avaient tout quitté
    n'avaient rien encore obtenu
    et où il n'y avait rien d'autre à faire qu'à attendre' ([1980] 1994, 48).

17 'En somme, Ellis Island ne sera rien d'autre qu'une usine à fabriquer des Américains, une usine à transformer des émigrants en immigrants, une usine à l'américaine, aussi rapide et efficace qu'une charcuterie de Chicago: à un bout de la chaîne, on met un Irlandais, un Juif d'Ukraine ou un Italien des Pouilles, à l'autre bout – après l'inspection des yeux, inspection des poches, vaccination, désinfection – il en sort un Américain' ([1980] 1994, 10–11).

18 'un nom bien américain que les autorités d'état civil n'auraient pas de mal à transcrire' ([1980] 1994, 17).

19 'C'est ainsi qu'il fut inscrit sous le nom de John Ferguson' ([1980] 1994, 18).

20 'Cette histoire est peut-être trop belle pour être vraie, mais il importe peu, au fond, qu'elle soit vraie ou fausse' ([1980] 1994, 18).

21 'c'est n'est jamais, je crois, par hasard, que l'on va aujourd'hui visiter Ellis Island' ([1980] 1994, 36).

22 'cinq millions d'émigrants en provenance d'Italie
   quatre millions d'émigrants en provenance d'Irlande
   un million d'émigrants en provenance de Suède
   six millions d'émigrants en provenance d'Allemagne
   trois millions d'émigrants en provenance d'Autriche et de Hongrie' ([1980] 1994, 24).

23 'quatre millions d'immigrants sont venus d'Irlande
   quatre cent mille immigrants sont venus de Turquie et d'Arménie
   cinq millions d'immigrants sont venus de Sicile et d'Italie
   six millions d'immigrants sont venus d'Allemagne
   quatre cent mille immigrants sont venus d'Hollande' ([1980] 1994, 68).

24 '*comment décrire?*
   comment raconter?
   comment regarder?
   sous la sécheresse des statistiques officielles,
   sous le ronronnement rassurant des anecdotes mille fois
   ressassées par les guides à chapeaux scouts,
   sous la mise en place officielle de ces objets quotidiens
   devenus objets de musée, vestiges rares, choses historiques,
   images précieuses,
   sous la tranquillité factice de ces photographies figées
   une fois pour toutes dans l'évidence trompeuse de leur
   noir et blanc
   comment reconnaître ce lieu?' ([1980] 1995, 37, my emphasis)

25 In *L'Obvis et l'obtus* (1982) Barthes explores the problem of representation, which is that it always already exists within a preconceived set of connotative values that facilitate interpretation, but which also mean that transparency in language is necessarily a myth. The sign always operates within a system of signification separate to the independence of its object. As Barthes states: 'Décrire consiste précisément à adjoindre au message dénoté […] une connotation […]: décrire ce n'est donc pas seulement être inexact ou incomplet, c'est changer de structure, c'est signifier autre chose que ce qui est.' / 'To describe precisely means adding a connotation to the denoted message: to describe is not simply to be inexact or incomplete, it is to change structure, it is to mean something other than what is' (Barthes 1982, 12).

26 'Un grand nombre, sinon la plupart, de ces choses ont été décrites, inventoriées, photographiées, racontées ou recensées. Mon propos dans les pages qui suivent a plutôt été de décrire le reste, ce que l'on ne note généralement pas, ce qui ne se remarque pas, ce qui n'a pas d'importance, ce qui se passe quand il ne se passe rien, sinon au temps, des gens, des voitures et des nuages.'

27 comment lire ces traces?
   comment aller au-delà
   aller derrière
   ne pas nous arrêter à ce qui nous est donné à
           voir
   ne pas voir seulement ce que l'on savait d'avance
           que l'on verrait?
   Comment saisir ce qui n'est pas montré, ce qui n'a pas
   été photographié, archivé, restauré, mis en scène?
   Comment retrouver ce qui était plat, banal, quotidien,
   ce qui était ordinaire, ce qui se passait tous les jours? ([1980] 1994, 37).

28 'cela ne veut rien dire, de vouloir faire parler des images, de les forcer à dire, ce qu'elles ne sauraient dire' ([1980] 1994, 41).

29 'la plénitude du vide'.

30 'par exemple:
   deux grands doubles éviers de faïence blanche,
   dont l'un est pourvu d'une essoreuse à main
   quatre chaises
   deux planches à repasser reposant sur de larges
   pieds de fonte, l'un de base rectangulaire' ([1980] 1994, 44).

31 'ne pas dire seulement: seize millions d'émigrants sont passés en trente ans par Ellis Island' ([1980] 1994, 51).

32 'ce que furent ces seize millions d'histoires individuelles,
   ces seize millions d'histoires identiques et différentes
   de ces hommes, de ces femmes et de ces enfants chassés
   de leur terre natale par la famine ou la misère,
   l'oppression politique, raciale ou religieuse,
   et quittant tout' ([1980] 1994, 51).

33 'Vive le Quatrième Monde, celui auquel on dit: "L'utopie est réalisée, que ceux qui n'y ont pas part disparaissent", celui qui n'a plus le droit de faire surface, *disenfranchised*, déchu de parole, voué à l'oubli, qu'on éjecte et qui va crever dans une fatalité de second ordre. *Disenfranchising*' (Baudrillard [1986] 2000, 222).

34 Parts of this section appear in my article 'From Legislative to Interpretive Modes of Travel Writing: Space, Ethics and Literary Form in Jean Baudrillard's *America*'. See Jein (2014).

35 See, for instance, Douglas Kellner (1989, 170), who sees in *America* the 'decline of Baudrillard's theoretical powers and the collapse of social analysis and critique – as well as politics.'

36 Equally, Caren Kaplan (1996, 100) describes Baudrillard's *America* in terms of a 'world-weary cultural relativism that masks an aggressive Eurocentrism'.

37 This piece follows Mike Gane's (1991) more nuanced categorization of Baudrillard's writing as both 'counter-modernist' and 'counter-postmodernist', and appropriates the text to examine the ethical implication of such modes of countering for travel writing.

38 'l'Amérique profonde des mœurs et des mentalités' (Baudrillard [1986] 2000, 12).

39 All quotations from *America* are drawn from the 1988 translation by Chris Turner.

40 'Nostalgie née de l'immensité des collines texanes et des sierras du Nouveau-Mexique: plongées autoroutières et supertubes sur la stéréo-Chrysler et vague de chaleur – la photo ponctuelle n'y suffit plus – il faudrait avoir le film total, en temps réel du parcours […] – non pour le seul plaisir du souvenir, mais parce que la fascination d'une répétition insensée et déjà là, dans l'abstraction du voyage' (Baudrillard [1986] 2000, 10).

41 Virilio ([1980] 1989) hypothesizes that new technologies from the motorcar to the airplane to the cinematographic camera produce hitherto unheard-of perceptions of time and space that definitively alter humanity's relationship to the real.

42 'Nous, en Europe, c'est la révolution de 1789 qui nous a marqués, mais non pas du même sceau: du sceau de l'Histoire, de l'Etat et de l'Idéologie. La politique et l'histoire restent notre scène primitive, non la sphère utopique et morale' (Baudrillard [1986] 2000, 150).

43 Gerry Coulter (2008, 146) uses this term to describe Baudrillard's belief and hope that despite the proliferation of systematization in the Western world it may collapse under the weight of its own excess.

44 'Nous sommes toujours au centre, mais au centre du Vieux Monde. Eux qui furent une transcendance marginale de ce Vieux Monde en sont aujourd'hui le centre neuf et excentrique. L'excentricité est leur acte de naissance' (1986, 161).

45 'J'ai cherché l'Amérique *sidérale*, celle de la liberté vaine et absolue des *freeways*, jamais celle du social et de la culture – celle de la vitesse désertique, des motels et des surfaces minérales, jamais l'Amérique profonde des mœurs et des mentalités. J'ai cherché dans la vitesse du scénario, dans le réflexe indifférent de la télévision, dans le film des jours et des nuits à travers un espace vide, dans la succession merveilleusement sans affect des signes, des images, des visages, des actes

rituels de la route, ce qui est le plus proche de l'univers nucléaire et énucléé qui est virtuellement le nôtre jusque dans les chaumières européennes. […] Cette forme nucléaire, cette catastrophe future, je savais tout cela à Paris. Mais pour la comprendre, il faut prendre la forme du voyage, qui réalise ce que Virilio dit être l'esthétique de la différence. Car la forme désertique mentale grandit à vue d'œil, qui est la forme épurée de la désertion sociale. […] L'inhumanité de notre monde ultérieur, asocial et superficiel, trouve d'emblée ici sa forme extatique. Car le désert n'est que cela: une critique extatique de la culture, une forme extatique de la disparition' (Baudrillard [1986] 2000, 17–18).

46 'Il n'y a pas pour moi de vérité de l'Amérique' / 'L'Amérique n'est ni un rêve, ni une réalité' / 'L'Amérique est un gigantesque hologramme' (Baudrillard [1986] 2000, 56–57).

47 'La situation coloniale a simplement été transférée en métropole, hors de son contexte originel' (Baudrillard [1986] 2000, 164).

48 'qu'en se formalisant dans l'abstraction [devient] aussi dévoratrice de singularité que la révolution l'est de ses enfants' ([1986] 2000, 165).

49 As Davis ([1990] 1992, 19–20) states, 'The ultimate world-historical significance – an oddity – of Los Angeles is that it has come to play the double role of utopia *and* dystopia for advanced capitalism. The same place, as Brecht noted, symbolized both heaven and hell.'

50 For an exploration of utopia and America, see Scott (2004).

51 'Tout est repris par la simulation. Les paysages par la photographie, les femmes par le scénario, les pensées par l'écriture, le terrorisme par la mode et les media, les événements par la télévision. Les choses semblent n'exister que par cette destination étrange. On peut se demander si le monde lui-même n'existe qu'en fonction de la publicité qui peut en être faite dans un autre monde' (Baudrillard 1986, 64).

52 'Où est le cinéma? Il est partout dehors, partout dans la ville' (1986, 111).

53 'le présupposé miraculeux d'une utopie incarnée' (Baudrillard 1986, 153).

54 'La conviction idyllique des Américains d'être le centre du monde, la puissance suprême et le modèle absolu n'est pas fausse. Et elle ne se fonde pas tant sur les ressources, les techniques et les armes, que sur le présupposé miraculeux d'une utopie incarnée, d'une société qui, avec une candeur qu'on peut juger insupportable, s'institue sur l'idée qu'elle est la réalisation de tout ce dont les autres on rêvé – justice, abondance, droit, richesse, liberté: elle le sait, elle y croit, et finalement les autres y croient aussi' ([1986] 2000, 153).

55 'Si l'utopie est réalisé, le malheur n'existe pas, les pauvres ne sont plus crédibles. Si l'Amérique est ressuscitée, alors le massacre des Indiens n'a pas eu lieu, le Vietnam n'a pas eu lieu. […] Les déshérités seront voués à l'oubli, à l'abandon, à la disparition pure et simple. C'est la logique du *must exit. Poor people must exit* (Baudrillard [1986] 2000, 221).

56 'Comme si le bien et le mal s'étaient développés séparément' (Baudrillard [1986] 2000, 175).

Conclusion

1 'La ville n'existe symboliquement, pour ses habitants, que quand ils sont en mesure de la jouer: de la faire exister dans leur imagination, dans leur langue, dans leur création'.

REFERENCES

Primary Texts

Baudrillard, Jean. (1986) 2000. *Amérique*. Paris: Descartes & Cie.
———. (1986) 1988. *America*. Translated by Chris Turner. London: Verso.
Dyssord, Jacques. 1932. *Londressecret*. Paris: Éditions de la Madeleine.
Janin, Jules. 1851. *Le Mois de mai à Londres et l'exposition de 1851*. Paris: Michel Lévy Frères.
Leroy, Alfred. 1946. *Londres et la vie anglaise*. Paris: Les Éditions Universelles.
Morand, Paul. 1930. *New York*. Paris: Ernest Flammarion.
Perec, Georges. (1980) 1994. *Récits d'Ellis Island: histoires d'errance et d'espoir*. Paris: Sorbier; Bry-sur-Marne: L'Institut national de l'audiovisuel.
———. 1995. *Ellis Island*. Translated by Harry Mathews. New York: The New Press.
Sartre, Jean-Paul. (1945) 1949. *Situations III*. Paris: Gallimard.
Vallès, Jules. (1876) 1951. *La Rue à Londres*. Paris: Les Éditeurs français réunis.

Secondary Texts

Abbeele, Georges Van Den. 1992. *Travel as Metaphor from Montaigne to Rousseau*. Minneapolis: University of Minnesota Press.
Abensour, Miguel. 1990. 'Saint-Just and the Problem of Heroism'. In *The French Revolution and the Birth of Modernity*, edited by F. Fehér, 133–49. Berkeley: University of California Press.
Adams, Annmarie. 1994. 'The Healthy Victorian City: The Old London Street at the International Health Exhibition of 1884'. In edited by Z. Çelik, D. Favro and R. Ingersoll, 203–12.
Adams, Percy G. 1983. *Travel Literature and the Evolution of the Novel*. Lexington: University Press of Kentucky.
Adler, Judith. 1989. 'Origins of Sightseeing'. *Annals of Tourism Research* 16: 7–29.
Adorno, Theodore W., and Max Horkheimer. (1944) 2002. *Dialectic of Enlightenment*. Translated by J. Cumming. New York: Continuum.
Agnew, John A., ed. 1984. *The City in Cultural Context*. London: Allen & Unwin.
———. 1989. 'The Devaluation of Place in Social Science'. In *The Power of Place: Bringing Together Geographical and Sociological Imaginations*, edited by John A. Agnew and James A. Duncan, 9–29. Boston: Unwin Hyman.
Agnew, John A., and James A. Duncan, eds. *The Power of Place: Bringing Together Geographical and Sociological Imaginations*. Boston: Unwin Hyman.
Alison, Jane et al. 2007. *Future City: Experiment and Utopia in Architecture*. New York: Thames & Hudson.
al-Khalil, Samir. 1991. *The Monument: Art, Vulgarity and Responsibility in Iraq*. London: André Deutsch.
Allen, Graham. 2002. 'Le Degré zéro de l'écriture'. *The Literary Encyclopaedia*. http://www.litencyc.com/php/sworks.php?rec=true&UID=10337 (accessed 1 November 2014).
Allport, Gordon W. 1954. *The Nature of Prejudice*. Cambridge, MA: Addison-Wesley.
Alsworth Ross, Edward. 1901. *Social Control: A Survey of the Foundations of Order*. New York: Macmillan.

Althabe, Gérard. 1984. *Urbanisme et réhabilitation symbolique: Ivry, Bologne, Amiens*. Paris: Éditions Anthropos.

———. 1990. 'Ethnologie du contemporain et enquête de terrain'. *Terrain* 14: 126–31.

Althabe, Gérard, and Mireille Meyer, eds. 1988. *Des Migrants et des villes*. Aix-en-Provence: IREMAM.

Anderson, Benedict. (1983) 2003. *Imagined Communities*. London: Verso.

Anderson, Jon. 2009. *Understanding Cultural Geography: Places and Traces*. London: Routledge.

Appadurai, Arjun. 1996. *Modernity at Large: Cultural Dimensions of Globalization*. Minneapolis, MN: University of Minnesota Press.

———. 2002. 'Deep Democracy: Urban Governmentality and the Horizon of Politics'. *Public Culture* 14 (1): 21–48.

Aprile, Sylvie. 2003. 'Voices of Exile: French Newspapers in England'. In *Exile from European Revolutions: Refugees in Mid-Victorian England*, edited by S. Freitag, 149–63. Oxford: Berghahn Books.

Arendt, Hannah. (1963) 1990. *On Revolution*. London: Penguin.

Arens, Katherine. 2007. '*Stadtwollen*: Benjamin's *Arcades Project* and the Problem of Method'. *Publications of the Modern Language Association of America* 122 (1): 43–60.

Aristotle. 1995. *Poetics*. Translated by S. Halliwell. Cambridge, MA: Harvard University Press.

Armstrong, Isobel. 2008. *Victorian Glassworlds: Glass Culture and the Imagination, 1830–1880*. Oxford: Oxford University Press.

Arnold, Dana. 2000. *Re-presenting the Metropolis: Architecture, Urban Experience and Social Life in London, 1800–1840*. London: Ashgate.

Aronson, Ronald, and Adrian Van den Hoven, eds. 1991. *Sartre Alive*. Detroit: Wayne State University Press.

Arscott, Caroline, and Griselda Pollock, with Janet Wolff. 1988. 'The Partial View: The Visual Representation of the Early Nineteenth-Century City'. In *The Culture of Capital: Art, Power and the Nineteenth-Century Middle Class*, edited by J. Wolff and J. Seed, 191–233. Manchester: Manchester University Press.

Attali, Jean. 2001. *Le Plan et le détail: une philosophie de l'architecture et de la ville*. Nîmes: Éditions Jacqueline Chambon.

Attridge, Steve. 2003. *Nationalism, Imperialism and Identity in Late Victorian Culture: Civil and Military Worlds*. London: Palgrave.

Auerbach, Erich. 1957. *Mimesis: The Representation of Reality in Western Literature* Translated by W. Trask. Garden City, NY: Doubleday Anchor.

Auerbach, Jeffrey. 1999. *The Great Exhibition of 1851: A Nation on Display*. New Haven, CT: Yale University Press.

Augé, Marc. 1986. *Un ethnologue dans le métro*. Paris: Hachette.

———. 1992. *Non-lieux: introduction à une anthropologie de la surmodernité*. Paris: Seuil.

———. 1994a. *Le Sens des autres: actualité de l'anthropologie*. Paris: Librairie Arthème Fayard.

———. 1994b. *Pour une anthropologie des mondes contemporains*. Paris: Aubier.

———. 1997. *L'Impossible Voyage: le tourisme et ses images*. Paris: Payot & Rivages.

———. 1998. *Les Formes de l'oubli*. Paris: Payot & Rivages.

Augustinos, Olga. 1994. *French Odysseys: Greece in French Travel Literature from the Renaissance to the Romantic Era*. London: Johns Hopkins University Press.

Aymes, Jean René, ed. 1983. *L'Espace romantique: témoignages de voyageurs français*. Paris: Métailié.

Babbage, Charles. 1851. *The Exposition of 1851: or Views of the Industry, the Science and the Government of England*. London: John Murray.

Babelon, Jean-Pierre. 1997. 'Le Louvre: demeure des rois, temple des arts'. In *Les Lieux de mémoire*, edited by P. Nora, II, 1803–30. Paris: Gallimard.

Bachelard, Gaston. (1957) 2001. *La Poétique de l'espace*. Paris: Presses Universitaires de France.

Bailey, Peter. 1978. *Leisure and Class in Victorian England*. London: Routledge.

Baird, George, and Charles Jencks, eds. 1969. *Meaning in Architecture*. London: Barrie and Rockliff.

Bakhtin, Mikhail Mikhailovich. 1981. *The Dialogic Imagination: Four Essays*, edited by M. Holquist. Translated by C. Emerson and M. Holquist. Austin, TX: University of Texas Press.

Balshaw, Maria, and Liam Kennedy, eds. 2000. *Urban Space and Representation* Sterling, VA: Pluto Press.

Barnett, Samuel. 1888. 'A Scheme for the Unemployed'. *Nineteenth Century* 24: 750–58.

Barth, Gunther. 1980. *City People*. New York: Oxford University Press.

Barthes, Roland. 1953. *Le Degré zéro de l'écriture*. Paris: Seuil.

———. 1957. *Mythologies*. Paris: Seuil.

———. (1962–1967) 2002. *Œuvres complètes*. 5 vols. Paris: Seuil.

———. (1962) 2002. 'L'Imagination du signe'. In *Œuvres complètes*. 5 vols. II: 460–65.

———. (1964) 2002. 'La Tour Eiffel'. In *Œuvres complètes*. 5 vols. II: 529–53.

———. (1967) 2002. 'Sémiologie et urbanisme'. In *Œuvres complètes*. 5 vols. II: 1277–86.

———. (1968) 1984. *Le Bruissement de la langue*. Paris: Seuil.

———. 1968. *Writing Degree Zero*. Translated by A. Lavers and C. Smith. Preface by S. Sontag. New York: Hill & Lang.

———. (1970) 2002. 'Un univers articulé de signes vides'. In *Œuvres complètes*, III: 649–54.

———. 1981. *Le Grain de la voix: entretiens 1962–1980*. Paris: Seuil.

———. 1982. *L'Obvie et l'obtus: essais critiques III*. Paris: Seuil.

———, Leo Bersani, Philippe Hamon, Michael Riffaterre and Tzvetan Todorov. 1982. *Littérature et réalité*. Paris: Seuil.

Baudelaire, Charles. (1857) 1972. *Les Fleurs du mal*. Paris: Librairie Générale Française.

———. 1983–1985. *Œuvres complètes*. Edited by C. Pichois. Paris: Gallimard.

———. (1869) 1987. *Le Spleen de Paris. Petits poèmes en prose. La Fanfarlo*. Edited by D. Scott and B. Wright. Paris: Garnier-Flammarion.

Baudrillard, Jean. (1970) 1976. *La Société de consommation: ses mythes, ses structures*. Paris: Gallimard.

———. (1972) 1974. *Pour une critique de l'économie du signe*. Paris: Gallimard.

———. (1972) 1981. *For a Critique of the Political Economy of the Sign*. Translated by C. Levin. St. Louis, MO: Telos Press.

———. 1973. *Le Miroir de la production: ou l'illusion critique du matérialisme historique*. Tournai: Casterman.

———. 1976. *L'Échange symbolique et la mort*. Paris: Gallimard.

———. 1977. *Oublier Foucault*. Paris: Galilée.

———. 1979. *De la séduction*. Paris: Denoël.

———. 1983. *Les Stratégies fatales*. Paris: Bernard Grasset.

———. 1987a. *Cool Memories 1980–1985*. Paris: Galilée.

———. 1987b. *The Evil Demon of Images*. Translated by P. Patton and P. Foss. Sydney: Power Institute Publications.

———. 1990. *Fatal Strategies: Revenge of the Crystal*. Translated by P. Beitchman and W.G.J. Niesluchowski. New York: Semiotext(e).

———. 1991. *La Guerre du Golfe n'a pas eu lieu*. Paris: Galilée.

———. 1993a. *Baudrillard Live: Selected Interviews*. Edited by M. Gane. London: Routledge.

———. 1993b. *Symbolic Exchange and Death*. Translated by I. H. Grant. London: Sage.

———. 1994. *The Illusion of the End*. Translated by C. Turner. London: Polity.

———. 1995a. *Le Crime parfait*. Paris: Galilée.

———. 1995b. *The Gulf War Did Not Take Place*. Translated by P. Patton. Bloomington: University of Indiana Press.

———. 1997. *Écran total*. Paris: Galilée.

———. 1999. *The Perfect Crime*. Translated by C. Turner. New York: Verso.

———. 2000. *The Vital Illusion*. Edited by J. Witwer. New York: Columbia University Press.

Baudrillard, Jean, Yves Dauge, Gilles Lipovetsky, Michelle Perrot, Pierre Yves Pétillon, Guy Petitdemange, Joël Roman, Paul Thibaud, Alain Touraine, Pierre Vidal-Naquet. 1991. *Citoyenneté et urbanité*. Paris: Seuil.

Baudrillard, Jean, and Sylvère Lotringer. 1986. 'Forgetting Baudrillard.' Interview. *Social Text* 15: 140–41.

Bauman, Zygmunt. 1987. *Legislators and Interpreters: On Modernity, Post-modernity and Intellectuals*. Cambridge: Polity Press.

———. 1988. 'Disappearing into the Desert'. *Times Literary Supplement* (December): 16–22.

———. 1996. 'From Pilgrim to Tourist – or a Short History of Identity'. In *Questions of Cultural Identity*, edited by S. Hall and P. Du Gay, 19–36. London: Sage

———. 2000. *Liquid Modernity*. Cambridge: Polity.

Beardmore, George. 1984. *Civilians at War, Journals 1938–1946*. London: John Murray.

Beaujour, Michel. 1981. 'Some Paradoxes of Description'. *Yale French Studies* 61: 27–59.

Beauvoir, Simone de. 1954. *L'Amérique au jour le jour*. Paris: Gallimard.

Beaver, Patrick. 1999. *The Crystal Palace. The Great Exhibition*. New Haven: J.A. Auerbach.

Bégout, Bruce. 2003. *Lieu commun: le motel américain*. Paris: Éditions Allia.

Bellanger, François, and Bruno Marzloff. 1996. *Transit: les lieux et les temps de la mobilité*. Paris: Éditions de l'aube.

Bellet, Roger, ed. (1975) 1990. *Jules Vallès: Œuvres*.2 vols. Paris: Gallimard.

Bendix, Regina F. 1997. *In Search of Authenticity: The Formation of Folklore Studies*. Madison, WI: University of Wisconsin Press.

Benjamin, Walter. 1969. 'Paris: Capital of the Nineteenth Century'. *Perspecta* 12: 163–72.

———. (1973) 1985. *Charles Baudelaire: A Lyric Poet in the Era of High Capitalism*. Translated by H. Zohn. London: Verso.

Benko, Georges and Ulf Strohmayer, eds. 1997. *Space and Social Theory: Interpreting Modernity and Postmodernity*. Oxford: Blackwell.

Bennett, Tony. 1988. 'Museums and "the people"'. In *The Museum Time-Machine: Putting Cultures on Display*, edited by R. Lumley, 63–86. London: Routledge.

———. 1995. *The Birth of the Museum*. London: Routledge.

———, ed. 1983. *Formations of Pleasure*. London: Routledge.

Bensimon, Fabrice. 2003. 'The French Exiles and the British'. In *Exile from European Revolutions: Refugees in Mid-Victorian England*, edited by S. Freitag, 88–102. Oxford: Berghahn Books.

Bentham, Jeremy. 1988. *The Principles of Morals and Legislation*. New York: Prometheus.

Berchet, Jean-Claude. 1985. *Le Voyage en Orient: anthologie des voyageurs français dans le Levant au XIXe siècle*. Paris: R. Laffont.

Berger, John. (1972) 2008. *Ways of Seeing*. Harmondsworth: Penguin.

Berlioz, Hector. 1852. *Les Soirées de l'orchestre*. Paris: Michel Lévy frères.

Berman, Marshall. (1982) 1988. *All that is Solid Melts into Air: The Experience of Modernity*. London: Penguin.

———. 1984. 'The Signs in the Street: A Response to Perry Anderson'. *New Left Review* 144: 114–23.

Bertho-Lavenir, Catherine. 1997. 'Suivre le guide?' *Les Cahiers de médiologie: la confusion des monuments* 7: 151–63.

Besant, Walter. (1882) 1997. *All Sorts and Conditions of Men*. Oxford: Oxford University Press.

Bhabha, Homi, ed. 1990. *Nation and Narration*. London: Routledge.

———. (1994) 2010. *The Location of Culture*. London: Routledge.

Birchall, Clare. 2011. 'Transparency, Interrupted: Secrets of the Left'. *Theory, Culture & Society* 28 (7–8): 60–84.

Blanc, Louis. (1861–1865) 2001. *Lettres sur l'Angleterre*. Paris: L'Harmattan

Blanqui, Adolphe. 1851. *Lettres sur l'Exposition universelle de Londres, précédées d'un préambule et suivies d'un rapport présenté à l'Institut National de France*. Paris: Capelle.

Blau, Judith R. 1988. 'Where Architects Work: A Change Analysis 1970–1980'. In *The Design Professions and the Built Environment*, edited by P. L. Knox, 127–46. London: Croom Helm.

Boden, Deirdre and Harvey Molotch. 1994. 'The Compulsion to Proximity'. In *Now/Here: Time, Space and Modernity*, edited by R. Friedland and D. Boden, 257–86. Berkeley, CA: University of California Press.

Bolton, Arthur Thomas. 1895. *The Influence of Literature on Architecture*. London: Royal Institute of British Architects.

Booth, Charles. 1891. *Life and Labour of the People in London*. vol. 2. London: Williams & Norgate.

Borm, Jan. 2000. 'In-Betweeners? On the Travel Book and Ethnographies'. *Studies in Travel Writing* 4: 78–105.

———. 2004. 'Defining Travel: On the Travel Book, Travel Writing and Terminology'. In *Perspectives on Travel* Writing, edited by G. Hooper and T. Youngs, 13–26. Aldershot: Ashgate Publishing.

Bourdieu, Pierre. 1984. *Distinction*. London: Routledge.

Bouvier, Nicolas. 1981. *Le Poisson-Scorpion*. Paris: Gallimard.

———. (1989) 2001. *Chronique japonaise*. Paris: Éditions Payot et Rivages.

———. (1990) 2001. *Journal d'Aran et d'autres lieux*. Paris: Éditions Payot et Rivages.

Bowen, Elizabeth D. C. 1945. *The Demon Lover and Other Stories*. London: Cape.

Boyer, M. Christine. 1995. 'The Great Frame-Up: Fantastic Appearances in Contemporary Spatial Politics'. In *Spatial Practices: Critical Explorations in Social/Spatial Theory*, edited by H. Liggett and D. C. Perry, 81–109. London: Sage Publications.

Boym, Svetlana. 2007. 'Nostalgia and Its Discontents'. *The Hedgehog Review*, Summer, 7–18. http://www.iasc-culture.org/eNews/2007_10/9.2CBoym.pdf (accessed 28 February 2016).

Brahimi, Denise. 1982. *Arabes des lumières et bédouins romantiques: un siècle de 'voyages en orient'. 1735–1835*. Paris: Le Sycomore.

Braidotti, Rosi. 1994. *Nomadic Subjects: Embodiment and Sexual Difference in Contemporary Feminist Theory*. New York: Columbia University Press.

Bredekamp, Horst. 1995. *The Lure of Antiquity and the Cult of the Machine: The Kunstkammer and the Evolution of Nature, Art and Technology*. Princeton: Markus Wiener.

Breton, Philippe. 1997. *L'Utopie de la communication: le mythe du village planétaire*. Paris: La Découverte.

Brewer, John. 1997. *The Pleasures of the Imagination: English Culture in the Eighteenth Century*. New York: Farrar, Strauss, Giroux.

Bridge, Gary and Sophie Watson, eds. 2002. *The Blackwell City Reader*. London: Blackwell.

Brind Morrow, Susan. 1997. *The Names of Things: Life, Language, and Beginnings in the Egyptian Desert*. New York: Riverhead Books.

Broadbent, Geoffrey, Richard Bent, and Charles Jencks, eds. 1980. *Signs, Symbols and Architecture*. Chichester: Wiley Press.

Brooker, Peter. 2001. *Modernity and the Metropolis: Writing, Film and Urban Formations*. Basingstoke: Palgrave.

Bruner, Edward M. 1994. 'Abraham Lincoln as Authentic Reproduction: A Critique of Postmodernism'. *American Anthropologist* 96 (2): 397–415.

Bryson, Norman, Michael A. Holly and Keith Moxey, eds. 1994. *Visual Culture: Images and Interpretations*. London: Wesleyan University Press.

Buck-Morss, Susan. 1989. *The Dialectics of Seeing: Walter Benjamin and the Arcades Project*. Cambridge, MA: MIT Press.

Budford, Norman. 1997. *French Literature in/and the City*. Amsterdam: Rodopi.

Bull, Michael. 2000. *Sounding out the City: Personal Stereos and the Management of Everyday Life*. London: Berg.

Burgess, Moira. 1998. *Imagine a City: Glasgow in Fiction*. Glendarnel: Argyll Publishing.

Burkart, Arthur John and Slavoj Medlik. 1974. *Tourism, Past, Present and Future*. London: Heinemann.

Burke, Edmund. (1757) 1998. *A Philosophical Enquiry into the Origins of our Ideas about the Sublime and the Beautiful*. Edited by A. Philips. Oxford: Oxford University Press.

Butor, Michel. 1960. *Degrés*. Paris: Gallimard.

———. 1962. *Mobile. Étude pour une représentation des États-Unis*. Paris: Gallimard.

Burnham, Scott. 2007. 'Customising the City'. *Icon* 50: 94–98.

Buzard, James. 2002. 'The Grand Tour and After, 1660–1840'. In *The Cambridge Companion to Travel Writing*, edited by P. Hulme and T. Youngs, 37–52. Cambridge: Cambridge University Press.

———. 2005. 'What Isn't Travel?' In *Unravelling Civilization: European Travel and Travel Writing*, edited by H. Schulz-Forberg, 43–61. Oxford: Peter Lang.

Byrne, David. 2001. *Understanding the Urban*. London: Palgrave.

Byron, George Gordon, Walter Scott, and Thomas Moore (1819–1824) 1859. *The Poetical Works of Lord Byron*. London: John Murray.

Cahen, Jules M. (1908) 1909. *Exposition franco-britannique de Londres*. Paris: Comité français des expositions à l'étranger.

Cahoone, Lawrence E. 1988. *The Dilemma of Modernity: Philosophy, Culture, and Anti-Culture*. Albany: State University of New York Press.

Calet, Henri. 1947. *America*. Paris: Minuit.

Calvet, Louis-Jean. 1994. *Les Voix de la ville: introduction à la sociolinguistique urbaine*. Paris: Éditions Payot et Rivages.

Campbell, Jan, and Janet Harbord, eds. 2002. *Temporalities: Autobiography and Everyday Life*. Manchester: Manchester University Press.

Campbell, Mary Baine. 1988. *The Witness and the Other World: Exotic European Travel Writing 400–1600*. London: Cornell University Press.

———. 1997. 'Renaissance Voyage Literature and Ethnographic Pleasure: The Case of André Thevet'. *Studies in Travel Writing* 1: 9–42.

———. 1999. *Wonder & Science: Imaginary Worlds in Early Modern Europe*. London: Cornell University Press.

Camus, Albert. (1965) 1975. 'Pluies de New York'. In *Œuvres completes*, edited by Jean Grenier. 3 vols. II: 1829–34.

———. 1978. *Journaux de voyage*. Paris: Gallimard.

Cannadine, David, and David Reeder, eds. 1982. *Exploring the Urban Past: Essays in Urban History*. Cambridge: Cambridge University Press.

Capetti, Carla. 1993. *Writing Chicago: Modernism, Ethnography and the Novel*. New York: Columbia University Press.

Caraion, Marta. 2003. *Pour fixer la trace: photographie, littérature et voyage au milieu du XIXe siècle*. Geneva: Droz.

Caretto, Carlo. 1979. *The Desert in the City*. London: Collins.

Castells, Manuel. 1977. *The Urban Question: A Marxist Approach*. London: Edward Arnold.

Çelik, Zeynep, Diane Favro, and Richard Ingersoll, eds. 1994. *Streets: Critical Perspectives on Public Space*. London: University of California Press.

Céline, Louis-Ferdinand. 1932. *Voyage au bout de la nuit*. Paris: Éditions Denoël et Steele.

Certeau, Michel de. (1969) 2005. *L'Etranger ou l'union dans la différence*. Paris: Editions du Seuil.

———. (1980) 1990. *L'Invention du quotidien*. Vol. 1, *Arts de faire*. 2nd ed. Paris: Gallimard.

———. 1984. *The Practice of Everyday Life*. Translated by Steven F. Rendall. Berkeley: University of California Press.

Chambers, William. 1773. *A Dissertation on Oriental Gardening*. Dublin: Wilson. Chamoiseau, Patrick. 2002. *Livret des villes du deuxième monde*. Paris: Monum.

Charton, Edouard. (1838) 1854–57. *Voyageurs anciens et modernes, ou choix des relations de voyages les plus intéressantes et les plus instructives depuis le cinquième siècle avant Jésus-Christ jusqu'au dix-neuvième siècle, avec biographies, notes et indications iconographiques*. 4 vols. Paris: n.d.

Chateaubriand, François-René de. (1811) 1968. *Itinéraire de Paris à Jérusalem*. Paris: Garnier-Flammarion.

———. 1836. 'Shakespeare'. *Revue de deux mondes* 5: 10–12.

———. (1847) 1992. *Mémoires d'outre tombe*. 4 vols. Paris: Larousse.

———. 1852. *Œuvres complètes*. Paris: Dufour.

Chevalier, Michel M. 1851. *L'Exposition universelle de Londres considérées sous les rapports philosophique, technique, commercial et administratif au point de vue français*. Paris: Librairie Scientifique Industrielle.

Choay, Françoise. 1965. *L'Urbanisme, utopies et réalités: une anthologie*. Paris: Seuil.

———. 1969. 'Urbanism and Semiology'. In *Meaning in Architecture*, edited by C. Jencks and G. Baird, 27–37. London: Barrie and Rockliff.

City of London Corporation. 1944. *Report on the Preliminary Draft Proposals for Post-War Reconstruction in the City of London*. London: City of London Corporation.

Clarke, Steve, ed. 1999. *Travel Writing and Empire: Postcolonial Theory in Transit*. London: Zed Books.

———. 2000. '"Bang at its Moral Centre": Ideologies of Genre in Butor, Fussell, and Raban'. *Studies in Travel Writing* 4: 106–125.

Clark, Timothy James. 1985. *The Painting of Modern Life: Paris in the Art of Manet and His Followers*. London: Thames and Hudson.

Clifford, James, and George E. Marcus, eds. 1986. *Writing Culture: The Poetics and Politics of Ethnography*. London: University of California Press.

Clifford, James. 1986. 'On Ethnographic Allegory'. In *Writing Culture: The Poetics and Politics of Ethnography*, edited by J. Clifford and G. E. Marcus, 98–121. London: University of California Press.

———. 1988. *The Predicament of Culture: Twentieth-Century Ethnography, Literature and Art*. Cambridge, MA: Harvard University Press.

Cobbett, William. 1822. 'Rural Rides'. *Cobbett's Weekly Register*. 5 January.

Cocker, Mark. 1992. *Loneliness and Time: British Travel Writing in the 20th Century*. New York: Pantheon Books.

Cohen, Erik. 1972. 'Towards a Sociology of International Tourism'. *Social Research*, 39: 164–82.

———. 1979. 'A Phenomenology of Tourist Experiences'. *Sociology* 13 (2): 179–201.

———. 1988. 'Authenticity and Commoditization in Tourism'. *Annals of Tourism Research* 15 (3): 371–86.

Cole, George, and Douglas Howard. 1956. *The Post-War Condition of Britain*. London: Routledge & Keegan.

Coleman, Nathaniel. 2005. *Utopias and Architecture*. London: Routledge.

Conrad, Joseph. (1902) 1973. *Heart of Darkness*. London: Penguin Books.

Conrad, Peter. (1998) 1999. *Modern Times, Modern Places*. London: Thames & Hudson.

Conrads, Ulrich, and Hans G. Sperlich, Hans G. (1960) 1963. *Fantastic Architecture*. Translated by C. Crasemann Collins and G. R. Collins. London: The Architectural Press.

Coppock, J.T. (1976) 2011. 'The Changing Face of England: 1850 – circa 1900'. In *A New Historical Geography of England after 1600*, edited by H.C. Darby, 295–373. Cambridge: Cambridge University Press.

Cormack, Bill. 1998. *A History of Holidays 1812–1990*. London: Routledge.

Corrigan, Philip and Derek Sayer. 1985. *The Great Arch: English State Formation as Cultural Revolution*. Oxford: Blackwell.

Cosgrove, Denis and Stephen Daniels, eds. 1988. *The Iconography of Landscape: Essays on the Symbolic Representation, Design and Use of Past Environments*. Cambridge: Cambridge University Press.

Coulter, Gerry. 2008. 'Baudrillard and Hölderlin and the Poetic Resolution of the World'. *Nebula* 5 (4): 146.

Cox, Edward Godfrey. 1935. *A Reference Guide to the Literature of Travel*. Seattle: University of Washington Publications in Language and Literature.

Craik, Jennifer. 1991. *Resorting to Tourism: Cultural Policies for Tourist Development in Australia*. North Sydney: Allen & Unwin.

———. 1997. 'The Culture of Tourism'. In *Touring Cultures: Transformations of Travel and Theory*, edited by C. Rojek and J. Urry, 1–19. London: Routledge.

Crang, Mike. 1996. 'Magic Kingdom or a Quixotic Quest for Authenticity?' *Annals of Tourism Research* 23 (2): 415–31.

Cresswell, Tim. 2004. *Place: A Short Introduction*. London: Wiley-Blackwell.

———. 2006. *On the Move: Mobility in the Modern Western World*. London: Routledge.

Crick, Malcolm. 1989. 'Representations of International Tourism in the Social Sciences: Sun, Sex, Sights, Savings and Servility'. *Annual Review of Anthropology* 18: 307–44.

Cronin, Michael. 2000. *Across the Lines: Travel, Language, Translation*. Cork: Cork University Press.

———. 2012. *The Expanding World: Towards a Politics of Microspection*. Winchester: Zero Books.

Culler, Jonathan. 1981. 'Semiotics of Tourism'. *American Journal of Semiotics* 1: 127–40.

———. 1990. *Framing the Sign: Criticism and Its Institutions*. Norman: University of Oklahoma Press.

Cunningham, Peter. 1863. *Handbook of London As It Is*. London: John Murray.

Curtis, William J. R. (1982) 2005. *Modern Architecture since 1900*. London: Phaidon.

Custine, Marquis de. (1843) 1975. *Lettres de Russie: La Russie en 1839*. Preface by P. Nora. Paris: Gallimard.

Damisch, Hubert. 1996. *Skyline: la ville narcisse*. Paris: Seuil.

Daniels, Stephen, and Denis Cosgrove. 1988. 'Introduction: Iconography and Landscape'. In *The Iconography of Landscape: Essays on the Symbolic Representation, Design and Use of Past Environments*, edited by D. Cosgrove and S. Daniels, 1–10. Cambridge: Cambridge University Press.

Davidson, Robyn, ed. 2000. *The Picador Book of Journeys*. Basingstoke: Macmillan.

Davin, Anna. 1996. *Growing up Poor – Home, School and Street in London: 1870–1914*. London: Rivers Oram Press.

Davis, Mike. (1990) 1992. *City of Quartz: Excavating the Future in Los Angeles*. London: Vintage.

Debray, Régis. 1997. 'Trace, forme ou message'. *Les Cahiers de la médiologie* 7, *La Confusion des monuments*. Paris: Gallimard: 27–44.

Delessert, Édouard. (1853) 1857. *Voyage aux villes maudites. Sodome. Gomorrhe. Seboim. Adama. Zoar. Suivi de notes scientifiques et d'une carte par M. F. de Saulcy*. Paris: Librarie nouvelle.

Deleuze, Gilles. 1990a. 'Post-scriptum sur les sociétés de contrôle'. Reproduced in *Pourparlers 1972–1990*: 240–245.

———. 1990b. *Pourparlers 1972–1990*. Paris: Minuit.

Deleuze, Gilles, and Félix Guattari. (1972) 1973. *L'Anti-Œdipe: Capitalisme et Schizophrénie*. Paris: Minuit.

———. (1980) 2004. *A Thousand Plateaus: Capitalism and Schizophrenia*. Translated by B. Massumi. London: Continuum.

———. 1980. *Mille Plateaux: Capitalisme et schizophrénie*. Paris: Minuit.

Depardon, Raymond. 2000. *Errance* Paris: Seuil.

Derrida, Jacques. 1974. *Glas*. Paris: Galilée.

Descartes, René. (1637) 1966. *Discours de la méthode*. Paris: Flammarion.

Designi, Silvia. 1999. 'Nécessité d'une réflexion sur la correspondance de Vallès'. *Les Amis de Jules Vallès – Vallès en toutes lettres. Correspondance d'exil*. http://pagesperso-orange.fr/jules.valles/exil.html (accessed 6 February 2007).

Dodd, Philip. 1982. *The Art of Travel: Essays on Travel Writing*. London: Cass.

Domosh, Mona. 1996. *Invented Cities: The Creation of Landscape in Nineteenth-Century New York & Boston*. London: Yale University Press.

Donner, Florinda. 1982. *Shabono: A Visit to a Remote and Magical World in the Heart of the South American Jungle*. New York: Delacorte Press.

Doré, Gustave, and Jerrold Blanchard. 1872. *London, a Pilgrimage*. London: Grant.

Douglas, Mary. 1986. *How Institutions Think*. Syracuse: Syracuse University Press.

Douyère-Demeulenaere, Christiane. 2003. *Séverine et Vallès. Le Cri du peuple*. Paris: Éditions Payot.

Drumond, Arianna. 2103. 'Contextualizing Authenticity in Tourism: An Examination of Postmodern Tourism Theory.' *Cultural Hybridity: Remix and Dialogic Culture* (blog), 14 December, https://blogs.commons.georgetown.edu/cctp-725-fall2013/2013/12/14/contextualizing-authenticity-in-tourism-an-examination-of-postmodern-tourism-theory/.

Dubeck, Paula, and Zane L. Miller. 1980. *Urban Professionals and the Future of the Metropolis*. London: Kennikat Press.

———. 1980. 'The Contemporary Metropolitan Crisis'. In *Urban Professionals and the Future of the Metropolis*, edited by P. Dubeck and Z. L. Miller, 117–22. London: Kennikat Press.

Du Bellay, Joachim. (1558) 1994. *Les Antiquités de Rome/Les Regrets*. Preface by F. Joukovsky. Paris: Flammarion.

Dubey, Madhu. 2003. *Signs and Cities: Black Literary Postmodernism*. Chicago: University of Chicago Press.

Duhamel, Georges. 1930. *Scènes de la vie future*. Paris: Mercure de France.

Dumas, Alexandre. 1857. *Causeries*. 2 vols. Leipzig: A. Durr.

Duncan, Carol, and Alan Wallach. 1980. 'The Universal Survey Museum'. *Art History* 3: 448–69.

Dutton, Denis. 1990. 'Jean Baudrillard'. *Philosophy and Literature* 14: 234–38.

———. 2003. 'Authenticity in Art'. In *The Oxford Handbook of Aesthetics*, edited by J. Levinson, 258–74. Oxford: Oxford University Press.

Dyos, Harold J. 1973. *Victorian Suburb: A Study of the Growth of Camberwell*. Leicester: Leicester University Press.

———. 1982. 'The Slums of Victorian London'. In *Exploring the Urban Past: Essays in Urban History*, edited by D. Cannadine and D. Reeder, 129–53. Cambridge: Cambridge University Press.

———, and Michael Wolff, eds. (1973) 1999. *The Victorian City: Images and Realities*. 2 vols. London: Routledge.

Eagleton, Terry. 1990. *The Ideology of the Aesthetic*. Oxford: Blackwell.

———. 1996. *The Illusions of Postmodernism*. Oxford: Blackwell.

Eco, Umberto. 1986. *Faith in Fakes: Travels in Hyperreality*. Translated by W. Weaver. London: Secker & Warburg.

Edwards, Catherine. 1996. *Writing Rome: Textual Approaches to the City*. Cambridge: Cambridge University Press.

Elias, Norbert. 1978. *The Civilizing Process*. 2 vols. I. *The History of Manners*. Oxford: Blackwell.

———. 1982. *The Civilizing Process*, 2 vols. II. *State Formation and Civilization*. Oxford: Blackwell.

Elsner, Jas, and Joan-Pau Rubiés. 1999. *Voyages and Visions: Towards a Cultural History of Travel*. London: Reatkion.

Énault, Louis. (1859) *Écosse, Irlande: Voyage pittoresque*. Paris: Morizot.

———. (1875) 1984. *Londres et les Londoniens en 1875*. Paris: Sacelp.

Engels, Friedrich. (1844) 1993. *The Condition of the Working Classes in England*. Oxford: Oxford University Press.

Esposito, Roberto. 2009. *Communitas: The Origin and Destiny of Community*. Translated by T. Campbell. Stanford, CA: Stanford University Press.

Esteban, Claude. 1985. *Traces, figures, traversées: essais sur la peinture contemporaine*. Paris: Galilée.

Exposition internationale. 1851. *Guide de l'étranger à Londres: comprenant une notice sommaire sur le palais de cristal, sa construction… avec un plan de Londres / Exposition universelle de 1851*. Havre: Brindeau.

Fainstein, Susan S., and Dennis R. Judd, eds. 1999. *The Tourist City*. London: Yale University Press.

Febvre, Lucien, and Henri-Jean Martin. 1958. *L'Apparition du Livre*. Paris: Albin.

Feifer, Maxine, and Michel Albin. 1985. *Going Places: The Ways of the Tourist from Imperial Rome to the Present Day*. London: Macmillan.

Feldman, David, and Gareth Stedman Jones, eds. 1989. *Metropolis-London: Histories and Representations since 1800*. London: Routledge.

Ferguson, Priscilla Parkhurst. 1994. *Paris as Revolution: Writing in the 19th Century City*. Berkeley: University of California Press.

Fijalkow, Yankel. 2007. *Sociologie des villes*. Paris: La Découverte.

Findlen, Paula. 1989. 'The Museum: Its Classical Etymology and Renaissance Genealogy'. *Journal of the History of Collections* 1: 59–78.

Fine, David M. 1977. *The City, the Immigrant and American Fiction, 1880–1920*. London: Scarecrow Press.

———. 2000. *Imagining Los Angeles: A City in Fiction*. Albuquerque: University of New Mexico Press.

Flanders, Judith. 2007. *Consuming Passions: Leisure and Pleasure in Victorian Britain*. London: Harper Perennial.

Forsdick, Charles. 2005. *Travel in Twentieth-Century French and Francophone Cultures: The Persistence of Diversity*. Oxford: Oxford University Press.

Forsdick, Charles, Feroza Basu, and Siobhán Shilton. 2006. *New Approaches to Twentieth-Century Travel Literature in French: Genre, History, Theory. Travel Writing Across the Disciplines.* New York: Peter Lang.

Forsdick, Charles, and Susan Morson. 2000. *Reading Diversity / Lectures du divers.* Glasgow: University of Glasgow French and German Publications.

Forsdick, Charles, and David Murphy, eds. 2003. *Francophone Postcolonial Studies: A Critical Introduction.* London: Arnold.

———. 2009. *Postcolonial Thought in the French-speaking World.* Liverpool: Liverpool University Press.

Foster, Shirley. 1990. *Across New Worlds: Nineteenth-Century Women Travelers and their Writings.* London: Harvester Wheatsheaf.

Foucault, Michel. 1963. *Naissance de la clinique: une archéologie du regard medical.* Paris: Presses universitaires de France.

———. 1966. *Les Mots et les choses: une archéologie des sciences humaines.* Paris: Gallimard.

———. (1967) 2001. 'Des espaces autres'. In *Dits et écrits*, edited by D. Defert and F. Ewald, 2 vols. II: 1571–81. Paris: Gallimard.

———. 1975. *Surveiller et punir: naissance de la prison.* Paris: Gallimard.

———. 1976. *Histoire de la sexualité*, 3 vols. I. *La Volonté de savoir.* Paris: Gallimard.

———. (1982) 2001. 'Espace, savoir et pouvoir'. In *Dits et écrits*, edited by D. Defert and F. Ewald, 2 vols. II: 1089–104. Paris: Gallimard.

———. 2001. *Dits et écrits 1954–1988.* Edited by D. Defert and F. Ewald. 2 vols. Paris: Gallimard.

Fowler, Corinne. 2007. *Chasing Tales: Travel Writing, Journalism and the History of Ideas about Afghanistan.* Amsterdam: Rodopi.

Freitag, Sabine, ed. 2003. *Exile from European Revolutions: Refugees in Mid-Victorian England.* Oxford: Berghahn Books.

French, Dorothea R. 1992. 'Journeys to the Centre of the Earth: Medieval and Renaissance Pilgrimages to Mount Calvary'. In *Journeys toward God: pilgrimage and crusade*, edited by B. N. Sargent-Baur, 61–64. Kalmazoo, MI: Medieval Institute Publications, Western Michigan University.

French, R. A. and Ian Frederick Edwin Hamilton. 1979. *The Socialist City: Spatial Structure and Urban Policy.* New York: John Wiley.

Frey, Jean-Pierre. 2000. 'La Ville des architectes et des urbanistes'. In *La Ville et l'urbain: l'état de savoirs*, edited by T. Paquot, M. Lussault and S. Body-Gendrot, 106–14. Paris: La Découverte.

Fried, Albert, and Richard E. Elman, eds. 1969. *Charles Booth's London: A Portrait of the Poor at the Turn of the Century, Drawn from His 'Life and Labour of the People in London'.* London: Hutchinson.

Friedland, Roger, and Deirdre Boden, eds. 1994. *Now / Here: Time, Space and Modernity.* Berkeley: University of California Press.

Friedman, Jonathan. 1995. 'The Past in the Future: History and the Politics of Identity. *American Anthropologist* 94 (4): 837–859.

Frisby, David. 2001. *Cityscapes of Modernity.* Cambridge: Polity.

Frisby, David, and Mike Featherstone, eds. (1997) 2006. *Simmel on Culture: Selected Writings.* London: Sage.

Fuchs, Rachel G. 2005. *Gender and Poverty in Nineteenth-Century Europe.* Cambridge: Cambridge University Press.

Furlough, Ellen. (1998). 'Making Mass Vacations: Tourism and Consumer Culture in France, 1930s to 1970s'. *Comparative Studies in Society and History* 40 (2): 247–86.

Fussell, Paul. 1980. *Abroad: British Literary Travelling Between the Wars.* New York: Oxford University Press.

———, ed. 1987. *The Norton Anthology of Travel.* New York: Norton.

Gallie, Duncan. 1983. *Social Inequality and Class Radicalism in France and Britain.* Cambridge: Cambridge University Press.

Gallingani, Daniela. 2002.'La Ville et ses auteurs: un paradigme seculaire de l'illusion et de la découverte de la modernité entre XVIII et XXe siècles'. In *Le Travail des Lumières*, edited by C. Jacot-Grapa, 675–89. Paris: Champion.

Gallo, Max. 1988. *Jules Vallès ou la révolte d'une vie*. Paris: Robert Laffont.

Galton, Francis. (1872) 2000. *The Art of Travel or Shifts and Contrivances Available in Wild Countries*. London: Phoenix Press.

Gandelsonas, Mario, and David Morton. 1980. 'On Reading Architecture'. In edited by G. Broadbent, R. Bent and C. Jencks, 243–73.

Gane, Mike. 1991. *Baudrillard: Critical and Fatal Theory*. London: Routledge.

Garsten, Christina, and Monica Lindh de Montoya. 2008. *Transparency in a New Global Order: Unveiling Organizational Visions*. Cheltenham: Edward Elgar.

Gates, Robert Allan. 1987. *The New York Vision: Interpretations of New York City in the American Novel*. Lanham, Maryland: University Press of America.

Gauthier, Maximilien. 1945. 'Le Candidat de la misère/Les Députés des fusillés'. *Gavroche* 39 (May). http://avocatdespauvres.over-blog.com/article-le-candidat-de-la-misere-le-depute-des-fusilles-souvenirs-sur-jules-valles-par-maximilien-gauthier-gavroche-numero-39-mai-1945–59505111.html> (accessed 2 November 2014).

Gautier, Théophile. 1852. *Caprices et zigzags*. Paris: Victor Lecou.

Gavard, Charles. 1895. *Un diplomate à Londres: lettres et notes, 1871–1877*. Paris: Plon Nourrie et cie.

Geertz, Clifford. 1988. *Works and Lives: The Anthropologist as Author*. Stanford: Stanford University Press.

Gellner, Ernest. 1964. *Thought and Change*. London: Weidenfield and Nicholson.

General Register Office. (1955) 1956. *Census 1951 of England and Wales*. London: H.M. Stationary Office.

Genette, Gérard. 1983. *Nouveau discours du récit*. Paris: Seuil.

———. 1986. 'Introduction à l'architexte'. In *Théorie des genres*, Gérard Genette, Hans Robert Jauss, Jean-Marie Schaeffer, Robert Scholes, Wolf Dieter Stempel and Karl Viëtor, 89–159. Paris: Seuil.

Genette, Gérard, Hans Robert Jauss, Jean-Marie Schaeffer, Robert Scholes, Wolf Dieter Stempel, and Karl Viëtor. 1986. *Théorie des genres*. Paris: Seuil.

Giddens, Anthony. 1991. *Modernity and Self-Identity*. Cambridge: Polity.

Giedion, Sigfried. 1967. *Space, Time and Architecture: The Growth of a New Tradition*. Cambridge, MA: Harvard University Press.

Giedion, Sigfried, Fernand Léger, and José Luis Sert. (1943) 1993. 'Nine Points on Monumentality'. In *Architecture Culture 1943–1968: A Documentary Anthology*, edited by Joan Ockman, 29–30. New York: Columbia University and Rizzoli International Publications.

Gilmore, Leigh. 1994. *Autobiographics: A Feminist Theory of Women's Self-Representation*. London: Cornell University Press.

Ginzburg, Carlo. (1986) 1990. *Myths, Emblems, Clues*. London: Hutchinson Radius.

Girardet, Herbet. 1999. 'Sustainable Cities: A Contradiction in Terms?' In *The Earthscan Reader in Sustainable Cities*, edited by D. Satterthwaite, 413–25. London: Earthscan Publications.

Gmelch, George, and Walter P. Zenner, eds. 1980. *Urban Life: Readings in Urban Anthropology*. New York: St. Martin's Press.

Goffman, Erving. 1959. *The Presentation of Self in Everyday Life*, Garden City, NY: Doubleday.

———. 1963. *Behavior in Public Places: Notes on the Social Organization of Gatherings*. New York: Free Press.

———. 1971. *Relations in Public: Microstudies of the Public* Order. New York: Basic Books.

Goldberg, Jacob J. 1995. 'Corporate Capital and the Techniques of Modernity: Problems in the Mass Production of Space, Image and Experience. *Journal of Architectural Education* 48 (4): 227–39.

Golomb, Jacob. 1995. *In Search of Authenticity: From Kierkegaard to Camus*. London: Routledge.

Gomes, Plinio Freire. 2005. 'Blank Variations: Travel Literature, Mapmaking, and the Experience of the Unknown in the New World'. In *Unravelling Civilization: European Travel and Travel Writing*, edited by H. Schulz-Forberg, 89–105. Oxford: Peter Lang.

Gottdiener, Mark, and Alexandros Ph. Lagopoulos, eds. 1986. *The City and the Sign: An Introduction to Urban Semiotics*. New York: Columbia University Press.

Grafmeyer, Yves. 1994. *Sociologie urbaine*. Paris: Nathan.

Graulund, Rune. 2006. 'Travelling the Desert: Desert Travel Writing as Indicator Species'. *Studies in Travel Writing* 10 (2): 141–59.

Green, David R. 1991. 'The Metropolitan Economy: Continuity and Change 1800–1939'. In edited by K. Hoggart and D. R. Green, 8–33.

Green, Nancy L. 2002. 'The Comparative Gaze: Travellers in France before the Era of Mass Tourism'. *French Historical Studies* 25 (3): 423–40.

Green, Nicholas. 1990. *The Spectacle of Nature: Landscape and Bourgeois Culture in Nineteenth-Century France*. Manchester: Manchester University Press.

Gregory, Alexis. 1998. *The Golden Age of Travel, 1880–1939*. London: Cassel.

Grimshaw, Jean. 1993. 'Practices and Freedom'. In *Up against Foucault: Explorations of some tensions Between Foucault and Feminism*, edited by C. Ramazanoglu, 51–72. London: Routledge.

Gropius, Walter. (1935) 1996. *The New Architecture and the Bauhaus*. Translated by P. Morton Shand. Cambridge, MA: MIT Press.

Guerolt, Adolphe. 1838. *Lettres sur l'Espagne*. Bruxelles: Société Typographiques Belge.

Gunn, Simon, and Robert J. Morris, eds. 2001. *Identities in Space: Contested Terrains in the Western City since 1850*. Aldershot: Ashgate.

Gustafsson, Lotten. 2000. 'Medieval Selves and Current Communities: Playing with Identity at an Intersection of Rootedness and Mobility'. In *Folklore, Heritage Politics and Ethnic Diversity. A Festschrift for Barbro Klein*, edited by P. Anttonen, A.-L. Siikala, S.R. Mathisen and L. Magnusson, 158–76. Botkyrka: Multicultural Centre.

Gympel, Jan. 1999. *The Story of Architecture: From Antiquity to the Present*. Cologne: Könemann.

Hall, Stuart, ed. 1997. *Representation: Cultural Representations and Signifying Practices*. London: Sage.

Halewood, Christopher, and Kevin Hannam. 2001. 'Viking Heritage Tourism: Authenticity and Commodification'. *Annals of Tourism Research* 28 (3): 565–80.

Hamon, Philippe. 1989. *Expositions: littérature et architecture au XIXe siècle*. Paris: José Corti

Hanne, Michael. 1993. *Literature and Travel*. Amsterdam: Rodopi.

Hannerz, Ulf. 1983. *Explorer la ville: éléments d'anthropologie urbaine*. Paris: Minuit.

Harbison, Robert. (1977) 2000. *Eccentric Spaces*. London: MIT Press.

Harding, Desmond. 2002. *Writing the City: Urban Visions and Literary Modernism*. London: Routledge.

Harris, Roy. 1987. *Reading Saussure: A Critical Commentary on the 'Cours de linguistique générale'*. London: Duckworth.

Harrison, Brian. 1971. *Drink and the Victorians: The Temperance Question in England, 1815–1872*. London: Faber & Faber.

Hartig, Irmgard and Alfred Soboul. 1977. *Pour une histoire de l'utopie en France au XVIIIe siècle*. Paris: Société des Études Robespierristes.

Harvey, David. 1985. *Consciousness and the Urban Experience*. Oxford: Blackwell.

———. 1989. *The Urban Experience*. Baltimore: Johns Hopkins University Press.

———. 2006. *Paris: Capital of Modernity*. London: Routledge.

Harvey, Penelope. 1996. *Hybrids of Modernity: Anthropology, the Nation State, and the Universal Exhibition*. London: Routledge.

Hawkes, Nigel. (1990) 1993. *Structures: The Way Things Are Built*. New York: Macmillan.

Healey, Kimberley J. 2003. *The Modernist Traveler: French Detours 1900–1930*. Lincoln: University of Nebraska Press.

Hegel, G. W.F. (1807) 1977. *Phenomenology of Spirit*. Translated by A.V. Miller. Oxford: Oxford University Press.

Heidegger, Martin. (1927) 1962. *Being and Time*. Translated by J. Macquarrie and E. Robinson. Oxford: Oxford University Press.

———. (1971) 2005. 'Building, Dwelling, Thinking'. In *Rethinking Architecture: A Reader in Cultural Theory*, edited by N. Leach, 98–124. London: Routledge.

Hewison, Robert. 1987. *The Heritage Industry: Britain in a Climate of Decline*. London: Metheun.

Hibbert, Christopher. 1987. *The Grand Tour*. London: Thames Metheun.

Highmore, Ben. 2005. *Cityscapes: Cultural Readings in the Material and Symbolic City*. London: Palgrave.

Hobsbawm, Eric. (1962) 1999. *The Age of Revolution: Europe 1789–1848*. London: Abacus.

———. 1989. *The Age of Empire*. London: Abacus.

Hoffenberg, Peter. 2001. *An Empire on Display: English, Indian and Australian Exhibitions from the Crystal Palace to the Great War*. Los Angeles: University of California Press.

Hoggart, Keith, and David R. Green, eds. 1991. *London: A New Metropolitan Geography*. London: Edward Arnold.

Hölderlin, Friedrich Johann. (1803) 1990. 'Patmos'. In *Hölderlin: Poems and Fragments*. Translated by Michael Hamburger. Oxford: Alden.

Holland, Patrick, and Graham Huggan, 2004. 'Varieties of Nostalgia in Contemporary Travel Writing'. In *Perspectives on Travel Writing*, edited by G. Hooper and T. Youngs, 39–52. Aldershot: Ashgate Publishing.

Hollinshead, John. 1862. *Underground London*. London: Groombridge and Sons.

Holloway, Steven W. 2001. 'Biblical Assyria and Other Anxieties in the British Empire'. *Journal of Religion & Society* 3. http://moses.creighton.edu/jrs/2001/2001–12.pdf (accessed 4 November 2014).

Hood, Christopher. 2006. 'Transparency in Historical Perspective'. In *Transparency: The Key to Better Governance?*, edited by C. Hood and D. Heald, 3–23. Oxford: Oxford University Press.

Hooper, Glenn, and Tim Youngs, eds. 2004. *Perspectives on Travel Writing*. Aldershot: Ashgate Publishing.

Hopper, Sarah C. 2002. *To Be A Pilgrim*. Sutton: Sutton Publishing.

Horne, Donald. 1984. *The Great Museum: The Re-Presentation of History*. London: Pluto.

Hseih, Yvonne Y. 1996. *From Occupation to Revolution: China though the Eyes of Loti, Claudel, Segalen and Malraux. 1895–1933*. Birmingham, AL: Summa Publications.

Hudson, Kenneth. 1975. *A Social History of Museums: What the Visitors Thought*. London: Macmillan.

Hugo, Charles. 1875. *Les Hommes de l'exil*. Paris: A. Lemerre.

Hulme, Peter, and Tim Youngs, eds. 2002. *The Cambridge Companion to Travel Writing*. Cambridge: Cambridge University Press.

Humphreys, Anne. 2002. 'Knowing the Victorian City: Writing and Representation'. *Victorian Literature and Culture* 30 (2): 601–12.

Hundertwasser, Friedensreich. 1999. *KunstHausWien*. London: Taschen.

Hunt, Lynn. 1994. 'Male Virtue and Republican Motherhood'. In *The French Revolution and the Creation of Modern Political Culture*, vol. 4 *The Terror*, edited by K. M. Baker, 195–210. Bingley: Emerald.

Huyssen, Andreas. 2007. 'Modernist Miniatures: Literary Snapshots of Urban Spaces'. *Publications of the Modern Language Association of America* 122 (1): 27–42.

Inwood, Stephen. 2005. *City of Cities: The Birth of Modern London*. London: Macmillan.

Islam, Syed Manzurul. 1996. *The Ethics of Travel: from Marco Polo to Kafka*. Manchester: Manchester University Press.

Jacobs, Jane. (1961) 1962. *The Death and Life of Great American Cities*. London: Jonathan Cape.

Jacot-Grapa, Caroline, ed. 2002. *Le Travail des Lumières*. Paris: Champion.

Jameson, Fredric. 1991. *Postmodernism, or, The Cultural Logic of Late Capitalism*. London: Verso.

Janin, Jules. 1836. *Le Chemin de traverse*. Vol. 1. Brussels: J.P. Méline.

Jarvis, Robin. 1997. *Romantic Writing and Pedestrian Travel*. London: Macmillan.

Jauss, Hans Robert. (1970) 1986. 'Littérature médiévale et théorie des genres'. In *Théorie des genres*, Gérard Genette, Hans Robert Jauss, Jean-Marie Schaeffer, Robert Scholes, Wolf Dieter Stempel and Karl Viëtor, 37–76. Paris: Seuil.

Jein, Gillian. 2014. 'From Legislative to Interpretive Modes of Travel: Space, Ethics and Literary Form in Baudrillard's *America*'. In *Travel and Ethics: Theory and Practice*, edited by C. Forsdick, C. Fowler and L. Kostova, 31–51. London: Routledge.

Jencks, Charles. 1986. *What is Post-Modernism?* London: St. Martin's Press.

———. (1995) 1997. *The Architecture of the Jumping Universe. A Polemic: How Complexity Science is Changing Architecture and Culture*. Chichester: Academy Editions.

———. 2002. *The New Paradigm in Architecture: The Language of Postmodernism*. London: Yale University Press.

Jeudy, Henri-Pierre. 2003. *Critique de l'esthétique urbain*. Paris: Sens & Tonka.

Johnson, James, and Colin Pooley, eds. 1982. *The Structure of Nineteenth-Century Cities*. London: Croom Helm.

Johnson, Richard. 1970. 'Education Policy and Social Control in Early Victorian England'. *Past and Present* 49: 96–119.

Jokinen, Eeva and Soile Veijola. 1997. 'The Disorientated Tourist: The figuration of the tourist in contemporary cultural critique'. In *Touring Cultures: Transformations of Travel and Theory*, edited by C. Rojek and J. Urry, 23–51. London: Routledge.

Jones, Colin. (2004) 2006. *Paris: Biography of a City*. London: Penguin Books.

Jones, Donna V. 2007. 'The Prison House of Modernism: Colonial Space and the Construction of the Primitive at the 1931 Paris Colonial Exhibition'. *Modernism/Modernity* 14 (1): 55–69.

Jordonova, Ludmilla. 1989. 'Objects of Knowledge: A Historical Perspective on the Museum'. In *The New Museology*, edited by P. Vergo, 21–40. London: Reatkin.

Jourdan, Annie. 1999. 'Robespierre and Revolutionary Heroism'. In *Robespierre*, edited by C. Haydon and W. Doyle, 54–74. Cambridge: Cambridge University Press.

Joyce, James. (1922) 1994. *Ulysses* London: Flamingo.

Jupilles, Fernand de. 1886. *La Moderne Babylone: Londres et les Anglais*. Paris: La Librairie Illustrée.

Kafka, Franz. (1946) 1962. *America*. Translated by E. Muir. New York: New Directions.

Kaplan, Caren. 1996. *Questions of Travel: Postmodern Discourses of Displacement*. Durham, NC: Duke University Press.

Kearns, Gerry, and Chris Philo, eds. 1993. *Selling Places: The City as Cultural Capital, Past and Present*. Oxford: Pergamon.

Keating, P. J. (1973) 1999. 'Fact and Fiction in the East End'. In *The Victorian City: Images and Realities*, edited by H. J. Dyos and M. Wolff, 2 vols. I: 585–602. London: Routledge.

Keith, Alexander. 1832. *Evidence of the Truth of the Christian Religion, Derived from the Literal fulfillment of Prophecy; Particularly as illustrated by the History of the Jews, and by the Discoveries of Recent Travellers*. New York: J.&J. Harper.

Keith, Michael, and Pile, Steve. 1993. *Place and the Politics of Identity*. London: Routledge.

Kelley, Wyn. 1996. *Melville's City: Literary and Urban Form in Nineteenth-Century New York*. Cambridge: Cambridge University Press.

Kellner, Douglas. 1989. *Jean Baudrillard: From Marxism to Postmodernism and Beyond*. Stanford, CA: Stanford University Press.

Kerouac, Jack. (1955) 1991. *On the Road*. London: Penguin.

Kierkegaard, Soren. 1960. *The Diary of Soren Kierkegaard*. Edited by P. Rohde. New York: Philosophical Library.

Kirshenblatt-Gimblett, Barbara. 1998. *Destination Culture: Tourism, Museums and Heritage*. Berkeley: University of California Press.

Klein, Norman M. 1997. *The History of Forgetting: Los Angeles and the Erasure of Memory*. London: Verso.

Knight, Diana. 1997. *Barthes and Utopia: Space, Travel, Writing*. Oxford: Clarendon Press.

Knopper, Françoise, and Jean–Marie Paul. 2000. *L'Homme et la cité allemande au XXe siècle: souffrance et résistance*. Nancy: Presses universitaires de Nancy.

Knox, Paul L., ed. 1988. *The Design Professions and the Built Environment*. London: Croom Helm.

Koolhaas, Rem. (1978) 1994. *Delirious New York: A Retroactive Manifesto for Manhattan*. New York: Monacelli Press.

Koolhaas, Rem, and Bruce Mau. 1995. *S, M, L, XL: Office for Metropolitan Architecture*. New York: Monacelli Press.

Kopp, Anatole. 1967. *Ville et révolution: architectures et urbanisme soviétiques des années vingt*. Paris: Éditions Anthropos.

Köstlin, Konrad. 1997. 'The Passion for the Whole: Interpreted modernity or modernity as interpretation'. *The Journal of American Folklore* 110 (437): 260–76.

Kostof, Spiro. 2001. *The City Shaped: Urban Patterns and Meanings through History*. London: Thames & Hudson.

———. 2004. *The City Assembled: The Elements of Urban Form through History*. London: Thames & Hudson.

Krier, Rob. 1979. *Urban Space*. Translated by C. Czechowski and G. Black. London: Academy Editions.

Kroes, Rob. 1999. 'America and the European Sense of History'. *Journal of American History* 86 (3): 1135–55.

Kuehn, Julia, and Paul Smethurst, eds. 2008. *Travel Writing, Form, and Empire: The Poetics and Politics of Mobility*. London: Routledge.

Kwinter, Sanford. 2001. *Architectures of Time: Toward a Theory of the Event in Modernist Culture*. London: MIT Press.

Laborit, Henri. 1971. *L'Homme et la ville*. Paris: Flammarion.

Laboulaye, Charles. 1856. *Essai sur l'art industriel: comprenant l'étude des produits les plus célèbres de l'industrie, à toutes les époques, et des oeuvres les plus remarquées à l'Exposition universelle de Londres, en 1851, et à l'Exposition de Paris, en 1855*. Paris: Dictionnaire des arts et manufactures.

Lackey, Kris. 1997. *Roadframes: The American Highway Narrative*. Lincoln: University of Nebraska Press.

Lamizet, Bernard. 2002. *Le Sens de la ville*. Paris: L'Harmattan.

Lang, Michael H. 1999. *Designing Utopia: John Ruskin's Urban Vision of Britain and America*. London: Black Rose.

La Pradelle, Michèle de. 2000. 'La ville des anthropologues'. In *La Ville et l'urbain: l'état de savoirs*, edited by T. Paquot, M. Lussault and S. Body-Gendrot, 45–52. Paris: La Découverte.

Lash, Scott. 1990. *Sociology of Postmodernism*. London: Routledge.

Lash, Scott, and Jonathan Friedman, eds. 1992. *Modernity and Identity*. Oxford: Blackwell.

Lash, Scott, and John Urry. 1994. *Economies of Signs and Space*. London: Sage.

Lassels, Richard. 1670. *An Italian Voyage, Or, a Compleat Journey through Italy*. London: John Starkey.

Laudéra, Jean. 1853. L'exposition universelle à Londres en 1851: poème…; suivi de: Le palais de cristal: chanson. Calais: E. Leleux et soeur.

Lauzanne, Alain. 1997. 'Jules Vallès à Londres, ou les mémoires d'un exilé'. *Arob@se*, 2. http://www.liane.net/arobase (accessed 22 August 2009).

Leach, Neil, ed. (1997) 2005. *Rethinking Architecture: A Reader in Cultural Theory*. London: Routledge.

Leask, Nigel. 2002. *Curiosity and the Aesthetics of Travel Writing, 1770–1840*, Oxford: Oxford University Press.

Le Breton, David. 2000. *Éloge de la marche*. Paris: Seuil.

Le Corbusier. 1925. *Urbanisme*. Paris: Crès.

———. (1943) 1996. *Manière de penser l'urbanisme*. Paris: Gonthier.

Lees, Lynn. (1973) 1999. 'Metropolitan Types: London and Paris Compared'. In *The Victorian City: Images and Realities*, edited by J. Dyos and M. Wolff, 2 vols. I: 413–28. London: Routledge.

Lefebvre, Henri. (1968) 2003. *Right to the City*. In *Writings on Cities*. Translated and edited by E. Kofman and E. Lebas, 63–181. Oxford: Blackwell.

———. 1972. *Le Droit à la ville*. 2 vols. Paris: Éditions Anthropos.

———. (1974) 1991. *The Production of Space*. Translated by D. Nicholson Smith. London: Basil Blackwell.

————. (1974) 2000. *La Production de l'espace*. Paris: Éditions Anthropos.

Le Goff, Jacques. (1977) 1988. *Histoire et mémoire*. Paris: Gallimard.

Legrand, Ignace. 1944. *Nos amis les Anglais*. London: Commodore Press.

Lehan, Richard. 1998. *The City in Literature: An Intellectual and Cultural History*. London: University College Press.

Leith, James A. 1991. *Space and Revolution: Projects for Monuments, Squares and Public Buildings in France, 1789–1799*. Montreal: Mc Gill-Queen's University Press.

Lennon, John, and Malcolm Foley. 2000. *Dark Tourism: The Attraction of Death and Disaster*. London: Continuum.

Le Palais de cristal. Ed. 1851. *Le Palais de cristal: journal illustré de l'exposition de 1851*. Paris: Le Palais de cristal.

Lepoutre, David. 1997. *Cœur de banlieue. Codes, rites et langages*. Paris: Odile Jacob.

Lepschy, Giulio C. 1970. *A Survey of Structural Linguistics*. London: Faber and Faber.

Leroy, Alfred. 1942. *Madame du Barry*. Paris: Le Club du livre selectionné.

————. 1946. *Aux bords de la Tamise*. Paris: Julliard.

————. 1965. *Histoire de la civilisation anglaise*. Paris: Didier.

Lévi-Strauss, Claude. (1958) 1996. *Anthropologie structurale*. Paris: Plon.

Levinas, Emmanuel. (1974) 1991. *Autrement qu'être ou au-delà de l'essence*. London: Kluwer Academic Publishers.

Ley, David, and Kris Olds. 1988. 'Landscape as Spectacle: World's Fairs and the Culture of Heroic Consumption'. *Environment and Planning D: Society and Space* 6: 191–212.

Lidchi, Henrietta. 1997. 'The Spectacle of the "Other"'. In *Representation: Cultural Representations and Signifying Practices*, edited by S. Hall. London: Sage: 151–222.

Liggett, Helen, and David C. Perry, eds. 1995. *Spatial Practices: Critical Explorations in Social/Spatial Theory*. London: Sage Publications.

Lionnet, Françoise. 2001.'Des clichés et des villes, entre Paris et Los Angeles'. *Esprit créateur* 41 (3): 3–8.

Lippmann, Walter. 1922. *Public Opinion*. New York: Harcourt Brace.

Locke, John. (1690) 2008. *An Essay Concerning Human Understanding*. Abridged with an introduction and notes by P. Phemister. Oxford: Oxford University Press.

Lofland, Lyn H. 1985. *A World of Strangers: Order and Action in Urban Public Space*. Prospect Heights, IL: Waveland Press.

Lumley, Robert. 1988. *The Museum Time-Machine: Putting Cultures on Display*. London: Routledge.

Lussault, Michel. 2000. 'La Ville des géographes'. In *La Ville et l'urbain: l'état de savoirs*, edited by Thierry Paquot, Michel Lussault and S. Body-Gendrot, 21–35. Paris: La Découverte.

Lynch, Kevin. 1960. *The Image of the City*. London: MIT Press.

————. 1981. *A Theory of Good City Form*. London: MIT Press.

Lynch, Patricia A., Joachim Fischer and Brian Coates. 2006. *Back to the Present, Forward to the Past: Irish Writing and History since 1798*. 2 vols. Amsterdam: Rodopi.

Lyotard, Jean-François. (1979) 1984. *The Postmodern Condition: A Report on Knowledge*. Translated by G. Bennington and B. Massumi. Foreword by Fredric Jameson. Manchester: Manchester University Press.

————. 1987. 'Re-writing Modernity'. *SubStance* 16 (3.54): 3–9.

————. 1998. '"Domus" et la mégapole'. *Po&sie* 44: 93–102.

MacCannell, Dean. 1973. 'Staged Authenticity: Arrangements of Social Space in Tourist Settings'. *American Journal of Sociology* 79 (3): 589–603.

————. 1976. *The Tourist: A New Theory of the Leisure Class*. London: Macmillan.

————. 2001. 'Tourist Agency'. *Tourist Studies* 1 (1): 23–37.

Macinardi, Patricia. 1985. 'The Political Origins of Modernism'. *Art Journal* 45 (1): 11–17

Madsen, Peter, and Richard Plunz. 2002. *The Urban Lifeworld: Formation, Perception, Representation*. London: Routledge.

Maillart, Ella R. 1991. *La Voie cruelle: deux formes, une Ford vers l'Afghanistan*. Paris: Éditions Payot.

Maille, Françoise. 2007. 'La Ville et l'industrie. Quelques aspects de Londres au milieu du XIX siècle'. *Cercles*, 17: 140–55.

Malcomson, Scott L. 1985. 'The Pure Land beyond the Seas: Barthes, Birch and the Uses of Japan'. *Screen*, 26 (3–4): 23–33.

Malinowski, Bronislaw. 1961. *Argonauts of the Western Pacific*. New York: E.P. Dutton.

Malthus, Thomas Robert. 1803. *An Essay on the Principle of Population, or a View of its Past and Present Effects on Human Happiness*. 2 vols. London: J. Johnson.

Mannheim, Karl. 1956. *Idéologie et utopie* Translated by P. Rollet. Paris: Éditions Marcel Rivière.

Maranhão, Tullio, ed. 1990. *The Interpretation of Dialogue*. Chicago, IL: University of Chicago Press.

Marin, Louis. 1973. *Utopiques: jeux d'espaces*. Paris: Minuit.

Marshall, Alfred. 1884. 'The Housing of the London Poor – Where to House Them'. *Contemporary Review*, 45: 226–32.

Martin, Sylvia. 2005. *Futurism*. London: Taschen.

Marx, Karl, and Friedrich Engels. (1848) 1967. *The Communist Manifesto*. Introduction by A. J. P. Taylor. Harmondsworth: Penguin.

Massey, Doreen. 2005. *For Space*. London: Sage.

Mathias, Peter. 1969. *The First Industrial Nation, an Economic History of Britain*. London: Metheun.

Mattéi, Jean-François. 1999. *La Barbarie intérieure: essai sur l'immonde moderne*. Paris: Presses Universitaires de France.

Mayhew, Henry, and Binny, John. 1862. *The Criminal Prisons of London and Scenes of Prison Life*. London: Griffin, Bohn.

McClung, William A. 1984. *The Architecture of Paradise: Survivals of Eden and Jerusalem*. London: University of California Press.

McClellan, Andrew. 1994. *Inventing the Louvre: Art, Politics, and the Origins of the Modern Museum in Paris*. Cambridge: Cambridge University Press.

McLuhan, Marshall. 1962. *The Gutenberg Galaxy: The Making of Typographic Man*. Toronto: University of Toronto Press.

———. (1964) 2002. *Understanding Media: The Extensions of Man*. London: Routledge.

Mehlman, Jeffrey. 2000. *Émigré New York: French Intellectuals in Wartime Manhattan, 1940–1945*. London: Johns Hopkins University Press.

Merker, René. 1970. Review of Jules Vallès's *Correspondance avec Hector Malot*. *The French Review*: 687.

Merleau-Ponty, Maurice. (1945) 2001. *Phénoménologie de la perception*. Paris: Gallimard.

Michael, Mike. 1996. *Constructing Identities: The Social, the Nonhuman and Change*. London: Sage.

Miles, Steven, and Malcolm Miles. 2004. *Consuming Cities*. London: Palgrave.

Mill, John Stuart. 1863. *Utilitarianism*. Glasgow: Fontana.

Mills, Sara. 1991. *Discourses of Difference: An Analysis of Women's Travel Writing and Colonialism*. London: Routledge.

Mirzoeff, Nicholas. 2006. 'On Visuality'. *Journal of Visual Culture* 5 (1): 53–79.

———. 2011. *The Right to Look: A Counterhistory of Visuality*. Durham, NC: Duke University Press.

Moncan, Patrice de. 2009. *Le Paris d'Haussman*. Paris: Éditions du Mécène.

Mondada, Lorenza. 2005. 'Seeing as a Condition of Saying: On the Discursive Construction of Knowledge in Travel Accounts'. In *Unravelling Civilization: European Travel and Travel Writing*, edited by H. Schulz-Forberg, 63–85. Oxford: Peter Lang.

Morand, Paul. 1923a. *Fermé la nuit*. Paris: Éditions de la nouvelle Revue Française.

———. 1923b. *Ouvert la nuit*. Paris: Éditions de la nouvelle Revue Française.

———. 1933. *Londres*. Paris: Plon.

———. 1997. 'Interview with Label France'. *Humanities* 28 (July): 28–34.

More, Thomas. (1516) 2003. *Utopia*. Translated and Introduced by P. Turner. London: Penguin.

Morin, Edgar, and Karel Appel. 1984. *New York: La Ville des villes, City of Cities*. Translated by A.P. Van Teslaar. Paris: Galillée.

Morrison, Arthur. 1889. 'Whitechapel'. *Palace Journal* 24 (April): 6–8.

————. 1894. *Tales of Mean Streets*. London: Methuen.

Mortier, Roland. 1974. *La Poétique des ruines en France. Ses origines, ses variations de la Renaissance à Victor Hugo*. Genève: Droz.

Moureau, François. 1996. *Le Second Voyage, ou, le déjà-vu*. Paris: Klincksieck.

Mullin, John R. 2000. 'Edward Bellamy's Ambivalence: Can Utopia be Urban?' *Utopian Studies: Journal for the society for Utopian Studies* 11 (1): 51–65.

Mumford, Lewis. 1938. *The Culture of Cities*. New York: Harcourt Brace.

————. 1961. *The City in History: Its Origins, its Transformations, its Prospects*. London: Harcourt Brace Jonanovich.

Nairn, Tom. 1977. *The Break-up of Britain*. London: New Left Books.

Nash, Dennison. 1981. 'Tourism as an Anthropological Subject'. *Current Anthropology* 22 (5): 461–81.

Nead, Lynda. 2005. *Victorian Babylon: People, Streets and Images in Nineteenth-Century London*. London: Yale University Press.

Needham, Rodney. 1973. *Right and Left. Essays on Dual Symbolic Classification*. London: University of Chicago Press.

Neill, William J. V. 2004. *Urban Planning and Cultural Identity*. London: Routledge.

Nematollahy, Ali. 2007. 'Jules Vallès and the Anarchist Novel'. *Nineteenth-Century French Studies* 35 (3/4): 575–89.

Nietzsche, Friedrich. 1964. *La Généalogie de la morale*. Paris: Nouvelle Revue Française.

————. (1885) 2003. *Beyond Good and Evil: Prelude to a Philosophy of the Future*. Translated by R.J. Hollingdale. London: Penguin.

Ni Loingsigh, Aedin. 2009. *Postcolonial Eyes: Intercontinental Travel in Francophone African Literature*. Liverpool: Liverpool University Press.

Nizet, François. 1988. *Le Voyage d'Italie et l'architecture européenne. 1675–1825*. Brussels: Institut historique belge de Rome.

Nora, Pierre, ed. 1997. *Les Lieux de mémoire*. 3 vols. Paris: Gallimard.

Norberg-Schulz, Christian. 2000. *Architecture: Presence, Language and Place*. Milan: Spiro Editions.

Norris, Christopher. 1992. *Uncritical Theory: Postmodernism, Intellectuals, and the Gulf War*. Amherst: University of Massachusetts Press.

Oakes, Penelope J., Alexander S. Haslam and John C. Turner. 1994. *Stereotyping and Social Reality*. Oxford: Blackwell.

Oakes, Timothy. 1997. 'Place and the Paradox of Modernity'. *Annals of the Association of American Geographies* 87 (3): 509–31.

O'Doherty, Brian. (1976) 1999. *Inside the White Cube: The Ideology of the Gallery Space*. London: University of California Press.

Olsen, Donald J. 1982. *Town Planning in London: Eighteenth and Nineteenth Centuries*. New Haven, CT: Yale University Press.

Olsen, Kjell. 2002. 'Authenticity as a Concept in Tourism Research: The Social Organization of the Experience of Authenticity'. *Tourist Studies* 2 (2): 159–82.

Online Etymological Dictionary. http://www.etymonline.com/ (accessed 29 February 2016).

Osborne, Peter. 1992. 'Modernity is a Qualitative, Not a Chronological Category'. *New Left Review* 192: 65–84.

Paquot, Thierry. 2000. 'De l'accueillance: essai pour une architecture et un urbanisme de l'hospitalité'. In *Éthique, architecture, urbain*, edited by C. Younès and T. Paquot, 68–83. Paris: La Découverte.

Paquot, Thierry, Michel Lussault, and Sophie Body-Gendrot, eds. 2000. *La Ville et l'urbain: l'état de savoirs*. Paris: La Découverte.

Parameshwar Gaonkar, Dilip, ed. 2001. *Alternative Modernities*. London: Duke University Press.

Parkhurst-Ferguson, Priscilla. 1994. *Paris as Revolution: Writing the Nineteenth-Century City*. Los Angeles: University of California Press.

Parsons, Deborah L. 2000. *Streetwalking the Metropolis: Women, the City, and Modernity*. Oxford: Oxford University Press.

Paschel, Ulrike. 1998. *No Mean City? The Image of Dublin in the Novels of Dermot Bolger, Roddy Doyle and Val Malkerns*. Frankfurt am Main: Peter Lang.

Pasquali, Adrien. 1994. *Le Tour des horizons: critique et récits de voyage*. Paris: Klincksieck.

Penguin English Dictionary. 2004. 2nd ed. London: Penguin Books.

Perec, Georges. 1967. *Un homme qui dort*. Paris: Denoël.

———. 1969. *La Disparition*. Paris: Denoël.

———. 1974. *Espèces d'espaces*. Paris: Galilée.

———. (1974) 1999. *Species of Space and Other Pieces*. Edited and Translated by John Sturrock. London: Penguin.

———. 1975. *W ou le souvenir d'enfance*, Paris: Denoël.

———. (1975) 1982. *Tentative d'épuisement d'un lieu parisien*. Paris: C. Bourgois.

———. 1978. *Je me souviens*. Paris: Hachette.

———. 1985. *Penser/classer*. Paris: Hachette.

Perkin, Harold. 1986. *Origins of Modern English Society*. London: Ark Paperbacks.

Peters, Edward, ed. 1998. *The First Crusade: The Chronicle of Fulcher of Chartres and other Source Materials*. Philadelphia: University of Pennsylvania Press.

Pétonnet, Colette. 1982. *Espaces habités: ethnologie des banlieues*. Paris: Galilée.

Picchi, Debra. 1983. 'Review of *Shabono: A Visit to the Remote and Magical World in the Heart of the South American Jungle* by Florinda Donner'. *American Anthropologist* 85 (3): 674–75.

Piedagnel, Alexandre. (1876) 1884. *Jules Janin*. Paris: Librairie Fischbacher.

Pierson, Stanley. (1973) 1999. 'The Way Out'. In *The Victorian City: Images and Realities*, edited by H.J. Dyos and M. Wolff, 2 vols. II: 873–78. London: Routledge.

Pile, Steve. 2002. 'Memory and the City'. In *Temporalities: Autobiography and Everyday life*, edited by J. Campbell and J. Harbord, 111–27. Manchester: Manchester University Press.

Pinkney, David H. 1958. *Napoleon III and the Rebuilding of Paris*. Princeton, NJ: Princeton University Press.

Pitkin, Thomas M. 1975. *Keepers of the Gate: A History of Ellis Island*. New York: New York University Press.

Poe, Edgar Allen. 1966. *Complete Stories and Poems of Edgar Allen Poe*. New York: Doubleday.

———. (1840) 1966. 'The Man of the Crowd'. In *Complete Stories and Poems of Edgar Allen Poe*, E. A. Poe, 215–21. New York: Doubleday.

———. (1841) 1966. 'A Descent into the Maelstrom'. In *Complete Stories and Poems of Edgar Allen Poe*, E. A. Poe, 108–20. New York: Doubleday.

Polezzi, Loredana. 2004. 'Between Gender and Genre: The Travels of Estella Canziani'. In *Perspectives on Travel Writing*, edited by G. Hooper and T. Youngs, 121–37. Aldershot: Ashgate Publishing.

Poovey, Mary. 1995. *Making a Social Body: British Cultural Formation, 1830–1864*. Chicago: Chicago University Press.

Porter, Denis. 1991. *Haunted Journeys: Desire and Transgression in European Travel Writing*. Oxford: Princeton University Press.

Pratt, Mary Louise. 1986. 'Fieldwork in Common Places'. In *Writing Culture: The Poetics and Politics of Ethnography*, edited by J. Clifford and G. E. Marcus, 27–50. Berkeley: University of California Press.

Pyne, Kathleen. 1994. 'Whistler and the Politics of the Urban Picturesque'. *American Art* 8 (3/4): 60–77.

Quincy, Quatremère de. (1815/1836) 1989. *Considérations morales sur la destination des ouvrages de l'art suivi de Lettres sur l'enlèvement des ouvrages de l'art antique à Athènes et à Rome*. Paris: Librairie Arthème Fayard.

Raban, Jonathan. (1974) 1998. *Soft City*. London: Harvill Press.

Ramazanoglu, Caroline, ed. 1993. *Up Against Foucault: Explorations of Some Tensions between Foucault and Feminism*. London: Routledge.

Rancière, Jacques. 2004. *The Politics of Aesthetics: The Distribution of the Sensible*. Translation by G. Rockhill. London: Continuum.

Raymond, Henri. 1984. *L'Architecture: les aventures spatiales de la raison*. Paris: Centre Georges Pompidou.

Read, Donald. 1972. *Edwardian England 1901–1915: Society and Politics*. London: George G. Harrap.

Réda, Jacques. 1986. *Châteaux des courants d'air*. Paris: Gallimard.

Redfern, Walter. 1992. *Feet First: Jules Vallès*. Glasgow: University of Glasgow French and German Publications.

Reichler, Claude and Roland Ruffieux. 1998. *Le Voyage en Suisse: anthologie des voyageurs français et européens de la Renaissance au XXe siècle*. Paris: R. Laffont.

Revest, Didier. 2007. 'Misère et Taudis dans le Londres du XIXe siècle. Problème moral ou structurel?' *Cercles* 17: 156–66.

Rich, Norman. (1970) 1977. *The Age of Nationalism and Reform 1850–1890*. London: W.W. Norton.

Richard, Jean. 1996. *Les Récits de voyage et de pèlerinages*. Turnhout: Brépolis.

Richarderie, G. Boucher de la. 1808. *Bibliothèque universelle des voyages, ou notice complète et raisonnée de tous les voyages anciens et modernes dans les différentes parties du monde classées par ordre des pays dans leur série chronologique*. 6 vols. Paris: n.p.

Richards, Ivor A. 1932. *The Philosophy of Rhetoric*. London: Oxford University Press.

Richer, Jean. 1981. *Études et recherches sur Théophile Gautier prosateur*. Paris: A.-G. Nizet.

Ricoeur, Paul. 1988. *Le Temps raconté*. Paris: Seuil.

———. 1990. *Soi-même comme un autre*. Paris: Seuil.

Ridon, Jean-Xavier. 2002. *Le Voyage en son miroir: essais sur quelques tentatives de réinvention du voyage au 20e siècle*. Paris: Kiné.

Ridon, Jean-Xavier, and Elodie Laüght, eds. 2005. *Nouvelles lectures de l'exotisme*. Nottingham: University of Nottingham.

Robbe-Grillet, Alain. 1970. *Projet pour une révolution à New York*. Paris: Minuit.

Robbins, Keith. (1983) 1997. *The Eclipse of a Great Power: Modern Britain 1870–1992*. London: Longman.

Rogozinski, Dolorès. 1982. 'La Parade des monstres: l'entre-sort'. *Revue des Sciences Humaines* 188: 93–115.

Rojek, Chris. 1993. *Ways of Escape: Modern Transformations in Leisure and Travel*. Basingstoke: Macmillan.

Rojek, Chris, and John Urry. 1997a. 'Transformations of Travel and Theory'. In *Touring Cultures: Transformations of Travel and Theory*, edited by C. Rojek and J. Urry, 1–19. London: Routledge.

———, eds. 1997b. *Touring Cultures: Transformations of Travel and Theory*. London: Routledge.

Rollwagon, Jack. 1980. 'New Directions in Urban Anthropology: Building an Ethnography and an Ethnology of the World System'. In *Urban Life: Readings in Urban Anthropology*, edited by G. Gmelch and W. P. Zenner, 370–82. New York: St. Martin's Press.

Ropars-Wuilleumier, Marie-Claire. 2002. *Écrire l'espace*. Paris: Presses Universitaires de Vincennes.

Ross, Kristen. 1995. *Fast Cars, Clean Bodies: Decolonization and the Reordering of French Culture*. Cambridge, MA: MIT Press.

Ross, Michael L. 1994. *Storied Cities: Literary Imaginings of Florence, Venice and Rome*. London: Greenwood.

Rossi, Aldo. 1982. *The Architecture of the City*. Introduction by P. Eisenmann. Translated by D. Ghirado and J. Ockman. London: Graham Foundation for Advanced Studies in the Fine Arts and the Institute for Architecture and Urban Studies by MIT Press.

Rotella, Carlo. 1998. *October Cities: The Redevelopment of Urban Literature*. London: University of California Press.

Rousseau, Jean-Jacques. (1750) 2011. *Discours sur les Sciences et les Arts*. Electronic Edition: Les Echos du Maquis. http://www.echosdumaquis.com/Accueil/Textes_(A-Z)_files/Discours%20sur%20les%20sciences%20et%20les%20Arts%20(1750).pdf

———. (1750) 1923. *The Social Contract and Discourses*. London: J.M. Dent.

———. (1782) 1997. *Les Rêveries du promeneur solitaire*. Paris: Flammarion.

Rowntree, Seebohm B. 1901. *Poverty: A Study of Town Life*. London: Macmillan.

Rubiés, Joan Pau. 2002. 'Travel Writing and Ethnography'. In *The Cambridge Companion to Travel Writing*, edited by P. Hulme and T. Youngs, 242–60. Cambridge: Cambridge University Press.

Ruskin, John. 1854. *The Opening of the Crystal Palace: Considered in some of its Relations to the Prospects of Art*. London: Smith, Elder.

Russel, Alison. 2000. *Crossing Boundaries: Postmodern Travel Literature*. New York: Palgrave.

Sadler, Simon. 1998. *The Situationist City*. London: MIT Press.

Said, Edward. (1978) 1979. *Orientalism*. New York: Vintage-Random.

Sala, George Augustus. 1864. 'The Streets of the World: Paris; The Passage des Panoramas'. *Temple Bar* 10: 61–65.

Saminadayer-Perrin, Corinne. 2000. 'Impressions londoniennes'. *Les Amis de Jules Vallès* 30: 7–10.

Samuel, Raphael. 1994. *Theatres of Memory*, 2 vols. I. *Past and Present in Contemporary Culture*. London: Verso.

Sansot, Pierre. 1996. *Poétique de la ville*. Paris: Armand Colin.

———. 1998. *Du bon usage de la lenteur*. Paris: Payot.

Sant'Elia, Antonio. 1914. 'Manifesto of Futurist Architecture'. *Lacerba* 2 (15): 228–31.

Sargent-Baur, Barbara N., ed. 1992. *Journeys toward God: pilgrimage and crusade*. Kalamazoo: Medieval Institute Publications, Western Michigan University.

Sarner, Éric. 1986. 'L'Image, la guerre, la ville'. *Autrement* 83: 6–9.

Sartre, Jean-Paul. 1945. 'La France vue d'Amérique'. *Le Figaro*, 24 January.

———. (1938) 1968. *La Nausée*. Paris: Gallimard.

———. 1945. 'Victoire du gaullisme'. *Le Figaro*, 25 January.

———. (1945) 1995. *L'Être et le néant*. Paris: Gallimard.

———. (1948) 1985. *Qu'est-ce que la littérature?* Paris: Gallimard.

———. (1956) 1961. *Les Jeux sont faits*. London: Metheun.

———. 1964. *Les Mots*. Paris: Gallimard.

Sassen, Saskia. 1991. *The Global City: New York, London, Tokyo*. Princeton, NJ: Princeton University Press.

———. 1998. *Globalization and Its Discontents*. New York: New York Press.

Satterthwaite, David. 1999. *The Earthscan Reader in Sustainable Cities*. London: Earthscan Publications.

Savage, Mike, Alan Warde and Kevin Ward. 2003. *Urban Sociology, Capitalism and Modernity*. Basingstoke: Palgrave.

Scheerbart, Paul. (1914) 1971. 'Glass Architecture (excerpt)'. In Kaus R. Scherpe, and Lisa Roetzel. 1992–1993. 'Nonstop to Nowhere City? Changes in the Symbolization, Perception, and Semiotics of the City in the Literature of Modernity'. *Cultural Critique* 23: 137–64.

Schivelbusch, Wolfgang. (1979) 1986. *The Railway Journey: The Industrialization and Perception of Time and Space in the Nineteenth Century*. Leamington Spa: Berg.

———. (1988) 1995. *Disenchanted Night: The Industrialization of Light in the Nineteenth Century*. Translated by A. Davies. London: University of California Press.

Schlesinger, Max. 1853. *Saunterings In and About London*. London: Nathaniel Cooke.

Schulz-Forberg, Hagen. 2005a. 'Framing the Senses: Inter-mediality and Inter-sensuality in French and German Urban Travel Writing on London, 1851 to 1939'. In *Unravelling Civilization: European Travel and Travel Writing*, edited by H. Schulz-Forberg, 263–86. Oxford: Peter Lang.

———, ed. 2005b. *Unravelling Civilization: European Travel and Travel Writing*. Oxford: Peter Lang.

———. 2006. *London–Berlin: Authenticity, Modernity, and the Metropolis in Urban Travel Writing from 1851 to 1936*. Brussels: Peter Lang.

Scott, David. 2004. *Semiologies of Travel: from Gautier to Baudrillard*. Cambridge: Cambridge University Press.

Scott, Geoffrey. (1914) 1954. *The Architecture of Humanism: A Study in the History of Taste Garden City*. New York: Doubleday.

Segalen, Victor. (1908) 1986. *Essai sur l'exotisme, une esthétique du divers; Textes sur Gauguin et l'Océanie/Segalen et l'exotisme*. Montpellier: Fata Morgana.

———. (1972/1976) 1996. *Chine, la grande statuaire/Les Origines de la Statuaire de Chine*. Paris: Flammarion.

Selbourne, David. 1993. *The Spirit of the Age*. London: Sinclair-Stevenson.

Sennett, Richard. (1990) 1993. *The Conscience of the Eye: The Design and Social Life of Cities*. London: Faber & Faber.

———. (1994) 2002. *Flesh and Stone: The Body and the City in Western Civilization*. London: Penguin.

———. 1996. *The Uses of Disorder: Personal Identity and City Life*. London: Faber & Faber.

Servier, Jean. (1967) 1991. *Histoire de l'utopie*. Paris: Gallimard.

Seton-Watson, Hugh. 1977. *Nations and States. An Enquiry into the Origins of Nations and the Politics of Nationalism*. Boulder, CO: Westview Press.

Shakespeare, William. (1609) 2005. *Cymbeline*. Edited by J. Pitcher. London: Penguin.

Sheppard, Francis. 1971. *London, 1808–1870: The Infernal Wen*. London: Seeker and Warburg.

Sherman, Daniel J. 1989. *Worthy Monuments: Art Museums and the Politics of Culture in Nineteenth-Century France*. London: Harvard University Press.

Sherman, William H. 2002. 'Stirrings and Searchings. 1500–1720'. In *The Cambridge Companion to Travel* Writing, edited by P. Hulme and T. Youngs, 17–36. Cambridge: Cambridge University Press.

Shields, Rob. 1991. *Places on the Margins*. London: Routledge.

Shklovsky, Victor. (1917) 2006. 'Art as Technique'. In *The Critical Tradition: Classic Texts and Contemporary Trends*, edited by D. H. Richter, 774–84. New York: St. Martin's Press.

Siegel, Kristi, ed. 2002. *Issues in Travel Writing: Empire, Spectacle, and Displacement*. Oxford: Peter Lang.

Simmel, Georg. (1903) 2002. 'The Metropolis and Mental Life'. In *The Blackwell City Reader*, edited by G. Bridge and S. Watson, 11–19. London: Blackwell.

———. (1903) 2006. 'The Metropolis and Mental Life'. In *Simmel on Culture: Selected Writings*, edited by D. Frisby and M. Featherstone, 174–85. London: Sage.

———. (1907) 1990. *The Philosophy of Money*. London: Routledge.

Simoën, Jean-Claude. 1989. *Le Voyage en Égypte: les grands voyageurs au XIXe siècle*. Paris: Lattès.

Sims, George Robert, ed. (1990) 1901. *Edwardian London*. 4 vols. London: The Village Press.

———, ed. 1901. *Living London*. London: Cassell.

Sirvent, Michel. 2007. *Georges Perec ou le dialogue des genres*. Amsterdam: Rodopi.

Sitte, Camillo. (1889) 1965. *City Planning according to Artistic Principles*. Translated by G. R. Collins and C. C. Collins. New York: Random House.

Skilton, David. 2007. 'Tourists at the Ruins of London: The Metropolis and the Struggle for Empire'. *Cercles* 17: 93–119.

Smart, Barry. 1993. 'Europe/America: Baudrillard's Fatal Comparison'. In *Forget Baudrillard?*, edited by C. Rojek and B. S. Turner, 47–69. London: Routledge.

Smith, Valene L. (1977) 1989. *Hosts and Guests: The Anthropology of Tourism*. Philadelphia: University of Pennsylvania Press.

Soja, Edward W. 1984. *The World, the Text, and the Critic*. London: Faber & Faber.

———. 1996. *Thirdspace: Journeys to Los Angeles and Other Real-and-Imagined Places*. Malden, MA: Blackwell.

———. 2000. *Postmetropolis: Critical Studies of Cities and Regions*. London: Blackwell.

Søltoff, Pia. 2001. 'Ethics and Irony'. In *The Concept of Irony*, edited by Robert L. Perkins, 265–88. Macon, GA: Mercer University Press.

Sontag, Susan. 1979. *On Photography*. Harmondsworth: Penguin.

Soper, Kate. 1995. 'Forget Foucault?' *New Formations* 25: 21–27.

Soussan, Myriam. 2002. 'La mémoire vivante des lieux: Perec et Bober'. *Le Cabinet d'amateur*. http://www.cabinetperec.org/articles/soussan/artsoussan.html (accessed 10 November 2007).

Southall, Aidan. 1998. *The City in Time and Space*. Cambridge: Cambridge University Press.

Spurr, David. 1993. *The Rhetoric of Empire: Colonial Discourse in Journalism, Travel Writing and Imperial Administration*. London: Duke University Press.

Starobinski, Jean. (1961) 1999. *L'Œil vivant: Corneille, Racine, la Bruyère, Rousseau, Stendhal*. Paris: Gallimard.

Stébé, Jean-Marc, and Hervé Marchal. 2010. *La Sociologie urbaine*. Paris: Presses Universitaires de France.

Stedman Jones, Gareth. 1971. *Outcast London: A Study in the Relationship Between Classes in Victorian London*. Oxford: Oxford University Press.

Steinberg, Sigfrid Henry. 1966. *Five Hundred Years of Printing*. Harmondsworth: Penguin.

Steiner, Carol J., and Yvette Reisinger. 2004. 'Understanding Existential Authenticity. *Annals of Tourism Research* 33 (2): 299–318.

Steve, Mary. 2003. *The Aesthetics and Politics of the Crowd in American Literature*. Cambridge: Cambridge University Press.

Stierle, Karlheinz. 2001. *La Capitale des signes: Paris et son discours*. Preface by J. Starobinski. Translated by M. Rocher-Jacquin. Paris: Éditions de la Maison des Sciences de L'Homme.

Stilltoe, Alan. 1997. *Leading the Blind: A Century of Guidebook Travel, 1815–1914*. London: Papermac.

Strange, Carolyn and Michael Kempa. 2003. 'Shades of Dark Tourism: Alcatraz and Robben Island'. *Annals of Tourism Research* 30 (2): 386–40. http://www.sciencedirect.com/science/journal/01607383 (accessed 4 November 2014).

Sullivan, Joseph Matthew. 1921. 'Criminal Slang'. *The Virginia Law Register* 7 (1): 9–17.

Sutcliffe, Anthony. 1970. *The Autumn of Central Paris: The Defeat of Town Planning, 1850–1970*. London: Edward Arnold.

———. 2006. *London: An Architectural History*. London: Yale University Press.

Tabori, Paul. 1972. *The Anatomy of Exile: A Semantic and Historical Study*. London: Harrap.

Tadier, Neferti Xina M. 1995. 'The Dream-Work of Modernity: The Sentimental Education in Imperial France'. *boundary 2* 22 (1): 143–83.

Tafuri, Manfredo. 1976. *Architecture and Utopia: Design and Capitalist Development*. Translated by B. Luigia. London: MIT Press.

Tagg, John. 1994. 'The Discontinuous City: Picturing and the Discursive Field'. In *Visual Culture: Images and Interpretations*, edited by M. Holly and K. Moxey, 83–103. London: Wesleyan University Press.

Taine, Hippolyte. (1872) 1923. *Notes sur l'Angleterre*. Paris: G. Crès.

Tally Jr., Robert T. 2012. *Spatiality*. London: Routledge.

———. 2014. *Literary Cartographies: Spatiality, Representation, and Narrative*. London: Palgrave Macmillan.

Taylor, Charles. 1980. *Hegel and Modern Society*. Cambridge: Cambridge University Press.

———. (1989) 2004. *Sources of the Self: The Making of Modern Identity*. Cambridge: Cambridge University Press.

———. 2001. 'Two Theories of Modernity'. In *Alternative Modernities*, edited by D. Parameshwar Gaonkar, 172–196. London: Duke University Press.

———. 2004. *Modern Social Imaginaries*. London: Duke University Press.

Taylor, John. 1994. *A Dream of England. Landscape, Photography and the Tourist's Imagination*. Manchester: Manchester University Press.

Taylor, John P. 2001. 'Authenticity and Sincerity in Tourism'. *Annals of Tourism Research* 28 (1): 7–26.

Tester, Keith, ed. 1994. *The Flâneur*. London: Routledge.

Tholoniat, Richard. 1976. 'La Pauvreté à Londres, à travers *Notes sur Angleterre* de Taine et *La Rue à Londres* de Vallès'. *Confluents* 1: 79–94.

———. 2007. 'D'une guerre à l'autre: le voyage à Londres; pierre de touche de l'Entente Cordiale. 1919–1929'. *Cercles* 17: 167–80.

Thompson, C.W. 2011. *French Romantic Travel Writing: Chateaubriand to Nerval*. Oxford: Oxford University Press.

Thompson, Grahame. 1983. 'Carnival and the calculable: consumption and play at Blackpool'. In *Formations of Pleasure*, edited by T. Bennett, 124–36. London: Routledge.

Thoreau, Henry David. (1854) 1995. *Walden; or, Life in the Woods*. New York: Dover Publications.

Timbs, John. 1865. *Walks and Talks about London*. London: Lockwood and Co.

Timms, Edward and David Kelley, eds. 1985. *Unreal City: Urban Experience in Modern European Literature and Art*. Manchester: Manchester University Press.

Tindall, Gillian. 1991. *Countries of the Mind: The Meaning of Place to the Writer*. London: Hogarth.

Tocqueville, Alexis de. (1831) 1835. *Democracy in America*. 4 vols. I. Translated by Henry Reeve. London: Saunders and Otley.

———. (1831) 1848. *De la démocratie en Amérique*. 4 vols. I. Paris: Pagnerre.

Todorov, Tzvetan. 1989. *Nous et les autres: la réflexion française sur la diversité humaine*. Paris: Seuil.

Tomasch, Sylvia and Sealy Gilles, eds. 1998. *Text and Territory: Geographical Imagination in the European Middle Ages*. Philadelphia: University of Pennsylvania Press.

Tönnies, Ferdinand. (1887) 2001. *Community and Civil Society*. Translated by Jose Harris and Margaret Hollis. Cambridge: Cambridge University Press.

Topping, Margaret. 2004. *Eastern Voyages, Western Visions: French Writing and Painting of the Orient*. Oxford: Bern.

Trigg, Dylan. 2006. *Aesthetics of Decay: Nothingness, Nostalgia and the Absence of Reason*. New York: Peter Lang.

Trilling, Lionel. 1972. *Sincerity and Authenticity*. Cambridge, MA: Harvard University Press.

Tristain, Flora. (1840) 1978. *Promenades dans Londres ou l'aristocratie et les prolétaires anglais*. Paris: Maspéro.

Tronnes, Mike, ed. 1995. *Literary Las Vegas: Portraits of America's Most Fabulous City*. Edinburgh: Mainstream.

Trousson, Raymond. 1975. *Voyages aux pays de nulle part: histoire littéraire de la pensée utopique*. Brussels: Éditions de l'Université de Bruxelles.

Turner, Katherine. 2001. *British Travel Writing in Europe 1750–1800: Authorship, Gender and National Identity*. Aldershot: Ashgate

Twying, John. 1998. *London Dispossessed: Literature and Social Space in the Early Modern City*. Basingstoke: Macmillan.

Tyler, Stephen A. 1984. 'The Poetic Turn in Postmodern Anthropology: The Poetry of Paul Friedrich'. *American Anthropologist* 86 (2): 328–36.

Urbain, Jean-Didier. 1991. *L'Idiot au voyage: histoires de touristes*. Paris: Plon.

———. 2000. 'I Travel therefore I am: The "Nomad Mind" and the Spirit of Travel'. *Studies in Travel Writing* 4: 141–64.

Urry, John. 1990. *The Tourist Gaze*. London: Sage.

———. 1995. *Consuming Places*. London: Routledge.

———. 2007. *Mobilities*. Cambridge: Polity.

Vallès, Jules. (1872–80) 1980. *Jacques Vingtras, Le Proscrit: correspondance avec Arthur Arnould* in *Œuvres complètes*, edited by L. Scheler. 15 vols. IV. Paris: Les Éditeurs français réunis.

———. (1848–71) 1953. *Le Cri du peuple* in *Œuvres complètes*. Edited by L. Scheler. Paris: Les Éditeurs français réunis.

———. (1862–84) 1968. *Correspondance avec Hector Malot* in *Œuvres complètes*. Edited by Lucien Scheler. 15 vols. IX. Paris: Les Éditeurs français réunis.

———. 1971. *Le Tableau de Paris* in *Œuvres complètes*. Edited by Lucien Scheler. 15 vols. XIII. Paris: Les Éditeurs français réunis.

———. 1972. *Correspondance avec Séverine* in *Œuvres complètes*. Edited by Lucien Scheler. 15 vols. XV. Paris: Les Éditeurs français réunis.

Vasili, Paul Comte. 1885. *La Société de Londres*. Paris: Nouvelle Revue Française.

Venter, Malcolm. 1992. *The Spirit of Place: An Anthology on Travel Writing*. Oxford: Oxford University Press.

Venturi, Robert. (1966) 1977a. *Complexity and Contradiction in Architecture*. New York: MOMA.

———, Denise Scott Brown and Steven Izenour. (1972) 1977b. *Learning from Las Vegas: The Forgotten Symbolism of Architectural Form*. Cambridge, MA: MIT Press.

Vergo, Peter. 1989. *The New Museology*. London: Reaktion.

Vidler, Anthony. 1992. *The Architectural Uncanny: Essays in the Modern Unhomely*. London: MIT Press.

Virilio, Paul. (1980) 1989. *Esthétique de la disparition*. Paris: Galilée.

Volney, Constantin-François. (1791) 1979. *Les Ruines ou Méditation sur les révolutions des empires*. Geneva: Slatkine Reprints.

Wallock, Leonard, and William Sharpe, eds. (1983) 1987. *Visions of the Modern City: Essays in History, Art, and Literature*. Baltimore: Johns Hopkins University Press.

Walton, John K., ed. 2005. *Histories of Tourism: Representation, Identity and Conflict*. Toronto: Channel View Publications.

Wang, Ning. 1999. 'Rethinking Authenticity in Tourism Experience'. *Annals of Tourism Research* 26 (2): 349–70.

———. 2000. *Tourism and Modernity: A Sociological Analysis*. Oxford: Elsevier.

Waugh, Patricia, ed. 2006. *Literary Theory and Criticism: An Oxford Guide*. Oxford: Oxford University Press.

Weber, Max. 1958. *The City*. London: Collier Macmillan Publishers.

Wegner, Philip E. 2002. *Imaginary Communities: Utopia, the Nation, and the Spatial Histories of Modernity*. London: University of California Press.

Weiner, Deborah E. B. 1989. 'The People's Palace: An Image for East End London in the 1880s'. In *Metropolis-London: Histories and Representations since 1800*, edited by D. Feldman and G. S. Jones, 40–55. London: Routledge.

West-Pavlov, Russell. 2013. *Temporalities*. London: Routledge.

White, Jerry. (2001) 2002. *London in the Twentieth Century: A City and Its People*. London: Penguin.

Wilde, Oscar. 1898. *The Ballad of Reading Gaol*. https://ebooks.adelaide.edu.au/w/wilde/oscar/w67p/chapter16.html (accessed 19 February 2016).

Williams, Rosalind H. 1982. *Dream Worlds: Mass Consumption in Late Nineteenth-Century France*. Berkeley: California University Press.

Wilson, A.N. (2003) 2006. *The Victorians*. London: Arrow Books.

———. (2005) 2006. *After the Victorians: The World our Parents Knew*. London: Arrow Books.

Wimsatt, William K. and Monroe C. Beardsley. (1954) 1970. *The Verbal Icon*. London: Metheun.

Winter, James. 1993. *London's Teeming Streets – 1830/1914*. London: Routledge.

Wirth, Louis. 1938. 'Urbanism as a Way of Life'. *The American Journal of Sociology* 44 (1): 1–24.

Wirth-Nesher, Hana. 1996. *City Codes: Reading the Modern Urban Novel*. Cambridge: Cambridge University Press.

Withey, Lynne. (1997) 1998. *Grand Tours and Cook's Tours: A History of Leisure Travel, 1750–1915*. London: Aurum Press.

Wolff, Janet and John Seed, eds. 1988. *The Culture of Capital: Art, Power and the Nineteenth-Century Middle Class*. Manchester: Manchester University Press.

Wolfreys, Julian. 1998. *Writing London: The Trace of the Urban Text from Blake to Dickens*. London: Macmillan.

Wolfzettel, Friedrich. 1996. *Le Discours du voyageur: pour une histoire littéraire du récit de voyage en France du Môyen Age au XVIIIe siècle*. Paris: Presses Universitaires de la France.

Wood, Robert E. 1998. 'Touristic Ethnicity: A Brief Itinerary', *Ethnic and Racial Studies* 21 (2): 218–41.

Woods, Robert A., W. T. Elsing, Jacob A. Riis, Willard Parsons, Everett J. Wendell, Ernest Flagg, William Jewett Tucker, Joseph Kirkland, Walter Besant, Edmund R. Spearman, Jessie White Mario and Oscar Craig. (1895) 1896. *The Poor in Great Cities: Their Problems and What is Being Done to Solve Them*. London: Kegan Paul.

Wright, Will and Steven Kaplan. 2003. *The Image of the City in Literature, Media and Society*. Pueblo: University of Southern Colorado.

Wunenburger, Jean-Jacques. 2000. 'Mythe urbain et violence fondatrice'. In *Cahiers Internationaux de Symbolisme* 95: 185–92.

——— 2002. *La Vie des images*. Grenoble: Presses Universitaires de Grenoble.

Ydewalle, Charles d'. 1945. *Ici, Londres*. Paris: Arthème Fayard.

Younès, Chris and Thierry Paquot, eds. 2000. *Éthique, architecture, urbain*, Paris: La Découverte.

Young, Ken and Patricia L. Garside. 1982. *Metropolitan London: Politics and Urban Change, 1837–1901*. London: Edward Arnold.

Young, Robert. 1990. *White Mythologies: Writing History in the West*. London: Routledge.

Youngs, Tim. 1994. *Travellers in Africa: British Travelogues, 1850–1900*. Manchester: Manchester University Press.

———. 2004. 'Where are we Going?' In *Perspectives on Travel* Writing, edited by G. Hooper and T. Youngs, 167–80. Aldershot: Ashgate Publishing.

Youngs, Tim, and Charles Forsdick, eds. 2012. *Travel Writing*. London: Routledge.

Yuill, Stephanie Marie. 2003. 'Dark Tourism: Understanding Visitor Motivation at Sites of Death and Disaster' (master's thesis, Texas A&M University). http://oaktrust.library.tamu.edu/bitstream/handle/1969.1/89/etd-tamu-2003C-RPTS-Yuill-1.pdf?sequence=1&isAllowed=y (accessed 29 February 2016).

Zane, Kathleen. 1984. *Paradigms of Place in Travel Literature: The Oriental Voyages of Nerval, Burton, Kinglake and Chateaubriand*. Ann Arbor, MI: University Microfilms Int.

INDEX